CHRISTIAN THEOLOGY IN CONTEXT

SERIE

Timothy Gorringe   S

G000109702

CHRISTIAN THEOLOGY IN CONTEXT

Any inspection of recent theological monographs makes plain that it is still thought possible to understand a text independently of its context. Work in the sociology of knowledge and in cultural studies has, however, increasingly made obvious that such divorce is impossible. On the one hand, as Marx put it, "life determines consciousness". All texts have to be understood in their life situation, related to questions of power, class, and modes of production. No texts exist in intellectual innocence. On the other hand texts are also forms of cultural power, expressing and modifying the dominant ideologies through which we understand the world. This dialectical understanding of texts demands an interdisciplinary approach if they are to be properly understood: theology needs to be read alongside economics, politics, and social studies, as well as philosophy, with which it has traditionally been linked. The cultural situatedness of any text demands, both in its own time and in the time of its rereading, a radically interdisciplinary analysis.

The aim of this series is to provide such an analysis, culturally situating texts by Christian theologians and theological movements. Only by doing this, we believe, will people of the fourth, sixteenth or nineteenth centuries be able to speak to those of the twenty-first. Only by doing this will we be able to understand how theologies are themselves cultural products—projects deeply resonant with their particular cultural contexts and yet nevertheless exceeding those contexts by being received into our own today. In doing this, the series should advance both our understanding of those theologies and our understanding of theology as a discipline. We also hope that it will contribute to the fast-developing interdisciplinary debates of the present.

Origen

Scholarship in the Service of the Church

Ronald E. Heine

OXFORD
UNIVERSITY PRESS

OXFORD
UNIVERSITY PRESS

Great Clarendon Street, Oxford ox2 6DP

Oxford University Press is a department of the University of Oxford.
It furthers the University's objective of excellence in research, scholarship,
and education by publishing worldwide in

Oxford New York

Auckland Cape Town Dar es Salaam Hong Kong Karachi
Kuala Lumpur Madrid Melbourne Mexico City Nairobi
New Delhi Shanghai Taipei Toronto

With offices in

Argentina Austria Brazil Chile Czech Republic France Greece
Guatemala Hungary Italy Japan Poland Portugal Singapore
South Korea Switzerland Thailand Turkey Ukraine Vietnam

Oxford is a registered trade mark of Oxford University Press
in the UK and in certain other countries

Published in the United States
by Oxford University Press Inc., New York

British Library Cataloguing in Publication Data

Data available

Library of Congress Cataloging in Publication Data

Library of Congress Control Number : 2010933142

Typeset by SPI Publisher Services, Pondicherry, India
Printed in Great Britain
on acid-free paper by
Clays Ltd, St Ives plc

ISBN 978–0–19–920907–1 (Hbk)
ISBN 978–0–19–920908–8 (Pbk)

1 3 5 7 9 10 8 6 4 2

To Gillian

Contents

Preface

Origen's life is somewhat unique among the Church Fathers because there is a major hiatus in the middle of it. He began his life, lived his formative years, and built a reputation as a Christian scholar and teacher in the thriving intellectual center of Alexandria. There he rubbed shoulders with some of the greatest pagan intellectuals of his day: philosophers, grammarians, physicians, mathematicians, poets, literary and textual scholars, geographers, and others. They came to Alexandria to study, do research, or teach. This center had also attracted some of the great intellectuals of the second- and third-century Church. Its legacy included the Gnostic thinkers Basilides and Valentinus, and the more orthodox Pantaenus and Clement.

Alexandria's population was a cosmopolitan mix of Greeks, Romans, Jews, and Egyptians. The city had earlier had one of the largest Jewish populations in the world, but this population had been greatly reduced as a result of Jewish revolts during the reigns of Trajan and Hadrian in the early second century AD. It was in Alexandria that Origen did what no other Christian theologian of his day had done, and very few did after him in the Patristic period. He learned the Hebrew language so that he could work with the Hebrew Scriptures.

In mid-life, because of disagreements between himself and the bishop of Alexandria, Origen left the city and settled permanently in Caesarea of Palestine. Caesarea was also a Hellenized, pagan city and a seat of Roman government but it must have seemed like an intellectual wasteland to an exile from Alexandria. There was, however, a thriving Synagogue and a famous rabbinical school in Caesarea. In this new context Origen was ordained a priest and entered fully into the life of the Church. He founded a Christian school and library, preached in the liturgical cycle of the Church, which he had not been allowed to do in Alexandria, counseled the persecuted, and seems to have interacted regularly with the rabbis in Caesarea. It was here that he produced the majority of his written works. These two local settings of Origen's life form the major divisions of this study. The first six chapters look at Origen's life and work in Alexandria, and Chapters 7–10 treat his activities in Caesarea.

I have made a serious attempt in this book to treat Origen's Alexandrian works and his Caesarean works separately, without throwing their contents into one bowl and stirring them together to give an homogenized view of his thought. It is in this rigorous separation of his works into their two settings with their unique contexts that this study differs from preceding books on Origen. This separation also distinguishes, consequently, between the thought of the young Origen and the old Origen. Neither of these distinctions has been taken very seriously in studies of Origen. He has, in fact, often been presented as having developed a system of thought in his early period in Alexandria and never deviated from it. This approach is partly the result of the focus on his Alexandrian work, *On First Principles*, as the most important of his works, and certainly the most convenient way into his thought. The argument in this book is that new situations brought new problems for Origen, and these new problems caused him to turn his attention in new directions, and sometimes, even to rethink old positions.

The majority of Origen's works are either commentaries or homilies on Scripture. His commentaries on Scripture are not like modern academic commentaries. His goal in writing commentaries was not to solve the problems associated with a book of Scripture and explain what it meant to its first audience. He wrote commentaries on Scripture to solve problems in the Church. This was especially true in his Alexandrian period. He used the particular Scriptural book that he commented on because he believed that this book, or some portion of it, addressed issues facing the Church and individual Christians of his day. This focus on specific theological or ecclesiastical problems is why his Alexandrian commentaries treat only selected portions of Biblical books. None of these early commentaries covered an entire book of the Bible. He was interested in commenting only on those parts used by opponents of the Church or what he considered erring members of it, in order to show their errors and refute their views. His scholarship was always in the context and service of the Church.

Origen had been thoroughly educated in the disciplines of Greek education. He was trained as a grammaticus and as a philosopher. His works show evidence of this Greek education both in the way that he approaches them and in some of the assumptions he brings to them. But he was first and foremost a man of Christian faith. He considered his Greek education only a "handmaid" to serve the Christian faith. His life was devoted to understanding, defending, and promoting the faith.

I wish to thank Peeters Publishers in Leuven for permission to use parts of my article, "Origen's Alexandrian *Commentary on Genesis*" in *Origeniana Octava*, ed. by L. Perrone (Leuven/Peeters, 2003), 63–73, in ch. 5, and Mohr Siebeck in Tuebingen for permission to use parts of my article, "Origen and the Eternal Boundaries", in their forthcoming *The Septuagint and Christian Origins*, ed. by H. Lichtenberger and S. Caulley, in ch. 3. I also wish to thank Northwest Christian University for some release time from teaching in the spring semester of 2009 for work on this book.

R. E. H.

All Saints Day, 2009

Abbreviations

ORIGEN'S COMMENTARIES AND HOMILIES

In the abbreviations of Origen's commentaries and homilies I have followed the style in *The Westminster Handbook to Origen*, though not always the exact abbreviations used there. Origen's commentaries and homilies are identified first by the type of material: *Com (Commentary)*, *Hom (Homily)*, *Frag (Fragment)*, and, in the case of part of the *Commentary on Matthew*, *Ser (Series)*. These are then followed by a standard abbreviation for the Biblical book being referenced: *HomJer (Homilies on Jeremiah)*, *ComJn (Commentary on John)*, *FragLam (Fragments on Lamentations)*, and, in the case of part of the *Commentary on Matthew*, *SerMt (Series Matthew)*. The numbers following these abbreviations are to the numbering systems used in the series, Die griechischen christlichen Schriftsteller der ersten drei Jahrhunderte, except for references to the *Commentary on the Canticles*, where the numbering system used in the two volumes in Sources chrétiennes are followed.

ORIGEN'S OTHER TREATISES

Cels	*Against Celsus*
Dial	*Dialogue with Heracleides*
EpGreg	*Epistle to Gregory*
EpistAfr	*Epistle to Julius Africanus*
ExhMart	*Exhortation to Martyrdom*
PEuch	*On Prayer (Peri Euches)*
Phil	*The Philocalia*
Princ	*On First Principles*
Strom	*Stromata*

OTHER CHRISTIAN WRITERS OF ANTIQUITY

Africanus, *EpistOr*	Africanus, *Epistle to Origen*
Clement, *EclProph*	Clement of Alexandria, *Eclogae Propheticae*

Clement, *Exc. Ex Theod*	Clement of Alexandria, *Excerpta ex Theodoto*
Clement, *Strom*	Clement of Alexandria, *Stromata*
Epiphanius, *Pan*	Epiphanius, *Panarion*
Eusebius, *H. E.*	Eusebius, *Ecclesiastical History*
Gregory, *Pan*	Gregory Thaumaturgus, *Panegyric to Origen*
Hippolytus, *Haer*	Hippolytus, *Refutation of all Heresies*
Irenaeus, *Dem*	Irenaeus, *Demonstration of the Apostolic Preaching*
Irenaeus, *Haer*	Irenaeus, *Against all Heresies*
Irenaeus, *Proof*	Irenaeus, *Proof of the Apostolic Preaching*
Jerome, *Ep*	Jerome, *Epistle*
Justin, *Dial*	Justin, *Dialogue with Trypho the Jew*

MODERN ABBREVIATIONS

ABD	*Anchor Bible Dictionary*
BETL	Bibliotheca Ephemeridum Theologiacarum Lovaniensium
BZ	*Byzantinische Zeitschrift*
CCSG	Corpus Christianorum, series Graeca
CSEL	Corpus Scriptorum Ecclesiasticorum Latinorum
FC	Fontes Christiani
FOTC	Fathers of the Church
GCS	Die griechischen christlichen Schriftsteller der ersten drei Jahrhunderte
HeyJ	*Heythrop Journal*
HTR	*Harvard Theological Review*
JECS	*Journal of Early Christian Studies*
JEH	*Journal of Ecclesiastical History*
JQR	*Jewish Quarterly Review*
JTS	*Journal of Theological Studies*
LCC	Library of Christian Classics
LCL	Loeb Classical Library
OCA	Orientalia Christiana Analecta
OECS	Oxford Early Christian Studies
P. Giss. Lit	*Mitteilungen aus der Papyrussammlung der Giessener Universitätsbibliothek, Literarische Stücke*

P.Oxy	*Oxyrhynchus Papyri*
P.Tebt.	*The Tebtunis Papyri*
PG	J. P. Migne, *Patrologiae Graecae*
SBL	Society of Biblical Literature
SC	Sources chrétienne
WUNT	Wissenschaftliche Untersuchungen zum Neuen Testament
ZAC	*Zeitschrift für antikes Christentum*
ZAW	*Zeitschrift für die alttestamentliche Wissenschaft*
ZKG	*Zeitschrift für Kirchengeschichte*
ZWT	*Zeitschrift für wissenschaftliche Theologie*

1

Alexandria near Egypt

Origen was born in Egypt, probably in Alexandria, around AD 185. He left Alexandria to reside in Caesarea sometime around AD 232 when he would have been approximately 47 years old. Alexandria and the Christian community in the city were major factors in the shaping of his life and thought. In this chapter we will look at the city that was his home in this long and important segment of his life. In the next chapter we will investigate the Alexandrian Christian community in which his faith was born and nurtured.

LOCATION, TOPOGRAPHY, AND POPULATION OF ALEXANDRIA

Alexandria was a Greek city on Egyptian soil. Alexander the Great chose the site during his unopposed sweep through Egypt in 332 BC before he turned east to push his conquests to the Indus River. When he died unexpectedly in 323 BC he left no heir to his kingdom. His more powerful comrades fought over territory for several years, and eventually three powerful families emerged in control of the major segments of his conquests. The Antigonids controlled the areas of Greece and Macedonia; the Seleucids the region of Syria, Mesopotamia, and Asia Minor; and the Ptolemies Egypt and Palestine as far north as Lebanon.

Alexander selected the narrow strip of land between the Mediterranean and Lake Mareotis on the western edge of the Nile Delta for his namesake city. Only a small fishing village called Rakotis stood on the site. It was a choice spot for a major port. A limestone shelf below the surface ran from Canopus in the east to several kilometers west of the site and would provide the foundation for the city's great buildings. The island of Pharos lay just over a kilometer out from the site, breaking the waves and currents of the Mediterranean. One of the early Ptolemies built a road called the Heptastadion to the island from the mainland, making two harbors, the Great Harbor to the east and the Eunostos Harbor to the west.[1] Origen's student Dionysius, bishop of Alexandria from AD 247, refers to Alexandria's harbors as "calm and waveless".[2]

It was Alexander's general, Ptolemy I Soter, who built the city on the site Alexander had chosen. Rakotis, along with a village on the island of Pharos, was incorporated into the city. On the eastern tip of the island of Pharos Ptolemy I Soter or II (Philadelphus) constructed the great lighthouse. It stood slightly higher than the American Statue of Liberty.[3] Underwater archaeology has discovered the remains of a huge male statue in the area sculpted as a pharaoh, and another of the Egyptian goddess Isis probably representing the pharaoh's wife. The statues originate, however, from the time of the Ptolemies. This suggests that the Greek rulers attempted to put an Egyptian façade on the city by depicting themselves as pharaohs. It is estimated that the two statues would have been more than 12 meters high when in place and that they stood at the base of the lighthouse, where they would have been seen by every ship entering the Great Harbor.[4]

Alexandria was planned by the Rhodian Dinocratês.[5] It was laid out as a grid, which was the normal plan of Hellenistic cities.[6] The east–west axis was the broad, colonnaded Canopic Way crossed near its center by a major north–south street running from Lake Mareotis on the south edge of the city to the Great Harbor. Strabo said these two streets were approximately 30 meters wide;[7] a more recent estimate puts them at 14 meters, still impressively wide. The Canopic Way stretched 5 kilometers from the Sun Gate, through which one entered from the east, to the Moon Gate in the west.[8] In his second-century AD novel, *The Adventures of Leucippe and Clitophon*, Achilles Tatius says that the first-time visitor is struck by the beauty of the city on catching sight of the double row of columns stretching all the way to the western gate. Proceeding along the Canopic Way, he adds, one comes to another column-lined street crossing it at right angles. The overall impression of the city's beauty, size, and population, he claims, were overwhelming (5.5.5–6).

Alexandria's population, it is thought, initially grew very rapidly. It may have reached 300,000 by the late third century BC, and may have had a modest growth again in the Roman empire.[9] A population of 400,000 seems a safe estimate in the Roman period with, perhaps, a decline in the late third

---

[1] Haas (1997), 21, 24–55.   [2] Eusebius, *H.E.* 7.21.4.   [3] Haas (1997), 25.
[4] Empereur (1998), 75–7; cf. Fowden (1993), 62–3.   [5] Bell (1948), 51.
[6] Haas (1997), 24; Tarn (1967), 310.   [7] *Geography* 17.1.8.
[8] Empereur (1998), 56, 53.   [9] Scheidel (2004), 21.

century AD.[10] Alexandria was the second largest city in the Roman empire. Rome was probably twice its size; Ephesus, the next largest city, had only half the population of Alexandria.[11] The population was mixed from the beginning. The largest racial groups were Greeks, Jews, and Egyptians, with Romans later. But because it was such a commercial crossroads there were numerous other races that could be seen and heard on the streets of Alexandria.[12]

The city was divided into five districts, with each district designated by one of the first five letters of the Greek alphabet. This division was made in the third century BC and was still in use in the fourth century AD.[13] The section occupied by the Greeks, and later the Romans, was called the Brucheion district in the Roman period.[14] It probably bore only a letter designation in the time of the Ptolemies. It lay in the northern and somewhat central section of the city, in the vicinity of the Great Harbor and reached at least as far south as the Canopic Way.[15] It was the location of the palace, state buildings, and temples, as well as the residential area of the Greeks and Romans. The Museum with its library probably also stood in this section, though its exact location is unknown. Four houses from the third century BC have been uncovered by archaeologists in the Brucheion district, and three additional ones just to the west near the Caesarion.[16] One of the houses to the west was a Roman villa probably built in the mid-second century AD and destroyed in the second half of the third century. Both the Hellenistic and the Roman houses are large, providing evidence that the Brucheion district and the immediate adjacent vicinity "was the site of grand residences".[17]

Philo, the first-century AD Alexandrian Jew, says that Jews made up the majority of two of the five sections of the city and that some lived also in the other sections.[18] The Greek geographer and historian Strabo asserts that the Jewish population inhabited a large portion of Alexandria, and that they were governed by a Jewish ethnarch.[19] The Jews inhabited the region which lay along the sea in the northeast of the city. Its western side bordered the Brucheion.[20] The ancient designation for this section of the city is not

[10] Stark (1997), 131; Scheidel (2004), 21, 31.   [11] Stark (1997), 131.
[12] Bell (1948), 52–3.   [13] Haas (1997), 47–8.   [14] Ausfeld (1904), 494–5.
[15] Ausfeld (1904), 496–7.
[16] The Caesarion was a temple for the worship of the Roman emperors on the waterfront of the Great Harbor. Cleopatra VII (reigned 51–30 BC) began its construction and Augustus completed it.
[17] Empereur (2000), 191; see also McKenzie (2007), 179–81.   [18] *Flaccus* 55–6.
[19] Quoted in Josephus, *Antiquities of the Jews*, 14.117.   [20] Haas (1997), 95.

known. Jews also inhabited the section of the city designated by the Greek
letter Delta. According to a papyrus letter from 13 BC the Delta section was
in the northwest region of the city, north of the Rakotis district.[21] The Ptolemies controlled Judaea until 200 BC and many Jews may have migrated to the
seat of political power during that period. In the Roman period, before the
time of Origen, this large Alexandrian Jewish population had been greatly
reduced by disastrous revolts of the Jews against the Romans in the time of
Trajan (AD 115–17) and, again, in that of Hadrian (AD 135).[22]

The southwest section of Alexandria, called Rakotis after the name of
the ancient village, was the section inhabited by native Egyptians. The Serapeon, the Ptolemies' temple for the god Sarapis, stood in the Rakotis district.
The city was always an attraction for people from rural Egypt but they seem
to have flooded it during the Roman rule. They came primarily for employ-
ment. Abd-el-Ghani notes that several papyri from the Roman period show
"the existence in Alexandria of a dense rural population from the villages
of Middle Egypt". He adds that among their motives for living in Alexandria the "first and foremost was the work in that wealthy city". Alexandria,
he says, "was the queen city of the eastern Mediterranean, the crossroads
of commerce between the Greco-Roman world and eastern and southern
nations, as well as the center of many industries."[23] One second century AD
papyrus indicates that there were middlemen whose job it was to provide
Alexandria with workers from the countryside, and another refers to a person who supplied acrobats as entertainers for the city.[24] In the early third
century the emperor Caracalla expelled numerous rural Egyptians from
Alexandria. A papyrus claiming to contain extracts from his edict demands
that "[a]ll Egyptians who are in Alexandria, and especially country people
who have fled from other districts...be expelled". He made exceptions for
those bringing pigs to the city, those working the riverboats, and those bringing fuel for the baths. Also excepted were those bringing sacrificial animals
for the festival of Sarapis, those on temporary business trips, and tourists.[25]

Alexandria was a city where several races and nationalities rubbed shoulders daily on the streets. It was not, however, a racial melting pot. Racial and
national distinctions were maintained. "Juxtaposition" rather than "fusion,
or mixture" is the current term used in the technical literature to describe
the relationship between Egypt's racial groups.[26] It has been argued that

---

[21] Pearson (2004), 110.   [22] Haas (1997), 104–5.   [23] Abd-el-Ghani (2004), 163.

[24] *P. Oxy.* 41.2981; *P. Oxy.* 38.2860; see Abd-el-Ghani (2004), 163–8.

[25] *P. Giss. Lit.* 6.3; quoted in Rowlandson and Harker (2004), 84.

[26] Bagnall (1993), 230–1.

Greek-speaking children were educated in a Hellenocentric way which ignored all Egyptian culture. Greeks and Egyptians, it is thought, coexisted but did not truly interact. The cultural program that Ptolemy I Soter intended his Museum and library to promulgate was totally Greek-centered. The books that were gathered were Greek books and, if not, they were translated into Greek. The Museum would promote "Greek learning, literature, art, and science". It was not until the Roman period that Greek was taught as a second language to Egyptian children.[27]

The marriage of Alexandria to Egypt was not a completely happy marriage. The Greek Alexandrians referred to their city as "near" or "by" Egypt.[28] The Egyptian priests in Upper Egypt, on the other hand, looked forward to the time when the Greeks would be gone and the site of the city would once more be only a place where fishermen dried their catch.[29]

Philostratus, who wrote in the first half of the third century AD, says that Egyptians who visited India spoke ill of the Greeks, claiming that they had obtained the rites of their religions from the Egyptians, and asserting that they were a worthless, treacherous people.[30]

POLITICS AND ECONOMICS

Ptolemy I Soter first ruled Egypt from Memphis but by 319 BC had moved the seat of government to Alexandria.[31] Alexandria remained the seat of government throughout the Greek and, later, Roman rule. It was never an Egyptian city; it was never under Egyptian control. When Augustus Caesar defeated Antony and Cleopatra at Actium in 30 BC Egypt fell under the control of the Roman emperor. It was the richest of all the lands under Roman control. Augustus guarded it jealously. He appointed a Prefect, responsible to the emperor alone, to govern the country. Most of the Greek administration of the country was left intact. Greek continued to be the language of government.[32] This governing structure continued throughout the Roman period. The Prefect governing the province continued to be responsible directly to the emperor. He and a few high Roman officials resided in Alexandria. Once a year he traveled outside Alexandria to a city in the Delta and to another in upper Egypt to hold court and review local administrations.[33]

---

[27] Maehler (2004), 3–7.   [28] Fowden (1993), 20.
[29] Lewis (1983), 201–2, 206.   [30] *Life of Apollonius* 3.32; Fowden (1993/1986), 15–16.
[31] Scheidel (2004), 23–4.   [32] Marlowe (1971), 207.   [33] Lewis (1983), 19–20.

In addition to Alexandria, Naukratis in the Delta, Ptolemais in upper Egypt, and Antinoopolis in middle Egypt were also Greek cities.[34] Citizens of these four cities enjoyed several economic privileges in the Roman period not available to Egyptians. They were exempt from the poll tax, which the subjected native population had to pay. Citizens of Alexandria and the other Greek cities could purchase public land when the government disposed of it; Egyptians could not.[35] Some citizens of Alexandria owned extensive estates in other areas of Egypt. These lands were not taxed and the families owning them were not liable to the expensive compulsory public services that the locals had to bear. Alexandrians had lost this exemption from local compulsory services, however, by the mid-third century AD.[36]

Nevertheless, the Roman occupation of Egypt demoted Alexandria from its political glory as the magnificent capital of the independent country of Egypt to the resident city of the Roman Prefect governing the province. Many Alexandrians resented the Romans. The Romans reciprocated by refusing the Alexandrians' repeated requests for their own city council to govern the city. These refusals were made more bitter by the fact that two, and perhaps all three, of the other Greek cities in Egypt were granted such councils in the tradition of Greek cities.[37] The Alexandrians' feelings toward the Roman rule were expressed in a secretive protest literature that flourished from the first to the third centuries. Modern scholars have labeled this literature *The Acts of the Alexandrians*, or, sometimes, *The Acts of the Pagan Martyrs*. The stories were clearly popular throughout Egypt in the Roman period. Papyri containing them have been found in cities and villages scattered throughout the land.[38] The stories claim to be records of hearings of Alexandrians before Roman emperors. The Alexandrians defy the emperor with contempt and, consequently, one, or more, of the defendants is executed.[39]

Two additional actions of Roman emperors in the early third century AD further lowered Alexandria's political standing. The first was Septimius Severus' granting that all the nome capitols in Egypt could form their own councils.[40] This lowered Alexandria's prestige not just to the level of the other three Greek cities in Egypt but also to that of all the Egyptian capitols in the various nomes. This took place in AD 199/200. In AD 212 the emperor Caracalla granted Roman citizenship to all free inhabitants of the

---

[34] Lewis (1983), 26.   [35] Lewis (1983), 27.
[36] *P. Oxy.* 40.2915; Abd-el-Ghani (2004), 174.   [37] Lewis (1983), 198.
[38] Rowlandson and Harker (2004), 94–6.
[39] Lewis (1983), 199. For the stories see *The Acts of the Pagan Martyrs* (1954).
[40] Nomes were the administrative divisions of the land of Egypt.

empire. Alexandrian citizenship had earlier been a status symbol in Egypt. It carried rights and privileges not open to Egyptians in particular. Being an Alexandrian citizen continued to have advantages, but it lost some of its significance after this blanket distribution of Roman citizenship.[41]

Roman Egypt's sociopolitical makeup has been compared to a pyramid. A few powerful Romans occupied the top. Under them was a larger, less privileged group comprising the urban Greeks and, in the earlier period, Jews. Below these two strata of privilege lay the remaining masses, "peasants, artisans, landowners, merchants, the rich few and the many poor, townspeople whose status bestowed certain benefits, and villagers enjoying no benefits at all". The Romans referred to the totality of the lower masses, regardless of their nationality, as "Egyptians". Very few in this lower group were able to advance to higher status.[42]

Soldiers constituted the largest group of Romans in Egypt. Normally two legions, which could consist only of Roman citizens, were garrisoned in Egypt along with auxiliary units made up of provincials under Roman commanders. Most provincials in the auxiliary units were from provinces other than Egypt. Those from Egypt were not drawn from the masses, but from the Greek population that traced its ancestry to the time of the Ptolemies. Auxiliary troops who were discharged honorably after 26 years service were given Roman citizenship. Native Egyptians, however, were not allowed to serve in the auxiliary units until the late second century AD.[43]

A contingent of these Roman soldiers was garrisoned just east of Alexandria at Nicopolis. The camp was in the vicinity of the hippodrome that Augustus had built. The soldiers were used occasionally to maintain order at the hippodrome. Their presence in the area also served as protection for travelers through the eastern region called Boukolia, where herdsmen and shepherds pastured their animals. These shepherds and herdsmen were notorious for assaulting travelers and one another.[44] Roman soldiers from the nearby camp must have been a common sight on the streets of Alexandria.

Although Alexandria was demoted politically by the Roman occupation, it continued to be the major economic power of the eastern Mediterranean.[45] Under the Ptolemies (323–30 BC) Alexandria had become the major port of the Mediterranean. Its harbors and docks bustled with activity. Had Carl Sandburg been an Alexandrian he could have aptly applied Chicago's epithet, "City of the Big Shoulders", to the city.[46] It became the commercial

---

[41] Haas (1997), 60.   [42] Lewis (1983), 18–19.   [43] Lewis (1983), 20.
[44] Haas (1997), 31–22; 39–40.   [45] Trapp (2004), 115.
[46] Carl Sandburg, "Chicago".

crossroads of the world for both sea and land trade. Trade routes ran down the Nile valley to the Thebaid and across to the port of Berenike on the Red Sea, where they turned east to the lands of Arabia and India bringing exotic spices to Alexandria's markets.[47] Two of the ships on which the apostle Paul was sent from Caesarea to Rome in the middle of the first century AD were Alexandrian ships carrying merchandise to Italy (Acts 27:6; 28:11). Near the end of the first century AD Dio Chrysostom praised Alexandria's commercial power. The city lay, he said, at the crossroads of the earth. Its harbors, fleets, and access to the Indian Ocean via the Red Sea put the trade of the entire world at its feet.[48]

Egypt had a monopoly on paper production from its papyrus grown in the Nile delta. It also was a large exporter of fine linen and glass. Archaeological discoveries of pottery and winepresses in the area around Lake Mareotis confirm that it was a wine-producing region.[49] A workshop producing two-handled wine jugs called amphorae dates from the time of the Ptolemies and seems to have continued in existence for nearly a thousand years.[50] A sunken ship discovered near Marseilles containing numerous amphorae like those found in the rubbish heaps of the potteries by Lake Mareotis shows that wine from there was shipped as far as the Rhone valley.[51] Strabo praised Mareotic wine (*Geo* 17.1.14), and Horace described Cleopatra as drunk with it (*Odes* 1.37.14). Clement of Alexandria refers to an Egyptian wine called Mendēsian and thinks that one should drink the wine from one's own country rather than imported wines (*Paed* 2.2.30).

The city's maritime location was connected with the Nile by the 20 kilometer-long Schedia canal. It ran from the western Canopic branch of the Nile to the southern side of the city. Branches of the canal cut through the city to each of Alexandria's harbors and also connected it with Lake Mareotis. This canal made it possible for the barges carrying Egypt's grain down the Nile to deliver their cargo to the granaries near Lake Mareotis for transport to the Great Harbor and shipment to the world markets.

The grain trade was the major source of Alexandria's wealth. At the height of the Roman empire, Rome received 83,000 tons of grain a year from Egypt.[52] All this grain passed through the granaries and docks of Alexandria. It has been estimated, on the basis of grain tax documents among the papyri, that the grain traffic alone on the Nile may have involved as many as 900 boats. Many of these were owned by the government, others

---

[47] Haas (1997), 43.   [48] *Or* 32.36; see Rowlandson and Harker (2004), 79.
[49] Haas (1997), 38; Rowlandson and Harker (2004), 90.   [50] Empereur (1998), 217.
[51] Empereur (1998), 218.   [52] Haas (1997), 42–3.

by wealthy landowners, some of whom resided in Alexandria.[53] The grain trade was the backbone of the Egyptian economy. It provided income for the farmers, the boat owners who transported it to Alexandria, the men who worked on the boats and loaded the ships, those who managed the granaries, and all those involved with the ships which transported it across the Mediterranean. In addition to these, the government's control of the shipment and storage of grain demanded a large number of clerical workers to manage the paperwork.[54]

The Schedia canal was a lifeline for Alexandria not only for boat traffic on the Nile but also as the primary source of the city's water supply. Below the city lay a system of cisterns linked by underground water channels.[55] More than a hundred have been discovered. The annual inundation of the Nile caused the canal to overflow, filling the cisterns. There are inscriptions and texts referring to the care of the canal. An inscription from the early first century AD acknowledges that Augustus had the Schedia dredged so that its waters flowed freely.[56]

Politically, the flower of Alexandria lost most of its petals in the Roman period, but commercially it continued to bloom. Rome needed Alexandria economically. It was a major food source and Rome's most convenient connection with the markets of the Far East.[57]

CULTURE

The earliest Ptolemies were responsible for two major institutions which were central to Alexandrian cultural life throughout the Greek and Roman periods. One was the creation of the god Sarapis and the construction of a temple in the Rakotis district called the Serapeon where he was worshipped. The other was the construction in the Brucheion of the great research center called the Museum with its famous library.

By Origen's time, and probably long before, the accounts of the origin of both the religion and the statue of Sarapis were confused and contradictory. He knows that Sarapis was a creation of Ptolemy for Alexandria and that prior to Ptolemy there had been no such god (*Cels* 5.37–8). Pausanius, who saw shrines of Sarapis all over Greece in the mid-second century AD, confirms the Ptolemaic origin of the god when he says the Athenians

---

[53] Bagnall (1993), 88–89; Lewis (1983), 142–3.   [54] Bagnall (1993), 34.
[55] McKenzie (2007), 24–5.   [56] Empereur (1998), 130–31; (2000), 192–3.
[57] Haas (1997), 21.

had taken Sarapis over from Ptolemy (Paus 1.18.4). Clement of Alexandria relates that some said the idol set up in Alexandria was an image of Pluto/ Hades, the Greek god of the underworld, sent to Ptolemy as a gift from the people of Sinope on the Black Sea. Others, Clement asserts, said the idol came from Pontus, while some said that it came from the Seleucids in the region of Antioch, and yet another that it was of ancient Egyptian origin being a combination of Osiris and Apis and called Osirapis by the Egyptians (*Protrept* 4.48.1–6).

The religion of Sarapis was probably intentionally syncretistic. Ptolemy I seems to have wanted a deity that would blend Greek and Egyptian worship. His new god absorbed the attributes of many deities. Origen says that Numenius described him as a god sharing the nature of all animals and plants (*Cels* 5.38). Tacitus says he was associated with the Greek healing god Asclepius, with Zeus, and with Pluto, god of the underworld.[58] He was clearly associated with the Egyptian gods Osiris and Apis. The name "Osor-Apis" was found in hieroglyphics translating the Greek name Sarapis in tablets discovered in the late-nineteenth-century excavation of the Serapeon in Alexandria.[59] Pausanius asserts that Sarapis' most famous shrine in Egypt was at Alexandria but the most ancient, he adds, was at Memphis (Paus 1.18.4). The latter was the seat of the worship of "the Memphite deity Osor-Hapi (in Greek Oserapis)".[60] A life-size statue of an Apis bull was found in a crypt of the Serapeon in the nineteenth-century excavations mentioned above. An inscription shows that the statue had been dedicated by the emperor Hadrian, who rebuilt the Serapeon in the second century AD. Osir-Apis was the god of the dead worshipped in the form of a bull at Memphis in the time of the Pharaohs.[61] The Greeks would naturally have associated this god with their own Hades/Pluto.

Although the Ptolemies may have wanted their new god to bring the Greeks and Egyptians in their kingdom together in religion, there is considerable evidence that suggests that this did not happen. For the Alexandrians Sarapis was a Greek god worshipped in a temple built after the Greek style, though some Egyptian objects were present in the temple and some Egyptians served as priests. In Memphis, however, Sarapis was no more than the name of Osor-Hapi and hardly any Greek elements were present at all.[62] Outside Alexandria temples continued to be constructed in the Egyptian style and the gods worshiped were Egyptian, even if they bore Greek names.[63]

[58] *Histories* 4.84; Empereur (1998), 90–2.   [59] Empereur (1998), 90–2.
[60] Fowden (1993/1986), 19.   [61] Empereur (1998), 90–2.
[62] Fowden (1993/1986), 20–1.   [63] Bagnall (1993), 48.

The catacombs of Kom el-Shuqafa in Alexandria provide some of the clearest evidence of the way the Greek and Egyptian religions were related in the minds of Alexandrians. The tomb of a husband and wife that can be dated to the end of the first or beginning of the second century AD contains elements of both Greek and Egyptian religion. There are symbols of Hermes, Dionysus, and Athena in the tomb, but above the sarcophagi are Egyptian scenes of the worship of the Apis bull and the mummification of Osiris by Anubis while Horus and Thoth stand beside him.[64] An adjacent tomb, labeled the tomb of Caracalla, has a double set of panels, one above the other. The upper panel shows the mummification of Osiris by Anubis with Isis and Nephthys standing on either side; the lower is the Greek scene of Hades taking Persephone to the underworld as Demeter and Hecate watch. There is no syncretism in these Alexandrian tombs, which are dated at least four hundred years after the Ptolemies had introduced their new god to the city. The people buried here have looked to each religion separately.[65] Stark has compared the way people respond to "religious risk" to the way they respond to financial risks: they *"diversify"*. If they cannot "determine which of an array of religious investments is the most secure," their "most rational strategy" is to "include all, or many, of them in" their "portfolio".[66] It is clear that the afterlife is of great concern to the persons buried in the tombs of Kom el-Shuqafa. They have, as it were, attempted to cover the options available in Alexandria so that they will not come up short beyond the grave.

Even if the Sarapis cult may not have achieved the dreams of its founders in melding Greek and Egyptian religion into one, it was, nevertheless, a huge success. It spread rapidly outside Egypt. Pausanius, as noted above, attests its presence throughout Greece, and it later found a home in Rome.[67] In Egypt it was as popular in the time of the Romans as in that of the Ptolemies.[68] The festival of Sarapis, celebrated annually on 25 April, was a major event. Even Caracalla's edict expelling rural Egyptians from Alexandria made an exception for those bringing sacrificial animals into the city for the festival.[69] The second-century AD novelist Achilles Tatius describes the torch-lit procession on the night of the Sarapis festival as the greatest spectacle he had ever seen. It lit up the city, he says, competing with the brilliance of

[64] Empereur (1998), 156.
[65] Empereur (1998), 170–3; Guimier-Sorbets and Seif el-Din (2004), 133–6.
[66] Stark (1997), 204.   [67] Empereur (1998), 90.
[68] Abd-el-Ghani (2004), 167.   [69] See above under "Location, etc.", p. 1.

the lights of the heavens.[70] Papyrus letters written from Alexandria refer
to praying to Sarapis for the addressee in the letter greetings so regularly
that the reference appears formulaic. A third-century AD letter written from
Alexandria to the writer's home in Oxyrhynchus concludes by saying, " '[B]y
the will of Sarapis I have been quite comfortable and I made supplication for
you, as I said, and for everyone'."[71] The religion of Sarapis was clearly still
very much a part of life in the Alexandria that Origen knew.

The Ptolemies' god Sarapis was by no means the only god worshipped
in Alexandria. Temples and shrines for numerous gods constituted a large
portion of the imposing buildings in central Alexandria. The snake god,
referred to as "Agathos Daimon" (i.e. the good demon), who appeared to
the founders of the city, had a prominent shrine in the Agora. A Greek-style
temple called the Tychaion stood in the central part of the city. Besides a
statue of the goddess Tyche (Fortune), it contained statues of many Greek
and Egyptian gods. A temple for Isis and Sarapis stood on the Canopic Way
and another for the Syrian goddess Rhea Kybele. The emperor Septimius
Severus constructed the latter in the late second or early third century AD,
probably influenced by his wife Julia Domna whose family was connected
with the priesthood of ancient Semitic religions.[72]

The landscape near the western end of the Great Harbor was dominated
by the Caesarion. Begun by Cleopatra VII in the last half of the first century
BC and completed by Augustus, it was home to the Roman imperial cult.
Busts of Roman emperors stood in the building for veneration.[73] The Caesarion can be precisely located because Augustus installed two obelisks near
its entrance. They had been made at Aswan a millennium before the founding of Alexandria. The obelisks stood in place until the nineteenth century.
An inscription on one of the bronze crabs on which the obelisks rested says
the obelisks were dedicated by Augustus in 13 BC. Excavations in the late
nineteenth century uncovered the foundation of a wall of the Caesarion 3.5
meters thick. Philo of Alexandria describes the temple as an immense, magnificent building sitting on a high point facing the harbors (*De Leg* 151). The
sanctuary was associated with the protection of sailors. A Greek inscription found in connection with the Caesarion and dated to the winter of AD
175–6, when Marcus Aurelius was in Alexandria, refers to his wife Faustina,
who had recently died on a sea voyage, as "Saviour of the fleet".[74]

---

[70] *The Adventures of Leucippe and Clitophon*, 5.2; cited in Rowlandson and Harker (2004), 88;
cf. Lesky (1966), 697. On the date of Achilles Tatius see Lesky (1966), 857, 865–6, esp. 865, n. 1.

[71] *P. Tebt.* 11.416; cited in Rowlandson and Harker (2004), 87.

[72] Haas (1997), 143.

[73] Empereur (1998), 116.

[74] Empereur (1998), 112–18.

The Emporion, where import and export duties were collected, stood near the Caesarion at the Western end of the Great Harbour.[75] There was a temple to the sea-god Poseidon in the region of the Caesarion and another on the island of Pharos. Both were built in the Ptolemaic era. A temple to Isis Pharia, goddess of sailors, stood on the island of Pharos, and a shrine to Aphrodite was located "on or near the Heptastadion". Kronos / Thoth, Egyptian god of commerce, and other appropriate gods had temples at the Emporion.[76] Around the fringes of the city stood shrines to other gods, predominantly Egyptian: Anubis, Hathor, Thoth, and the non-Egyptian Mithras, god especially of soldiers.[77]

The religion of Hermes Trismegistus seems to have arisen in Egypt during the time the Romans were in control. The Hermetic literature, at least, stems from this period in Egypt. It is attributed to Hermes Trismegistus, Asclepius, and other deities associated with him. There are philosophical texts of a Platonic sort but clearly not produced by significant philosophers, and texts on such subjects as magic, alchemy, and astrology. The philosophical texts are dated between the first and third centuries AD.[78]

Hermes Trismegistus was a syncretistic god, a blend of the Egyptian Thoth and the Greek Hermes. Thoth was the moon god and, as such, regulated time and individual destinies through his control of "the stars, seasons, months and years." He presided over the temple cults, sacred texts and formulae, and magic. He was also considered to be in charge of knowledge, language, and science, and could be regarded as personified Reason. His powers included healing and, at death, it was he who conducted the dead to the region of the gods. The Greeks associated their Hermes "with the moon, medicine and the realm of the dead". He was also the Logos or personified Reason who interpreted "the divine will to mankind" (cf. Acts 14:12) and, for the Stoics, he had the additional role of demiurge (creator).[79] The Hermetic treatise called *Poimandres* is a religious text in which the prophet of the god Poimandres claims to be a guide for humans teaching them how to be saved (*Poim* 29).

In addition to the Serapeon and the religion of Sarapis, the Museum with its great library was the other major culture-shaping institution founded in Alexandria by the early Ptolemies. The Museum was not a University, in the sense of a modern state-funded educational institution, nor, do I think, was it exactly an ancient version of a think-tank to give advice on national or commercial problems, though it was probably closer to the latter than to

[75] Haas (1997), 26.   [76] Haas (1997), 144–5.   [77] Haas (1997), 145.
[78] Fowden (1993 / 1986), xxi, 11.   [79] Fowden (1993 / 1986), 22–4.

the former. From the evidence that survives, much of the work done by the scholars of the Museum was literary, especially the collection, preservation, and correction of ancient Greek texts. Some of the scholars functioned occasionally as tutors for the royal children. Ptolemy II had been a student of Zenodotus, one of the early librarians. It has been argued that this early influence by Zenodotos gave him the idea of encouraging the Museum scholars to reconstruct the original text of Homer's works from the multiple copies that had become available in Alexandria. The project of correcting the text of the Greek classics may "have had its origin in considerations of cultural policy" by Ptolemy II. Homer's epic, along with the ancient texts of the Greek lyric poets and dramatists, was the basis of the education "which legitimized the rule of Greeks over Egyptians".[80] The attempt to produce an accurate and standardized text of Homer may, therefore, have been the result of the political agenda of the early Ptolemies.

The name "Museum" indicates that it was a shrine to the Muses. There was an official resident priest "called an *epistates*, or director, appointed by analogy with the priests who managed the temples of Egypt." Legally the Museum was set up like "Plato's school in Athens, where a school required religious status to gain the protection of Athenian law".[81] In its earliest days scholars were lured to Alexandria by the lucrative offering of the Ptolemies. Ptolemy I endowed the Museum. Its scholars received an ample tax-free salary, along with food and board. Their quarters were located in the palace and they shared a common dining room.[82] The Museum library was not a public library, but was the closed preserve of the resident state-supported scholars.[83] Not everyone admired the Museum and the work of its members. The second-century BC sceptic philosopher Timon of Phlius referred to the Museum's scholars as "'cloistered bookworms'" who argued "'endlessly in the chicken-coop of the Muses'".[84] Diogenes Laertius relates that when Aratus asked Timon how he could get "a trustworthy text of Homer" the latter replied, "'You can, if you can get hold of the ancient copies, and not the corrected copies of our day'", referring, by the latter, to those produced by the scholars of the Museum.[85]

The early Ptolemies set in motion a vast book-collecting project of borrowing, buying, and stealing Greek manuscripts. Ptolemy III Euergetes is said to have requested texts of the Greek tragedians Euripides, Aeschylus, and Sophocles from Athens for copying. He had the texts copied, then

---

[80] Blum (1991), 110.   [81] MacLeod (2000), 3–4.   [82] Casson (2001), 33–4.
[83] Staikos (2004), 165.   [84] *Timon*, frg. 12 Diels; cited in Barnes (2000), 62.
[85] *Diogenes Laertius* 9.113; tr. R. D. Hicks, LCL, Vol. 2, 523; see Staikos (2004), 167.

returned the copies and kept the originals. Galen, the second-century AD physician, relates a similar procedure. He says that books would be confiscated from ships docking in Alexandria's harbors, copied, and the copies returned to the ships. The originals were then put in the library and catalogued under the category "From the ships".[86]

The collection of books was almost entirely Greek. There is some evidence that the library's scope was intended to include the most significant works of other cultures as well. Irenaeus relates, in connection with his account of the translation of the Septuagint, that Ptolemy Soter intended to include the most significant writings of all peoples in the Alexandrian library.[87] The *Letter of Aristeas* (9), which is our oldest source concerning the Alexandrian library, also indicates that the collection was intended to be universal in its scope. The history of Babylonia, written in Greek by the third-century BC Chaldean priest Berosus, was known in Alexandria and may have been a part of Ptolemy's collection. A large book on Zoroastrianism by Hermippus, a student of the third-century BC Museum scholar Callimachus, implies a collection of material on the Persian faith in Alexandria. There may also have been Buddhist materials in Alexandria "as the result of an exchange of embassies between Asoka of India and Ptolemy II Philadelphus". And there is a strong tradition, which will be discussed in Chapter 3, that the translation of the Jewish Law into Greek at Alexandria was initiated by the Greeks for the purpose of making this work a part of the Museum library.[88] The twelfth-century Byzantine scholar Ioannes Tzetzes relates that the books in Ptolemy's library came not only from the Greeks but from "all other peoples, including the Jews". The non-Greek books, he adds, "were submitted to scholars of the respective people who were proficient in Greek and in their own language and were translated into Greek".[89] The library was clearly for Greek-speaking scholars.

The library eventually grew to perhaps 400,000 volumes. A second, daughter library was established in the Serapeon and this library is thought to have housed 90,000 volumes. Whether these were overflow volumes from the great library or copies made from works in the great library and placed in the Serapeon for a more general public is not known for certain. The large open court within which the temple of Serapis stood was surrounded by roofed stoa fronted with large columns. In the late fourth century AD Aphthonius wrote a description of the Serapeum. McKenzie

---

[86] *Commentary on Hippocrates Epidemics* III, XVIIA, 606K; cited in MacLeod (2000), 4–5.

[87] *Haer* 3.21.2; cf. Eusebius, *H.E.* 5.8.11.

[88] El-Abbadi (2004), 170.

[89] Cited in Blum (1991), 104–5.

thinks the complex he describes was probably essentially the one built by the Romans "in the late second or early third century AD".[90] In his description, Aphthonius refers to "precincts... of the stoas... built inside, some as storehouses... for the books, open to those eager to study", and says that these "lift the entire city up to the possibility of acquiring wisdom". Other sections in the stoa "were erected to venerate the traditional gods".[91] This suggests that the Serapeon library was not so limited in relation to those who might use it as the library in the Museum. This library was destroyed in the late fourth century when Theophilus, bishop of Alexandria, incited a mob of Christians to destroy the temple of Sarapis, "the quintessential symbol of paganism in the city".[92]

Some think the Museum library was destroyed in the fire set by Julius Caesar to protect himself and his troops from the Alexandrian army in 48 BC.[93] Others think that the references to books destroyed by the fire point to the destruction of some warehouses near the harbor where newly acquired books were stored before being processed into the library. The first view is based on Plutarch (*Caes* 49) and the second on Dio Cassius (*Rom Hist.* 42.38.2). There are reasons for accepting the view that the Museum library itself was not destroyed in Caesar's fire but continued to exist into the late third century AD, when the whole palace area was destroyed in the emperor Aurelian's suppression of the uprising by Queen Zenobia of Palmyra.[94] Suetonius relates, for example, that Claudius, emperor in the mid-first century AD, built an addition to the Alexandrian library, where one of his two books of history was read to a public audience every year. His other book was read elsewhere in the original library.[95] Suetonius also says that in the early second century AD the emperor Domitian sent scholars to Alexandria to copy books after the Roman library had been destroyed by fire.[96]

Many things changed in relation to the Museum and the library in the Roman period. Augustus included a bilingual library in the Caesarion which one scholar, at least, thinks may have been intended to replace the libraries in the Serapeon and the Museum "in accordance with the new cultural policy" to show that Egypt was now a Roman province and to remove the "symbolism of the Alexandrian Library as the intellectual centre of

[90] McKenzie (2007), 198–9.

[91] Aphthonius, *A Description of the Temple of Alexandria in the Midst of the Acropolis*, trans. by A. T. Reyes in McKenzie (2007), 200–1.

[92] Staikos (2004), 176.

[93] El-Abbadi (2004), 172.

[94] See Casson (2001), 45–7; Barnes (2000), 70–3; Staikos (2004), 208.

[95] *Claudius*, 42.2; cited in Casson (2001), 111.   [96] *Domitian*, 20; Barnes (2000), 72–3.

Mediterranean civilization".[97] The members of the Museum were no longer exclusively scholars and literary men. Men distinguished in government and military service received appointments, as did also distinguished athletes. In the middle of the first century AD a non-scholar, government and military man Tiberius Claudius Balbillus, was even appointed director of the library.[98] An official letter from the senate of Hermopolis written in AD 267 congratulates Aurelius Plution, one of its distinguished citizens, on his return from Rome. The honorific title with which he is addressed in the greeting is "member of the Museum". Nothing is known of his connection with scholarship, but he had been a distinguished athlete in his youth and later a procurator.[99]

The names are known of 11 members of the Museum in the Roman period who were not scholars.[100] State support of Museum members seems to have continued through the Roman period. An inscription at Antinoe honors one of the city's citizens as belonging to "the company of those maintained tax-free in the Museum, Platonic philosopher and councilor of Antinoe".[101] Caracalla, emperor from AD 211–17, when Origen was still resident in Alexandria, threatened to cut off the free board and privileges of the Museum scholars.[102]

One of the greatest contributions of the Museum and library to Alexandria was the trickle-down effect they had on Alexandrian life. Numerous teachers and students were attracted to Alexandria from the Mediterranean world. The city became known for its famous schools and teachers outside those officially connected with the Museum. Some of the most famous people associated with learning in the Hellenistic and Roman periods spent time studying, teaching, or working in Alexandria. In the following list, some of the people were connected with the Museum and others were not.

Herophilos of Chalcedon performed the first medical post-mortem examination in Alexandria; Ktesibios developed a water clock; Aristarchos of Samos perceived the heliocentric universe; and Archimedes of Syracus came and studied there. Euclid composed a large part of his Geometry in Alexandria. Zenodotos of Ephesus was probably the first to divide and publish Homers work in 24 songs; Aristophanes of Byzantium founded scientific lexicography and introduced the still valid system of accents; and the grammar which Aristarchus of Samotrace produced is still valid today.[103]

[97] Staikos (2004), 204–5.   [98] Casson (2001), 45–7.
[99] C.P. Herm. 125.ii; cited in Turner (1968), 85–6.   [100] Lewis (1963), 257–61.
[101] F. Preisigke, et al., *Sammelbuch gr. Urkunden aus Ägypten*, 6012; cited in Turner (1968), 86.
[102] Staikos (2004), 206.   [103] Orru (2002), 34.

This list can be supplemented with intellectuals of the second century AD such as "the grammarians, Apollonius, Herodian and Hephaestion; the mathematician, Menelaus; the geographer, Nicanor; the poets Dionysius the Periegete, Areius and Pancrates" and, from the first century AD, Philo Judaeus.[104]

In the middle of the second century AD Galen left Asia Minor to spend four to six years in Alexandria studying medicine. He considered the advances made in the study of anatomy in third-century BC Alexandria not to have been surpassed until his own century, and he thought the Alexandrian anatomist Numisianus to have re-established Alexandria's superiority in anatomical studies for the Roman period.[105] Also in third-century BC Alexandria, Herophilus had discovered the nervous system, and "Erasistratus mapped the blood-vascular system".[106] Rufus and Soranus, noted physicians of Ephesus, had both studied medicine in Alexandria before Galen in the second century AD. There is evidence for the presence of physicians in Egypt in the second century AD from "Athens, Cilicia, Pontus, Smyrna, Ephesus, Pergamum, and Syrian Antioch".[107]

Alexandria was the place where Greeks living in other Egyptian cities sent their children for education beyond that of the gymnasia. Sometimes, however, the reputation exceeded the reality and the students were disappointed with their Alexandrian teachers. A young man sent to Alexandria to study under its famous teachers wrote home to his father:

For now in my search for a tutor I find that both Chaeremon the teacher and Didymus son of Aristocles, in whose hands there was hope that I too might have some success, are no longer in town, but [the teachers are all] trash, in whose hands most pupils have taken the straight road to having their talents spoiled.[108]

Plotinus initially had a similar experience in his search for a teacher. Porphyry tells us that Plotinus had been recommended to the philosophers in Alexandria who had high reputations as teachers, but he found their lectures so disappointing that he was depressed. On telling a friend of his experience, the friend sent him to the Alexandrian philosopher Ammonius Saccas. Plotinus found Ammonius to be a worthy teacher and continued his study with him for the next 11 years.[109]

Alexandria throbbed with intellectual energy. It had a long history of literary scholarship and scientific investigation which gave it the kind of

---

104 Trapp (2004), 126.   105 Staden (2004), 180–1.
106 Vallance (2000), 97.   107 Staden (2004), 185.
108 *P. Oxy.* XVII, 2190; cited in Rowlandson and Harker (2004), 86–7.
109 *Life of Plotinus*, 3.

intellectual momentum one finds in old European university cities today. Tradition was important to the scholars at Alexandria, as shown in the concern they displayed for the textual tradition of Homer in the development of critical instruments to determine and preserve the accuracy of the text. There was, however, a critical attitude towards the tradition. Zenodotus, the Homeric specialist at Alexandria, wanted to produce a new, accurate text of Homer's works, but he did not want to eliminate the textual tradition which he had received. He developed, consequently, a system for marking additions and omissions which left the original text with which he worked intact.

In the second and first centuries BC the Jewish authors Philo the Epic Poet and Theodotus rewrote Biblical history in the Greek hexameters of Homer; Ezekiel the Tragedian retold the story of the exodus in the iambic meter of the Greek tragedians; Aristobulus the Jewish philosopher combined aspects of the Jewish law and Greek philosophy; and Demetrius the Chronographer wrestled with problems in Biblical chronology in the scientific manner of the Greeks. It cannot be said with certainty that all these men worked in Alexandria, but Alexandria is the location favored by most modern scholars as their provenance. The fragmentary remains of these Jewish authors suggest a lively intellectual community in the Delta quarter where the Jews lived in Ptolemaic Egypt. In the first century AD Philo Judaeus labored as a philosopher and interpreter of the Jewish Scriptures in Alexandria. He represents a kind of innovation in the Scriptural tradition with his philosophical interpretation. He was not the first Jew to apply philosophical understandings to the Jewish Scriptures but he did it most extensively, it seems.

ORIGEN IN ALEXANDRIA

Where and how should we think of Origen in this large, dynamic, multi-racial city? It is not possible to provide anything like a street address for Origen. It is possible, however, in my opinion, to eliminate some possibilities and, thereby, to shrink, at least, the dimensions of the city where we might expect his activity to have been concentrated. A few things may also be concluded concerning his race, family, education, and circle of acquaintances. Consideration of his Christian roots and relationships are postponed until the next chapter. Here I am concerned with what we might surmise about Origen in relation to the aspects of Alexandria and Alexandrian life that I have sketched in this chapter. Most of what I say in this section must be inferential. In his many writings Origen says next to nothing about Alexandria or his life there.

It is unlikely that Origen was an Egyptian, although his fourth-century antagonist Epiphanius claims that he was.[110] His Egyptian name, which means "descendant of Horus", cannot be used to argue that he was Egyptian. It has been shown that personal names do not provide a clear way of identifying ethnicity in Egypt. A father, for example, writing to have his four children enrolled in the official records lists their names: the first name is Greek, the second Roman, the third has both a Greek and Egyptian name, and the fourth has an Egyptian name. All four children had the same father and mother.[111]

Origen's education, privileges, and connections suggest that his family was Greek. It has been pointed out that Alexandria's "educational institutions were...class specific, largely restricted to the wealthy and more cultured elements of the populace".[112] Porphyry refers to Origen as "a Greek, educated in Greek subjects".[113] Origen began his working life as a teacher, probably a *grammatikos*, which was the rough equivalent of a teacher at the secondary level today.[114] This suggests he was Greek, and not Egyptian.[115] The first stage of Greek education was referred to as the study of grammar. Since evidence from other cities of Roman Egypt suggests that the same occupations were handed on in families from generation to generation, Origen's father was probably a *grammatikos* before him.[116] Eusebius refers to Origen's father advancing the boy in his Greek lessons and also refers to his insistence that Origen study the divine Scriptures as well as the normal curriculum of Greek lessons. These statements suggest that Origen's father was an educator and that he was in charge of at least the early education of his son (*H.E.* 6.2.7–8, 15).

Origen's family probably resided among the Greek inhabitants of Alexandria on the fringes of the Brucheion. In the first half of the second century AD Apollonius Dyscolus, the Alexandrian grammarian, lived in the Brucheion district "'near the road'", which probably means the Canopic Way.[117] There were numerous Greek administrators, clerical workers, and teachers in Alexandria. The Greek satirist Lucian of Samosata, for example, held an appointment in the court system in Alexandria in the late second century AD. His job seems to have involved that of court clerk, registrar, and keeper of records.

---

[110] *Pan.* 64.2; followed by Heisey (2000), 29.   [111] Bagnall (1993), 232–3.
[112] Haas (1997), 62.   [113] Eusebius, *H.E.* 6.19.7.
[114] See Chapter 2 in "The ecclesiastical school directed by Origen in Alexandria", p. 60.
[115] Eusebius, *H.E.* 6.3.1; cf. 6.3.8.
[116] Haas (1997), 57–8.
[117] Blank (1982), 5, 65–6.

He refers to it as an unimportant job but well salaried.[118] Ammianus Marcellinus refers to the Brucheion as home to many significant personalities and authors such as Aristarchus, Herodian, and Ammonius Saccas.[119] It has been argued, on the basis of Eusebius' reference to the escape of many Christians from the Brucheion during a siege of that section of the city by the Romans in the late third century AD, that the Brucheion was the location of the orthodox Church and the Alexandrian catechetical school.[120]

Origen was befriended by two wealthy residents of Alexandria. After his father's martyrdom and the confiscation of the family property he was taken in by a wealthy Alexandrian woman who had a home large enough to provide for a second Christian man at the same time, whom Eusebius refers to as a heretic from Syria (*H.E.* 6.2.12–14). Later, Origen was befriended by a wealthy Alexandrian named Ambrose who, Eusebius relates, was converted from the heresy of Valentinus at the time many educated persons were seeking Origen out for instruction. Ambrose later provided Origen with the necessary stenographers for him to carry out his publication of commentaries on Scripture.[121] We do not know the source of wealth for either of Origen's benefactors, but the most common source associated with Alexandria's upper class in the papyri was "the ownership of agricultural land in the chora.... Some of these upper-class property owners possessed a house (or houses) in Alexandria, a house situated in an up-country nome metropolis, as well as several tracts of agricultural land."[122] The Brucheion is the most likely place of residence for both of Origen's benefactors, and this would put Origen himself there. The Brucheion is also the most likely location for the educated persons, referred to by Eusebius, to have had contact with Origen or to have heard of his reputation.

Alexandria's busy harbors facilitated the extension of Origen's reputation and influence beyond Egypt. Boats, not roads, were the primary means of mobility for people in the Roman empire.[123] All the major cities of the empire were port cities. Alexandria's ports served not only the commercial, but also the personal needs of its citizens. Origen was a very mobile person during the time he lived in Alexandria. Eusebius catalogues six major journeys he made to other cities of the empire. He traveled from Alexandria to

---

[118] *Apology for the "Salaried Posts in Great Houses"* 12; Mackie (1904), xii.

[119] *Res Gestae* 22.16.16; cited in Andresen (1979), 449–50.

[120] Andresen (1979), 440–1, 449–50.

[121] Eusebius, *H.E.* 6.18.1–2; 23.1–2; Jerome, *Ep.* 43.1. See Chapter 4 in "Ambrose, the Valentinians, and Origen's *Commentary on John* 1:1a", p. 89.

[122] Haas (1997), 55.

[123] Stark (2006), 74.

Rome (*H.E.* 6.14.10), Arabia (*H.E.* 6.19.15), Caesarea (*H.E.* 6.19.16), Antioch of Syria (*H.E.* 6.21.3), again to Caesarea and on to Greece (*H.E.* 6.23.4), and, finally, he made a permanent move from Alexandria to Caesarea (*H.E.* 6.26.1). On all of these trips Origen would have departed on ships sailing from Alexandria's harbors.

Origen would not have had access to the famous Museum library. This library was reserved for use by the state-supported scholars. Nor would Origen have made use of the library in the Serapeon or that later established by the Romans in the Caesarion. The Serapeon was a temple to Alexandria's most famous pagan god and the Caesarion was the shrine of the Roman imperial cult. It is inconceivable that Origen, the young Christian scholar whose father had been martyred for his allegiance to the Christian faith and who held his father's martyrdom in highest esteem would have frequented any such establishment in the early third century when pagan–Christian tensions still ran high.[124]

The Alexandrian intellectual milieu, nevertheless, made a definite impression on Origen. Alexandria was a city of books outside those in the great libraries. This was part of the trickle-down effect mentioned above. Alexandria was known for its books. People living outside Alexandria ordered books from booksellers in the city.[125] Origen himself had gathered a collection of non-Christian ancient writings as a young man that was sufficient in size to provide him with very modest daily living expenses when he later sold it because he had decided to devote his attention completely to the study and teaching of divine subjects.[126] When he later moved to Caesarea, one of the things that he did there was to establish a Christian library which was still in existence in the fourth century and used by Eusebius, Rufinus, and Jerome. The bookish side of Alexandrian society had been impressed on the young Origen.

Origen's scholarly interests and methods were also imprinted with the mark of Alexandrian literary scholarship. One of the tasks undertaken by the scholars of the Museum library was the establishment of an accurate text of the most important of the Greek classics, especially the texts of Homer. Zenodotus, in particular, collected numerous texts of Homer, compared them, and developed a system of marking additions or omissions from his new standard text by the use of asterisks (*) and obelisks (†) so that he might preserve the traditions from which he produced his new text. Origen, much later in Alexandria, gathered several Greek translations of the Hebrew Scriptures and copied them side by side in a massive

---

[124]   Origen, *HomEz.* 4.8; cf. Eusebius, *H.E.* 1.1–2.6.

[125]   *P. Oxy.* 18.2192; cited in Abd-el-Ghani (2004), 177–8.   [126]   Eusebius, *H.E.* 6.3.9.

textual study known as the *Hexapla*.[127] Origen's reasons for this work are not known for certain, but one purpose was to establish where the Septuagint translation, which had been made in Alexandria by the Jews a few centuries before Origen, differed from the Hebrew text. Origen applied the critical signs invented by Zenodotus to mark where the Septuagint either added to the Hebrew text or lacked things that were in that text.

The literary scholars of the Alexandrian Museum also produced numerous commentaries on the classical works collected in the library. Aristarchus of Samothrace (216–144 BC) was tutor to the children of Ptolemy VI and instructor of a large group of other pupils. He was an authority on the writings of Homer and developed the method of interpretation which later went under the heading of interpreting Homer by Homer. He used evidence within Homer's writings themselves, in other words, to interpret Homer's words and sentences. Origen later applied this methodology to the study of the Bible and referred to it as "interpreting spiritual things by spiritual".[128] Aristarchus, "[u]nlike most editors of that time, who delivered their notes on the text orally in the lecture room ... wrote lengthy ... commentaries (*hypomnemata*) on the works he edited". One source puts the number of his books of commentaries at 800.[129] In the second half of the first century BC, when Rome had brought the Ptolemaic rule of Egypt to an end, the Museum scholar Didymus, nicknamed "Bronze-guts", produced between 3,500 and 4,000 books, most of which were commentaries and glossaries.[130] Origen, who produced more commentaries on the Bible than any other early Christian author, grew up in an intellectual environment where the reading and writing of commentaries on ancient texts was commonplace. He took over the format of commentary literature that had been developed by the commentators on Greek literature and applied it to the production of Christian commentaries on Scripture.[131] There is a papyrus from the second century AD which appears to have been a school exercise. It is a rather "garbled" list of librarians of the Museum.[132] If this was, in fact, a school exercise, it shows that the librarians of the Museum library were a subject of study in the curriculum and, if their names were memorized by

---

[127] See the section on the Hexapla in Chapter 3 below.

[128] Heine (1997a), 135–6.

[129] Staikos (2004), 183.

[130] Casson (2001), 44–5.

[131] Heine (1995a), 3–12; Neuschäfer (1987), 58–84; 139–246. See Chapter 4 below, "The Biblical commentaries produced at Alexandria", p. 84.

[132] *P. Oxy.* 1241; cited in Barnes (2000), 69.

students, surely something of their accomplishments was also studied. It has been surmised that "[k]nowledge of the work of the scholars of Alexandria probably reached the general public through the schoolmasters, who attended their lectures and read their commentaries".[133] This would mean that Origen would have been exposed to the library scholars and their methods of working as a part of his early educational experience.

Alexandria was especially known as a center of philosophy. Alexandrian Platonism was a significantly modified form of Plato's system that had adopted viewpoints from other philosophical schools.[134] Its most famous representatives were the late-second-century Platonist Ammonius Saccas, and Plotinus, who taught in the early third century and is considered to have been the founder of Neo-Platonism. It has been common fare in studies of Origen to assume that he had been a student of Ammonius Saccas with whom Plotinus studied for 11 years. This can no longer be simply assumed or, perhaps, even convincingly defended. A plausible case has been made that there were two men named Ammonius in Alexandria, one the Platonist who taught Plotinus and didn't write anything, and the other a Christian who produced the Christian writings with which Eusebius incorrectly associated the Platonist Ammonius.[135] Porphyry's reference to Origen as a "hearer" of the Platonist Ammonius[136] may be correct, in contrast to "student" or "follower" of Ammonius. The term "hearer" "can refer to a single, or repeated, attendance at a lecture which does not result in a student relationship".[137]

In a letter of Origen preserved by Eusebius (*H.E.* 6.19.11–14) he refers to going to the lectures of an unnamed teacher of philosophy in Alexandria in order to become more conversant with Greek philosophy so that he would be able better to answer those cultured people, sometimes heretics, who were seeking him out. Origen does not identify this teacher as Ammonius and we should not do that either.[138] If Origen did attend a few lectures of Ammonius Saccas, it must have been only shortly before his departure from Alexandria to Caesarea in AD 232, for Ammonius may have

---

[133] Turner (1968), 109.

[134] Although it is old, Bigg (1968/1886) is still a good introduction. See also Edwards (2002).

[135] *H.E.* 6.19.10. There were also two men in Alexandria named Origen: Origen, the Christian who probably was not a student of Ammonius, and Origen, the pagan who was a student of Ammonius. For the latter see Porphyry, *The Life of Plotinus*, ch. 3 (*Plotinus* 1 (1989), 11).

[136] Cited in Eusebius, *H.E.* 6.19.6.

[137] Schwyzer (1983), 36.

[138] Schwyzer (1983), 21–36; cf. Edwards (1993), 169–81.

begun teaching not long before AD 231.[139] If this date for the beginning of Ammonius Saccas' teaching in Alexandria is correct, then the philosopher to whom Origen refers in the above-mentioned letter could not have been Ammonius Saccas. Origen says that Heraclas had already been studying with this teacher of philosophy for five years when he began to attend his lectures.[140] Origen did become conversant with Greek philosophy for he is able to think and reason with the tools of philosophy.[141] It seems likely, however, that this ability was attained through the instruction of someone other than the Platonist Ammonius Saccas.

[139] Schwyzer (1983), 34, 36. Schwyzer's argument is based on Porphyry, *The Life of Plotinus* 3 (*Plotinus* 1 (1989), 9), where he relates that Plotinus was 28 years old when he first made contact with Ammonius and that he continued as his student until his 39th year, when he joined Gordian's army to fight the Persians, which Schwyzer dates in 242. This means that Plotinus joined Ammonius in 231. Schwyzer assumes that Ammonius had begun teaching only a short time before Plotinus found him.

[140] Eusebius, *H.E.* 6.19.13.

[141] Heine (1993a), 89–117.

2

Alexandrian Christianity and the Formation of Origen's Thought

When and how Christianity first came to Alexandria is a mystery. Evidence from archaeology and the non-literary papyri for Christianity in Egypt before the fourth century is essentially non-existent.[1] The New Testament also is silent about Christianity in Alexandria. There were Jews from Egypt and neighboring Cyrene present in Jerusalem at Pentecost (Acts 2:10), and there were Jews from Alexandria and Cyrene, members of "the synagogue of the Freedmen" in Jerusalem, who debated with Stephen. It appears that it was these particular Jews who set the process in motion that resulted in Stephen's arrest and execution (Acts 6:9–14 NRSV). Nothing is said, however, of *Christian* Alexandrian Jews in either of these contexts.

THE JERUSALEM ORIGINS OF CHRISTIANITY IN ALEXANDRIA

The general consensus among most current scholars of early Egyptian Christianity is that "Christianity reached Egypt from Palestine in a form strongly influenced by Judaism."[2] Ritter has argued that those who took Christianity to Alexandria came from Peter, James the brother of Jesus, and John the son of Zebedee, the three that Paul refers to as "pillars of the Church" in Jerusalem.[3] The Christian community in Alexandria was so strongly Jewish, it is suggested, that no clear distinction between Christians and Jews was made until sometime in the second century. It may even be an

---

[1] Pearson (2006), 331.

[2] Based on the work of Roberts (1979), 49. See also Klijn (1986), 162–4; Runia (1993), 193–4; Pearson (2004), 283; Paget (2004), 157; Bagnall (1993), 278; and Jakab (2001), 53–64, who follows Daniélou, however, in thinking that the community originated after the fall of Jerusalem in AD 70. This whole school of thought regarding the Jewish/Jerusalem origin of Alexandrian Christianity grew out of a negative reaction to the theory put forth by W. Bauer that the earliest Christian community in Alexandria was a Gnostic Christian community using the *Gospel of the Egyptians* as their Gospel; Bauer, (1934/1971), 44–60.

[3] Ritter (1987), 163–5.

anachronism to call these earliest Jesus believers in Alexandria Christians. They were simply a new variant among the many variants of Judaism in the city.[4] Barnard suggested that the author of *The Epistle of Barnabas* was a converted rabbi from the Alexandrian Synagogue. He dates the *Epistle* "c. A.D. 117–19" and thinks it presupposes a "long tradition of worship, catechesis, and liturgy". On the basis of the strong Jewish elements in the Epistle he argues that there were Christians of Hebrew descent "in Egypt at an earlier period".[5] Paget sees commonality between the Jewish and Christian communities in Alexandria in their use of the Septuagint, their focus on Scriptural exegesis, and their attempt to relate their Biblical faith to the Greek heritage in which many of them had been raised.[6]

Apollos is the one Jewish Christian who is identified as an Alexandrian in the New Testament. He makes his first appearance as a Christian missionary in Ephesus. He is identified as "a Jew . . . a native of Alexandria . . . well-versed in the scriptures". He was a Christian before he went to Ephesus, for Luke describes him as one who "taught accurately the things concerning Jesus" and who could show from "the scriptures that the Messiah is Jesus" (Acts 18:24–8; NRSV). What Luke does not tell us is where Apollos had first heard of Jesus. It is well-known that the text of Acts 18:25 in the fifth century Codex Bezae (D) says that Apollos had been "instructed in the word in his fatherland". That these words stood in the original text of Acts, however, is strongly questioned by scholars. Their absence, on the other hand, does not negate the possibility that it was in Alexandria that Apollos first learned of Jesus. If we assume that the latter is correct, that must mean that there was a Christian community in Alexandria by the mid-first century for by c. AD 54, when Paul wrote 1 Corinthians, Apollos had already taught in Corinth and Paul had encouraged him to visit Corinth again (1 Cor. 1:12; 3:5–9; 16:12).[7] I will show in what follows that all of the evidence, such as it is, points to a date in the first half of the first century for the presence of a Christian community in Alexandria and most of it suggests that the community came from Jerusalem.

Eusebius asserts that the evangelist Mark first took Christianity to Alexandria and that a multitude of believers sprang up in the city. Eusebius' understanding of the establishment and rapid growth of Christianity in Alexandria, however, was based on his view that Philo's treatise *On the*

---

[4] Pearson (2004), 283.   [5] Barnard (1966), 47–52.

[6] Paget (2004), 158–9. In this regard see the discussion in Chapter 1 at the end of the section on "Culture", p. 19, of Philo the Epic Poet, Theodotus, Ezekiel the Tragedian, Aristobulus, and Demetrius the Chronographer, as well as the work of Philo Judaeus.

[7] See Ritter (1987), 160.

Contemplative Life about the therapeutae on Lake Mareotis described the Christian community in Alexandria (*H.E.* 2.16.1–17.24). Eusebius' Christian interpretation of Philo's treatise has not been accepted, though the precise identity of Philo's group remains a mystery.[8] Eusebius adds that, in the eighth year of Nero's reign (AD 61), Annianus succeeded Mark in his ministry at Alexandria (*H.E.* 2.24), thus providing the terminal date for his understanding of Mark's time in Alexandria. The earliest extant reference to a visit of Mark to Alexandria is in the letter of Clement of Alexandria to Theodore, if it is a genuine letter of Clement.[9] In the letter Mark is said to have gone to Alexandria from Rome after Peter's death, which would have been in the reign of Nero. The letter does not suggest, however, that Mark was the first to evangelize Alexandria. It assumes, rather, the existence of a Christian community there when he arrives.[10]

The fourth-century Pseudo-Clementine *Homilies* present Barnabas as a missionary in Alexandria. Clement of Rome is said to have heard that the Son of God had appeared in Judea. He set sail from Rome to Judea to learn about him but his ship was blown off course and landed in Alexandria, where Clement asked some philosophers if there was anyone there who had heard of the one said to be Son of God who appeared in Judea. They informed him that there was a man named Barnabas from Judea who claimed to be one of the man's disciples living in Alexandria. Clement met Barnabas, who was hurrying to return to Judea for an unspecified festival. Clement followed Barnabas to Judea a few days later where he was introduced to Peter, who was preparing to leave on a missionary journey which would culminate in his preaching in Rome (*ClemHom* 1). There is no evidence to verify this story. There are, however, two interesting points reflected in the story that may suggest some connection with ancient traditions. One is the close connection assumed between Christianity in Alexandria and the Church in Judea, and the other is the early date that the story suggests for the presence of Christianity in Alexandria. It assumes Christian missionary work in Alexandria by the Jewish-Christian community in Judea before Peter had gone to Rome.[11]

---

[8]   See the summary discussion by F. H. Colson, *Philo* 9 (1995/1941), 104–11. Grant (1986), 180, argued that Philo's therapeutae provided the most plausible precedent for the later Christian school in Alexandria.

[9]   Smith (1973), 446–53.

[10]   Pearson (1986), 138.

[11]   Paget (1994), 36, gives some credence to a visit of Barnabas to Alexandria. He also notes that it is only in works associated with Alexandria that there are references to the Epistle of Barnabas and suggests that an actual visit of Barnabas to Alexandria would make sense of the attachment of his name to a letter written there.

It has been suggested that the letter of the emperor Claudius to the Alexandrians dated in November AD 41 may allude to Jewish-Christian missionaries from Palestine when it forbids the Jews of Alexandria to invite in Jews from Syria who foment trouble.[12] While there is no proof that Claudius' reference is to Christian Jews from Syria (i.e. Palestine), it is a possibility.[13] The presence of Jewish-Christian preachers in Alexandria in the early forties would certainly fit with the references to the Alexandrian Christian Jew Apollos in Acts and 1 Corinthians.

CONTINUITY BETWEEN EARLY ALEXANDRIAN JEWISH CHRISTIANITY AND THE LATER ALEXANDRIAN CHRISTIAN COMMUNITY

The Alexandrian Jewish population was severely reduced in the revolt during Trajan's reign, but it was not exterminated. The Alexandrian Jews sent an embassy to Hadrian c. 119 to defend the Jewish community against charges made by the Greek community. This suggests that there was still some communal organization in the Alexandrian Jewish community after the revolt in the time of Trajan.[14] A papyrus text in Hebrew from Oxyrhynchus laments "the misfortunes suffered by the Jews 'in the days of our oppressors'—which the editor identifies as the period following the revolt of 115–17".[15] The Alexandrian Jewish community, however, seems not to have recovered in the same way that other Mediterranean Jewish communities did after the Bar Cochba revolt which Hadrian put down c. AD 135. Evidence concerning Jews in Alexandria in the second and third centuries AD is very scarce.[16]

---

[12] See Pearson (1986), 134–5. The letter is *P. Lond 1912*, and can be found in *Select Papyri* (1934), 78–89.

[13] Jakab (2001), 43–5, thinks this not possible and concludes, because of lack of hard evidence to the contrary, that "Christianity by-passed Alexandria in its ancient apostolic period". Koester (1982), 219, on the other hand, represents the view more generally accepted concerning Christian beginnings in Alexandria when he admits that "there is no direct evidence for the beginnings of Christianity in Egypt" but thinks "there can be little doubt that the Christian mission must have reached Alexandria during I CE". Barnard (1966), 43–4, thinks the letter may refer to the Jewish reinforcements that poured into Alexandria from other Jewish centers after the pogrom when Flaccus was governor of Egypt.

[14] Haas (1997), 103.

[15] Haas (1997), 121, citing F. Klein-Franke, "A Hebrew Lamentation from Roman Egypt", ZPE 51 (1983), 80–4.

[16] Haas (1997), 105. Bagnall (1993), 278, considers Hadrian to have virtually eliminated the Jewish community in Alexandria.

Should we, then, think that the early Jewish Christianity of the first and early second century left an imprint on Alexandrian Christianity that was still discernible in the time of Origen? There is some papyrological evidence that there were still Jews in Alexandria in Origen's time.[17] There is also evidence in Origen's Alexandrian works of contacts with Jewish Christians in the city. A fragment from the *Commentary on John*, which would have been a part of one of the books written in Alexandria, suggests that Origen knew Christians there who were circumcised and "wished to embrace Judaism openly" (*FragJn* 8). While it is not impossible, it is not likely, that these were Gentile Christians. It is much more likely that they were Jews who had become Christians but still wished to continue Jewish religious practices. He also refers to the rarity of believers from the Hebrews in the first book of his *Commentary on John* (1.7), and implies that they fall far short of reaching the number of 144,000 mentioned in Revelation 7:4. This statement, however, does not seem to have been directed specifically to the situation in Alexandria but to have been a general statement about the number of Jewish believers in the Church universal.

There was a teacher in Alexandria who influenced Origen's thinking on several subjects whom he refers to as "the Hebrew". He is mentioned in the Alexandrian portions of the *Commentary on John*, in a fragment from his Alexandrian commentary on the Psalms, and in the *On First Principles*.[18] This man must have been a Christian teacher in Alexandria of Hebrew origin. He may have been the same Jewish-Christian teacher Origen later mentions who had fled to Alexandria because he had abandoned the law and accepted the Christian faith (*HomJer* 20.2). Origen also knew a *Gospel according to the Hebrews*, which is thought to have been used by the Jewish-Christian community in Alexandria.[19] He has clearly read the work and, while he does not seem to have accepted it himself, he does not speak against it or those who use it (*ComJn* 2.87–8). There is no evidence for significant contact between Origen and a Jewish community in Alexandria. The Jews he knew in Alexandria appear to have been Christian Jews, such as the Hebrew teacher whom he highly regarded, and the community that used the *Gospel according to the Hebrews*.

There is a suggestion in Athanasius, the fourth-century bishop of Alexandria, that Jewish practices had left a lasting imprint on the Alexandrian Church. Athanasius recommends a psalm to be recited on the first, second, fourth, and sixth days of the week (*Letter to Marcellinus* 23). The psalms he

---

[17] Tcherikover and Fuks (1957–64), 225ff.   [18] *ComJn* 1.215; *Phil* 2.3; *Princ* 1.3.4; 4.3.14.

[19] *New Testament Apocrypha* (1963/1959), 158–65.

recommends for these four days are the same as those the *Mishnah* says the Levites sang in the temple on those four days of the week (*m. Tamid* 7.4). One of the more obvious traces of the continuing imprint of its early Jewish-Christian origins is the acceptance and use of the works of Philo in a segment, at least, of the Alexandrian Christian community. Van den Hoek has shown the importance of Philo for Clement of Alexandria, though Clement rarely mentions him by name.[20] Runia has made a similar argument for the importance of Philo for Origen, though again Philo is referred to by name only rarely. Runia notes that in most of Origen's anonymous references to Philo he is referred to as a *"predecessor"* and thinks this suggests that Origen saw himself standing in an exegetical tradition reaching back at least as far as Philo.[21] It is also significant that Origen never criticizes Philo's exegesis in these citations. He sees himself and Philo as "being on the same side" so to speak. The discovery of third-century papyrus texts of Philo in Christian households in provincial towns far removed from Alexandria shows the extent to which Philo's thought "had penetrated Christian circles".[22] The key to the importance of Philo for Origen and for the ways Origen treats his thought, it seems to me, is that an earlier segment of the Christian community in Alexandria had embraced Philo's works, and Origen had inherited this legacy.[23] There were several lines, some more direct than others, connecting third-century Alexandrian Christianity with the Jewish matrix in which it had been born in the first century. We will have occasion to notice the influence of several of these connections in the formation of Origen's thought as we examine his work in the chapters to come.

THE STRUCTURE OF THE ALEXANDRIAN CHRISTIAN COMMUNITY IN THE SECOND CENTURY

Eusebius provides a list of seven men who allegedly led the Christian community in Alexandria in the time between Mark, whom he asserts first evangelized Alexandria, and bishop Demetrius in the time of Origen.[24] He

---

[20] Van den Hoek (1990), 185.   [21] Runia (1993), 163.   [22] Runia (1993), 23–4.

[23] Jakab (2001), 53–64, holds a view similar to this. He thinks the group in which Christianity took root in Alexandria was middle-class, educated Hellenized Jews who were spiritual heirs of Philo, as well as proselytes to Judaism, and pagan sympathizers (God-fearers). This group bequeathed the works of Philo, along with the LXX, to Alexandrian Christianity "after the disappearance of the Jewish community of the city" (55).

[24] *H.E.* 2.16.1; 2.24; 3.14; 3.21; 4.1; 4.4; 4.5.5.

appears to want these men to be understood as bishops of the Alexandrian Christian community but the language he uses is elusive. Only Cerdo, who died around AD 109, is referred to with the term bishop (*episcopos*) (*H.E.* 4.1). Nor does Eusebius flesh out these names with any details beyond the times of their appointments and their deaths. No other ancient Christian writers mention them. If they were leaders in the Alexandrian Church it is unclear exactly what their offices may have been. It seems rather certain that they were not bishops of Alexandria and that, in all probability, there was no one prior to Demetrius to whom this title can be applied in the sense of a monarchial episcopate.

Ritter thinks the Jerusalem origin of Alexandrian Christianity may explain why there was no monarchical bishop there until Demetrius in the time of Origen. He argues that the community was led by a presbyter system on the model of the Synagogue of the diaspora.[25] Jerome, who accepted Eusebius' view that Mark evangelized Alexandria, says that from the time of Mark the evangelist up to the episcopates of Heraclas and Dionysius in the mid-third century the presbyters at Alexandria always chose one from among themselves to become bishop (*Ep* 146.1.6). While this statement refers to a bishop, it underlines the tradition of the existence of a powerful body of presbyters in the Alexandrian Christian community.

What evidence there is suggests that the earliest Christian community in Alexandria was led by presbyters and teachers. Dionysius, bishop of Alexandria in the mid-third century, refers to summoning "the presbyters and teachers" in the region of Arsinoë (Eusebius, *H.E.* 7.24.6). Van den Broek raises the question of whether or not this structure of presbyters and teachers was a continuation of the structure of the Alexandrian Synagogue, with the Christian presbyter continuing the role of the Jewish presbyter and the Christian teacher continuing that of the rabbi. He makes the interesting observation that, "[a]ccording to later Egyptian tradition there were 12 presbyters in the Alexandrian Church from the beginning". He thinks this tradition must be ancient because, "[t]he same number of presbyters is also indicated in the Jewish-Christian Ps.-Clementines for Antioch and Caesarea and even specified in the Syrian *Testamentum Domini*". He notes the predominance of the number 12 in the organization and leadership of the people of Israel and concludes that "[i]t would not be surprising if the Alexandrian Christians had organized themselves in this manner as the new people of God after the destruction of the Jewish community".[26] The importance of teachers in the leadership structure of early Jewish

[25] Ritter (1986), 163–5.   [26] Van den Broek (1996), 189–91.

Christianity is made clear in the Jewish-Christian document called *The Shepherd of Hermas*, which, as we will see below, Origen had read at Alexandria. Hermas joins teachers with apostles, bishops, and deacons in a list of those who have faithfully served the people of God (*Vis* 3.5.1), and links them three times with apostles as people who proclaim the word of God (*Sim* 9.15.4; 16.5; 25.2).

Jakab has suggested that Origen's discussion of the community of Israel and the Levitical order at the beginning of his *Commentary on John* reflects the structure of the Alexandrian Christian community at the beginning of the third century. He thinks the Alexandrian Christians were divided into three distinct groups on the pattern of the ancient Jewish religious community: the masses, who had no particular religious functions; the priests and Levites devoted to the word and worship of God, whom he identifies with the Christian presbytery; and the high priest in the order of Aaron.[27] This is an interesting suggestion and, if it should be so, we may be able to see hints of some of the structure that has been discussed above as well as a hint of the tension Origen was already feeling between himself and the Alexandrian bishop Demetrius in this text. Origen was never made a presbyter in the Alexandrian Christian community. The question is where he considers himself to stand, if this analogy with ancient Israel is intended to depict the community in Alexandria. He might be thought to include himself among the masses since he speaks in the first person when he says, "Most of us who approach the teachings of Jesus...would perhaps be those from the tribes who have a little fellowship with the priests and support the service of God in a few things" (*ComJn* 1.10). He then switches to the third person when he says, immediately after this, that "those who devote themselves to the divine Word and truly exist by the service of God alone will properly be said to be the Levites and priests" (*ComJn* 1.10). On the other hand, he uses the first person again shortly after this when he asserts that his every action as well as his entire life is "dedicated to God" (*ComJn* 1.12).[28] This would seem to place him in the Levitical category of priests and Levites. What this may suggest is that the organizational model based on the Synagogue, suggested by Van den Broek above, in which the community was led by presbyters *and* teachers was the community structure in which Origen worked. He functioned as a teacher and, as such, held a position in the community different from but parallel to that of the presbyters.

---

[27] Jakab (2001), 194–6.
[28] Translations from *Origen: Commentary on the Gospel according to John Books 1–10* (1989), 33–4.

The analogy with the ancient community of Israel described in Leviticus may also contain hints of changes in this structure that Demetrius was introducing which Origen found disturbing. Origen emphasizes that there can be "high priests according to the order of Aaron, but not according to the order of Melchisedech" (*ComJn* 1.11).[29] High priests in Aaron's order should be men who "excel all others" and who hold the highest rank in their generation. The high priesthood of Melchisedech is inimitable for all except Christ. Origen's contrast between high priests in the order of Aaron and in the order of Melchisedech might suggest that Demetrius had, in some way, assumed an authority in Alexandria that earlier "high priests" chosen out of the group of Alexandrian presbyters had not. He might even be hinting subtly that Demetrius is not even qualified to be a high priest in Aaron's order.

CHRISTIAN LITERATURE OF THE SECOND CENTURY ASSOCIATED WITH ALEXANDRIA

My concern here is to look at some of the literature produced by Christians in Alexandria and not works produced elsewhere which were used by Alexandrian Christians, such as the various writings of the New Testament for which there is an abundance of evidence of their early usage in the literary papyri found in Egypt. I also do not attempt to provide an exhaustive list of second-century Alexandrian Christian literature, but to select some of the literature which can, with a reasonable degree of probability, be considered to have originated in Alexandria.[30] The purpose of this brief survey is to get some idea of how Christians in second-century Alexandria thought about their faith.

I begin with three documents which, though extant only in a few fragments, seem most likely to have originated in Alexandria: The *Kerygma Petrou* or *Preaching of Peter,* *The Gospel of the Hebrews,* and *The Gospel of the Egyptians.* The *Kerygma Petrou* appears in early Christian literature only in citations in the writings of Clement of Alexandria and in a reference in Origen, who says the Valentinian Heracleon had cited it.[31] Clement clearly

---

[29] Translations from *Origen: Commentary on the Gospel according to John Books 1–10* (1989), 33–4.

[30] For a much more exhaustive listing and discussion see Pearson (2006), 332–4, and (2004), 43–81.

[31] Clement *Strom* 1.29.182–3; 2.15.68.2; *EclProph* 58; *Strom* 6.5.39.2–40.2; 6.5.41.2–6 (cf. Origen, *ComJn* 13.104); 6.7.58.1–2; 6.5.43.3; 6.6.48.1; 6.15.128.1.

considered the work to be a writing of Peter himself. Origen, on the other hand, rejected its authenticity when he wrote the *On First Principles*, if we may assume that the title in Rufinus' translation, *The Teaching of Peter*, refers to the *Kerygma Petrou* (*Princ* 1. Pref. 8).[32] The document appears to have been a form of early Christian apologetic attacking the way of worshipping God by both Gentiles and Jews, somewhat reminiscent of Romans 1–2.[33] I am not suggesting any kind of literary knowledge of Romans 1–2 on the part of the author, but only that both may reflect the earliest general form of Jewish-Christian apologetic. Christians are said to be a third race living under a new covenant with God because "the things belonging to the Greeks and the Jews are old".[34]

The author of the *Kerygma Petrou* identifies Christ as both Nomos (law) and Logos (word), the latter, of course, being an important concept in the philosophy of the time.[35] This may suggest the kind of Alexandrian Jewish thinking represented in Philo's treatises where the law and philosophy are joined, with the law providing the textual framework for discussion and philosophy the interpretative model and content of the interpretation. In Jewish-Christian fashion the author emphasizes the oneness of God who created all things. Clement says, however, that Peter, when speaking of the one god "who made a beginning of all things" reveals "the first begotten Son, since he understands accurately the statement, 'In the beginning God made heaven and earth'". If the joining of the Son with the opening statement in Genesis is the work of the author of the *Kerygma Petrou*, and not Clement's interpretation of what he said, there is an important link here between the *Kerygma Petrou* and the theology of Origen, for the latter, as I will point out in Chapter 5, saw a reference to the Son in the term "beginning" in Genesis 1:1. There is an even stronger link between Origen and this passage in the *Kerygma Petrou* in the immediately following statement that "this Son is called Wisdom by all the prophets". Origen's statement first identifies "beginning" in Genesis 1:1 with Wisdom and then identifies Wisdom with the Son.[36] Another interesting connection between Origen and this fragment of the *Kerygma Petrou* occurs in the latter's statement that the Son, as God's Wisdom "educates and perfects what is from above from the first foundation of the world" (*katabolēs kosmou*). The phrase *katabolēs*

---

[32] He rejects it again, but not so strongly, a little later in Caesarea in *ComJn* 13.104, where it appears in a citation of Heracleon.

[33] Clement, *Strom* 6.5.392–40.2; 6.5.41.2–3.

[34] Ibid., 6.5.41.4–6.

[35] Ibid., 1.29.182.3; 2.15.68.2; *EclProph.* 58.

[36] Ibid., 6.7.58.1–2; for Origen see Chapter 5, in "The *Commentary on Genesis*", p. 104.

kosmou is not frequently used in the Greek Bible to refer to creation.[37] It appears also, however, in this usage in *The Epistle of Barnabas* (5.5), another second-century Christian work that may have originated in Alexandria. It receives a special discussion and plays a key role in Origen's understanding of the creation of the world and the beings that inhabit it in his Alexandrian treatise *On First Principles* (3.5.4). These observations suggest that some of Origen's thinking about creation may be part of an Alexandrian Jewish-Christian interpretive trajectory.

There is one additional point of importance to make here about the teachings found in the *Kerygma Petrou*. The author and the community with which he was associated placed a strong emphasis on Scripture and its exegesis. "We say nothing without Scripture", he asserts. He refers explicitly to "the books of the prophets" in which, he says, his community had found the coming of the Christ disclosed along with "his death, the cross and all the other punishments the Jews inflicted on him, along with his resurrection and being taken up into heaven before the destruction of Jerusalem". These disclosures of Christ in the prophets are found "sometimes in parables, sometimes enigmatically, [and] sometimes directly with precise words".[38] This last statement reveals that the community in which the *Kerygma Petrou* originated did not read the prophets literally, but in the freer allegorical method associated with Philo Judaeus in first-century AD Alexandria. This same language of Christ being spoken of in parables in the prophets appears in other Christian literature associated with second-century Alexandria. In the *Epistula Apostolorum* Christ is said to have spoken "in parables through the patriarchs and prophets".[39] In the *Epistle of Barnabas* Exodus 33:3 is said to be a parable of our Lord (*Barn* 6.10) and, more broadly, the general message of Scripture is said to be in parables (*Barn* 8.7).[40] A similar attitude is expressed in the statement that certain things are clear to Christians but obscure to Jews because the latter "did not listen to the voice of the Lord" (*Barn* 8.7). The latter statement points to sayings of Jesus such as those found in Luke 24:44 and John 5:46.

The *Gospel of the Hebrews* also most likely originated in second-century Egypt, probably in Alexandria.[41] Clement of Alexandria cites a saying

---

[37] See Heine (2002), 49–51. The phrase does not appear in the works of Philo. See Borgen, Fuglseth, and Skarsten (2000), 188. The closest Philo comes to this idea is with the use of the phrase *katabolē geneseōs* to refer to the origin of the Hebrew people (Moses 1.279).

[38] Clement, *Strom* 6.15.128.1.

[39] *New Testament Apocrypha* (1963 / 1959), 192.

[40] See Harl (1982), 342 and Paget (1994), 238–9.

[41] Klijn (1988), 4008; Pearson (2004), 43; Koester (1982), 223.

from it, and Jerome says that Origen frequently used it.[42] It is cited only twice, however, in Origen's extant writings and it is the same citation both times—Christ refers to the Holy Spirit as his mother.[43] Koester notes that this saying would come most naturally from a Semitic language because the noun spirit is feminine in these languages.[44] Origen does not give his approval to the saying, but does treat it with respect.[45] Jerome cites a passage from this Gospel, which also treats the Holy Spirit. The "whole fount of the Holy Spirit" is said to descend on and remain on Jesus at his baptism, and say, "My Son, I was waiting for you in all the prophets that you should come and I might rest in you. For you are my rest; you are my first-begotten Son who reigns forever."[46] Klijn has noted the following differences between this account and the reports of the descent of the Holy Spirit on Jesus in the canonical Gospels: there is no mention of a dove, no report of heaven being opened, and no voice from heaven speaks. Here it is the Spirit which speaks. Jerome connects the story with Isaiah 11:2. Klijn believes the thought derives from Jewish Wisdom theology and that it is a good example of Jewish-Christian wisdom thinking.[47]

Jerome also quotes a story he assigns to the *Gospel of the Hebrews* which privileges James, the brother of Jesus, as a witness of the resurrection. James, the story goes, had taken an oath not to eat anything from the time he had "drunk the cup of the Lord" until he saw him risen from the dead. The risen Lord, then, appears to James, has a table set, and in eucharistic fashion, takes bread, blesses and breaks it, and gives it to James saying, "'My brother, eat your bread, for the Son of man is risen from among them that sleep.'"[48]

Koester suggests that the Alexandrian Jewish Christians may have used several writings connected with the name of James such as the first and second *Apocalypses of James* found at Nag Nammadi and the *Apocryphon of James*. The latter contains sayings of Jesus similar to but not identical with material found in "the Gospel of John, the *Gospel of Thomas*, and the Synoptics".[49]

---

[42] Clement, *Strom* 2.9.45.5; 5.14.96.3; Jerome, *VirInl 2*.

[43] *ComJn* 2.87; *HomJer* 15.4. There is also a reference to a "Gospel which is called according to the Hebrews" in *ComMt* 15.14, but Klijn (1988), 4020, thinks this citation comes from the *Gospel of the Nazaraeans*.

[44] Koester (1982), 223.

[45] This will be discussed more fully in Chapter 4.

[46] *New Testament Apocrypha* (1963/1959), 163–4, translation modified.

[47] Klijn ((1988), 4015; so also Koester (1982), 223–4, who notes Wis 7:27 and Sir 24:7, and Van den Broek (1996), 184.

[48] *New Testament Apocrypha* (1963/1959), 165, translation modified. 1 Cor. 15:7 speaks of a resurrection appearance to James.   [49] Koester (1982), 224.

The title of the *Gospel of the Egyptians* suggests that it comes from a community of native Egyptians, since they were the only ones so designated in Alexandria. It has been associated especially with the area of the city called Rakotis, where most native Egyptians lived.[50] It is mentioned almost exclusively by Clement of Alexandria in the early Church.[51]

Clement's references to the *Gospel of the Egyptians* all involve conversations between Salome and Jesus. He says that the Saviour says in this Gospel, "I came to destroy the works of the female." Clement quotes this as a theme-setting statement for the Gospel (*Strom* 3.9.63.2). On the basis of this statement, which he is confident comes from the *Gospel of the Egyptians*, he says that he thinks the following statements quoted by some who oppose marriage also come from this Gospel:

When Salome asked, 'How long does death have power?' the Lord replied, 'So long as you women give birth.'

When she replied, 'I did well, then, in not having children,' . . . the Lord replied, 'Eat every plant, but do not eat the plant that is bitter.'[52]

Clement has one further saying that he attaches with confidence to the *Gospel of the Egyptians*. "When Salome asked when her inquiries would be answered, the Lord said, 'Whenever you trample on the garment of shame, and whenever the two become one and the male is with the female neither as male nor female'" (*Strom* 3.13.92.2). Statements with strong similarities to this last saying appear in *2 Clement* 12.2 and in the *Gospel of Thomas* 22. Here I only note these similarities. Something more will be said about them when *2 Clement* is discussed below.

From what Clement of Alexandria has preserved, the *Gospel of the Egyptians* would seem to come from a Christian community with a strong ascetic tendency. Sexuality is considered as something to be ignored, at best, and harmful at worst. Birth is the source of death. Rearing children, as Clement understands the saying at least, is considered "bitter" because it demands time that should be devoted to God. Clement identifies his opponent who uses these sayings as Julius Cassianus, a second-century Alexandrian Christian encratite who wrote a book with the title, *Concerning Continence and Celibacy* (*Strom* 3.13.91–3), but Cassianus was not the author of the *Gospel of the*

[50] Van den Broek (1996), 184–5.

[51] Hippolytus, Ref. 5.7.7–9, says the Naassenes derived their teachings about the soul from this Gospel, and Epiphanius, *Haer.* 62.2–4, says the Sabellians took their error from it. Hennecke and Schneemelcher (1963 / 1959), 170, are on target when they say of Epiphanius' statement that although the Sabellians may have used the Gospel of the Egyptians, no conclusions concerning it can be drawn from Epiphanius' remarks.

[52] *Strom* 3.6.45.2 (cf. *EclTheod* 67.2; *Strom* 3.9.64.1); 3.9.66.1–2.

Egyptians. There is another unidentified saying of Jesus in *2 Clement* (5.2–4) which some have suggested might come from the *Gospel of the Egyptians.*[53] This saying pushes the ascetic tendency beyond that of disregarding marriage to the willingness to die a martyr's death. When Jesus describes the disciples as lambs among wolves, Peter asks him, "Will the wolves, then, rip the lambs apart?" Jesus replies "Let the lambs not fear the wolves after they die. And you, do not fear those who kill you and can do nothing further to you."

I add four additional second-century Christian writings that many argue originated in Alexandria, although their Alexandrian origins are on less certain ground than the previous three: the *Epistula Apostolorum*, the *Epistle of Barnabas, 2 Clement* and the *Apocalypse of Peter.*[54] The *Epistula Apostolorum*[55] uses the format of a Gnostic revelation discourse to argue against Gnosticism.[56] The risen Jesus teaches the 11 apostles. What he teaches, however, is not something to be kept secret, but something to be taken openly to the whole world, beginning with the 12 tribes (*EpistApost* 30). The following teachings found in the treatise show its anti-Gnostic orientation: the connection of Jesus with the prophecies of the Old Testament (*EpistApost* 3, 19, 31), the resurrection in the flesh of both Jesus and his followers (*EpistApost* 21, 24), and the freedom that everyone has to choose to believe in the light (*EpistApost* 39). The treatise often uses the language of the synoptic Gospels and John. Nathanael, for example, who appears only in John's Gospel, is one of the apostles named as recipients of the teachings.

It is the attitude towards Paul in the *Epistula Apostolorum*, however, that is especially interesting. Koester notes that there are allusions to Pauline letters but they are not "cited as authoritative words of the apostle".[57] Klijn thinks that the work contains a defense of Paul in a setting where he is not accepted.[58] The crucial passage represents the risen Jesus telling the 11 about Paul. He is referred to as "the last of the last" who, as a Jew, will take the gospel to the Gentiles. The 11 are to teach him about the fulfillment of the Scriptures in Christ so that he might be the means of salvation for the Gentiles.[59] Paul is clearly not considered to be a primary authority here. He is subordinated to

---

[53] *Early Christian Fathers* (1953), 187.

[54] As I indicated above, my list here is not exhaustive for literature which can be associated with Alexandria.

[55] The work is assigned to Egypt by Klijn (1980), 162–3, 168 and Koester (1982), 236–8. Pearson (2004), 49–50, accepts the arguments of Hill (1999), 1–53, who places its origin in Asia Minor.

[56] Koester (1982), 236–7.

[57] Ibid., 237.

[58] Klijn (1986): 174.

[59] *Epistula Apostolorum* 31; trans. Hennecke and Schneemelcher *New Testament Apocrypha* (1963/1959), 213.

the 11 in what he will know and teach about Christ. The authority of his message will rest in his understanding, learned from the 11, of the fulfillment of the Scriptures in Christ.

What makes this presentation of Paul interesting is that a faint echo of it can be detected in Clement and Origen. Clement refers to Paul as being "inferior [to the earlier apostles] so far as time goes, since he flourished immediately after the Lord was taken up. His writing, therefore, depends on the old covenant, getting its life and voice from that source" (*Strom* 4.21.134.2). In another passage Clement refers to the "true tradition of the blessed teaching" deriving from "the holy apostles Peter, James, John, and Paul" (*Strom* 1.1.11.3). Here Paul is included among the apostles and is a source of the "true tradition" but he stands last in the list of the four apostles considered important to mention. These are not hostile attitudes towards Paul, and Clement's writings have numerous citations from Paul. They do, nevertheless, suggest a slight limitation on Pauline authority. A similar attitude can be found in one of Origen's Alexandrian works. Origen lumps all of the epistles of apostles together and refers to their authors as wise men whose writings depend on the "words of the law and the Prophets" for their credibility. They are beneficial but they do not stand "on a par with, 'Thus says the Lord almighty'". He thinks Paul considered his own words to carry apostolic authority, but not to be divinely inspired.[60] There is another interesting statement of Origen in the fragment on 1 Corinthians 7:12 concerning Paul's remark, "To the rest, I say, not the Lord." He asserts that "the Laws of Moses consist of some from God and some from Moses". Then he points to the distinction Jesus made between the two. "Moses", Origen says, "being a servant of God, gave second laws in addition to the laws of God. And Paul, being a servant of the gospel gave second laws pertaining to matters related to the churches after the laws from God through Jesus Christ. "Now it is better", he adds, "to listen to laws from the Lord than from Paul the apostle. For even though he is a saint, his laws are very inferior to those of the Lord."[61] These comments probably come from Origen's Caesarean period, but they reflect what seems to have been the earlier Alexandrian attitude towards Paul.

Pearson considers the *Epistle of Barnabas* to be "one of the most important sources we have for early-second-century...Christianity in

---

[60] *ComJn* 1.15–16; trans. *Origen* (1989), 35.
[61] *FragCor* 35.128.61–72; *JTS* 9 (1908), 505. This same distinction in the law of Moses based on the words of Jesus in Mt 15:4 and 19:8, but not with the application to Paul, can be found in the Gnostic Ptolemaeus' *Letter to Flora*. Ptolemaeus even calls Moses' divorce legislation a "second" and a "lesser" law inferior to the legislation from God. The text of *The Letter to Flora* is translated in Grant (2003), 63–8.

Alexandria".[62] Barnard considered the work to have originated in Alexandria and argued that the author was "a converted Rabbi who brought into Christianity the exegetical and homiletic traditions of the Alexandrian Synagogue".[63] Like much of the Christian literature from the second century, its provenance cannot be proven and other locations of origin have been argued. Paget, after sifting through the evidence for and against locating its origin in Alexandria, concluded that there are "good grounds for thinking Alexandria/Egypt the most likely provenance".[64] The earliest references to the work are in Clement of Alexandria,[65] who may have considered it Scripture. Eusebius says that Clement, in his (now lost) *Hypotyposeis*, commented on it along with the other works considered disputed in their canonical status: the catholic epistles, Barnabas, and the *Apocalypse of Peter* (*H.E.* 6.14.1). Origen cites the epistle in a list of what he labels proofs from Scripture on the existence of good and bad angels (*Princ* 3.2.4). The inclusion of the passage certainly shows that the community reading Origen's treatise in Alexandria would consider it a significant citation.

The *Epistle of Barnabas* falls into two sections. The first and larger section provides a Christian reading of the Jewish law (1–17); the second is a discourse on the two ways (18–21), much like that found in the *Didache*. The first section asserts that the Mosaic covenant was lost by the Jews at Sinai when the people made the golden calf and Moses threw down the tables of the law (4.6–8; 13.1; 14.1–4). At that time the covenant passed to Jesus to be held in store for those who would believe in him. This meant for Barnabas that the law was not intended to be read literally. I noted above in the discussion of the *Kerygma Petrou*, that Barnabas speaks of Scripture being parabolic in its assertions. He is convinced that there is a deeper knowledge (*gnōsis*) hidden in the ancient Jewish texts. He announces at the beginning of his work that he wants to enable his readers to have "perfect knowledge" along with their faith (1.5). To uncover this hidden knowledge he applies the kind of exegetical technique to reading the law that the Jewish philosopher Philo had used in the first century AD and Clement of Alexandria and Origen would use in the late second and early third centuries.

---

[62] Pearson (2004), 50. Barnard (1966), 51, calls it "our earliest certain evidence for Christianity in Egypt".

[63] Barnard (1966), 47.

[64] Paget (1994), 36. For a survey of the arguments for and against Alexandrian provenance see ibid., 30–42. Lightfoot (1926), 240, assumed Alexandria to be its place of origin, and thought its "picture... of feuds between Jews and Christians" to be "in keeping with the state of the population of that city".

[65] References are given below in "Second Century Christian Works Read by Clement of Alexandria and Origen", p. 46.

Barnabas' exegesis, however, lacks the philosophical sophistication the latter three possess. The community in which the *Epistle of Barnabas* was produced and read found the story of Jesus latent in the legal and prophetic texts of Scripture.[66]

There was also a sense of living in the last days in the community in which the epistle was produced. The section that precedes the author's launching into uncovering the story of Jesus in the Jewish Scriptures is a warning about living in the last days when "the final stumbling block approaches" (4.1–3). The author picks this up again before he closes this preface-like section with another warning about the "stumbling blocks that are about to appear". His readers must be on their guard that "the dark one" does not slip in during these dangerous times (4.9). This reference to "the dark one" may also anchor the ethical section on the two ways at the end of the epistle in this awareness of living in the end times. The two ways are designated the ways of light and darkness in the epistle, rather than the ways of life and death as in the *Didache*. The second way is introduced as the "way of the dark one" when its characteristics are listed.[67]

As with the *Epistle of Barnabas* and the other second-century Christian literature considered in this section, the precise provenance of *2 Clement* cannot be proven. Koester notes that only a few scholars locate its origin in Alexandria but he proceeds to make a rather convincing case for thinking it might have come from there.[68] One of the stronger arguments in favor of this location is the appearance in *2 Clement* 12.2 of the quotation from the *Gospel of the Egyptians* which also appears in the *Gospel of Thomas*.[69] References to the *Gospel of the Egyptians* appear almost exclusively in Clement of Alexandria, as noted above. Koester takes the saying to be Gnostic but the interpretation given to it in *2 Clement* 12:3–5 to be non-Gnostic. Another indication of an anti-Gnostic concern in the work is the definition of Christian *gnōsis* as the refusal to deny Christ, and the definition of confessing Christ as positive Christian moral action (3.1–4.5). The confession of Christ is extended, also in a non-Gnostic way, as far as actually dying for him if necessary (5.1–5). All of these points cut across what we know of Gnostic views on confessing or denying Christ and martyrdom. Further, contrary to Gnostic teachings, *2 Clement* argues that Christ became flesh and, consequently, the flesh has positive value and will be raised and judged

---

[66] See, for example, Chapters 2 and 5.

[67] Cf. the angel of darkness contrasted with the prince of light in IQS 3–4.

[68] Koester (1982), 233–6.

[69] See the discussion of the *Gospel of the Egyptians* above in this section. It was noted above also that there may be another quotation from the *Gospel of the Egyptians* in *2 Cl* 5.2–4.

(9.1–5). Koester thinks *2 Clement* is "the first tangible evidence for the existence of anti-gnostic Christianity in Egypt before the middle of II CE".[70]

A parallel interpretation of Christ and the Church based on Genesis 1:27 to *2 Clement* 14.1–2 is found later in both Origen's Alexandrian and Caesarean works. *2 Clement* refers to the "first Church" being "spiritual" and being "created before the sun and the moon". He then anchors this view in Genesis 1:27, saying,

I do not think you are ignorant that the living Church is the body of Christ. For the Scripture says, 'God made humanity male and female'. The male is Christ; the female is the Church. And I do not think you are ignorant that the books and the apostles say clearly that the Church does not exist now, but exists from the beginning, for she was spiritual, as also our Jesus, but she [or he] became visible in the last days to save us (*2 Clement* 14.1–2).

The historian Socrates states that in the ninth volume of the Genesis commentary Origen "proved in great detail that Adam is Christ and Eve is the Church". He then adds that Pamphilus and Eusebius defended this interpretation by pointing out that Origen was not the first to treat the subject in this way but that he was "interpreting the mystical tradition concerning the Church".[71] The seventh-century abbot of the monastery of St Catherine, Anastasius Sinaita, claimed that Papias, Clement, Pantaenus, and Ammonius all understood *the entire Hexaemeron* of Christ and the Church (*PG* 89.860B-C; my italics). This would be an interesting chain of tradition involving Pantaenus, whom Origen knew as a teacher in Alexandria, reaching down to Origen, but no one has been able to verify Anastasius' statement.[72] There is also no explicit evidence in Origen's extant Alexandrian works that he had read *2 Clement*.[73] Origen had, however, read the *Shepherd of Hermas*, which identifies the Church with the aged woman who is said to have been the first of all created things (*Hermas* 4.2.1). However, Hermas does not make any explicit connection between Eve and the Church. Koester thinks *2 Clement* 14.1–2 was an interpretation to counter "gnostic speculation about Gen 1:27 concerning the heavenly aeons Christ and the church".[74] It seems most likely to me that the Genesis speculation in *2 Clement* had its ultimate roots in the statements in Ephesians 5:31–2.

There is a hint of the understanding of Adam and Eve as Christ and the Church in Origen's Alexandrian *De Principiis* (4.3.7), where the interpretation

---

[70] Koester (1982), 236.

[71] *H.E.* 3.7.8. Origen's *ComGn* has been lost except for a few fragments (see Chapter 5).

[72] See the attempts by Daniélou (1964), 299–301, and Roncaglia (1977), 219–26.

[73] See the following section, p. 46.   [74] Koester (1982), 235–6.

is tied to Ephesians 5:31–2. There are also hints of this understanding of Adam and Eve in several of his Caesarean works.[75] In the *Commentary on Matthew* he says, for example, that Paul's statement in Ephesians 5:31, that "the two shall be one flesh", was made of Christ and the Church. This then informs his understanding of the creation statement in Genesis 1:27. "He who at the beginning created Him 'who is in the form of God' after the image, made Him male, and the church female, granting to both oneness after the image" (*ComMt* 14.17). We do not have Origen's theological understanding preserved in the fragment of his commentary on Ephesians 5:31. Jerome, however, in my opinion, preserves it in the following words:

But this same example is interpreted allegorically in Christ and the Church, so that Adam prefigures Christ and Eve the Church.... And just as the whole human race is born from Adam and his wife, so the whole multitude of believers has been produced from Christ and the Church.

He then explains how this multitude becomes the one body of Christ, relying again on the creation account. "This multitude ... is again placed in the side of Christ and the place of the rib is filled up and the one body of a man is formed."[76] Eve, in other words, as the Church, again becomes a part of the body of Adam who is Christ. It is this understanding of Adam and Eve that allows Origen to say in his *Commentary on Canticles* that the Church has been the bride of Christ "from the beginning of the human race and from the very foundation of the world".[77]

If Jerome's subsequent comment on Ephesians 5:32 has its ultimate source in Origen's commentary on Ephesians it would indicate that the tradition that Anastasius Sinaita connected with Pantaenus and the other three exegetes was known in Alexandria, that is, that the *whole Hexaemeron* is about Christ and the Church. Jerome asserts that "[i]t is not, as many think, that the whole story which has been written of Adam and Eve in Genesis can readily be related to Christ and the Church, but only what stands in the present passage".[78] I suggested above in discussing the *Kerygma Petrou* that some of Origen's speculation on Genesis may have come from an Alexandrian Jewish-Christian interpretative trajectory. His interpretation of Genesis 1:27 may belong to that same trajectory. There is no proof that he had read *2 Clement* itself, but he is certainly aware of the viewpoint that is found in *2 Clement* on the meaning of Genesis 1:27.

---

[75] *HomGn* 9.2; *ComCant* 2.3.13–14; *ComJn* 19.23; *CatJn* 45; *ComRom* 5.1.
[76] *ComEph* on Eph. 5:31; trans. Heine (2002), 240.
[77] *ComCant* 2.8.4; trans. *Origen* (1957), 149.
[78] *ComEph* on Eph. 5:32; trans. Heine (2002), 240.

The *Apocalypse of Peter* was considered authentic by some in the early Church. It is listed as an accepted book in the Muratorian Canon, but with the added note that some did not want it read in Church. Eusebius rejected it as spurious (*H.E.* 3.3.2; 3.25.4) but noted that Clement of Alexandria in his *Hypotyposeis* had included it among the Scriptures on which he wrote explanations (*H.E.* 6.14.1). Clement cites the work three times in his extant writings, all in the *Eclogae Propheticae* (41.2; 48.1; 49.1). Each time he introduces the quotations as coming from Peter in the Apocalypse. The three citations all address either the fate of aborted babies or the punishments of those who aborted their babies.

The Apocalypse begins with Jesus addressing his disciples on the Mt of Olives concerning the signs of the end of the world. Peter becomes a dialogue partner with Jesus in a short section concerning the interpretation of the parable of the fig tree (2).[79] The subject quickly turns to the judgment and punishments of the wicked. The latter, in great detail, occupy the larger part of the text (5–12).[80] Peter appears again at the end of the work as the person who has been addressed and chosen to take the message to the world (14–17).[81] The text originated in a community of Christians who had a very strong doctrine of the resurrection of the flesh. Even humans who have been devoured by birds and beasts will be restored for the judgment, "for nothing perishes for God" (4).[82] Among those being tortured will be those who worshipped "images of cats and lions, of reptiles and wild beasts and the men and women who manufactured the images" (10).[83] This statement about the worship of images of animals along with the citations of the work as a writing of Peter by Clement of Alexandria have led some to consider Alexandria, or at least Egypt, as its place of origin.[84]

If we ask of these seven works, which can, with some degree of certainty, be assigned to second-century Egypt, who the heroes were of the Christian community in Alexandria, excluding Jesus of course, Peter's name stands at the head of the list, followed perhaps by that of James the brother of Jesus. This fits well with the assumption of a Jewish-Christian majority in the city

---

[79] *New Testament Apocrypha* (1965/1964), 668–9.

[80] The text is extant in Ethiopic and Akhmim, both of which are translated in *New Testament Apocrypha* (1965/1964), 668–83. There are also a few Greek fragments which have recently been edited and translated into German and English in *Das Petrusevangelium und die Petrusapokalypse* (2004).

[81] *New Testament Apocrypha* (1965/1964), 679–83.

[82] Ibid., 670.

[83] Ibid., 677.

[84] Ibid., 664. Pearson (2004), 43–4 lists it among works he considers to be "indisputably or most probably of Egyptian provenance".

which originated from a Jerusalem-based mission. Paul's name is notably absent in these documents from Alexandria. They do not attack him; he is simply not a major player in their understanding of Christian faith.

Most of the works indicate a strong focus on Old Testament Scripture interpreted in relation to Jesus. Some read the Old Testament in the allegorical tradition while others treated it literally. The early chapters of Genesis were applied to Christ and the Church. Jewish wisdom traditions influenced Christological understandings. Sayings of Jesus were important, but not all came from our four Gospels.[85] The immediacy of the end time, the resurrection of the flesh, and the rewards and punishments of the flesh are emphasized in areas of the literature. There were also ascetic leanings in parts of the Christian community represented in these documents. The Christian community behind these documents was diverse in its understanding of Christian faith and life.

SECOND-CENTURY CHRISTIAN WORKS READ BY ORIGEN AND CLEMENT AT ALEXANDRIA

By cataloguing the second-century Christian works which Origen either mentions or quotes verbatim in his Alexandrian treatises, and by doing the same for Clement of Alexandria, we can form an idea of the Christian writings that Origen and the Alexandrian Church were reading. Among those works called the Apostolic Fathers, Origen quotes once from *1 Clement*, identifying the author as a "disciple of the apostles" (*Princ* 2.3.6), once from the *Epistle of Barnabas* (*Princ* 3.2.4), and six times from *The Shepherd of Hermas*.[86] In all but the first of these references involving Hermas the writing is identified explicitly. These six references to the *Shepherd of Hermas* show that Origen was quite familiar with the entire writing. It is a strongly Jewish-Christian treatise. This observation is significant in relation to the

---

[85]   Klijn calls attention to several papyri found in Egypt containing non-canonical stories about Jesus and sayings of Jesus, along with the Secret Gospel of Mark, which the Letter of Clement to Theodore claims was composed in Alexandria, the Gospel according to the Hebrews, and the Gospel according to the Egyptians referred to by both Clement and Origen, and concludes that Christianity in Egypt was centered on the life of Jesus (Klijn (1986),167). The papyri are *P. Oxy* 654.1 and 655; *P. Eger.* 2; frag. From Fayyum; *P. Oxy.* 840; *P. Cair.* 10.735; and *P. Oxy.* 1224. They can be found in English in the *New Testament Apocrypha* (1963/1959, 85–116).

[86]   *Princ* 1. Pref. 4; 1.2.3; 2.1.5; 3.2.4; 4.2.4; and *ComJn* 1.103. For a similar cataloguing of works cited by Origen and Clement see Van den Hoek (1995), 93–113, who catalogues the works for a different purpose and who does not limit herself to Origen's Alexandrian writings.

Jewish matrix of Alexandrian Christianity that was pointed out in the previous section. The *Shepherd* did not originate in Alexandria, but found a ready reception there. While he was not one of the Apostolic Fathers, mention must also be made of Melito's treatise *On God being Corporeal*, which Origen refers to in a fragment from his *Commentary on Genesis* written before he left Alexandria.[87]

Origen also refers to *The Acts of Paul* (*Princ* 1.2.3), *The Gospel of the Hebrews* (*ComJn* 2.87), the *Prayer of Joseph*,[88] and the *Sentences of Sextus*. The latter, while not named, is quoted verbatim in the prologue to the Alexandrian *Commentary on the Psalms* preserved by Epiphanius (64.7.3). I mention also the *Kerygma Petrou* or *Preaching of Peter*, which Origen quotes once in a volume of the *Commentary on John* which would have been written not too long after his move to Caesarea. The quotation appears within a citation of the Valentinian Heracleon whose work Origen was reading in Alexandria. Origen raises the question of the genuineness of the writing but postpones a decision until a later time (*ComJn* 13.104). It appears that the reference to *The Teaching of Peter*, which he says is not one of the books used by the Church, nor is it a work of Peter or of any other inspired author (*Princ* 1. Pref. 8), is a reference to this same work. All the other references and quotations from this work are to be found in Clement of Alexandria, which has led scholars to see it as a work produced in Alexandria.[89] Origen quotes Heracleon's commentary on John twice in his Alexandrian works (*ComJn* 2.100–4; 137–9). Marcion, Valentinus, and Basilides are occasionally mentioned together in *On First Principles*, but no writing is ever specified, nor is anything ever quoted. They are most often mentioned in conjunction with a reference to the doctrine of pre-ordained natures which Origen asserts they held.

In contrast to Origen, Clement of Alexandria relies much more on quotations. He mentions and quotes from the following: Valentinus,[90] Basilides,[91] followers of Basilides,[92] Basilides' son Isidore,[93] followers of Carpocrates (*Strom* 3.2.5), Carpocrates' son Epiphanes (*Strom* 3.2.5–9), and Julius Cassianus.[94] Clement also cites Tatian (*Strom* 3.12.81; *EclProph* 38), the *Acts of John*,[95] the *Gospel of the Egyptians*,[96] and the *Apocalypse of Peter*.[97]

---

[87] See Heine (2005), 134.

[88] *ComJn* 1.221; 2.188–90; *Phil* 23.15, 19 from a fragment of Book 3 of the *ComGn*. Daniélou (1964), 188, considers the document to be Jewish Christian.

[89] The references are conveniently collected, translated, and discussed in Hennecke and Schneemelcher (1963/1964), 94–102.

[90] *Strom* 2.8.36, 20.114; 3.7.59; 4.13.89.   [91] *Strom* 4.12.81–3; 4.24.153,165; 5.1.3.

[92] *Strom* 2.8.36, 20.112; 3.1.1–2.   [93] *Strom* 2.20.113; 3.1.2–3.

[94] *Strom* 3.13.91, 93–14.95.   [95] *Adumbr* 3.

[96] *Strom* 3.6.45, 9.63, 66, 13.92–3; *Exc. Ex Theod* 67.   [97] *EclProph* 41; 48–9.

I have already mentioned above his citations of the *Gospel of the Hebrews*. Clement has more than 20 citations from Tatian. Among the writings of the Apostolic Fathers he cites 52 passages from *1 Clement*[98] (once incorrectly identifying it as Barnabas (*Strom* 6.8.64)), 24 passages from the *Epistle of Barnabas,* and 21 passages from Hermas.[99] Both Clement of Rome and Barnabas are identified as apostles by Clement of Alexandria. Barnabas is also referred to as one of the 70 and the co-worker of Paul.

If Clement and Origen are representative of the reading of at least the more educated of the Alexandrian Christians, then Hermas and *1 Clement* were the most read Christian writings outside the Scriptures. They were also quite open to reading books of authors who fell outside the circle of what many would have considered orthodoxy. Some of these works are cited in order to argue against the viewpoint presented, but others are cited without any concentrated effort to refute them, and sometimes they are even cited as corroborative evidence for the point being made. Others in Alexandria besides Clement and Origen must have been reading these books as well, and this suggests again the diversity of viewpoints in the Christian community in Alexandria in the late second and early third centuries.

CHRISTIAN SCHOOLS IN SECOND-CENTURY ALEXANDRIA

Eusebius refers to a teacher named Pantaenus heading "the school of the believers" in Alexandria around AD 180. He adds that there was a long tradition of a "school of sacred learning" in the Christian community there and that such a school had continued down to his own time. Pantaenus, however, is the earliest teacher Eusebius can name. According to Eusebius, Pantaenus continued as leader of the school in Alexandria until his death.[100] Eusebius asserts that Pantaenus had been Clement's teacher (*H.E.* 5.11.1–2) and that Clement "succeeded" him in the leadership of "the instruction". Later, he adds, Origen became a disciple of Clement (*H.E.* 6.6.1). Origen, Eusebius asserts, was made leader of "the school of instruction" by bishop Demetrius (*H.E.* 6.2.3; 6.8.1–3, 6). Origen was followed, as leader of the school, by his disciple Heraclas (*H.E.* 6.15; 6.26), and he in turn by Dionysius, another of Origen's disciples in Alexandria (*H.E.* 6.29.4). What

---

[98] *Strom* 1.7.38; 4.17.105; 6.8.65.

[99] The numbers come from the index of Stählin and Treu (1980), 26–9. There are a number of other Christian writings which are listed with a few references.

[100] Eusebius, *H.E.* 5.9; 5.10.1–4.

Eusebius pictures is a school in Alexandria connected with the leadership of the Church which reached back into the shadowy foreground of the early second-century Christian community that came into full light near the end of that century with the rise of Demetrius as bishop and Pantaenus, Clement, Origen, Heraclas, and Dionysius as successive leaders of the school.

Eusebius' picture of a Christian school in Alexandria under the auspices of the bishop of the city with a unified history and succession of teachers appears almost certainly to be his own creation.[101] What would appear to be trustworthy in the account is that there were Christian schools in Alexandria in the second century, reaching back perhaps to the early part of the century. Pantaenus was the earliest teacher whose name Eusebius knew, or wished to mention.[102] Eusebius appears to have obtained most, if not all, of his information about Pantaenus from the writings of Clement of Alexandria, especially the *Hypotyposeis,* which we no longer have (*H.E.* 5.11.1–5).

There were, in all probability, Christian schools in Alexandria prior to the time of Pantaenus. There was, however, almost certainly no direct connection between these schools and anyone who could have been considered anything like a bishop of Alexandria before the time of Demetrius and Origen. It is much more in keeping with the little evidence we have of Christianity in second-century Alexandria to speak of schools led by stellar personalities in the Christian community. There were five major personalities who, in all probability, led schools in the city in the second century: Basilides, Valentinus, Pantaenus, the teacher Origen refers to as "the Hebrew", and Clement of Alexandria. There were also others less well-known. The author of the *Epistle of Barnabas* was a teacher and may have had a school in Alexandria. Apelles spent some time in Alexandria after his break with Marcion and could have had a school of followers there. Among the Gnostics, Carpocrates, Epiphanes, and Heracleon, whose commentary on the Gospel of John Origen knew, taught there also.

Ancient schools most often met in the home of the teacher and were quite small, consisting of a few disciples and a teacher. Snyder, studying primarily philosophical schools, notes that a school could be as small as

---

[101] See Bardy (1937); Hornschuh (1960), 1–3; Bienert (1978), 81–7; Neymeyr (1989), 42–5; Scholten (1995); Van den Broek (1996), 197–205. Van den Hoek (1997) is less skeptical of Eusebius' account than the majority of modern scholars.

[102] He almost certainly knew that Basilides and Valentinus had taught there in the early part of the second century, but he considered them to have been heretical teachers and not to belong to the succession he assumed.

a teacher and a single student. The school might "perish with its teacher, or ... survive under a successor". Schools were also not necessarily "'academic' in our modern sense of the term".[103] Fowden credits the origin and validation of such schools to "the powerful personalities of individual holy men". He points to Porphyry's description of the circle of students around Plotinus, and Eunapius' description of Iamblichus and his disciples. The devotion of disciple to teacher could sometimes be "almost hysterical".[104] Brown refers to the teachers of the Christian schools of the second century as "spiritual guides" leading "[s]mall study-circles" of intense disciples who would "gather for years on end around" their guide.[105] We can detect something of this spirit in the *Panegyric* Gregory Thaumaturgus addressed to Origen later after being his disciple for several years at Caesarea. In Gregory's language of adoration Origen was one who had the appearance of a man but was, in reality, in the process of migration to deity (*Pan* 2.10). While Gregory mentions a broad curriculum of subjects that was pursued and a great freedom to range through Greek philosophical literature, it was primarily a school to form character (*Pan* 11.133–44; 13.150–14.173).

Snyder has noted that most ancient schools were "oriented to texts, and could be described as textual communities".[106] He proposes three models of how teachers interacted with the texts that were important for their schools: "(1) text functions as teacher, (2) text and teacher act in concert, and (3) teacher as text".[107] Most of the teachers he considers fall within the second category, which is where I would place the Christian teachers of Alexandria as well. He notes a further division within this second category between teachers who ordered their teaching by the structure of the text being considered and those who structured their teaching topically and used texts for support. Among those who structured their teaching by the order of the text he places Alexander of Aphrodisias and other Aristotelians who produced commentaries, called *hypomnēmata*, on Aristotle's works,[108] and in the other category he places Epictetus, whose works are topical but for whom texts were important.[109] If we look at Clement and Origen, the two Christian teachers of late second- and early third-century Alexandria from whom

---

[103] Snyder (2000), 8; see also Knauber (1968), 182.   [104] Fowden (1993/1986), 189.

[105] Brown (1988), 104.   [106] Snyder (2000), 10.   [107] Ibid., 224.

[108] Praechter, K. (1909), 523, considered most of the commentaries on Aristotle to have arisen from oral lectures delivered in a school setting.

[109] Snyder (2000), 225–6. He thinks Philo belongs to the first model, "text as teacher". Unlike the commentators in the second model, Philo does not refer to his own works as *hypomnēmata* (commentaries). In *De Cherubim* 49 he speaks of encountering the prophet Jeremiah and becoming his disciple, an experience which could only have been mediated by a text (cf. *De Migratione Abrahami* 23; Snyder (2000), 132–6).

we have extant written works, Clement's work would fall in the second sub-division. He structured his works topically but drew heavily on texts in the development of his teaching. Origen, on the other hand, has works that fit into both of the sub-divisions. His commentaries follow the structure of the Biblical text just as the Peripatetic commentaries of Alexander of Aphrodisias followed the order of the texts of Aristotle. But Origen also produced works structured topically, such as the *On First Principles, On the Resurrection, On Prayer*, etc. These works draw just as heavily on the texts of the Bible as the commentaries, but they do not follow the order of any text.

The Christian schools of second-century Alexandria should be conceived along the lines described by Snyder. They were small groups of disciples drawn to a magnetic personality who led them in the reading and interpretation of texts considered important in the Christian community. Some of the schools may have existed simultaneously. Most of them perished with the teacher's death or departure from the city.

The school of Basilides

Basilides taught in Alexandria during the reign of Hadrian (AD 117–38) and was succeeded by his son Isidore as leader of his school.[110] A few fragments from his works have been preserved, primarily by Clement of Alexandria and Origen.[111] Löhr thinks the thought of Basilides and his school was determined by two points of tension. On the one side he detects a philosophical eclecticism drawing on all four of the major schools of Greek philosophy but showing no attachment to any one of the schools in particular and on the other stood the Jewish-Christian tradition. In the fragments which remain he finds traces of philosophy in those treating the meaning of Christian faith, the understanding of the human soul, and the problem of theodicy. "Basilides and Isidor", he says, "were not school philosophers,

---

[110] Löhr (1996), 325; cf. Lietzmann (1953), 280; Clement *Strom* 7.17.106.4; Epiphanius 24.1.1. Irenaeus, *Haer* 24.1 also locates Basilides in Alexandria.

[111] Löhr (1996), 42–254 has the Greek texts, German translations, and extensive discussions of teachings attributed to both Basilides and his followers. His study is the most comprehensive one we have of Basilides. He thinks the reports of Basilides' teachings by the heresiologists are (1) unreliable, and (2) almost completely dependent on the report of Irenaeus. The latter, he says, measured Basilides by the "rule of truth" he had formulated and found him wanting. Basilides denied the identity of the creator and the highest God, pitted the God of redemption and the God of creation against one another, had a "nous-Christology" which was docetic and which led him to neglect the salvation of the flesh, and further to have a libertine attitude towards morals, approve of magic, and treat martyrdom as a thing of no consequence (Löhr (1996), 324–5).

but Christian theological teachers and pastors."[112] Philosophy was seen, perhaps, as serving theology, as Origen would later state it (*EpGreg* 1). Löhr cautions, however, against thinking too simply about the relationship between the two.[113] On the other hand, the relationship between the two was anything but simple for Origen also. Löhr suggests that the philosophical side of the tension "evokes questions that were interesting, provocative, and pointed and that the Biblical discourse of God and man leads to declarations which exceed the philosophical horizon".[114]

Origen says that Basilides wrote a Gospel (*HomLk* 1.2). Exactly what this may have been is unknown. The passages cited below show that he made use of Matthew's Gospel. Others have seen evidence of Luke's parable of the rich man and Lazarus (Lk 16:19–31) in a fragment preserved by Hegemonius.[115] Basilides' followers were concerned about the chronology of Jesus' life, providing the day and month of his baptism and his death (*Strom* 1.21.146.1–4). This might suggest that Basilides' "Gospel" was something on the order of Tatian's *Diatessaron,* which tried to harmonize the four Gospels.[116] We know from the Rylands fragment (P52) that John's Gospel was being used in Egypt by the time of Basilides and we know that John's chronology differs in several places from that of Matthew and the Synoptics. Eusebius cites a work by Agrippa Castor which refers to Basilides writing 24 books on "the gospel".[117] The use of the singular "gospel" might suggest that Basilides had produced a single Gospel from two or more of what later became the canonical Gospels and then produced a commentary in 24 books on this Gospel.

Basilides seems to have written several books of commentaries, but whether they were on various Biblical books or on a single Gospel and employed citations from other Biblical books in the one exposition cannot be known with certainty. With the exception of Origen's remark noted above about Basilides writing a gospel, there is no reference to his having written anything other than commentaries. His commentaries were still available in Alexandria in the time of Clement. The latter says that one of his quotations from Basilides comes from the twenty-third book of his *Commentaries* (*Strom* 4.81.1).[118] The quotation in question relates to 1 Peter 4:12–19 and the problem of the con-

---

[112] Löhr (1996), 327.   [113] Ibid., 330.   [114] Ibid.

[115] See *New Testament Apocrypha* (1963/1959), 347; text in Löhr (1996), 219–21.

[116] See *New Testament Apocrypha* (1963/1959), 346–8; Zahn (1975/1888–92), 1.770–2 suggested a harmony drawn from Matthew, Luke, and perhaps John.

[117] *H.E.* 4.7.5–7; see Löhr (1996), 12.

[118] Origen uses the same term, *exēgētica* (*commentaries*) of the twentieth book of his *Commentary on John* (20.422).

nection between suffering and sin. The same quotation gives a periphrastic interpretation of Matthew 5:21–2 and 27 which locates guilt in intentions as well as in actions, and quotes Job 14:4, making what appears at least to be an application of it very similar to what Origen later made (*Princ* 4.4.4) concerning the problem of Jesus suffering as an innocent human being.[119] Clement does not identify the sources of his other citations, except to connect them with Basilides. Three of his additional citations and one from Origen involve the interpretation of one or more passages of Scripture. In one, Clement gives an interpretation of Matthew 19:11–12 concerning abstinence from marriage which, he says, is that of Basilides' followers (*Strom* 3.1.1). Origen preserves an interpretation of Basilides on Romans 7:7–10 (*ComRom* 5.1), which he says was the basis for Basilides' doctrine of the transferal of souls into different bodies, and Clement has two further citations from Basilides where interpretations of the Old Testament are involved. One is on Genesis 23:4, which is applied to a doctrine of reincarnation of souls, and the other is on what appears to be Numbers 15:22–31 involving a statement about what sins can be forgiven (*Strom* 4.165.3; 4.153.3). These brief fragmentary remains suggest that in his school Basilides read and commented on the authoritative texts of the Christian community. Löhr thinks Basilides and his school stand at the source of "the Alexandrian theological tradition which first displayed itself in Clement and Origen".[120]

The school of Valentinus

Valentinus is associated with Egypt and Alexandria by Epiphanius, who says that there was a tradition that his home was in the Egyptian delta and that he obtained a Greek education in Alexandria (*Pan* 31.2). He moved to Rome between 136 and 140.[121] If he taught in Alexandria before he went to Rome, then he must have taught in Alexandria during the reign of Hadrian at the same time that Basilides was teaching there. If one limits oneself to the few fragments preserved, mostly in Valentinus' own words, by Clement of Alexandria, his connection with Gnosticism, including that of the later writers said to belong to the school of Valentinus, becomes quite tenuous.[122]

---

[119] Origen made frequent use of this verse in Job. *Biblia Patristica* (1991), 197, has 26 listings.

[120] Löhr (1996), 332.

[121] *The Gnostic Scriptures* (1987), 217; Markschies (1992), 335, thinks 136. Valentinus' presence in Rome is based on Irenaeus, *Haer* 3.4.3.

[122] This point has been forcibly made by the major study of Valentinus done by Markschies (1992) and the earlier, more limited study of Stead (1980). For an English translation of the texts see *The Gnostic Scriptures* (1987), 223–353.

Markschies, who has examined minutely the fragments that can be attributed to Valentinus with certainty, thinks "[h]is exegesis and theology indicate . . . a theologian who should be considered a predecessor of Clement of Alexandria rather than a teacher of Ptolemaeus and founder of Valentinian Gnosis".[123] His interpretation of Biblical texts, Marckschies says, is in the style of the " 'Biblical Platonism' of the Alexandrian exegesis of a Philo or Clement". The fragments of Valentinus, he continues, "do not primarily throw light on the history of Gnosticism, but rather on the dim history of early Alexandrian Christianity and its theology".[124] Stead's earlier study of Valentinus is in essential agreement with that of Markschies. He refers to Valentinus as a "biblical Platonist" and points to the use of "a Greek Genesis" in fragment 1, what appear to be texts from Matthew's Gospel (5:8; 7:19; 12:45; and 19:17) in fragment 2, and "faint echoes" of Romans 2:15 and Hosea 2:25 in fragment 6.[125] In his view, "the fragments of Valentinus . . . give no ground for supposing anything but a Platonizing biblical theologian of some originality, whose work hardly strayed beyond the still undefined limits of Christian orthodoxy".[126]

It would appear from the recent studies on Basilides and Valentinus cited above that the two earliest Christian schools that can, with some degree of certainty, be assumed to have existed in Alexandria were schools devoted to the exegesis of the Christian Scriptures within a strongly philosophical framework. They fit nicely into Snyder's model of "textual communities",[127] and stood somewhere, in their hermeneutics and theology, between Philo's allegorical, philosophical reading of the Jewish Scriptures and Clement's allegorical, philosophical reading of the Christian Scriptures.

The school of Pantaenus

There is a long gap in our knowledge of names of teachers in Alexandria from the reign of Hadrian in the late second and early third quarters of the second century, when Basilides and Valentinus taught there, to the reign of Commodus in the fourth quarter of the second century when Eusebius says Pantaenus taught there (*H.E.* 5.9). Pantaenus is identified as Clement's teacher by Eusebius on the basis of a now lost work of Clement called the

---

[123] Markschies (1992), 404.   [124] Ibid., 404–5.
[125] Stead (1980), 78–9; the numbering of the fragments follows Völker (1932), 57–9.
[126] Stead (1980), 75.   [127] Snyder (2000), 10.

Hypotyposeis, where he is said to have referred to Pantaenus as his teacher (*H.E.* 5.11.1–2). The only passage in Clement's works where he explicitly mentions Pantaenus is in the *Eclogae Propheticae 56*, where he refers to him as "our Pantaenus". Eusebius also thinks that it is Pantaenus whom Clement praises as his teacher in the first book of his *Stromateis* (*H.E.* 5.11.2–5; *Strom* 1.1.11.2). I think Eusebius is correct in this identification, as do several others,[128] but Pantaenus is not named in the passage.

If Eusebius' identification is correct, Pantaenus was a Christian teacher of Hebrew birth, for Clement refers to the teacher he praises as a Hebrew born in Palestine whom he had found in Egypt. Van den Broek relates a statement from Photius asserting that in the *Apology for Origen* written by Pamphilus and Eusebius in the fourth century, Pantaenus "is said to have been the pupil of teachers who had known the apostles and even" to have "heard some of the apostles themselves".[129] Pantaenus' teaching, Clement says, was drawn from the prophetic and apostolic Scriptures (*Strom* 1.1.11.2–3). Eusebius describes him as "very distinguished in his education", influenced by Stoicism, an ardent evangelist who had preached the gospel as far away as India, and as one who "commented on the treasures of the divine doctrines orally and in books" (*H.E.* 5.10.1–4). On the basis of this statement of Eusebius and his assertion that in the *Hypotyposeis* Clement both named Pantaenus as his teacher and "published his interpretations of scriptures and his traditions", Bardy concluded that Pantaenus was primarily an exegete (*H.E.* 6.13.2).[130] Neymeyr thinks Pantaenus belonged to a group of old Alexandrian "presbyters" who were Scriptural scholars and Biblical theologians.[131] Clement's one explicit reference to Pantaenus fits this picture of a Biblical exegete. He says, "Our Pantaenus used to say that prophecy usually presents its texts without limits of time, using present tense for both future time and past time" (*EclProph* 56). Eusebius' allusion to the influence of Stoicism on Pantaenus, cited above, is also not to be neglected. Origen too, in a fragment of a letter preserved by Eusebius, refers to Pantaenus' accomplishments in philosophical studies and says that his example in this was influential in his own decision to become proficient in philosophy (*H.E.* 6.19.12–13). These few surviving bits and pieces from and about Pantaenus suggest that the instruction in his school, like that in

---

[128] Griggs (1991), 57; Le Boulluec (2000b), 206–11; cf. Bardy (1937), 71–2.

[129] Photius *Bibliotheca*, Cod. 118, Van den Broek (1996), 198.

[130] Bardy (1937), 65–90, esp. 74.

[131] Neymeyr (1989), 40. He bases his information about the presbyters on Clement's *EclProph* 27.1 which refers to presbyters who did not write. On this basis he questions the veracity of Eusebius' statement about Pantaenus' writing (Neymeyr (1989), 45).

the schools of Basilides and Valentinus nearly half a century before him, focused on interpreting Biblical texts in the context of a perspective gained from Greek philosophy.

The school of "the Hebrew"

In the works he produced at Alexandria, Origen refers to a man he designates simply as "the Hebrew".[132] We have no knowledge of this teacher outside of Origen's references to him. The man is never given a name, and he seems to have been dead by the time Origen began writing, for he always uses the past tense when he mentions the teachings of "the Hebrew". This would place the man in Alexandria at approximately the same time that Pantaenus was teaching there.[133] "The Hebrew" was a Christian, for Origen refers to an interpretation he gave of the two seraphim in Isaiah's throne vision as being the Son and the Holy Spirit (*Princ* 1.3.4). This, plus the designation "the Hebrew", suggests that this teacher, like Pantaenus, was a Christian of Hebrew birth.

Origen never calls "the Hebrew" his teacher,[134] but he was obviously deeply influenced by some of the views the man had expressed. He cites a story concerning hermeneutics told by "the Hebrew" which highlighted the obscurity of Scripture and the necessity of searching through the whole of Scripture to find the key to the meaning hidden in specific texts (*Phil* 2.3), and he accepted "the Hebrew's" interpretation of the two seraphim in Isaiah's throne vision which he relates in *On First Principles* 1.3.4 and 4.3.14, for he uses it later, without mentioning "the Hebrew", in his homilies on Isaiah (*HomIs* 1.2; 4.1). It is probably also a story from the same Hebrew teacher to which he alludes in his discussion of divine sovereignty and human freedom in the twentieth homily on Jeremiah (*HomJer* 20.1–2); and it is an insight from "the Hebrew" that he applies to the subject of the purpose of divine punishments when he discusses the hardening of Pharaoh's heart in a commentary on Exodus (*Phil* 27.7). "The Hebrew" would appear to have been a significant Christian teacher in late second-century Alexandria. In line with the other Christian schools that had existed there, his school

---

[132] *Phil* 2.3 (a citation from the Alexandrian commentary on the Psalms); *Princ* 1.3.4; 4.3.14; *ComJn* 1.215. There is also a reference to "the Hebrew" in *Phil* 27.7 which comes from a commentary on Exodus probably written in Caesarea.

[133] I have a study in the process of preparation for publication which argues that "the Hebrew" and Pantaenus refer to the same person. I treat them separately here, however, since the credibility of that argument has not yet been critiqued by other scholars.

[134] In spite of Butterworth's translations in *Origen: On First Principles (1973)*, 32, 131.

was certainly focused on Biblical interpretation. Origen makes no mention of philosophy in connection with this man, but some of the subjects with which he connects him were subjects of concern to the philosophical schools of the time, such as divine sovereignty and human freedom and the question of theodicy, which "the Hebrew" seems to have discussed in relation to the Biblical story of the hardening of Pharaoh's heart.

The school of Clement

Clement of Alexandria is the first Christian teacher of second-century Alexandria from whom we have an abundance of extant writings.[135] His writings, as Campenhausen says, "are rooted in his teaching activity" and, therefore, provide an indirect "source of major importance for the Alexandrian educational system of the time".[136] Clement seems not to have been a native of Alexandria.[137] He refers, at least, to traveling widely in his search for instruction from Christian teachers before finally finding a teacher in Egypt who satisfied his spiritual longings (*Strom* 1.1.11.2). This teacher was, in all probability, Pantaenus. Clement probably left Alexandria permanently during the persecution in the reign of Septimius Severus (AD 193–211) in which Origen's father was martyred (Eusebius, *H.E.* 6.1).[138]

Clement's goal in his instruction was to lead a person from simple faith to knowledge (*gnosis*).[139] He stands in an Alexandrian intellectual tradition with his emphasis on the importance of knowledge supplementing faith. One of his pedagogical predecessors in Alexandria, the author of the *Epistle of Barnabas*, though lacking the philosophical finesse of Clement, had also expressed the desire that his students have "perfect knowledge" along with their faith (1.5). In Clement's understanding the two complement one another. He looks at Paul's statement in Romans 1:17, that "the righteousness of God is revealed *from faith to faith*", and argues that Paul understands faith to exist in a twofold manner. The "common faith" serves as the "foundation", but it is capable of "growth and perfection" (*Strom* 5.1.2.3–4;

---

[135] We have the following complete: *Protrepticus, Paidagogus, Stromata, Excerpta ex Theodoto, Eclogae Propheticae, Quis dives salvetur,* plus numerous fragments of other works.

[136] Campenhausen (1969/1953), 198.

[137] Van den Hoek (1990), 179.

[138] See Neymeyr (1989), 49–50; Van den Hoek (1990), 184. Whether he settled in Cappadocia or Jerusalem depends on how one interprets the fragments of a letter of Alexander preserved by Eusebius (*H.E.* 6.11.6; see Neymeyr (1989), 46–7).

[139] I will render *gnōsis* as "knowledge" and *ho gnōstikos* as "the person with knowledge" (rather than the more traditional "Gnostic") in this discussion, as I think this better represents what Clement means.

5.4.26.1). One cannot, Clement argues, have "knowledge without faith or faith without knowledge" (*Strom* 5.1.1.3). One cannot have knowledge without faith because all first principles, or ultimate causes, lie beyond the realm of intellectual demonstration and must be apprehended by faith (*Strom* 2.4.13.4–14.1). Faith draws on knowledge, and knowledge builds on faith (*Strom* 5.1.1–4; 5.1.5.2; 5.4.26.4). He can even define knowledge as "the perfection of faith" (*Strom* 6.18.165.1).

Clement considered God to be the author of Greek philosophy as well as of the Hebrew Scriptures. God gave "commandments to the one and philosophy to the other", thereby leaving both without excuse if they failed to believe, and leading both to the perfection that comes through faith (*Strom* 7.2.11.1–2; 6.6.44.1). Philosophy is the schoolmaster to bring the Greek mind to Christ, just as the law is for the Hebraic mind.[140] It is a preparatory discipline, providing "the preliminary cleansing and training required by the soul for the reception of the faith, on which foundation the truth builds up the edifice of knowledge".[141] The modern reader may receive the impression that there is more philosophy than Scripture in Clement's work, but Clement would not have agreed. He considered his work to lead out the meaning of the Scriptures. His words, he says, may sound different to the Scriptures, but one should know that "they breathe and live from Scripture, having their origin and meaning from that source" (*Strom* 7.1.1.4).

Clement occasionally drops a few hints of the curriculum followed in his school. In the second book of his *Stromata* he refers to the standard Graeco-Roman general education called the *engkuklios paideia* (*Strom* 2.1.2.3). Marrou notes that this phrase could be somewhat ambiguous, but when used by philosophers it usually meant what was later called the literary "*Trivium*—grammar, rhetoric and dialectic" along with "the four mathematical branches of the *Quadrivium*—geometry, arithmetic, astronomy and the theory of music".[142] Clement does not list the contents of the curriculum here, but joins with it astrology, mathematics, magic, and sorcery, and notes that all Greeks think these to be the greatest sciences. The discussion here does not give any clear idea of Clement's use of this curriculum in his teaching. Later, however, when he describes the person with knowledge in the sixth book, he refers to music, arithmetic, geometry,

---

[140] *Strom* 1.5.28.3. Clement did think, however, that most of Greek philosophy had been plagiarized from Moses and the prophets (*Strom* 5.1.10.1).

[141] *Strom* 7.3.20.2; trans. *Alexandrian Christianity* (1954), 104, modified.

[142] Marrou (1964/1956), 244–5.

astronomy, and dialectics, five of the seven subjects included in the *eng-kuklios paideia*, in a way that strongly suggests that these were a part of the education in his school (*Strom* 6.10.80.1–4). The person with knowledge, he asserts, "takes what is useful for the truth from each lesson" (*Strom* 6.10.80.1). Origen makes a similar statement when he urges Gregory, who had been his student in Caesarea, to take from philosophy "general lessons (*engkuklia mathēmata*) and preparatory instruction" for Christianity. He refers to the Greeks studying geometry, music, grammar, rhetoric, and astronomy as preparatory for philosophy and suggests that philosophy itself might serve this function for the study of Christianity. Origen also asserts that the study of geometry and astronomy is useful for interpreting the Scriptures (*EpGreg* 1).

Clement argues that the person with knowledge will not be deficient in the subjects that help him progress in the "general lessons" (*engkuklia mathēmata*) and Greek philosophy, but progress in these disciplines is only a secondary goal. "The general lessons (*mathēmata*)," he says, "are aids for philosophy, and philosophy itself is an aid for comprehending the truth" (*Strom* 6.11.91.1). There are three levels of study implied in this statement: the general lessons, philosophy, and the truth. The primary goal is to use the abilities gained in these disciplines to pass on the truth accurately and to defend it when it is threatened (*Strom* 6.10.82.4–83.1). This provides an important insight into the ultimate goal of Clement's school. It did not reach its desired goal in the formation of a scholar of the Biblical texts, but in the formation of an evangelist or an apologist. The seventh book of the *Stromata* has the description of the completed product of this schooling as its primary goal. Here Plato and Scripture flow into one another to describe the beatific goal of the person with knowledge.

This, then, is the activity of the person with knowledge who has reached maturity: to associate with God through the great High Priest, while being made like the Lord, so far as possible, by means of all his service to God. This service relates to the salvation of humanity connected with the kindness of God's care for us, and is performed in worship, teaching, and doing good deeds (*Strom* 7.3.13.2).

Not everyone, however, liked the approach Clement took in his school. Some could see no point in the study of the subjects contained in the *eng-kuklios paideia*. They considered them irrelevant to the performance of one's duties. Greek philosophy, seen in its better light, was thought to be mere human wisdom incapable of teaching truth (*Strom* 6.11.93.1). In its worst light, it was feared for its capacity to lead people astray (*Strom* 6.10.80.5; 6.11.89.1). This was more than the grumbling of a disgruntled student.

It was an objection to Clement's educational model by a segment of the Alexandrian Christian community. It may be that the attitude expressed in these grumblings is a later echo of the school of someone like the earlier author of the *Epistle of Barnabas*. Pearson, arguing backwards from the "the Christian "halachic" traditions reflected in the *Epistle of Barnabas*, especially the 'Two Ways' tradition", to the first century suggested that there were "less intellectually sophisticated varieties of Christianity" in Alexandria in the first century than the variety that might be seen in a trajectory running from Clement of Alexandria through "such second-century texts as the *Teachings of Silvanus*...to a first-century religious Platonism represented on the Jewish side by Philo and on the Christian side by Apollos".[143] Since citations of the *Epistle of Barnabas* appear in both Clement's and Origen's writings, and show that it was a highly respected work in Alexandria,[144] one might with confidence, then, project forward from the *Epistle* to the time of Clement and suspect that there were still those in the Alexandrian Christian community who shared the views of that writing. Clement treats the objection seriously and presents a justification for his approach. He argues that this kind of study equips a person to recognize what is true and false; he cites Scriptures which he understands to speak of the power of truth against falsehood; he appeals to the ability of Christians trained in dialectics to defend the truth against Sophists; he argues that the person with knowledge does not consider these disciplines as ends in themselves, but as aids for communicating the truth; and he tries to show that a number of these disciplines can be found in the Bible itself (*Strom* 6.10.81.1–6.11.91.1).

The ecclesiastical school directed by Origen in Alexandria

According to Eusebius, Origen began work as a teacher when he was quite young to support himself after his father's martyrdom. Marrou notes that in antiquity teaching was "a humble, somewhat despised occupation" and very poorly paid.[145] Eusebius seems to have thought that Origen was an exception in his rewards for teaching (*H.E.* 6.2.15). This first teaching had nothing to do with Christian faith but was in secular subjects (*H.E.* 6.2.15–3.1). In all probability Origen worked as a *grammatikos*, or teacher of grammar, as his father before him had also probably done.[146] The *grammatikos* taught at

---

[143] Pearson (1986), 149.
[144] See above in "Christian literature of the second century associated with Alexandria", p. 34.
[145] Marrou (1964/1956), 203–4.   [146] See Chapter 1, in "Origen in Alexandria", p. 19.

the second level of a child's education, after the child had been taught the basics of reading—letters, syllables, simple short texts—by a teacher called a *grammatistēst*. The *grammatikos* taught the child the classical authors, especially the poets. Homer, of course, headed the list but the tragic authors and comic poets were also studied, along with such prose authors as Herodotus, Xenophon, and Thucydides. This fits well with Eusebius' statement that when he decided to stop teaching secular subjects and devote himself completely to Christian teaching Origen sold all his volumes of ancient literature (*H.E.* 6.3.9).

The *grammatikos* treated a text in four stages: (1) criticism to determine what the ancient author had written; (2) reading and recitation, which included memorizing the text for recitation; (3) explanation of the text, which included the meaning of unusual words, the explanation of unusual grammatical forms, etymology, and the explanation of the content or story of the text; and (4) judgment, or the moral teaching of the text.[147] Marrou points out that from the first century BC the analysis of the grammar of a text had also been introduced into the education delivered by the *grammatikos*.[148] Apollonius Dyscolus wrote his study of Greek syntax in the Brucheion district of Alexandria in the first half of the second century AD, so the study of grammar was alive and well in Alexandria in the time of Origen and probably formed a part of the education he delivered to the children who came to him for instruction.[149]

It was while he was engaged in teaching as a *grammatikos* that Origen was approached by some non-Christians wanting to "hear the word of God". All other Christian teachers had fled the city in fear of an impending persecution by the local governor, and there was no one left, Eusebius asserts, devoted to teaching the elements of the faith. Two brothers, Plutarch and Heraclas, sought Origen out for instruction, and this could well have been the size of his first student body.[150] Eusebius slides from this story, which he derived from some written statement of Origen himself (*H.E.* 6.3.1), into the statement that "Origen was eighteen years old when *he was set over the instruction of the school*" (*H.E.* 6.3.3, my italics). This implies some kind of official appointment to the position of teacher of the school, but there is nothing explicit about this in the text at this point. Eusebius goes immediately into recounting the great reputation Origen quickly attained among the faithful; however, it was not for his teaching, as the story relates, but for the boldness of his

---

[147] See Marrou (1964/1956), 224–35.   [148] Ibid., 235–8.
[149] Blank (1982), 5–6.   [150] *H.E.* 6.3.1–2. See Snyder's remarks above at note 103.

support of the martyrs in the persecution (*H.E.* 6.3.3–4). Then Eusebius switches back to Origen the teacher. He was instructing so many in the faith that soldiers were placed around his house because of the rage of the unbelievers against him.[151] This implies that Origen's students met in his home for instruction.[152] It is at this point that Eusebius asserts that "Demetrius, bishop of the Church, had turned the school of instruction over to Origen alone" (*H.E.* 6.3.8). The point at which Eusebius introduces this remark into the story implies that Origen had been teaching for some time before Demetrius made this decision. The remark appears in the story when the number of students seeking Origen's instruction in Christian faith had grown to the point that he decided to stop his teaching as a *grammatikos* and sold his library of Greek literature (*H.E.* 6.3.8–9). At this point the focus of Origen's teaching seems to have been on instructing those seeking baptism. Eusebius refers to many of his pupils coming to the faith, and from this number he names the following nine who were martyred in the persecution, some it seems soon after their baptism: Plutarch, who was one of the first two to seek Origen out for instruction, Serenus, Heraclides, Hero, a second named Serenus, a woman named Herais, Basilides, a woman named Potamiaena, and her mother Marcella (*H.E.* 6.4.1–5.7).

Later, after perhaps a few years, the number of students under Origen's instruction became so large that he had no time for his own "examination and interpretation of the sacred writings". Consequently, he divided the students between those needing elementary instruction in Christian faith and those who had been studying with him for some time, giving the first group over to his student Heraclas for instruction and keeping the more advanced students for himself (Eusebius, *H.E.* 6.15). It was after this division of the school, at least as Eusebius has presented the material, that Origen learned the Hebrew language, gathered some copies of the Hebrew Scriptures along with various Greek translations of the Hebrew Scriptures, and began his massive work called the Hexapla, which will be considered in the next chapter.

It is only after Origen divided his school and took over the more advanced students, leading them, presumably in examining and interpreting the sacred writings, that his teaching activity resembles that of the

---

[151] Eusebius *H.E.* 6.3.5. It is unclear whether the soldiers were placed there to protect him, or to confine and capture him. It may well have been the second, for the next statement refers to Origen moving from house to house as the persecution raged against him.

[152] See the remarks above at note 103.

earlier schools examined in this section. We do not know the curriculum Origen followed in his school in Alexandria. We can, however, get a rather accurate idea of it by extrapolating backwards from what we know of his teaching in Caesarea, which is what Eusebius has probably done in his description of the Alexandrian curriculum (*H.E.* 6.18.2–4). Grant believed that Gregory Thaumaturgus' description of Origen's teaching at Caesarea shows us "Origen's Alexandrian teaching somewhat more fully developed but not essentially changed".[153] The second part of Gregory's speech in praise of Origen describes Origen's school syllabus at Caesarea.[154] It "began with dialectic... progressed to physics, geometry, astronomy... and ethics... and reached its climax in the study of theology."[155] Grant observed that though the poets and historians were a big part of the normal Greek school curriculum and they were a part of the Christian curriculum of the second-century apologists and Clement of Alexandria, there is no trace of them in Origen's curriculum. Origen, in fact, criticizes the study of Greek literary works and rhetoric in a homily on the Psalms for being devoid of anything that would contribute to knowledge of God.[156] He also includes philosophy, dialectic, geometry, astronomy, and music in this same critique, but most of these appear as a part of the preparatory studies in his own curriculum. Grant suggests that this reflects the influence of Plato who had banned the study of the poets from his curriculum but had insisted on the study of the mathematical sciences.[157]

The apex of Origen's school curriculum can best be seen in his *Letter to Gregory* written sometime in his Caesarean period. He advises Gregory to study Greek philosophy for the same reason that the Greeks study geometry, music, grammar, rhetoric, and astronomy. They treat these as handmaids to the study of philosophy. Origen suggests that philosophy may be viewed as the general studies preparing one for the study of Christianity (*EpGreg* 1). The goal of the curriculum, however, is the study of the Scriptures. They must be read "with close attention" (*prosechein*)—the word or a cognate is repeated five times in eight lines—and in prayer, searching for the hidden meaning that most of them contain.[158] Parts at least of Origen's commentaries on Scripture, such as those on the Gospels of John and

[153] Grant (1986), 185.
[154] Gregor der Wundertäter (1996), 160–200 (chs. 7–15); see Knauber (1968), 193–6; Nautin (1977), 185; Trigg (1983), 168–71; Crouzel (1989), 26.
[155] Heine (1993b), 264; see also *EpGreg* 2.1; *Cels* 3.58.
[156] *HomPs 36* 3.6; Grant (1986), 185.
[157] Grant (1986), 185–6.
[158] Gregor der Wundertäter (1996), 220 (ch 4 (3)).

Matthew, may be edited versions of his lectures to his students taken down by the shorthand writers provided for him by Ambrose.[159]

Origen's school, like Clement's before him, was not intended to form specialists in texts or ideas, whether secular or sacred, but to form a Christian person. The real subject was the virtues: practical wisdom, self-control, justice, and courage (*Pan* 9.22). In Origen's school, Gregory Thaumaturgus says, students were incited to virtue more by his works than by his words (*Pan* 9.126); his example caused his students to love the virtues (*Pan* 12.147–9). Gregory judged the ultimate goal of Origen's school to be that a person should progress through all the virtues and "having been made like God, with a pure mind, approach him and remain in him" (*Pan* 12.149). This statement, with its echo of Plato, is very similar to the goal of Clement's school in Alexandria noted above.

There are some common trajectories running through the Alexandrian schools surveyed in this section. They were schools focused on texts, they all had a strong emphasis on the study of Scripture, and they all approached Scripture in a philosophical context. Many of their questions were issues that the larger philosophical community was discussing. Their method of interpreting Scripture had also been derived from the philosophical schools. The written remains of most of these schools are too meager to ascertain what they desired their finished products to be. The schools of Clement and Origen, however, are an exception and both appear to have had very similar goals for the outcome of their educational efforts. They wanted to produce not so much learned people, as devout servants of God. They wanted to imprint the Christian virtues on the lives of their students to the extent that they would achieve the Platonic goal of becoming like God, so far as possible (*Theaet* 176b).

---

[159] Heine (1993b), 261–6; see Chapter 4.

3

Origen and the Bible of the Alexandrian Christians

Alexandria was the city in which the Hebrew Old Testament was first translated into the Greek language. That translation is referred to as the Septuagint or the Seventy, abbreviated with the Roman numeral LXX. The oldest account of the translation is found in the *Letter of Aristeas*, which says that the initiative came from the court of Ptolemy II Philadelphus who ruled Egypt and wanted to add the Jewish laws to the royal library in the Museum.[1] A request was sent to the high priest in Jerusalem to send scholars capable of the translation work to Alexandria. Seventy-two translators were sent, said to represent six from each of the 12 tribes of Israel. These translators were taken to a house on the island of Pharos where they worked together, translating, comparing their translations, bringing them into agreement, and making a final copy. When the project was completed it was read to the Jewish community in Alexandria whose leaders pronounced that it was so excellent and accurate that no alterations should ever be made to it. This account indicates that only the books of law were translated into Greek by the translators in the time of Ptolemy.[2]

The main lines of this story are repeated in the later Jewish accounts of the translation found in Aristobulus and Josephus.[3] Philo of Alexandria also repeats this story but embellishes it with the addition that the individual translators were inspired and each wrote identical translations as if the words had been dictated to them.[4] Philo also adds that the Alexandrian Jews held an annual festival on the island of Pharos to celebrate the

---

[1] It is not possible to give a precise date for the document. Dates from the late third century BC to the early first century AD are possible. Considerable argument has been given for a date c. 170 BC (see Jellicoe (1968), 47–52).

[2] *Aristeas* 301–11; see also 10. On modern understandings of this story see Swete (1902/1968), 1–28; *The Apocrypha and Pseudipigrapha* 2 (1968/1913), 83–4; Jellicoe (1968), 29–58; Collins (2000); Boulluec (2000a), 56–69.

[3] Aristobulus (Eusebius, *Praeparatio Evanglica* 13.12.2); Josephus, *Antiquities* 12.11–109.

[4] *De Vita Mosis* 2.25–42.

translation of the Jewish laws.[5] There is no mention in the Jewish sources of the translation of the other books of the Old Testament into Greek. Such translations had been made, however, by the late second century BC, for the prologue to Sirach, written in this time period, refers to the impossibility of translating exactly from Hebrew into another language and illustrates this by pointing to significant differences between the original and the translation in the cases of the law, the prophecies, and the other books (Sirach, prologue).

IRENAEUS' VERSION OF THE TRANSLATION STORY AND ITS INFLUENCE IN ALEXANDRIA

The earliest Christians adopted this Greek version of the Old Testament as their Scripture.[6] They applied the title Septuagint to the entirety of the Greek Old Testament, and the story of the translation of the law, as embellished with the motif of the divine inspiration of the translators by Philo, was repeated by the Christians in relation to the complete Greek Old Testament. The earliest mention of the translation by a Christian is in Justin's *First Apology*.[7] He does not speak of the law or laws being translated, however, but of prophecies (*1 Apol* 31.1). Justin says Moses was "the first of the prophets", but Isaiah is introduced a little later in the same chapter as "another prophet" whose prophecy agrees with that of Moses (*1 Apol* 32.1, 12).[8] Clearly more than just the books of Moses were understood by the term prophecies which had been translated.

Irenaeus' report of the translation legend broadens the contents of the original translation in the time of Ptolemy even more. He says it is the Jewish "Scriptures" which the Seventy elders translated into Greek.[9] He then

---

[5] *De Vita Mosis* 2.41–2.   [6] Hengel (2002), 22–3; Heine (2007), 31–8.

[7] See Hengel (2002), 26–7.

[8] Later, in *Dial* 84.3, Justin shows explicitly that he considered the translation made in the time of Ptolemy to have included Isaiah (see Hengel (2002), 31). See also Ps.-Justin, *Cohortatio*, 13 and Tertullian, *Apology* 18.5–8. The latter does not mention the divine inspiration of the translations. Tertullian does say, however, that the Hebrew texts could still be seen in his day in the library of Ptolemy in the temple of Serapis.

[9] Eusebius *H.E.* 5.8.11–12; Irenaeus, *Haer* 3.21.2. Christian sources consistently refer to the translation being done by 70. In the Jewish sources, the *Letter of Aristeas* speaks of six elders from each tribe consistently and even says the work was completed in 72 days (*Letter of Aristeas* 307). Neither Aristobulus nor Philo mention the number of translators. Josephus, on the other hand, begins by speaking of six elders from each tribe (*Ant* 12.39, 48, 56), but later in the story refers to 70 elders (*Ant* 12.57, 86).

verifies this translation as the true version of the Church by using Philo's account of the translation which claimed that the translators were inspired by God in their work. This was not unique, he argues, because Ezra had earlier been inspired when he reproduced the Jewish Scriptures which had been destroyed in Babylon (*2 Ez* 14:23–46). In the same way, he says, God "has preserved for us the unaltered Scriptures in Egypt", meaning the Greek version of the Seventy done in Alexandria (*Haer* 3.21.3). In addition, he asserts that the Septuagint was the translation used by the apostles (*Haer* 3.21.2–3). In this way he puts the apostolic stamp of approval on the Greek translation of the Hebrew Scriptures which he believed had been done in the time of Ptolemy I, Lagos. The additional books Irenaeus included as Scripture, based on what can be found in his own works, include the stories of Susanna (*Haer* 4.26.3) and Bel and the Dragon (*Haer* 4.5.2), the Wisdom of Solomon (*Haer* 4.38.3; Eusebius *H.E.* 5.8.8), and Baruch (*Proof* 97). These citations indicate that Irenaeus included more than the books accepted by the Hebrews in his recognized books, and may also suggest that he accepted the complete corpus that made up the Christian Septuagint.

Irenaeus' version of the translation was known to Clement of Alexandria.[10] Like Irenaeus, he refers to 70 elders, not 72,[11] and says that what was translated were the Scriptures of both the law and the prophets.[12] He also says, like Irenaeus, that the translation was done in the time of Ptolemy, son of Lagos, though he notes that others say Philadelphus.[13] There are a number of other verbal parallels between Clement's account and that of Irenaeus which show clearly that he was repeating the story as Irenaeus had told it. Like Irenaeus, Clement combines the Ezra legend with the account of the translation, and uses it as a paradigm for God inspiring the work of the 70 translators. This shows that Irenaeus' version of the translation of the Hebrew Scriptures, combined with the Ezra legend, was known in Alexandria in the time of Origen. The Ezra legend (*4 Ez* 14) also included the division of books into the 24 which were for

---

[10] *Strom* 1.22.148.1–149.3; cf. *Irenaeus, Haer* 3.21.2. A papyrus fragment of Irenaeus' *Haer* (*P. Oxy* 405) shows that the work was being read in Egypt in the late second or early third century (*The Oxyrhynchus Papyri* (1903), 10; C. H. Roberts (1979), 23, 53). Cf. also Clement *Strom* 7.18.109.2–110.1 and Irenaeus *Haer* 5.8.2.

[11] *Strom* 1.22.149.1; Irenaeus, *Haer* 3.21.2.

[12] *Strom* 1.22.148.1.

[13] *Strom* 1.22.148.1; Irenaeus, *Haer* 3.21.2. The Jewish sources noted above put the translation in the reign of Ptolemy Philadelphus. Among Christian accounts, Tertullian, *Apology* 18.5–8, which falls in the approximate time frame of Clement, also identifies Ptolemy as Philadelphus. The other early Christian accounts simply call the ruler Ptolemy (Ps.-Justin, *Cohortatio*, 13; Justin, *Apology I* 31.1–5).

everyone to read and the 70 which were kept for "the wise" alone (4 *Ez* 14:44–7). The use of the Ezra legend in conjunction with the story of the translation of the Septuagint could have been a factor in the early Christian assumption that the whole of the Old Testament had been translated in the time of the Ptolemies. It could also have suggested a larger group of inspired books written originally in Hebrew, but not contained in the Hebrew books accepted as Scripture.

Origen refers to the Ezra legend in a fragment on Joshua, and again in a fragment from his commentary on the Psalms.[14] If Hilary is drawing on Origen in the prologue to his *Commentary on the Psalms*, as he most likely is, then Origen also put the Ezra legend and the translation story together as Irenaeus had done.[15] Hilary refers to Ezra restoring the psalms which were out of order, and then adds that "the seventy elders... were ... commissioned by king Ptolemy with the charge of translating the whole law from the Hebrew into the Greek language".[16] Irenaeus also claimed that it was the translation of the Seventy that the apostles had used as Scripture. Origen defended the Church's use of the books that made up the larger collection of the Christian Septuagint because he believed these books came down from the apostles.[17]

THE BOOKS OF OLD TESTAMENT SCRIPTURE RECOGNIZED BY ORIGEN

In addition to the 39 books of the Hebrew Scriptures, Origen cites 11 additional texts not found in the Hebrew text:[18] the Epistle of Jeremiah, Baruch, Tobit, Judith, 1 and 2 Maccabees, Sirach, the Wisdom of Solomon, and the three expansions which form part of the text of Daniel in the Septuagint. These additional books are normally cited as Scripture and treated as Scripture. The only exceptions are Baruch, which is never called Scripture but is once introduced with the formula "it is written" which introduces quotations from Scripture; Judith, which is not referred to as Scripture but whose words are cited in conjunction with those of other Biblical personalities with no hint that their words have any different status than hers; and 1 Maccabees. No statement is made about the status of the latter book.[19]

---

[14] PG 12.824B and 1076B.   [15] Goffinet (1965), 26–30.
[16] *S. Hilarii Tractatus super Psalmos* (1891), 9.   [17] See *ComRom* 8.6–7.
[18] *Biblia Patristica* (1991).
[19] For a full discussion of Origen's use of these books see Heine (forthcoming b).

Sirach and the Wisdom of Solomon were the most important of these additional books for Origen.[20] They are frequently introduced as Scripture, and interpreted and applied as Scripture. Two passages in particular receive considerable attention: Wisdom 7:17–21, and Wisdom 7:25–6. The latter passage has a defining role in his doctrine of Christ.[21] There is a major exegesis of the passage in *On First Principles* 1.2, with a similar detailed treatment in the ninth homily on Jeremiah (*HomJer* 9.4) and an abbreviated version in *Against Celsus* (*Cels* 8.14). Clement of Alexandria never cites these verses.[22] They were, however, used in Christological thinking in Alexandria for they appear in the non-Gnostic treatise from Nag Hammadi known as *The Teaching of Silvanus* (112.37–113.12),[23] which is thought to have originated in Alexandria in approximately the time of Origen.[24] These verses of Wisdom also continued to be used in Alexandrian Christological thought after Origen's time. Dionysius, who had been Origen's student and was bishop of Alexandria[25] in the mid-third century, uses them to argue, like Origen, that the Son is co-eternal with the Father,[26] and in the fourth century Didymus of Alexandria makes the same argument from these verses.[27] Wisdom 7:17–21 is also interpreted in a line-by-line study in the *Commentary on the Song of Songs* (*ComCt* 3.13.28).[28]

There were Christians, however, who did not accept the Wisdom of Solomon as Scripture.[29] In the prologue to the *Commentary on the Song of Songs*, written after he had moved to Caesarea, Origen himself does not include it or Sirach among the works of Solomon. He says, "The churches...have accepted three volumes written by Solomon", and lists Proverbs, Ecclesiastes, and the Song of Songs (*ComCt* Prol 3.1; 4.31). Elsewhere in this commentary, however, he treats the Wisdom of Solomon as Scripture and occasionally refers to it this way.[30] Origen did not, in my opinion, consider either Sirach or the Wisdom of Solomon to have been written

---

[20] In the codices from the fourth and fifth centuries, Vaticanus, Sinaiticus, and Alexandrinus, only Wisdom, Sirach, Judith, and Tobit appear in all three (Harrington (2002), 198–9).

[21] These verses are cited 36 times either together or separately; *Biblia Patristica* (1991), 222.

[22] Stählin and Treu (1980), 7–8.

[23] See Schoedel (1975), 191–2.

[24] Van den Broek (1996), 195; Pearson (2004), 78–9; Zandee (1977), 1–2; *The Nag Hammadi Library in English* (1977), 347.

[25] Eusebius, *H.E.* 6.29.4; 6.35.

[26] Quoted in Athanasius, *On Dionysius* 15.

[27] Gronewald (1968) II, 354.

[28] For a full discussion of these passages see Heine (forthcoming b).

[29] *Princ* 4.4.6. See also *ComJn* 28.122, but cf. his use of Wis. 7:25–6 in *ComJn* 6.295 and 13.153.

[30] *ComCt* 2.5.34; 3.7.23–4; 3.13.16–28.

by Solomon.[31] The statement about Solomon writing only three books,
moreover, is crucial to this section of Origen's prologue. He is dealing with
a question common to the schema of topics addressed by ancient commentators on philosophical literature.[32] The question is about the place of the
writing being considered in the order of reading the works of the particular author. The order of reading Plato's works had been arranged in three
groups by the later commentators—ethics, physics, and theology—and the
works were to be read in that order. Origen argues that the three works of
Solomon represent the three categories of philosophy and correspond to
the same order of reading the treatises, thus placing the Song of Songs at
the pinnacle of the writings of Solomon. The reference to three books of
Solomon has to come from Origen himself. The attribution of Sirach and
the Wisdom of Solomon to Solomon in Origen's writings is the work of
Rufinus and the other unknown translator of Origen's works into Latin.

Rufinus clearly attributed Sirach to Solomon in his translation of Origen's eighteenth homily on Numbers, where a quotation from Sirach is
introduced in the following manner: "In the book which *we* include among
the books of Solomon and call Ecclesiasticus but the Greeks call the Wisdom of Jesus son of Sirach, it is written, 'All wisdom is from God'."[33] That
statement shows that Rufinus and the Latin-speaking Church of his day
considered Sirach to be a book of Solomon[34] and suggests that his tendency would be to insert that viewpoint into Origen's texts when he cites
Sirach. Origen most likely introduced the quotation from Sirach simply
with the title of the work, and said, "It is written in the Wisdom of Jesus
son of Sirach." I have argued elsewhere that those places where Origen's
texts refer words from Sirach or the Wisdom of Solomon to Solomon are
the work of Rufinus or the unknown translator of parts of the *Commentary
on Matthew*.[35] If this argument is correct, and Origen did not consider the

[31] Hippolytus indicated that Proverbs, Wisdom, Ecclesiastes, and the Song of Songs were
attributed to Solomon by the Church (PG 10.628D–629A). Clement of Alexandria sometimes
introduced quotations from the Wisdom of Solomon as the words of Solomon, and at other
times he does not mention the author but uses only the title Wisdom; he referred to quotations from Sirach, on the other hand, sometimes as being said by Solomon, and sometimes
as coming from the Wisdom of Jesus [son of Sirach] (Wisdom of Solomon: *Strom* 6.11.93.9;
6.14.110.1, 114.1; 6.15.120.3; 2.1.5.1; Sirach: *Strom* 2.5.24.1, 5; 1.3.27.1, 9.47.3).

[32] See Praechter (1909), 516–38, and Hadot (1987), 99–122.

[33] *HomNum* 18.3; PG 12.714B,C, my italics. For further texts suggesting that the attribu-
tions to Solomon are the work of Rufinus, see Heine (forthcoming b).

[34] Jerome, of course, did not (*Biblia Sacra* (1969), 2. 957).

[35] Heine (forthcoming b). There is only one Greek text which apparently introduces a passage from the Wisdom of Solomon as said by Solomon (Glaue (1928), 6.12).

Wisdom of Jesus son of Sirach and the Wisdom of Solomon to have been written by Solomon, then his statements in the prologue to the *Commentary on the Song of Songs* about the Church accepting three books of Solomon have no relation to his view of the authority of these two books.

Origen defends the three additions to the book of Daniel in the Septuagint in spite of their dismissal by the Jews and some Christians.[36] He is sensitive to their absence from the Hebrew Scriptures, but this does not deter him from treating them as a part of the book of Daniel. In his *Letter to Africanus*, written to defend the Church's use of Susanna, he mentions that in addition to the story of Susanna, that of Bel and the Dragon and numerous additional passages in the Old Testament do not appear in the Hebrew texts.[37]

The story of Susanna was an important text in the early Church. Hippolytus included it in his *Commentary on Daniel*, though he knew it was not in the text of Daniel used by the Jews. He thought they had excluded it because of the shameful actions of the Jewish elders in the story.[38] This appears to have been a common explanation used by the Church to explain the absence of the story in the Hebrew text. In his brief Alexandrian commentary on Susanna,[39] Origen refers to someone he calls "the Hebrew" who identified the elders in the Susanna story with the elders Ahab and Zedekiah mentioned in Jeremiah (*Jer* 36:21–3).[40] The same man is mentioned again on the same subject in the *Letter to Africanus* (*EpistAfr* 11.(7)). This was most likely the same man Origen refers to in his Alexandrian works, where it is clear that he was a Christian of Jewish origin.[41]

Julius Africanus thought the story of Susanna was "spurious". His major arguments were that the story is absent from the copies used by the Jews, and that the Greek etymological connections between the names of the trees and the punishments of the elders are not possible in Hebrew.[42] Origen answers the first argument by appealing to Christian tradition. He argues that all churches have accepted the story of Daniel containing the

[36] The three additional texts are Susanna, The Prayer of Azariah and the Song of the Three Young Men, and Bel and the Dragon.

[37] *EpistAfr* 3–8, *La lettre à Africanus* (1983), 522–32.

[38] *ComDan* 1.14; Maurice Lefèvre (ed. and trans.), *Hippolyte commentaire sur Daniel*, SC 14, Paris, 1947, 96.

[39] In Book 10 of his lost *Stromata*, but quoted by Jerome in his own *ComDan* 13.

[40] C. H. E. Lommatzsch (ed.), *Origenis Opera Omnia*, Vol.16, Berlin, 1844, 70–1.

[41] See *Phil* 2.3, from *ComPs* 1; *Princ* 1.3.4; 4.3.14; *ComJn* 1.215; *Phil* 27.7, from scholia on Ex. This latter reference cannot be located or dated with certainty. The previous four are all from works written at Alexandria, as is the reference in the *Stromata* under discussion.

[42] Africanus, *EpistOr* 1–9.

three additions (*EpistAfr* 8). Africanus' other objection is philological and concerns the play on the Greek words for the names of the trees and the punishments prescribed for the two elders in Susanna 54–9. Origen's reply is that he has asked some Jews about the corresponding Hebrew names for the trees, and no one has been able to give him Hebrew names for these trees. Consequently, he says that he is hesitant to say that no such correspondence is possible in the Hebrew language (*EpistAfr* 10).

When Origen discusses the absence of the story in the Hebrew copies, he introduces the Hebrew man mentioned earlier in his *Stromata*, and whom I have suggested was a Jewish Christian. This man, he argues, was a learned *Hebrew* who did not question the story of Susanna but identified the elders with Zedekiah and Ahab in Jeremiah (*EpistAfr* 11). He then introduces a second Hebrew who had passed on traditions "about these elders". It is not clear, however, that this second Hebrew actually discussed the Susanna story. Origen may have assumed this because the second man discussed the actions of the elders Ahab and Zedekiah, whom the first Hebrew had identified with the elders in the Susanna story (*EpistAfr* 12). Origen may have known only one Hebrew who accepted the story of Susanna, but he was a Christian and had probably accepted the Christian canon of the Greek Old Testament.

Origen, like Hippolytus, suggests that the absence of the Susanna story from the Hebrew copies is the result of a Jewish attempt to protect the integrity of their elders. He thinks that some of these stories had been preserved in Hebrew apocrypha; and that later Hebrew scholars had translated the Susanna episode into Greek (*EpistAfr* 15). The translators either found exact equivalents for the word play in Susanna 54–9 (which Origen doubts), or used words which were analogous for the translation.[43]

Origen must have been aware that other books of the Christian Septuagint did not appear in the Hebrew texts,[44] but he never refers to the absence of other books. The additions to Daniel were a special case because this book was present in the Hebrew copies. All its parts, therefore, must be accountable for from a Hebrew original that had been translated into Greek. This was the problem for Origen and Africanus with the expanded text of Daniel in the Septuagint.[45]

---

[43]   See Moore (1992), 22; Mendels (1992), Collins (1993).

[44]   His work on the Hexapla would have made this obvious, as would his listing of the books accepted by the Hebrews in his commentary on the Psalms (*H.E.* 6.25.2).

[45]   For a fuller discussion of the argument between Origen and Africanus see Heine (forthcoming b).

Origen was not willing to give up any of the texts that made up the Christian Septuagint. His resolution on this point, in my opinion, was based on a conviction that the Christian text of the Septuagint, as he knew it, was the text the apostles had used. In his *Commentary on Romans* he notes a difference between the Septuagint and the Hebrew copies and accepts the reading of the Septuagint because "the apostle" recorded the Septuagint reading, thus putting his approval on the Septuagint version over the Hebrew copies (*ComRom* 8.6, 7). I think Origen had been influenced by Irenaeus' identification of the Septuagint with the Scriptures used by the apostles.[46]

ORIGEN'S HEXAPLA

The Hexapla was a massive compilation of six texts of the entire Old Testament arranged in parallel columns. It has been estimated that the complete work would have comprised a minimum of 6,500 pages.[47] The first column contained the Hebrew text, the second a transcription of the Hebrew text in Greek letters, the third the translation of Aquila, the fourth that of Symmachus, the fifth the Septuagint, and the sixth the translation of Theodotion.[48] The translations of Aquila, Symmachus, and Theodotion were done in the second century AD. Aquila and Theodotion were Jews; Symmachus, according to tradition, was an Ebionite (Jewish) Christian.[49] These translations are lost except for some fragments. Theodotion's translation of Daniel, however, was preserved and used by the Church rather than the Septuagint text.

There are differing and conflicting views on Origen's intentions in his work on the Hexapla. Hanson accepted, with minor adjustments, Kahle's view that Origen considered the Hebrew text to have greater authority than a translation from it and wanted to bring the Septuagint into agreement with the Hebrew.[50] I do not think this was the case. This would have demanded a comparison between only the Hebrew and Septuagint texts.

---

[46] See above, in "Irenaeus' version of the translation story and its influence in Alexandria, p. 66", and Heine (forthcoming b).

[47] Jellicoe (1968), 101.

[48] This is the order of the texts in the fragment of Psalm 44 in the Milan palimpsest. The Hebrew text, however, is not present in this fragment (Klostermann (1896), 336–7). Eusebius says that in the Psalms Origen included three additional translations which he had discovered in various places but whose translators were unknown (*H.E.* 6.16.1–3; see also Grafton and Williams (2006), 89).

[49] Eusebius, *H.E.* 6.17.

[50] Hanson (1959), 177–8.

Origen argues in his *Letter to Africanus* that texts absent from the Hebrew but present in the Septuagint are authoritative for the Church (*EpistAfr* 3–7). Furthermore, if his goal was to correct the Septuagint by the Hebrew, the answer to his rhetorical question to Julius Africanus—when he asks if he thinks the churches should reject the Septuagint they have been using and ask the Jews for pure copies that have no forgeries (*EpistAfr* 8)—would be "yes", but that is clearly not the answer Origen intended. Bigg placed the stimulus for Origen's work on the Hexapla in the context of his disputations with Jews who could annul his arguments with the simple statement that the text he was citing was not in the Hebrew Bible.[51] This was certainly a serendipity of the work, as Origen himself indicates (*EpistAfr* 9), but I do not think this was the reason he undertook it. Jellicoe's suggestion is closer to the truth when he says that "[t]he primary object of the Hexapla was the establishment of a correct text, which Origen recognized as essential both for exegesis and apologetic".[52] Origen's work on the Hexapla, in my view, began during his early work as a teacher in Alexandria when he became acutely aware of the divergences between copies of the Septuagint. His desire was to establish an accurate text of this translation for his exegetical and doctrinal work as a teacher. In all probability he never intended the work to be published, but to be his teaching tool.

Origen had worked as a *grammatikos* teaching the classics of Greek literature before he began teaching Christian subjects. A *grammatikos* in the Hellenistic period, as we noted in Chapter 2, followed a four-step syllabus in teaching texts. The first step in the syllabus was called *diorthōsis*, the emending or correcting of the text being studied. This was necessary because, as Marrou noted, manuscripts "were such a fluid medium that . . . there were hardly ever two copies alike". The *diorthōsis* of the school syllabus was not the careful scientific approach that goes under the title of textual criticism today. It was primarily concerned with bringing the pupils' copies into agreement with the copy being used by the teacher.[53]

As a *grammatikos* using the texts of the Greek classics, Origen was keenly aware of the differences between copies of the same text. When he stopped teaching classical Greek literature and began teaching Biblical literature he would have continued the same basic steps in the teaching syllabus, beginning with *diorthōsis* for, as Haines-Eitzen remarks,

---

[51] Bigg (1968 / 1886), 124–5.

[52] Jellicoe (1968), 101. Cf. Grafton and Williams (2006), 117–19.

[53] Marrou (1964 / 1956), 230. On the fluidity of ancient texts see also Haines-Eitzen (2000), 105–11.

"Christian literature during the second and third century is ... marked by the malleability of texts."[54] Origen's first need for teaching was to have as accurate as possible a text to read with the students. He was aware of the numerous divergences in the manuscripts of books in both the Greek New and Old Testaments. He refers at various places in his writings to the differences between the "copies" (*antigrapha*). Noting that there are significant differences which had developed between copies of the Gospels, he attributes some to the "shoddy work of copyists" and others to emendations made to the text based on nothing more than the corrector's "own opinions" (*ComMt* 15.14). In the same passage he also notes disagreements between copies of the Septuagint. He is aware, when working with the Septuagint, that he has other resources to use in his *diorthōsis* than simply other copies of the Septuagint. He knows, of course, that the Septuagint is a translation from a Hebrew text which itself exists in numerous copies containing textual variations. And he knows, in the earliest stages of his work, of the translations of the Hebrew Scriptures done by Aquila, Symmachus, and Theodotion.[55] He thought, rather naively it seems, that he could use these latter translations to sort out differing readings in the copies of the Septuagint because these later translations had "not yet been corrupted" (*ComJn* 6.212; cf. 6.40). This same optimistic attitude towards the other three translations is repeated in his later *Commentary on Matthew*, where he says, "We discovered that the disagreement among the copies of the old covenant are cleared up ... when we use the other versions as a criterion. By using the other versions to make decisions regarding passages which were ambiguous in the Septuagint because the copies disagreed, we preserved accord among them" (*ComMt* 15.14). His reference to "disagreements among copies of the old covenant" can only mean copies of the Septuagint. This same method of correcting copies of the Septuagint by the other versions appears again in a homily on Jeremiah when he notes that "most copies of the version of the Seventy do not have it this way", and then adds, "Later, when we had examined the other versions we knew the passage contained an error" (*HomJer* 15.5). These statements suggest that the Hexapla was intended to clarify the text

---

[54] Haines-Eitzen (2000), 111, who also cites Origen's *ComMt* 15.14 as an example.

[55] See *ComJn* 6.40 where, in a discussion of a variant in Psalm 10:7, he refers to the reading in "the accurate copies [which must mean accurate copies of the LXX as opposed to other copies of the same he knows] and in the translations other than the Septuagint, and in the Hebrew" (trans. *Origen: Commentary on the Gospel according to John Books 1–10* (1989), 179).

of the Septuagint, and that Origen was working with multiple copies of the Septuagint.

If the locus of the Hexapla was Origen's need for an accurate text in the classroom, then Eusebius' account of the Hexapla becomes more credible. He places Origen's study of the Hebrew language, and his beginning of work, on the text of the Septuagint after he had divided the catechetical school in Alexandria and given the instruction of elementary subjects over to Heraclas.[56] This would make the Hexapla Origen's first scholarly work and mean that the work on the Hexapla was well-advanced, if not completed, in Origen's Alexandrian period. The references to the three other translators of the Hebrew Scriptures in the Alexandrian work on Lamentations suggest that work on the Hexapla was underway, at least, before the *Commentary on Lamentations* was written.[57] In Book 6 of the *Commentary on John* Origen refers in the past tense to learning Hebrew, comparing the Hebrew manuscripts with those of the Christians, meaning the Septuagint, and comparing also the translations of Aquila, Theodotion, and Symmachus (*ComJn* 6.212; cf. 6.40). The prologue to Book 6 makes it clear that this was the first book Origen wrote after he moved to Caesarea (*ComJn* 6.8–12). This suggests that most, if not all, of the work on the Hexapla had been done in Alexandria before he moved to Caesarea.

Origen describes his methodology in the Hexapla in a passage in his *Commentary on Matthew* (15.14). "We marked some passages", he says, "with an obelus since they do not appear in the Hebrew text. We were not so audacious as to remove them altogether. We added other passages and marked them with asterisks that it might be clear that they do not appear in the Septuagint but were added by us from the other translations in agreement with the Hebrew text." This was the methodology and system of markings developed approximately four centuries earlier by the Alexandrian Museum scholar Zenodotus in his work to produce a more accurate text of Homer.[58]

---

[56] H.E. 6.15.1–16.1. Epiphanius, *Pan* 64.3.1–5, appears also to think the Hexapla was Origen's first work, but his report of Origen's life is so garbled that little weight can be given to his assertions. Jellicoe (1968), 117–18, esp. n. 4, has suggested that the *EpistAfr* might be dated as early as 230, being written during Origen's first visit to Greece [c. 226–30]. If this dating should be correct, then the Hexapla would, in all probability, have been completed before this date.

[57] In *FragLam* 3, for example, he remarks that the translations of Aquila and Theodotion are not extant on Lamentations but only those of Symmachus and the Seventy; in *FragLam* 116 he gives the translations of Aquila and Symmachus for a phrase (in contradiction to his statement in *FragLam* 3).

[58] See Chapter 1, in "Origen in Alexandria", p. 19.

ORIGEN AND THE NEW TESTAMENT

Origen had a definite concept of an Old Testament and a New Testament, which together comprised Christian Scripture. He also knew and maintained the Christian tradition concerning the contents of each. I have discussed his defense of the Christian tradition concerning the books of the Septuagint above. We will see in what follows that he has the same concern to maintain the tradition relating to books of the New Testament. He uses, in fact, very similar phraseology to refer to the tradition in both cases. In discussing the Septuagint he refers to it as "[used] in [all] the churches under heaven" (*EpistAfr* 9). Likewise, he says that the four Gospels are "not disputed in the Church of God under heaven".[59]

Origen uses the terminology of Old and New Testament in the prologue of the first book of his *Commentary on John*.[60] This text is Alexandrian, and it appears in a book preserved complete in a Greek manuscript tradition. If my arguments in Chapter 4 are correct, this was Origen's first published work. Since he sets his discussion in the prologue in the context of "the Scriptures which are in circulation in all the churches of God",[61] its references to the books considered to be Scripture most likely represent the general consensus among orthodox believers in Alexandria and elsewhere, and not Origen's idiosyncratic view.

Origen does not use the term "canon" in his discussion of Scripture in the prologue to the first book of his *Commentary on John*, but he has a clear concept of books that are accepted in the churches. He begins his discussion by referring to "the Scriptures which are in circulation in all the churches of God and are believed to be divine".[62] He refers to Moses, the prophets, four Gospels, the Acts of the Apostles, the epistles of the apostles, and the Apocalypse of John. In the category of epistles, he mentions the writings of Paul and Peter (*ComJn* 1.14–26). He thinks the four Gospels are the most

---

[59] Quoted in Eusebius, *H.E.* 6.25.4; cf. *ComJn* 1:14.

[60] *ComJn* 1. 17, 19, 25, 36, 64, 80, beyond the prologue in 1.228, and several times in the later books. A reference to the New and Old Testaments also appears in *FragJn* 1, which is on John 1:1. The contents of this fragment read like Origen's work, but it does not appear in the *ComJn*, so it is not clear where to locate it.

[61] *ComJn* 1.14, trans in *Origen: Commentary on the Gospel according to John Books 1–10* (1989), 35.

[62] Ibid.; Hanson (1954), 138, 143, who does not think Origen uses the term "canon", suggests that it is the Greek phrase, "in circulation in the churches", which Rufinus has translated as "canon" in those places where the word appears in the Latin texts. Hanson (1954), 138, n.3 provides the following list where this phrase appears in Origen: *ComJn* 19.152; *Cels* 6.21, 31; PG 12.1140A; and *EpistAfr* 1 (incorrect references corrected).

important of all Scripture, and that the Gospel of John is the most important of the four Gospels. The apostolic epistles are trustworthy and helpful,
but they rely on the words of the Law and the Prophets for their authority.
Their words do not stand "on a par with, 'Thus says the Lord almighty'".[63]
He raises the question of whether even Paul himself considered his own
words to be "divinely inspired". While he does not state it in these words, it
is clear that the criterion by which he classifies the writings in this prologue
is their testimony to Christ and his divinity.

There are four Gospels, Origen says, because they constitute the "elements" of the Church's faith (*ComJn* 1.21). This is an allusion, of course,
to ancient Greek scientific thought, which believed that all things in the
world derived from four basic elements. Irenaeus had used a similar argument when he asserted that the Church must have no more nor less than
four Gospels because there are four inhabited zones in the world and four
winds. He pushed his analogy further, however, listing Biblical examples
of foursomes also.[64] Origen takes the significance of the correspondence
between the number of Gospels and the elements to lie in the fact that
God's reconciliation is for the whole world. He names the Gospels: Matthew, Mark, Luke, and John (*ComJn* 1.22).

In the first book of his *Commentary on Matthew*, written late in his residence in Caesarea, Origen refers to the four Gospels which alone "are not
disputed in the Church of God under heaven", and proceeds to relate what
he has learned from tradition concerning these Gospels.[65] What he says
about Matthew and Mark resembles in some points what Eusebius relates
that Papias had said about these two Gospels.[66] Matthew, who had been
a tax-collector, wrote a Gospel in the Hebrew language for Christians of
Hebrew origin, and Mark wrote his Gospel under Peter's guidance. Going
beyond what we know, at least, of Papias' account, Origen says that Luke

---

[63] *ComJn* 1.15–16, trans. in *Origen: Commentary on the Gospel according to John Books 1–10*
(1989), 35.

[64] *Haer* 3.11.8. While this is not the place to carry out such an investigation, it seems to me
that it might be fruitful to look more closely at the possibility of an influence of Irenaeus, *Haer*
3.11.7–9 on Origen's view of the Gospels. I noted above in the section on the LXX that there
are two passages in the writings of Clement of Alexandria which are drawn from Irenaeus,
and that there is also papyrological evidence that Irenaeus' work had reached Egypt by the
time of Clement and Origen. I also suggested in that same section that Irenaeus' version of
the LXX translation legend may have influenced Origen's thinking.

[65] This book has not been preserved. The remarks about the Gospels are quoted in Eusebius, *H.E.* 6.25.3–6.

[66] Eusebius, *H.E.* 3.39.15–16. Eusebius does not preserve any remarks from Papias on Luke
and John.

wrote the Gospel "praised by Paul" for Gentile Christians, and that John's Gospel was last.

In his first homily on Luke, also composed during his residence in Caesarea, Origen asserts that "[t]he Church has four Gospels, but heresy has many". He then lists some of the Gospels of the heretics: a Gospel according to the Egyptians, one according to the 12 Apostles, and others according to Basilides, Thomas, and Matthias. He adds that he has read numerous others and concludes, "[I]n all these we approve nothing other than what the Church approves, namely that only four Gospels are to be received" (*HomLk* 1.2). In all these discussions of the Gospels it is obvious that Origen is conscious of the fact, and thinks it important, that he stands firmly in line with what is accepted by all the churches. On the other hand, he tentatively cites the *Gospel of the Hebrews* three times in his extant works,[67] the *Gospel of Peter* once, the *Kerygma Petrou* twice, and a saying about prayer from an unknown source, which he connects with Jesus.[68] Each citation of the *Gospel of the Hebrews* is introduced by the phrase, "If one accepts". Origen uses this phrase once when introducing a passage from the Wisdom of Solomon (*ComJn 28.122*). Because of the strong evidence for his acceptance and use of this writing as Scripture in other places, however, it would not seem to suggest that Origen himself did not accept the book but only that he was aware that there were others who did not. On the other hand, in the case of his use of the phrase in relation to the *Gospel of the Hebrews*, Origen makes such firm statements elsewhere about the Church having only four Gospels that it would be contradictory for him to regard this Gospel on the same level with the four accepted ones. His treatment of it, however, may indicate its acceptance by some in Alexandria who were not considered heretical.[69] In his *Commentary on Matthew* Origen says that some, wishing to preserve Mary's virginity after the birth of Jesus, use a tradition from the *Gospel according to Peter* to argue that his siblings were the children of Joseph from a previous marriage (*ComMt 10.17*). He does not give his view of the status of the book, but he is in agreement with the sentiments of the argument based on the tradition. In the prologue to *On First Principles* Origen speaks quite strongly against the *Teaching of Peter*,

---

[67] See Chapter 2, n. 43.

[68] *Gospel of the Hebrews*: *ComJn* 2.87; *HomJer* 15.4; *ComMt* 15.14; *Kerygma Petrou*: *Princ* Prol 8; *ComJn* 13.104; unknown saying: *PEuch* 2.2; 14.1; 16.2; *ComMt* 16.28; *Cels* 7.44.

[69] See the discussion of this Gospel in Chapter 4, in "Monarchians, Heracleon, and the Alexandrian Theological Milieu in Origen's *Commentary on John* 1:1b–3", p. 97.

saying it is not among the Church's books, and does not derive from Peter or from any inspired author (*Princ* Prol 8). In Book 13 of the *Commentary on John*, where he notes that Heracleon had cited it, his negative attitude is still evident, though expressed more cautiously, when he says that one must examine whether the writing "can possibly be genuine, or is spurious, or a mixture" (*ComJn* 13.104).

Eusebius relates that in his *Homilies on Hebrews* Origen discussed the authorship of the book. Origen says he knew a tradition that attributed Hebrews to Clement of Rome, and another which attributed it to Luke. He thinks the style of Hebrews suggests that it contains Pauline ideas related from memory by a disciple who also added some interpretation. This, plus the fact that the ancients had considered it to be Paul's, led him to conclude that it should be treated as a Pauline letter.[70] This is perhaps the reason that whenever he cites it in his writings he always introduces the citation as coming from Paul.

In a fragment from the fifth book of the *Commentary on John*, written in Alexandria, Origen discusses the authenticity of the Petrine and Johannine epistles. He says Peter left one letter which is accepted and a second which is disputed. John, likewise, left one brief letter plus two additional ones which some do not think are genuine. In this same fragment he says John also wrote the Apocalypse.[71] In the discussion of the siblings of Jesus noted above in conjunction with the *Gospel according to Peter,* Origen also refers to the *Protevangelium Jacobi* (9.2), which he calls the *Book of James*, as a source of the view that Joseph had children from a previous marriage (*ComMt* 10.17). As with the *Gospel according to Peter*, he makes no comment about his own opinion on the authority of the book.

Did Origen consider any of the works known today as the Apostolic Fathers as Scripture?[72] He introduces a quotation from *1 Clement* by referring to Clement as a "disciple of the apostles" (*Princ* 2.3.6), and in another citation he identifies him with Paul's fellow-worker mentioned in Philippians 4:3 (*ComJn* 6.279).[73] The fact that he knew a tradition which attributed the Epistle to the Hebrews to Clement of Rome, as I noted above, may have inclined him to look favorably on *1 Clement* which was attributed to the same author. A reference to Barnabas is introduced as coming from "the

---

[70] Eusebius, *H.E.* 6.25.11–12.   [71] Eusebius, *H.E.* 6.25.8–10.

[72] Layton (2004), 141, points out that in fourth century Alexandria Didymous "incorporated into his exegesis writings traditionally treasured by the Egyptian church as Scripture: *1 Clement, the Didache, the Letter of Barnabas,* and the *Shepherd of Hermas.*"

[73] See Hanson (1954), 139, n. 7, who also lists *HomJosh* 3.4 and a fragment on Ez 8:3 in PG 13.767–836.

general epistle of Barnabas" (*Cels* 1.63). In a much earlier passage Barnabas stands in a list of citations to prove that thoughts may be suggested to humans by good or bad angels. The list begins with a reference to Tobit, followed by one to the *Shepherd of Hermas*, and is concluded by a reference to an assertion made "by Barnabas in his epistle" (*Princ* 2.3.4).

Origen clearly regarded the *Shepherd of Hermas* highly. He cites Mandate 1.1 five times in the *On First Principles* and the *Commentary on John*.[74] The creed-like statement concerning God and creation in the prologue to *On First Principles* begins by quoting *Hermas* Mandate 1.1, but without naming the source. The quotation is repeated later in the same treatise, where it is ascribed to Hermas (*Princ* 1.3.3), and is paraphrased and attributed to "the angel of repentance in the *Shepherd of Hermas*" in the first book of the *Commentary on John*, which was written at Alexandria (*ComJn* 1.103). In this last context the statement from Hermas is joined with the statement made by the mother of the seven martyrs in 2 Maccabees 7:28. These same two passages are joined also in *On First Principles* 2.1.5, where 2 Maccabees is cited as "scriptural authority" for the doctrine of creation presented and the statement from the *Shepherd of Hermas* is cited as additional support. The same statement is repeated again, without an ascription of source, in the last book of the *Commentary on John*, where it appears in Origen's Greek and matches that of Hermas exactly (*ComJn* 32.187). I noted above the inclusion of the *Shepherd of Hermas*, along with Tobit and the *Epistle of Barnabas*, in an argument about angels (*Princ* 2.3.4). In another passage he refers to the *Shepherd* as a book which some people disregard. He obviously does not, for he proceeds to use a passage from it to illustrate his view that Scripture consists of three levels of meaning (*Princ* 4.2.4). He cites the *Shepherd* again to support an understanding of the work of angels in his Caesarean *Homilies on Luke* (35.3). Again in conjunction with a doctrine of angels, he cites the *Shepherd* as a "Scripture in circulation among the churches but not considered to be divine by all" (*ComMt* 14.21). He considered the author of the *Shepherd* to have been the Hermas mentioned by Paul in Romans 16:14, and in this context refers to the writing as "very useful" and "divinely inspired" (*ComRom* 10.31). Hanson considered Origen's enthusiasm for the work to have cooled, however, in his later writings, where his citations are prefaced by phrases such as, "if it should seem to someone that that book is to be received".[75] I do not think that the three passages he cites necessarily

---

[74] Irenaeus also cites this passage (see Van den Hoek (1995), 102).
[75] Hanson (1954), 140; *HomNum* 8.1, cf. *SerMt* 53, *HomPs* 37.1 (SC 411, p. 270).

suggest that Origen's own regard for the book had declined. They need suggest no more than that he had become aware of a number of Christians who did not consider the book so highly.

But what was Origen's evaluation of these three books from the Apostolic Fathers? He seems to have thought of the Epistle of Barnabas as a general epistle written by the companion of Paul. Since he believed that the author of *1 Clement* was the fellow-worker of Paul also, he may have considered *1 Clement* in the same category as well. If, however, one looks at the lists of Origen's citations of the seven general epistles in *Biblia Patristica 3* in comparison to the few times that he cites Barnabas and *1 Clement*, then one must assume that he did not think of *1 Clement* and Barnabas as on a par with the other seven.[76] Only second and third John, which Origen noted some did not accept, with 11 and 4 citations respectively, might be compared with the number of citations from *1 Clement* and Barnabas. There are six columns of references to 1 John, seven-and-a-half columns of references to 1 Peter, 52 references to 2 Peter, and 104 to James. His attitude towards the *Shepherd of Hermas* may have been different. He locates Hermas, as he did Clement and Barnabas, within the circle of Pauline associates. How he classified the work is not clear. It is neither an epistle nor a Gospel, and he never refers to it as an apocalypse. His most usual way of designating the work is that of the *Shepherd*. Because he refers to it once as divinely inspired, and cites it with such high regard, we must, it seems, hold open the possibility that he considered it among the recognized books. It is not impossible that the shadow of Irenaeus might be detected here again. tn Hoek has called attention to the fact that Hermas is the only book of the Apostolic Fathers that Irenaeus cites, but, she adds, "he treats it as scripture".[77]

---

[76] *Biblia Patristica* (1991), 457–66.

[77] Van den Hoek (1995), 102. She cites Irenaeus, *Haer* 1.15.5; 22.2; 2.2.4; 6.2; 30.9; 4.20.2; *Dem* 4.

4

The Beginnings of Origen's Published
Biblical Scholarship

Origen produced two major compendia of his understanding of the Christian faith: the *On First Principles* in Alexandria and the *Against Celsus* in Caesarea. One is a kind of first attempt at systematic theology and the other is a classic defense of the Christian faith against the educated attack of a second-century Platonizing rhetorician.[1] These two works might be viewed as the "bookends" of Origen's theology, one coming relatively early in his career as a theologian and the other near its end. Otherwise, with the exception of a few treatises focused on individual theological issues, Origen did his theology by writing commentaries on the canonical scriptures of the Church in the manner that his contemporaries who were Aristotelian or Platonic philosophers did their philosophy by writing commentaries on the works of the earlier philosophers.[2] Longinus, for example, said that Plotinus' philosophy was a better exposition of "the principles of Pythagorean and Platonic philosophy" than that of any of his predecessors.[3] In all of his Alexandrian writings Origen is concerned to defend what he considers to be the Christian faith whose roots derive from the apostles. In this chapter we will look at his theology as he develops it in his earliest major Alexandrian writing, the *Commentary on John*.

Origen's Alexandrian writings probably fall in the period of AD 216/217–231/232.[4] The latter date is relatively certain, for Eusebius says Origen left Alexandria in the tenth year of the reign of Alexander Severus.[5] What cannot be dated precisely is the beginning point of Origen's literary activity. Eusebius

---

[1] The *Against Celsus* will be discussed in Chapter 10.

[2] See Synder (2000), 14–65, who argues that Stoics and Epicureans tended not to write commentaries on the works of their founding fathers but used written texts in different ways in their educational endeavors.

[3] Quoted in Porphyry on the *Life of Plotinus* 20.70, trans. *Plotinus* 1 (1989), 61. See also Mansfeld, (1994), 158–9.

[4] The usual dates given are 222–32. I will provide a basis below for thinking that Origen's writing may have begun a few years earlier than 222.

[5] Eusebius, *H.E.* 6.26. Alexander Severus reigned from 222–35.

gives the following list of the Alexandrian writings based on information from remarks of Origen in some of his works in the Caesarean library: the first five books of the *Commentary on John*, the first eight books of the *Commentary on Genesis*, a commentary on the first 25 psalms, a commentary in five books on Lamentations, a treatise *On the Resurrection*, the *On First Principles*, and ten books entitled *Stromata*. Earlier, Eusebius also places Origen's work on the *Hexapla* in Alexandria.[6] Jerome refers to a *Commentary on the Song of Songs* in two books written in Origen's youth, which must have been written in Alexandria.[7] Norelli also lists a work *On Natures* among Origen's Alexandrian writings.[8] Two works by Origen discovered among the papyri found at Tura in 1941 are unmentioned in all the ancient references to his works. One is the treatise *On the Passover*, and the other is the *Dialogue with Heraclides*. No one knows when to date these works, though most scholars have placed them among Origen's Caesarean writings. Chadwick thought it possible, at least, that the *Dialogue with Heraclides* might have been composed before 230, which would place it in the Alexandrian period.[9]

The two books of the youthful *Commentary on the Song of Songs* to which Jerome refers must have been written considerably earlier. All that survives from the work is one paragraph in the *Philocalia* (7.1). This earliest writing shows Origen already thoroughly knowledgeable of the conventions of commentary literature. The paragraph is an attempt to explain why readers find Scripture obscure, which was one of the topics addressed in the prologues of the secular commentaries.

THE BIBLICAL COMMENTARIES PRODUCED AT ALEXANDRIA

One of the conventions that Origen adopted from the format of the secular commentary literature of the time was that of the topics treated in the prologue to a commentary.[10] There was a standard list of topics which a

---

[6] Eusebius, *H.E.* 6.24 and 6.16. Epiphanius (*Pan.* 64.3.5), whose account of Origen's early life does not appear very trustworthy, refers to the Hexapla as Origen's first work.

[7] Jerome, *Ep.* 33.4. The introductory remarks of the compilers of the *Philocalia*, where a paragraph of the work is preserved, also refer to it as a work of Origen's youth.

[8] This work is known from a citation in Victor, bishop of Capua in the mid-sixth century, who reproduces it from a text of John the Deacon; Norelli (2000), 299. For the citation see Nautin (1977), 252.

[9] *Alexandrian Christianity* (1954), 432.

[10] See Praechter (1909), 516–38; Hadot (1987), 99–122; Neuschäfer (1987), 57–84; Heine (1995a), 3–12; Heine (2001), 421–39.

teacher took up with his students when he began the exegetical study of an ancient text with them.[11] Origen must have followed this format in his instruction of students in Alexandria. It has been noted that this list of topics was referred to by the technical phrase, "What comes before the study of ...". It is worth noting that this phrase appears in the conclusion to the prologue of Origen's *Commentary on John*,[12] and that six of the topics in the standard list are treated in that prologue.[13]

None of the commentaries in Eusebius' list of Origen's Alexandrian works exist today in their complete form. The *Commentary on John* is the most complete. We have the first two books, a fragment each from Books 4 and 5 preserved in the *Philocalia*, and 15 rather brief fragments, which might be from the books written in Alexandria,[14] preserved in catena commentaries.[15] There are only fragments of the commentaries on the first 25 psalms, on Genesis, and on Lamentations.

There is a peculiarity common to all of these commentaries that can be seen even in their fragmentary form. None of them offer comments on an entire Biblical book. The *Commentary on John*, which was completed in Caesarea, contained 32 books but stopped at John 13:36, the *Commentary on Genesis*, also completed in Caesarea in 13 books, ended at Genesis 4:26, the last fragment of the *Commentary on Lamentations* is on Lamentations 4:22, and the *Commentary on Psalms* covered only the first 25 psalms. We must not think of Origen's commentaries as one thinks of modern academic commentaries on Scripture, in which the commentator sets out to solve the problems connected with the Biblical book in question and to elucidate its meaning. Origen wrote in response to problems confronting the Church. The popularity of Genesis and the Gospel of John among Gnostic groups may have been a factor in his decision to write commentaries on these books. C. H. Roberts has observed that according to the papyrological remains, the Psalms, Genesis, and the Gospel of John were the three most read Biblical texts in Egypt.[16] Origen considered Lamentations, the other

---

[11] See Praechter (1909), 523–6; Heine (2001), 422–3.

[12] *ComJn* 1.88. Mansfeld (1994), 26, 98.

[13] See Heine (1995a), 7–12.

[14] The first text cited for discussion in Book six is John 1:19 (*ComJn* 6.12–13), although the discussion begins with John 1:16–18 to refute an interpretation of the Gnostic Heracleon. *FragJn* 13 is on John 1:18 but does not repeat anything found in *ComJn* 6.

[15] Catena commentaries was a genre of Biblical commentary that arose in the fifth century. The name, *catena*, is the Latin word for "chain". They consisted in excerpts from earlier Church Fathers following one another like links in a chain, arranged by chapter and verse of the Biblical book.

[16] Roberts (1979), 61.

book he commented on in Alexandria, along with the letter of Jeremiah, to form a part of the one book of Jeremiah.[17] Jeremiah, along with Isaiah, follows the Psalms and Genesis in the list of the most read Old Testament books in early Christian Egypt.

Origen was interested in treating those parts of the Bible his opponents used in order to expound the "correct" understanding of the text in question. He is doing polemical theology in all of his mature works at Alexandria. It is not polemical in the way that the later Caesarean *Contra Celsum* is, but it is polemical. What Origen attempts in his commentaries is to provide an interpretation that he considers correct and that will appeal to an intelligent, educated person. He will oppose, he says, "heretical fabrications *by adducing in opposition the sublimity of the gospel message*" (my italics).[18]

Origen is concerned about the disparity among Christians related to some of the most important doctrines of the faith (*Princ* 1. Pref. 2). He considers doctrinal variations between Churches to be unacceptable (*Dial* 1.25–6). He is, in fact, working out his own theological vision in these Alexandrian commentaries against the backdrop of what he considers to be aberrant views.

THE *COMMENTARY ON JOHN*

While Eusebius provides a list of the writings Origen produced at Alexandria, he gives no chronology for their composition. He knows, from a note in Origen's own hand in the Caesarean library copy, that the ten books of the *Stromata* were written during the reign of Alexander Severus (*H.E.* 6.24). From references in the *On First Principles* it is clear that some of the books of the *Commentary on Genesis* had been written before the *On First Principles*, as had the commentary on the second Psalm, at least, and the two books *On the Resurrection*.[19] There are no cross-references between the *Commentary on John* and the other Alexandrian writings. There is, however, a time reference in the opening book of the commentary itself. Origen refers to having been separated from his friend Ambrose and now recently having "come home to Alexandria". He wants to devote the first fruits of all his future activities, he says, to the first fruits of all Scripture, which he has identified as the Gospel of John (*ComJn* 1.12–13, 20).

---

[17] Eusebius, *H.E.* 6.25.2. Eusebius says this list comes from Origen's commentary on the first Psalm (*H.E. 6.25.1*).

[18] *ComJn* 5.8; trans. *Origen: Commentary on the Gospel according to John Books 1–10* (1989), 166.

[19] *Princ* 1.2.6; 2.3.6; 2.4.4; 2.10.1.

Preuschen identified this absence from Alexandria with Origen's secret flight from the city to Caesarea at the time of Caracalla's massacre of the population of Alexandria in 215.[20] Caracalla visited Alexandria on his way to a war against Parthia. When he passed through Thrace, he had identified himself with Alexander the Great and, among other things, adopted Macedonian dress, named a select group of his troops the "Macedonian phalanx", and ordered statues of Alexander and, it seems, of himself as Alexander to be erected in every city.[21] This order would have included Alexandria and, perhaps because it was the most important of Alexander's namesake cities, we should think that Caracalla was especially concerned to be honored as Alexander there. C. R. Whittaker points out that "the value of such an identification was ... an 'indirect method of emperor worship' ".[22] When he reached Alexandria Caracalla set up headquarters in the Serapeum, the temple of Alexandria's preeminent god.[23] There he lived, and from there he issued his orders concerning the city.

Precisely what happened in Alexandria is not clear because the two primary sources give slightly different versions of the events.[24] There is a papyrus fragment, however, which records a trial held by Caracalla in Alexandria in which he blames the Prefect Septimius Heraclitus for a recent riot in the city during which images were destroyed. The editors of the papyrus suggest that the images referred to in the papyrus are the images of Caracalla as Alexander that he had ordered erected in the city.[25] Whether

[20] *Origenes Werke* (1903), lxxix; see Eusebius, *H.E.* 6.19.16; so too *Eusebius The Ecclesiastical History* (1928), 206. Nautin (1977), 366–8, however, wants it to be the conflict with Demetrius referred to in the prologue to *ComJn* 6 to which Eusebius refers when he mentions the "warfare" in Alexandria. There are two points in Eusebius' account which I think point to Caracalla's massacre. First is Eusebius' statement that this warfare broke out "in the city" (*kata tēn polin*). This suggests something larger than a dispute between the bishop and a teacher. The other is the verb Eusebius chooses to designate Origen's departure—*hupexerchesthai*. The usual meaning of this word is a secret, unnoticed departure (see, for example, Josephus, *Antiquities* 14.16). I can see no reason for Origen's departure to have been secretive had he been leaving because of Demetrius' animosity towards him. But if it refers to his departure at the time when Caracalla's army was slaughtering the inhabitants of Alexandria randomly and at will, it would have had to be secretive.

[21] Herodian, 4.8.1–2. Herodian refers to some pictures with two half-faces, one of Alexander and the other of Caracalla.

[22] *Herodian* (1970), 413, n. 2.

[23] McKenzie (2007), 196, notes that Caracalla "is described as Philosarapis [Friend of Serapis] on some columns found in the harbour [of Alexandria] in 1997". She argues that the Serapeum, which was burned in the late second century AD, was reconstructed by the Romans between AD 181 and 215/16, and was probably completed by Caracalla (ibid. 195–6).

[24] Dio Cassius 78.22–3; Herodian 4.8.6–9.8.

[25] P. Benoît and J. Schwartz, *Études de Papyrologie* vii (1948), 17–33, cited in, *The Acts of the Pagan Martyrs* (1954), 229–30. Musurillo is cautious but favors a view connecting the contents of the papyrus with the massacre that occurred in Alexandria.

the riot had occurred prior to Caracalla's arrival or during his presence is not clear. The editors of the papyrus, again, suggest that it occurred in the course of the religious procession welcoming Caracalla to Alexandria. The emperor, maddened by the disgrace, then summoned the people to a public gathering and ordered his troops to surround and execute them. When the Alexandrians resisted, a prolonged general massacre of the city's population followed.[26]

Caracalla's visit to Alexandria was not an overnight stop. He seems to have arrived in September of 215. The massacre occurred early in his visit. The slaughter and plunder was random and massive. The net of destruction fell over foreigners and locals alike; even some of his own army fell prey when they were unidentified (Dio Cassius 78.22.2–23.1). There are papyri which suggest that Caracalla was still in Alexandria in January or February 216 (*P. Flor.* 382; *BGU* 1.266). The exact date of his departure is not known, but he was in Antioch in May of 216.[27] He was, therefore, in Alexandria for at least five months, and perhaps as long as six or eight. It was during this time that he issued the edict expelling all rural Egyptians from Alexandria except those with special reasons for being there.[28] Before he left, he ordered that free association among the city's population be disrupted by the construction of a wall through the city with guards stationed at intervals (Dio Cassius 78.23.3).

The autumn of 215 through the spring of 216 was an uneasy time in Alexandria even after the massacre had ceased. It was a good time for a young Christian scholar to slip away to Caesarea. He would not have thought of it as fleeing martyrdom, for the slaughter and oppression in Alexandria had nothing to do with the Christian faith. There is no information about how long Origen was absent. It must have been at least a year, perhaps two. He may have stayed away until after Caracalla's death in the spring of 217, which would have assured that the latter's animosity towards the Alexandrians would not flare up again. Origen may even have entertained thoughts of remaining in Palestine, as he was warmly received by the bishops of both Caesarea and Jerusalem, who seem to have encouraged his scholarly activity. Both bishops had invited him to expound the Bible in their respective Churches (Eusebius, *H.E.* 6.19.16–17). He must also have engaged in some kind of research in this period, for it was during this time in Palestine in the reign of Caracalla that he obtained a copy of the Psalms

---

[26] See *The Acts of the Pagan Martyrs* (1954), 230–1.   [27] *Herodian* (1970), 428, n. 2.

[28] Lewis (1983), 202; Dio Cassius 78.23.2; see the discussion of the edict above in Chapter 1, in "Location, Topography, and Population of Alexandria", p. 1.

found in a jar at Jericho which would provide one of the extra columns for the Psalms in the Hexapla (Eusebius, *H.E.* 6.16.3). It was only after Demetrius sent deacons to Palestine with a letter asking Origen to come back to his duties at Alexandria that he returned (*H.E.* 6.19.19).

Such a long absence gives meaning to Origen's remarks about his separation from Ambrose in the prologue to the *Commentary on John* (*ComJn* 1.12). This way of reading the texts also makes the *Commentary on John* the first of Origen's Biblical commentaries. Origen would have been in his early thirties when he began work on the commentary. He begins his literary career by trying to sort out the thorny Christological issues centered largely on the Gospel of John which divided the late second-and early third-century Church. T. E. Pollard argued that the Johannine Christology forced the church of the first four centuries to explicate the double problem of "the relationship between the pre-existent Logos-Son and the godhead", and "the relationship between the divine and the human in Jesus Christ".[29] John's Gospel, Origen claims, is the most important Gospel because it expresses Jesus' divinity more fully than the other three (*ComJn* 1.21–2).

AMBROSE, THE VALENTINIANS, AND ORIGEN'S *COMMENTARY ON JOHN* 1:1A

The immediate stimulus for Origen to write on John came from his friend Ambrose, who requested a study of the Gospel from him.[30] Ambrose did far more, however, than request a commentary from Origen. At his own expense he set up for Origen a scriptorium, the ancient version of a publishing house. Grafton and Williams have called attention to an earlier example of such a publishing undertaking. They have shown from the library of Philodemus (first century BC) found at Herculaneum that Philodemus had a staff of scribes with specialized skills who copied and produced the manuscripts of his works. They suggest that the staff and resources necessary for the production of Philodemus' works were provided by a wealthy patron, perhaps Calpurnius Piso in

[29] Pollard (1970), 5–6.
[30] *ComJn* 1.21; cf. Eusebius, *H.E.* 6.23.1. Eusebius, at best, provides a kind of relative chronology of events in Origen's life. He groups things within the reigns of specific emperors, but within these individual reigns, his chronological references are vague. The conversion of Ambrose from Valentinianism is related in the section defined by the reign of Caracalla (AD 211–17) and is introduced with the expression "at this time also" (*H.E.* 6.18.1). The beginning of Origen's writing of Biblical commentaries is placed in the section defined by the reign of Alexander Severus (AD 222–35) and is introduced with the phrase, "and from that time also" (*H.E.* 6.23.1).

whose villa Philodemus' books were found.[31] Ambrose provided Origen with seven stenographers to take down his dictation, seven scribes for copying the books, and an unspecified number of young women who could do calligraphy.[32] Haines-Eitzen has suggested that this staff of copyists was made up of slaves of Ambrose who had been educated within his own household for scribal work.[33] Ambrose obviously had in mind something more than a single private copy of a commentary on John's Gospel. In the prologue to the fifth book of the commentary Origen refers to "agreements" which he and Ambrose have entered into with one another concerning the production of books (ComJn 5.2), and remarks that he has already produced "many books", which may suggest multiple copies of the books he had been writing (ComJn 5.1).

Ambrose had been a Valentinian before he met Origen (H.E. 6.18.1). He knew the attractive power of the Gnostic writings on educated people and wanted to offer them "the theology of Origen", which he himself had found to be an effective antidote to the lure of Gnosticism.[34] The Valentinians usually accepted the same Scriptures as the Church. Their writings were not intended to replace Christian Scripture, but to interpret it. They claimed to bring out the meaning of Scripture by the application of allegorical interpretation to its texts.[35] They appear to have justified the application of this hermeneutic to the Gospels on statements drawn from Jesus himself. The Valentinian Theodotus said, "The Savior taught the apostles first in a figurative and mystical manner, then, in parables and enigmas, and thirdly, when they were alone, clearly and straight forwardly." Matthew 13:10, John 16:25, Mark 4:10, and Luke 9:18 have been suggested as the bases of these statements.[36] This made the Valentinian teachings appear especially subversive to the orthodox because they worked with the same texts that the latter accepted and, by the application of the allegorical hermeneutic, could show that the deeper meaning of these texts taught Valentinian doctrines.

[31] Grafton and Williams (2006), 50–2. For the contribution of Atticus to the publication of Cicero's works see Reynolds and Wilson (1968), 22–3.

[32] Eusebius, H.E. 6.23.1–2. Ambrose must have provided these same services for Origen when he moved to Caesarea. Origen remarks in the beginning of ComJn 6 (6.9) that one of the reasons he had not previously resumed work on the Commentary on John was that the "stenographers" were not present to take down his dictation. But in the next paragraph he says that he is now ready to "dictate" the succeeding books. This suggests either that the Alexandrian stenographers have now arrived in Caesarea or that he has taken on a new group of stenographers there.

[33] Haines-Eitzen (2000), 59–60, 64, cf. 44–7 on female scribes.

[34] Vogt (1999), 187–8.

[35] The Gnostic Scriptures (1987), 272–4.

[36] The Excerpta Ex Theodoto of Clement of Alexandria (1934), 83, Clément d'Alexandrie Extraits de Théodote (1970), 191.

In the prologue to Book 5 of the *Commentary on John* Origen provides his rationale for undertaking the writing of Biblical commentaries. He notes that the heterodox were producing numerous commentaries on the texts of the Gospels and the apostles and worries that if people such as himself who are grounded in the faith and capable of expounding it "are silent and do not present the true...teachings in opposition to them, the heterodox will prevail over inquisitive souls". Consequently he is convinced that he "must intercede...on behalf of the teaching of the Church and *refute those who pursue what is falsely called knowledge*" (my italics).[37] This statement puts opposition to the numerous Gnostic writings interpreting the Christian Scriptures at the center of Origen's agenda for producing commentaries in Alexandria. The scriptorium Ambrose provided made this kind of undertaking possible.

Valentinus had been born in the Nile Delta and educated in Alexandria in the early second century. He taught in Alexandria in the second quarter of the second century and still had cells of followers in the city in Origen's day.[38] Ambrose himself had been one of those followers. Valentinus and his followers made considerable use of John's Gospel.[39] Irenaeus presents a Valentinian exegesis of the prologue of John's Gospel by the followers of Ptolemaeus (*AdvHaer* 1.8.5). The Gospel of John plays a significant role in the Valentinian *Excerpts of Theodotus* preserved among the works of Clement of Alexandria. The Nag Hammadi treatise referred to as *The Gospel of Truth*, and often attributed to Valentinus himself,[40] paraphrases and interprets numerous passages from the Christian Scriptures. Of all the Scriptures used in the work, however, "the Johannine literature...had the most profound theological influence upon Valentinus's thought".[41] A follower of Valentinus named Heracleon may have written the first commentary on John's Gospel.[42] Origen had a copy of it and argued with Heracleon's interpretations at several places throughout his own commentary. Ambrose may have provided Origen with this copy of Heracleon's work on John, as he much later seems to have provided him with a copy of Celsus' *The True Doctrine* for refutation (*Cels* 1.1, 3; 3.1).

The prologue to John's Gospel (John 1:1–18) was especially important to the Valentinians, providing a scriptural basis for some of the basic points

[37] *ComJn* 5.8; trans. *Origen: Commentary on the Gospel according to John Books 1–10* (1989), 166, translation modified.

[38] *The Gnostic Scriptures* (1987), 217. See Origen, *Princ* 2.9.5, which might suggest a continuing school of Valentinians in Alexandria in Origen's time.

[39] See Pagels (1973).

[40] Rudolph (1983/1977), 319, however, disagrees and thinks it not a work of Valentinus, but to have only "vague affinities with the Valentinian school".

[41] *The Gnostic Scriptures* (1987), 251.　　[42] See Heine (2004c), 120–1.

of their myth.[43] The Valentinian Ptolemaeus produced an exegesis of it, as did Theodotus and Heracleon, and there are allusions to it in *The Gospel of Truth*. The Valentinians were not the only ones using the Johannine prologue to undergird their doctrines in the late second and early third centuries. However, responding to their understanding of the opening verses of John was a priority for Origen. He had a copy of Heracleon's commentary on John before him, and his wealthy patron whom he had led out of Valentinianism a few years earlier was prodding him for a study of John that would rival that of the Valentinians in its appeal to bright, educated people. Origen responded by devoting the first five books of his commentary to the Johannine prologue. He poured the full weight of his philological, philosophical, and theological skills into these volumes.[44] He had reached only John 1:7 at the end of Book 2, and when he begins Book 6 in Caesarea he is finishing off his discussion of John 1:16–18.[45]

Valentinus' name appears only once in the extant books of *The Commentary on John*, and that appearance is to identify Heracleon as his disciple (*ComJn* 2.100). Origen refers, however, to heterodox views which parallel views that can be documented as Valentinian in other authors. He refers, for example, in discussing John 1:4, to those "who have invented the mythology concerning aeons in pairs, and who think Logos and Life have been produced by Intellect and Truth" (*ComJn* 2.155).[46] Irenaeus mentions these same two pairs in his report of Valentinus' myth except that where Origen has "Intellect" Irenaeus has "Father" so that Father and Truth produce Logos and Life (Irenaeus, *AdvHaer* 1.11.1).

Origen is not concerned, however, with the views of Valentinus himself, but with those of his followers such as Heracleon. Although he does not mention Heracleon in the first book of his commentary, I will show that he does argue against Valentinian views in the first book. Whether this means that Heracleon had not commented on what Origen discusses there or that Origen presents Heracleon's views at places in the first book without naming him is not known. It is the Valentinian exegesis of the prologue to John's Gospel done by Ptolemaeus that displays the views Origen takes up in the first book of his commentary.[47]

---

[43] See Pagels (1973), 23–50.

[44] On Origen's use of Greek philological tools in his exegesis see esp. Neuschäfer (1987); on his use of Stoic logic, see Heine (1993a).

[45] We have complete texts of only Books 1 and 2 of the first 5 books of the commentary. In the prologue to Book 6 Origen makes it clear that he is no longer working in Alexandria.

[46] Trans *Origen: Commentary on the Gospel according to John Books 1–10* (1989), 135, modified.

[47] Ptolemaeus' exegesis is found in Irenaeus, *AdvHaer* 1.8.5, where Irenaeus claims to quote the very words of Ptolemaeus.

After the general prologue to the commentary, which treats some of the standard topics discussed in the prologues of commentaries on secular literature,[48] the first book of the *Commentary on John* investigates the opening statement of the Gospel, "In the beginning (*archē*) was the Word (*Logos*)." Origen wants to establish the meaning of the two nouns in this sentence, *archē* and *Logos*, both of whose meanings may vary depending on the contexts in which they appear. The word *archē*, usually translated "beginning" in John 1:1, can also mean "principle" or "first principle". The Greek title of Origen's treatise, *On First Principles*, is *Peri Archōn*, a plural form of *archē*. The Greek noun *Logos*, usually translated "Word" in John 1:1, also is used for "reason" and "speech".

Origen follows the Stoic principle of verbal ambiguity in his investigation of the meaning of the two nouns.[49] He refers to six different uses of the noun *archē* (*ComJn* 1.91–118). He concludes that the proper meaning of the term in the Johannine prologue is established by its appearance in connection with wisdom in Proverbs 8:22 so that when John says the *Logos* was in *archē* he means that the *Logos* was in wisdom. This is a key concept for understanding Origen's Christology. It sets his understanding in the context of Alexandrian Jewish and Jewish-Christian wisdom speculation, as we noted in chapter two.[50] Wisdom is a more fundamental concept in Origen's Christology than *Logos*. The latter can even be subsumed under the concept of Wisdom, as one of the ways in which Wisdom functions (*Princ* 1.2.3). Of all the titles used to describe the Son in the Bible, Origen suggests those adhering most closely to his nature are wisdom, *Logos*, life, and truth, and when he provides such a list, wisdom always stands at its head.[51] *The Teaching of Silvanus*, a non-Gnostic Christian document from Nag Hammadi which stems from late second-or early third–century Egypt, possibly from Alexandria, represents the kind of Jewish-Christian wisdom tradition which appears to have instructed Origen's Christological thinking. Silvanus describes the *Logos* in the language of Wisdom of Solomon 7:25–6.

[H]e is a light from the power of God, and he is an emanation of the pure glory of the Almighty. He is the spotless mirror of the working of God, and he is the image of his goodness. For he is also the light of the Eternal Light. He is the eye which looks at the invisible Father, always serving and forming by the Father's will. He

---

[48] *ComJn* 1.1–89. For the topics see above in "The Biblical commentaries produced at Alexandria, p. 84".

[49] See Heine (1993a), 93–7.

[50] Origen applies two passages from Jewish wisdom literature to Christ: Prov. 8:22–5 (*Princ* 1.2.1–3; *ComJn* 1.111.115, 243–6, 289) and Wisd. 7.25–6 (*Princ* 1.2.4–13).

[51] *ComJn* 1.118, 123; see Heine (2004a), 93–5.

alone was begotten by the Father's good pleasure. For *he is an incomprehensible Word, and he is Wisdom and Life.*[52]

Origen devotes the entire chapter on Christ in *On First Principles* 1.2 to a discussion of Christ as the wisdom of God. He bases his understanding primarily on Proverbs 8:22–5 and Wisdom of Solomon 7:25–26. *On First Principles* 1.2.5–13 contains a clause-by-clause exposition of Wisdom of Solomon 7:25–6, applying it all to Christ.

One of the possible ways of understanding *archē*, which Origen mentions but rejects in his survey of the possible meanings of the word, identifies the term with God. "But someone", Origen says, "will say with good reason that the God of all things is clearly an *archē* too, proposing that the Father is *archē* of the son, and the creator is *archē* of the things created and, in general, God is *archē* of the things which exist. And", he adds, "by understanding the Son to be the *Logos*, he will justify his view by the statement, 'In *archē* was the *Logos*', because what is said to be in the Father is in *archē*."[53] The person holding the view is identified with the impersonal pronoun, "someone", which was Origen's standard way of referring to the views of a predecessor. Origen is respectful of the view. He notes that an argument can be made in its favor. He does not ridicule it, nor does he argue against it; it is simply mentioned and passed over.

The view expressed in Origen's brief summary is similar to that of the Valentinian Ptolemaeus, though the latter identifies *archē* as the Son, the first of God's productions.[54] Ptolemaeus understood the prologue of John's Gospel to be about the origin of the Ogdoad, the first eight deities of the Valentinian hierarchy of deities called the *Plērōma*. The term *archē* was very important in Ptolemaeus' understanding. John, he says, wanting to explain how the *plērōma* derives from the Father,

lays down a certain *archē* as a foundation, that which was first begotten by God, which he has also called Son and Only-begotten God, in whom the Father put forth all things as seed.... Since, therefore John is speaking of the first origin, it is well that he proceeds in his teaching from the *archē*, that is from the Son and the *Logos*. John speaks in these words, 'In *archē* was the *Logos*, and the *Logos* was with God, and the *Logos* was God. This one was in *archē* with God.' He first distinguished

[52] 113.1–16; my italics, *The Nag Hammadi Library* (1977), 359. See Schoedel (1975), esp. 169–70, 174, 194.

[53] *ComJn* 1.102; trans. *Origen: Commentary on the Gospel according to John Books 1–10* (1989), 54–5, modified.

[54] There is a very ambiguous statement near the end of the quoted excerpt which may identify God as the *archē*: "'And the *Logos* was with God' for he was indeed the *archē*."

the three: God, *archē*, and *Logos*, and then united them that he might show the emanation of each of them, of both the Son and the *Logos* and their unity with one another and, at the same time, with the Father. For the *archē* is in the Father and of the Father, but the *Logos* is in the *archē* and of the *archē*. Well then did he say, 'In the *archē* was the *Logos*', for he was in the Son. 'And the *Logos* was with God' for he was indeed the *archē*. 'And the *Logos* was God', of course, because what has been begotten of God is God. 'This one was in *archē* with God.' He showed the order (*taxis*) of the emanation (Irenaeus, *AdvHaer* 1.8.5).

Origen does not engage in direct polemics against a specific Gnostic interpretation in his exploration of the possible meanings of the term *archē* in John 1:1. This excerpt from Ptolemaeus' exposition of the verse, however, shows the importance of Origen's long survey of the multifaceted term as he begins his commentary for the former Valentinian Ambrose. It may also suggest part, at least, of the reason why Origen treats the term *Logos* as he does. Ptolemaeus identifies *Logos* with the Son and seems not to have discussed any of the other titles applied to the Son in the Bible. When Origen begins his investigation of the term *Logos* in John 1:1 he asks why "some" stop with this designation for the Son and either ignore all the others, or treat *Logos* differently from the others as though it somehow defines the meaning of Son in a way the other titles do not (*ComJn* 1.125, 151).

Origen focuses his polemic against the use of the term *Logos* to define the nature of the son especially on those who argue that Psalm 45:1 describes his origin: "My heart uttered a good word (*logos*)."[55] They seem to think, Origen says, that "the Son of God is an expression of the Father occurring in syllables". No one, he argues, can possibly believe that a spoken word is a son.[56] There were, nevertheless, Christian teachers in the second and third centuries who had proposed that this verse provided the way to understand the generation of the *Logos*, and they were not all among the heterodox. The second-century apologist Theophilus of Antioch, and the Latin-speaking Tertullian (early third century) had both understood Psalm 45:1 to provide a description of the origin of the Son.[57] Whether Origen knew of Theophilus' work is not known. There is little likelihood that he knew of Tertullian's Latin works. Origen more

---

[55] See Heine (1997a), 28–32.

[56] *ComJn* 1.151–2; trans. *Origen: Commentary on the Gospel according to John Books 1–10* (1989), 64.

[57] Theophilus, *Aut* 2.10, 22; Tertullian, *Prax* 7.1; *Hermog* 18.6; *Marc* 2.4.1. See Grant (1986), 130; (1990), 72–3.

likely knew Valentinian interpretations along this line. Irenaeus accused the Valentinians of claiming to explain the generation of the *Logos* by the analogy of the production of words by the human tongue (*AdvHaer* 2.8.5). He, and Origen, may have been thinking of Valentinian statements similar to those in *The Gospel of Truth* where Valentinus says that "the Word that is in the heart of those that speak it, has come forward. It is not just a sound, but it became a body" (*GT* 26.1–8). This is not a precise statement about the *Logos* Son, but it uses incarnational language in reference to speech. A more precise statement occurs when Valentinus asserts that "the name of the father is the son" and seems to describe the process of generation in his reference to it pleasing the father "that his uttered name should be his son".[58]

Origen must have had even more problems with similar views in the Jewish-Christian wisdom tradition which I suggested above was a major factor in his thinking about Christ. *The Teaching of Silvanus* seems to understand the generation of the *Logos* Son within the framework of Psalm 45:1 when it says, "It is Thou who hast given glory to Thy Word in order to save everyone, O Merciful God. (It is) *he who has come from Thy mouth and has risen from Thy heart.*"[59]

Origen places *Logos* as a Christological concept on the level with all the other terms applied to Christ in the Bible and argues that it must be treated in the same way as these are treated by examining what particular aspect of Christ each term illuminates. He concludes that *Logos* should be understood of Christ in its usage related to reason, and that as *Logos* Christ takes away our irrationality and makes us rational beings who glorify God in all our actions (*ComJn* 1.267).

The foundational concept for Origen's Christology is "Son". This may have been the result of the importance the Gospel of John played in Egyptian Christianity,[60] for, as T. E. Pollard points out, "The regulative christological concept of the Gospel [of John] is not *Logos*, but *the Christ, the Son of God.*"[61] All the other concepts, for Origen, including *Logos* and even Wisdom, are titles (*ComJn* 1.123). Son is what he is. It carries implications of his substance both as a being independent of the Father and yet also identical with him. His basic objection to the use of Psalm 45:1 to describe the generation of the Son is that an uttered word lacks substance (*ComJn* 1.151–2).

---

[58] *GT* 40.23–5; trans. *The Gnostic Scriptures* (1987), 257, 263. See Daniélou (1964), 157–63.

[59] *Silvanus* 112.30–4; my italics; trans. *The Nag Hammadi Library* (1977), 359.

[60] Roberts (1979), 61.   [61] Pollard (1970), 6–7.

MONARCHIANS, HERACLEON, AND THE ALEXANDRIAN THEOLOGICAL MILIEU IN ORIGEN'S COMMENTARY ON JOHN 1:1B–3

At the beginning of the second book of the *Commentary on John* Origen states what he considers he did in the first book. He says he discussed (1) "what the *archē* is in which the *Logos* was" and (2) "what *Logos* was in the *archē*." He then says that in the second book he will discuss "how 'the *Logos* was in the *archē*' " (*ComJn* 2.1).[62] This discussion arises out of the distinction between the meaning of the Greek verbs *einai* (to be) and *ginesthai* (to come to be or to become). The first verb appears in the past tense in each of the four clauses in John 1:1–2: "In *archē was* the *Logos* and the *Logos was* with God, and the *Logos was* God. This one *was* in *archē* with God." The other verb, *ginesthai*, appears in the opening verses of several prophetic books in the Old Testament when it is stated that the *Logos* of the Lord *came to be* with such and such a prophet (*ComJn* 2.2–3). Origen's argument runs along the lines that what "comes to be" has a beginning; what "is" has no beginning. It is the past form of the verb "is" that appears in John 1:1–2 (*ComJn* 2.8–9). "The *Logos was* with God." Therefore, the Logos was/is eternally with God, which means that there has always been a second divine being with the Father. This is the "how 'the *Logos* was in the *archē*' " that Origen proposes to discuss in Book 2.

Origen treats the four clauses of John 1:1–2 as four propositions of Stoic logic.[63] "The Word" is the subject of each of the propositions. Each proposition ascribes a different predicate to the subject: The Word was in the beginning, . . . was with God, . . . was God, . . . was in the beginning with God. Origen thinks the order of the four propositions important. We should recall that the Valentinian Ptolemaeus also considered the order of these same four statements of John to be important, showing the order of the emanation of *archē* and *Logos* from the Father.[64] Origen draws a different meaning than Ptolemaeus from the order, but the order is very important to his argument. The first proposition shows that the Word always existed and that he always existed in Wisdom; the second distinguishes the Word from God but also establishes that he was always with God. The third proposition shows, based on its order after the second, that

---

[62] Trans. *Origen: Commentary on the Gospel according to John Books 1–10* (1989), 95, modified.

[63] *ComJn* 2.11, 34–5. See Heine (1993), esp. 92–100. I shall, from this point, use Word instead of *Logos* and beginning instead of *archē* in citing the verses of John's prologue.

[64] See the quotation from Irenaeus, *AdvHaer* 1.8.5 above in the preceding section.

the reason the Word is God is because he is always with God. The fourth proposition, Origen argues, sums up the previous three in one embracing statement.[65] What Origen has established in this exegesis is that there has always been a second person with God the Father and that this second person can properly be designated "God" but is, nevertheless, to be distinguished from God the Father.

What was the existential setting of this exegesis? I have noted already the concurrence of Origen's emphasis on the order of the clauses for establishing their meaning with the exegesis of Ptolemaeus. This is an agreement in one point of method between the two, but Origen's conclusions are not directly related to the argument of Ptolemaeus. There was, however, a Christological controversy of major proportions that was rending the unity of the Church in the late second and early third centuries. This was the Monarchian controversy. The Monarchians were concerned with the problem of how to recognize the Son as God along with the Father without falling into the error of believing in two Gods. They emphasized the "monarchy" of God, that is, there can be only one God just as there can be only one king. They tried to solve the problem of how to regard Jesus in one of two ways. Either he was God the Father in the flesh, so that there was no distinction between the two, or they believed that Jesus was a normal human whom God adopted at his baptism and endowed with a special outpouring of his Spirit for the mission he was to carry out. Johannine texts were of major importance to both sides of the argument. T. E. Pollard was convinced that "[t]he central theological task of the third century ... was that of giving clearer definition to the Johannine paradox of the Son's unity with and distinction from the Father".[66]

Origen was very much aware of the Monarchian issue. A few years earlier, before he had fled to Caesarea in 215, he had made a brief trip to Rome when Zephyrinus was bishop there (c. AD 199–217) because, he says in a letter partially preserved by Eusebius, he wanted to see "the most ancient church of the Romans" (*H.E.* 6.14.10–11). This may suggest some kind of respect Origen had for the Church in the capital, even a feeling that it was the keeper of the most ancient faith. He met the *Logos* theologian Hippolytus while he was there,[67] and must have met Zephyrinus, and Callistus who succeeded Zephyrinus as bishop of Rome. The visit laid to rest, however, any hopes Origen had that he would find there the ancient faith practiced in its pristine apostolic purity. The Church at Rome, in

---

[65] See Heine (1993a), 98–9.   [66] Pollard (1970), 52.

[67] Jerome, *Lives of Illustrious Men*, 61.

the time of Zephyrinus, was a seething kettle of hostile debate about the relationship of the Son to the Father. Callistus, and it seems Zephyrinus as well, had accepted a form of Monarchian theology which blurred the distinction between Father and Son. Hippolytus, who disliked Callistus, violently rejected Monarchian theology and pitted the Logos theology of the second-century Greek apologists with its two divine beings against it.[68] The Gospel of John provided central texts for this debate.[69]

Origen brings up the Monarchian question in the context of his discussion of the four propositions in John 1:1–2. Many very religious people, he says, trying to avoid proclaiming two Gods, "either deny that the individual nature of the Son is other than that of the Father" (that is, the Son is the Father in the flesh), or "deny the divinity of the Son and make his...nature and essence...to be different from the Father" (that is, the Son was a human adopted by the Father).[70] Origen does not attack those holding these views. In fact, he treats them very gently (*ComJn* 2.17–18). Tertullian identified the Monarchian theology with the simple in the Church and noted that this group is always the largest group of believers (*Prax* 3.1). This majority group usually took the first approach noted above—they identified the Father with the Son. In the larger context of the Monarchian discussion here Origen refers to a group, which he identifies as *the multitude of believers*, who appear to be Monarchians (*ComJn* 2.27, 29). It would appear that the majority of the ordinary people who made up the Christian community in Alexandria, as well as in other places, understood the relationship between the Father and the Son in a Monarchian manner which identified the Son completely with the Father.[71] Origen does not mention the simple in this discussion, but he makes frequent reference to them in his writings in general, including the Alexandrian *On First Principles*. His references always show him at odds with them, or they with him. They are vocal theological opponents who have some distinct theological perspectives which Origen considers mistaken, but they are not considered among the heterodox, who are always listed separately. Indeed, he had found Monarachian theology defended by those holding

---

[68] See Heine (1998).   [69] See Tertullian, *Against Praxius* 20–5.

[70] *ComJn* 2.16, trans. *Origen: Commentary on the Gospel according to John Books 1–10* (1989), 98.

[71] See Hällström (1984), 7, who says, citing Origen's Caesarean *HomJos* 17.2, that "Origen explicitly states that the simple believers are in the majority, whereas the advanced Christian is an exception in the Church." Harnack (1905), 305–6 seems to have accepted Epiphanius' statement concerning the monarchianism of the *Gospel of the Egyptians*, for there is no monarchianism in any of the other extant fragments. If this should be correct it would certainly make monarchianism an Alexandrian issue, and perhaps a widespread one, but cf. the remarks in n. 51 in Chapter 2, p. 38.

the highest offices in the Church in Rome. This may have been the reason Origen did not designate those holding this view as heretics, and why he treads so gently in his polemic against them. Many who held the Monarchian view were very powerful people in the Church.[72] Beryllus, bishop of Bostra, whose Christological views Origen was called upon to correct in oral dialogue, appears to have held a Monarchian doctrine of Christ (Eusebius, *H.E.* 6.33.1–3). It is not impossible that Demetrius, Origen's bishop in Alexandria, held Monarchian views. It was, at least, after Origen had begun writing the *Commentary on John,* and before he had finished his exposition of the Johannine prologue, that the disagreements between himself and Demetrius became so intolerable that he left Alexandria.

The *Dialogue with Heraclides,* which I noted earlier might have come from Origen's Alexandrian period perhaps even preceding his visit to Rome, shows him in discussion with a bishop somewhere who held a belief in the unity of the Father and Son which, if not Monarchian, in Origen's opinion at least, leaned towards it. Heraclides begins the discussion by stating his faith in the words of John 1:1–3. Origen then probes Heraclides' understanding of John 1:1–3 to see if he recognizes that there are two distinct beings referred to as God in these verses.

Origen said: '... Explain what you mean, for perhaps I didn't follow you.
    The Father is God?'
Heraclides said: 'Of course.'
Origen said: 'The Son is distinct from the Father?'
Heraclides said: 'Of course, for how could He be son if He were also father?'
Origen said: 'And while being distinct from the Father, the Son is Himself
    also God?'
Heraclides said: 'He is Himself also God.'
Origen said: 'And the two Gods become a unity?'
Heraclides said: 'Yes.'
Origen said: 'We profess two Gods?'
Heraclides said: 'Yes, [but] the power is one.'[73]

Origen, then, satisfied with Heraclides' reply, sets out to explain from Scripture how such a paradoxical doctrine can be true. It is not his explanation, however, that is of interest here, but the way that he addresses those who question this way of understanding Father and Son. He does not call them "heterodox", but "brothers". "But since our brothers", he says, "stumble over the statement that there are two Gods, we must exercise special care

---

[72] Hagemann (1864), 303–4.
[73] *Dial.* 2.15–27, trans. *Origen: Treatise on Passover and Dialogue* (1992), 58–9.

concerning this teaching and show in what way they are two and in what way the two are one God" (*Dial* 2.7–9). Holding an improper understanding of the Johannine teaching on the relationship between the Father and Son may not yet have ranked in Origen's mind on the level of the Gnostic Heracleon's views of Christ and his work, but he certainly recognized it as a delicate and potentially dangerous issue.

Origen turns his attention to the Monarchians again in his exegesis of John 1:3, "All things were made through him." Does the "all things", he wonders, include the Holy Spirit (*ComJn* 2.73)? There are, he argues, three possible alternatives. He presents the first two as more or less the standard options. If one accepts the statement of John 1:3, that all things which have a beginning receive that beginning from the Word, and one believes that the Holy Spirit had a beginning, then one must conclude that the Spirit was made through the Word. The alternative to this is to assert that the Holy Spirit is unbegotten. This places the Spirit outside the realm covered in John 1:3. But, Origen says, a "third person teaches that the Holy Spirit has no distinctive essence different from the Father and the Son" (*ComJn* 2.74). This was the view of the Monarchian Callistus of Rome. Using the words of John 4:24, "God is spirit", he argued that the Spirit did not have an existence apart from the Father but was the essence of the Father. He further argued that the way Father and Son were one and yet distinct was that the Son was the visible human aspect in which the spirit of the Father dwelt.[74]

Origen dismisses the second and third options for explaining the origin of the Holy Spirit and embraces the first as his own, but it is not a simple answer that he gives. Father, Son, and Holy Spirit, he says, are "three hypostases". "[O]nly the Father", he asserts, "is unbegotten." This makes the Father the source of the other two hypostases. The Son is "the only begotten", being "by nature a son from the beginning".[75] The latter is a hint at the doctrine of the eternal generation of the Son that Origen develops a little later in *On First Principles* (1.2.2, 9; 1.4.4). The Holy Spirit ranks above all other things made through the Word but, nevertheless, needs the ministrations of the Son for both his existence and functions (*ComJn* 2.75–6). Only a little later, when he writes the *On First Principles*, Origen, as most Christians well into the fourth century, is confident about the teachings of Scripture on the functions of the Holy Spirit, but hesitant about explanations of the Spirit's origin. He believes that the apostles taught that

---

[74] See Heine (1998), 70; Hagemann (1864), 306.

[75] *ComJn* 2.73–76, trans. *Origen: Commentary on the Gospel according to John Books 1–10* (1989), 113–14.

the Holy Spirit "is united in honour and dignity with the Father and the Son", but whether he should be considered as "begotten or unbegotten, or as being himself also a Son of God or not" is unclear, he thinks.[76]

Before he leaves the subject of the origin of the Holy Spirit Origen raises another question which shows the multifaceted nature of the theological milieu with which he was in discussion in Alexandria. He has concluded that the Holy Spirit was among the things made through the Word referred to in John 1:3. Then he recalls a statement in the *Gospel according to the Hebrews* that refers to the Holy Spirit as the mother of the Savior.[77] How can the Holy Spirit be the Savior's mother if the Savior made the Holy Spirit? The few fragments remaining from the *Gospel according to the Hebrews*, found primarily in Origen, Clement of Alexandria, and Jerome, plus its title suggest that this was a Gospel used by a Greek-speaking Jewish-Christian group in Alexandria.[78] Origen has obviously read this Gospel and knows people who accept its teachings as authoritative. He does not treat them as belonging to the heterodox. He takes the statement in the *Gospel according to the Hebrews* seriously and provides a way to reconcile it with what he has concluded about the origin of the Holy Spirit in his discussion of John 1:3 (*ComJn* 2.87–8).

It is in his discussions of John 1:3 that Origen first introduces the Valentinian Heracleon, whose views he will oppose at numerous points throughout the commentary. Origen's approach to Heracleon's views differs radically from the way he approached the Monarchians and those accepting the *Gospel according to the Hebrews*. Heracleon is identified as a disciple of Valentinus and is said to have interpreted John 1:3 in a way that is "forced and without evidence". First, Heracleon limited the expression "all things" made through the Word to the material realm of the cosmos, excluding everything in the higher realm of the spirit. Second, he made the Word of John 1:3 to be the cause of creation, not its agent. Another, he claims, created under the impulse of the Word. Heracleon's exegetical moves and conclusions fit within the framework of Valentinian hermeneutics and theology as we know it.[79] Origen's attack on Heracleon's interpretation is dismissive and moves on the level of ridicule. Heracleon shamelessly, Origen claims,

---

[76] *Princ* 1. Pref. 4, trans. *Origen: On First Principles* (1973), 3.

[77] The Valentinian *Gospel of Philip* (55.24–6) also identifies the Holy Spirit as female, but not as the mother of Christ (*The Nag Hammadi Library* (1977), 134).

[78] See *New Testament Apocrypha* (1963/1959), 158–65.

[79] For Heracleon's exegetical approach see Pagels (1973), 25–31. On the theology behind the elevation of the *Logos* over the creator see *The Tripartite Tractate* 100.19–36; 114.7–8, and the remarks of Quispel and Zandee in *Tractatus Tripartitus* (1973), 384–5.

adds to and deletes from the text "to suit his own purpose". His statements, he continues, are "distorted", "contrary to obvious facts", "absurd", and based on a misunderstanding of the ordinary use of language. Heracleon does not use "plausible argument" but thinks he can speak with the authority of "the prophets or apostles". Consequently, his interpretation of John 1:3 does not deserve the time it would take to refute it.[80] The only place in his entire attack on Heracleon's exegesis of John 1:3 where Origen actually advances arguments to counter Heracleon's views concerns his misunderstanding of the grammatical language of agency where the Johannine text says "all things were made *through* him".

It is obvious that Heracleon's understanding of the *Logos* of John 1:1–3 and his relationship to both the higher deity and the creation fall completely outside of Origen's Christological frame of reference. He can sympathize with the Monarchian fear of expounding two Gods; he can even conceive of a way of thinking of the Holy Spirit as the mother of the Son; but he cannot make the *Logos* higher than the creator, nor limit his creative function to the material world.

Origen's Christology was strongly influenced by the Gospel of John read in the context of the Christological controversies of the late second and early third centuries, and in the context of the theological milieu of Alexandria which included Jewish-Christian wisdom speculation and Gnostic speculation on the Johannine prologue. Origen's Christological thinking, as we will see, spilled over into his other Alexandrian works as well.

---

[80] *ComJn* 2.100–3, trans. *Origen: Commentary on the Gospel according to John Books 1–10* (1989), 120–1).

5

The Alexandrian Commentaries on the Old Testament

Origen seems to have been working on several treatises in the same time frame. While there are no explicit cross-references in the *Commentary on John* to other works, if, as I argued earlier, this was his first major *Commentary*, then he must have worked on the *On First Principles* while writing the first five books of the *Commentary*, for he is only on Book 6 of the *Commentary on John* when he moves to Caesarea permanently in 232, and the *On First Principles* was written at Alexandria before he left. *On First Principles* 2.3.6 refers to his treatment, in another work, of Genesis 1:1, but in the first book he indicates that he had not yet reached Genesis 1:26 in this other work (*Princ* 1.2.6). This other work was the *Commentary on Genesis* and Genesis 1:26 would have been treated somewhere in Books 4–8 of the *Commentary*.[1] This suggests that Origen had started the *Commentary on Genesis* while working on the Johannine prologue. It is likely that he was led to the opening words of Genesis from the opening words of John, "In the beginning…", and treated the two phrases more or less identically.

THE *COMMENTARY ON GENESIS*

There is a fragment from the *Commentary on Genesis* that suggests that Origen speculated on the meaning of "beginning" in the Genesis commentary in much the same way that he had in the *Commentary on John*. It comes from the sixth-century commentary on the creation by the Alexandrian philosopher John Philoponus. He may have had access to Origen's *Commentary on Genesis*. He does not refer to Origen by name, but introduces a statement that parallels Origen's conclusion about the meaning of "beginning" in his *Commentary on John* with the words, "some say": "But some say that 'in the beginning' means 'in wisdom'. For God made all things in wisdom, that is,

---

[1] See Heine (2005), 132–6.

in the Son."[2] There is also a fragment that is identified with the first book of the *Commentary on Genesis* in Pamphilus' defense of Origen.[3] It relates to the opening discussion of Book 2 of the *Commentary on John*, where it is argued that the Son has always existed with the Father and did not come into existence at some time. The fragment from the Genesis commentary asserts that God has always been a father, which implies, of course, that the Son has always existed. This connection with the discussion of the Johan- nine prologue in the *Commentary on John*, along with that of the previous fragment, suggests that the two commentaries were being worked on at the same time.

Although the *Commentary on Genesis* is extant only in fragments[4] we can still say three things about the overall structure of the original work on the basis of these fragments.[5] First, just as in the *Commentary on John*, each book of the commentary began with a prologue which followed the general lines of the ancient Greek secular commentaries.[6] There are fragmentary refer- ences to the prologues to Books 1 and 9 of the commentary on Genesis.[7] Second, it appears to have followed the approach known as "problems and solutions".[8] Philo had composed a *Questions and Answers* commentary on Genesis in Alexandria and, as I will show later, there is evidence that some of the heterodox Christians in Alexandria had used a kind of "Questions and Answers" approach to Genesis. Third, it extended only through the story of Seth in Genesis 4.[9] This means that Origen's agenda was to write a commentary on the creation narrative and the events immediately con- nected with the story of Adam and Eve in Genesis.[10] There was precedence for the study of the creation narrative in isolation from the rest of Genesis. The Jews regarded the creation narrative as constituting a special unit of study in the Scriptures and to be one of four such units which were to be avoided by the young.[11] Origen also had the example of Philo of Alexandria,

---

[2] *Johannes Philoponos* (1997), 90, my translation. See Heine (2005), 124–5; cf. Origen, *HomGn* 1.1.

[3] PG 17.560C–561A, also quoted in Eusebius' *Contra Marcellum* 1.4.

[4] See Heine (2005), 122–42.

[5] The material which follows on the *Commentary on Genesis* is based on Heine (2003), 63–73, esp. 64–72.

[6] See Chapter 4, n.10.

[7] PG 17.544A–545A=PG 12.45A–46B; Eusebius, *H.E.* 6.24.2.

[8] See Perrone (1995), 151–64.

[9] *Cels* 6.49.

[10] There is evidence that Origen commented on later texts in Genesis but not in the form of what he called commentaries. These later texts appear to have been treated in the genre the ancients referred to as scholia (see Lake and New (1932), 218 and Junod (1995), 133–49, esp. 144–5).

[11] Origen, *ComCant* Prol. 1.6–7.

who had written a commentary on the creation narrative.[12] Eusebius tells us that the early Christian writers Rhodo, Apion, and Candidus also each wrote commentaries on the narrative of the six days of creation.[13]

Genesis 1–4 were the chapters used by the heterodox Christians in Alexandria. It is well known that the Gnostics had a great interest in the creation narrative and in Seth, whose birth is related in Genesis 4:25.[14] In the Sethian document from Nag Hammadi, known as the *Apocryphon of John*, the "detailed retelling of Genesis stops with the birth of Seth" in Genesis 4:25.[15] The Valentinian *Excerpts of Theodotus* 54.1–2 sets the same limit on the discussion of the story in the opening chapters of Genesis as Origen says he had set for his *Commentary on Genesis*.[16] Both quote Genesis 5:1 as the end marker for the story.

Heterodox Christianity was by no means the only Alexandrian influence on Origen's commentary. Philo's influence is often apparent,[17] as is that of Clement of Alexandria occasionally. Origen gives us a glimpse of the theological viewpoints with which he was in dialogue in Alexandria at the time he was writing the *Commentary on Genesis* in his *On First Principles* that was being written at the same time.[18] He refers to Jews who insisted on reading Scripture literally, heretics, who separated the Creator God of the Jews from the God revealed by the Savior and composed myths, the simple whose beliefs about God were often unworthy of deity, and finally, those who read the Bible spiritually.[19] There are three fragments of the commentary in which he attacks the literal interpretation of the text,[20] once specifying Melito, the late second-century bishop of Sardis, as holding the viewpoint being contradicted. Some of his interpretations seemed similar to Gnostic understandings to later critics, but Origen never adopted any of the essentials of the Gnostic myth in relation to the creation story, such as the distinction between the creator God and the true God or the superiority of the human created to the God who created him.

It would appear that the overall agenda of the commentary was set by heterodox concerns in Alexandria. I noted earlier that Origen undertook the composition of his *Commentary on John* at the request of his friend

---

[12] *De Opificio Mundi.*   [13] Eusebius, *H.E.* 5.13.8; 5.27.

[14] See Roberts (1979), 52; Pagels (1986), 257–85.

[15] *The Gnostic Scriptures* (1987), 23.   [16] *Cels* 6.49.

[17] See Van den Hoek (2000), 44–121.   [18] See *Origenes Werke: De Principiis* (1913), x.

[19] *Princ* 4.2.1–2, trans. *Origen: On First Principles* (1973), 269–72.

[20] On Gen 1:26 (the image of God); Gen 2:8–9 (the trees in Paradise); and Gen 3:21 (the garments of skin).

Ambrose whom he had converted from Valentinianism.[21] This is also true of the treatise *On Prayer* that was written in Caesarea when Origen was completing the *Commentary on Genesis*.[22] The first four chapters of Genesis would have been a set of Biblical texts that had been important to Ambrose as a Valentinian, and it would have been natural for him to have requested that Origen produce a commentary on these chapters.

Against Celsus 6.49 is a crucial text for understanding Origen's *Commentary on Genesis*. The passage provides a minor table of contents for the beginning of the commentary. It suggests that Origen's discussion of the opening verses of Genesis took the "problems and solutions" approach noted earlier. Origen says that the commentary addressed the following problems: (1) "What was the heaven and the earth that was made 'in the beginning'?" (2) "What was 'the invisible and unformed part of the earth'?" (3) "What was the abyss and the darkness upon it?" (4) "What was the water and the Spirit of God moving to and fro upon it?" (5) "What was the light which was created?" (6) "What was the firmament as distinct from the heaven made in the beginning?"[23]

The list follows the key concepts in the Genesis passage. The questions, however, are of a completely different kind than those a modern interpreter would address to the passage. The way the questions are stated puts a particular twist on them that is foreign to modern concerns related to the opening verses of Genesis. Origen asks what each of these things was. The questions reflect issues which had been and were being discussed in theological circles in Alexandria in relation to the opening verses of Genesis.

Interest in these issues among the heterodox and the framing of them as particular problems can be illustrated from *The Testimony of Truth*, which may have come from the region of Alexandria in the late second or early fourth century and reflects Valentinian influence.[24] The author poses the following questions of the creation account:

And what is the light? And what is the darkness? And who is the one who has created [the earth]? And who is God? [And who] are the angels? And what is the soul? And what is spirit? And where is the voice? And who is the one who speaks? And who is the one who hears?[25]

---

[21] *ComJn* 1.9; 2.1; *H.E.* 6.18.1.   [22] *PEuch* 2.1.

[23] Trans. *Origen: Contra Celsum* (1965), 366, modified. *Cels* 6.49–52, and 60 seem to contain numerous hints of how Origen treated Gn 1–4 in his *ComGn*.

[24] *The Nag Hammadi Library in English* (1977), 406.

[25] Ibid., 410 (NH IX,3 41.28–42.3). I am indebted to M. A. Williams for calling this passage to my attention.

A discussion of creation in the Sethian *Apocryphon of John*,[26] which has similarities to the Valentinian account of creation,[27] shows how one group of Gnostics thought about such questions. The issues relating to Genesis are integrated into the Gnostic creation myth.

> Then the mother began *to move to and fro*. She became aware of the deficiency when the brightness of her *light* diminished. And she became *dark* because her consort had not agreed with her. But I said, "Lord, what does it mean that she *moved to and fro*?" And he smiled and said, "Do not think it is, as Moses said, '*above the waters*'. No, but when she had seen the wickedness which had happened, and the theft which her son had committed, she repented. And forgetfulness overcame her in the *darkness* of ignorance and she began to be ashamed."[28]

The interpreter's comment relating the statement to Moses' words points clearly to Genesis 1:2.[29] The italicized words point to the author's use of Genesis 1:2–6. The text as a whole from *The Apocryphon of John* constitutes what Painchaud has called a "rereading of Genesis".[30]

If we turn to Irenaeus' report of the Valentinian Ptolemy's account of the creation of the material cosmos we pick up subtle allusions to some of the same verses and themes. Achamoth, who is the source of the material creation, was banished from the Pleroma to "places of shadow and empty space" where "she was without light", and "without form and shape".[31] These are allusions to the formlessness of the earth in Genesis 1:2, and the "places of shadow and empty space" are the "darkness" and the "abyss" in the same verse.[32] The "light" which has forsaken Achamoth is identified as "Christ" in Ptolemy's explanation of creation.[33] These were Valentinian solutions to some of the problems posed by Origen in his commentary.

Philo had given a different set of answers to many of these same questions. To Origen's first question about the identity of the heaven and the earth, said in Genesis 1:1 to have been made in the beginning, Philo had

---

[26] See Turner (1986), 55–86, esp. 56.

[27] Irenaeus says that Valentinus adapted earlier Gnostic teachings "'into the proper form of a school'" (*Haer* 1.11.1). See Williams (1996), 33–7.

[28] *NH II*, 1 13.14–14.34 (italics indicating Scriptural words and phrases mine), trans. *The Nag Hammadi Library in English* (1977), 106–7. Cf. Irenaeus, *Haer* 1.30.1.

[29] See Painchaud (1996), 129–47. Dawson (1992), 130, refers to this process as "interpretation as composition" in which the old story is retold as a new story but the new story "contains oblique, sometimes nearly subliminal, echoes of the old story".

[30] Painchaud (1996), 137. See also *NH II*, 5 97.30–101.9, where there are allusions to darkness, light, abyss, water, day, beginning, word, spirit moving to and fro over the waters, separation of the watery substance from the dry substance, and the creation of heaven and earth (cf. Painchaud (1996), 138–40).

[31] *Haer* 1.4.1.   [32] *Haer* 1.4.2.   [33] *Haer* 1.4.5; cf. 1.8.2.

·COLOGNE·&·COTTON·

JOIN OUR MAILING LIST TO ENTER OUR COMPETITION & WIN
£150.00 voucher to spend on Cologne & Cotton bed linen

NAME

ADDRESS

EMAIL ADDRESS   POSTCODE

SEND CATALOGUE ☐

Please fill in your details to join our valued customer list and we will keep you informed
via email of all our sales, promotions and special offers

L. T. PIVER 'VETIVER'

£57.50   100 ml

answered that this was not the material heaven and earth that we know, for the earth made in Genesis 1:1 is said to be "invisible" in the Septuagint, but rather, it is the intelligible world which, like a city plan in the mind of an architect, exists only in the divine *Logos* (*Op* 12, 15–20, 29).

Clement of Alexandria had also addressed some of Origen's problems and given answers similar to Philo's. The heaven and earth created on day one and the light referred to in Genesis 1:3 are the invisible heaven, the formless earth, and the intelligible light. These belong to the world of thought and are archetypal for the material image which will follow. The abyss is without bounds and the firmament is the "solid heaven" perceptible to the senses.[34]

Unfortunately, none of the fragments preserved from Origen's *Commentary on Genesis* relate directly to these questions. There is, however, an allusion in *On First Principles* which suggests how Origen treated the first and sixth questions in the list: "What was the heaven and the earth that was made in the beginning?" and "What was the firmament as distinct from the heaven made in the beginning?" In *On First Principles* Origen refers to his fuller discussion of the words, "In the beginning God created heaven and earth," in his treatment of them in the *Commentary on Genesis*. He indicates that he had distinguished as separate creations the "heaven" referred to in Genesis 1:1 and the "firmament" of Genesis 1:8, as also the "earth" of Genesis 1:1 and the "dry land" of Genesis 1:10.[35]

Origen addresses the question of the distinction between the heaven made on the first day of creation and the firmament, which is also identified as heaven, made on the second day later in his first homily on Genesis. There the firmament, or "material heaven", is identified as "our outer person" and the heaven made on the first day of creation is identified as "spiritual substance" which is further identified as "our mind which is ... spirit".[36] In the much later *Against Celsus* Origen again refers the same understanding of Genesis 1:1 back to his *Commentary on Genesis*. He distinguishes Genesis 5:1, "This is the generation of humanity, in the day in which God made heaven and earth", from Genesis 1:1 by referring Genesis 1:1 to the creation of spiritual realities and Genesis 5:1 to material things.[37] When we join this with the statements in the first homily on Genesis which associates the creation of "spiritual substance" or "mind" with the heaven referred to in Genesis 1:1, then we must connect a discussion of Origen's doctrine

---

[34] *EclProph* 2.2; *Strom* 5.14.93.5–94.1.   [35] *Princ* 2.3.6.

[36] *HomGn* 1.2; trans. *Origen: Homilies on Genesis and Exodus* (1981), 48–9. See also *HomPs* 2.4 and 5.4.

[37] *Cels* 6.50–1.

of the creation of spiritual substance with his exposition of Genesis 1:1 in the *Commentary on Genesis*. This means that the commentary on Genesis 1:1 set out in some fullness the doctrine that is briefly set forth in *On First Principles* 2.9.1, which discusses the "beginning of creation" in Genesis 1:1 and identifies this as the creation of "spiritual creatures or minds". This truth, Origen says, is what "Moses somewhat obscurely introduces when he says, 'In the beginning God made the heaven and the earth'. For it is certain that these words refer not to the 'firmament' nor to the 'dry land', but to that heaven and earth from which the names of the ones we see were afterwards borrowed."[38]

In the third book of the *Commentary on Genesis* Origen discussed issues connected with astrology related to the statement in Genesis 1:14 that the stars were made to indicate "signs, seasons, days, and years".[39] While the ancient Greeks and Egyptians both had doctrines of fate, the "calculable connection" between the position of the planets and human activity, which is "the fundamental presupposition of astrology", appears only "in the aftermath of Alexander's conquests, through a fusion of Greek with Egyptian and Babylonian ideas".[40] Astrology reached Egypt in the second century BC, where its discovery was attributed "to a mythical Egyptian king Nechepso and his priest Petosiris". Tarn considered Alexandria to have been a "secondary centre" from which astrology "spread over the Mediterranean world".[41] Philo had complained of the Babylonian astrology which recognized no God beyond the visible heavenly bodies and made these the source of all things good and bad for human beings (*Migr Abr* 179: cf. *Op* 45–7, 58–61). A papyrus found at Oxyrhynchus and dated to AD 14 or later provides a horoscope for someone named Tryphon.[42] Even the famous second-century AD Alexandrian scientist, Ptolemy, whose *Almagest* was considered the premier work on astronomy until it was overturned by the work of Copernicus in 1543, wrote a work on astrology called *Tetrabiblos*. He considered his work on astronomy to make it possible to determine the position of the stars and planets and his accompanying work on astrology to treat their effects on human life. Some of the literature connected with the Egyptian god Hermes applies astrology to "the diagnosis and cure of disease". Hermes

---

[38] *Princ* 2.9.1; trans. *Origen: On First Principles* (1973), 130, n.16.

[39] The excerpt is preserved in *Phil.* 23.1–11 and Eusebius, *Praeparatio Evangelica* 6.11.

[40] Fowden (1993/1986), 91.

[41] Tarn (1967), 346.

[42] *P. Oxy* 235; text in *Papyrological Primer* (1965), 143–4.

was so frequently associated with astrological literature that "other generally acknowledged authorities in this field—the gods Asclepius and Isis, for example the priest Petosiris and King Nechepso—were all thought of as pupils of Hermes, or at least as expositors of Hermetic doctrine".[43] In *On First Principles* Origen alludes to the prevalence of astrological lore in Alexandria when he refers to "the secret and hidden philosophy of the Egyptians and the astrology of the Chaldaeans and Indians, who profess a knowledge of high things".[44]

Origen thinks it is of highest importance that he discuss the phrase in Genesis 1:14 concerning the purpose of the heavenly bodies because not only is it so many non-Christians who believe that all events on earth are determined by the planets and stars but also numerous Christians. He passes over the non-Christians completely and focuses his discussion on people who have embraced the Christian faith and yet worry that all things human may be controlled by the groupings of the stars. He is concerned, in the first instance, with the negative repercussions astrology has on Christian doctrine. Such a belief, he thinks, obliterates free will and all rewards and punishments for human conduct, annuls the message of the Bible and the work of Christ, attributes an individual's faith in God or lack of it to movement of the stars, and frees humans of guilt, placing the blame on God instead.[45]

Origen appears to be thinking of Gnostics in his description of those who try to blend Christian faith and astrology. He says they recognize two Gods, one higher and one lower who creates. They shield the higher God from charges of responsibility for evil by ascribing this to the creator God. The Alexandrian Valentinian Theodotus reflects a view similar to some points, at least, of Origen's description. Theodotus refers to invisible "powers", some good and some evil, which govern the stars.[46] It is these powers which direct births. "[T]he stars themselves do nothing but display the activity of the dominant powers."[47] The Lord's mission in coming to earth was to rescue us from this battle of the powers and give us peace. The appearance of the strange new star at the birth of the Lord was to annul "the old astral decree".[48]

[43] Fowden (1993/1986), 1–2; cf. 22, 93–4. See also, Chapter 1, in "Culture", p. 9.

[44] *Princ* 3.3.2, trans. *Origen: On First Principles* (1973), 224.

[45] *Phil* 23.1. Scott (1991), 144–5 makes the same observation.

[46] See ibid, 95–7, on astrological speculation in Gnosticism.

[47] *Exc. Ex Theod* 69–70; trans. *The Excerpta Ex Theodoto* (1934), 85.

[48] *Ibid.* 73–74; trans. 85, 87.

Origen's exposition adopts the basic point of Theodotus' understanding of the role of the stars: they do not cause things but reveal them. He admits, because Genesis 1:14 says that "the stars are for signs", that the stars are indicative of events, but not that they cause them. Mortals, however, are not capable of reading these signs; only the heavenly "powers" can do so. He structures his ensuing discussion in a problems and solutions manner. He will discuss (1) how God can have foreknowledge and humans, at the same time, have free will, (2) in what way the stars do not cause human events but only indicate them, (3) that humans cannot read the signs of the stars accurately, but only the heavenly powers, and (4) why God made the signs for the powers to know (*Phil* 23.6). Of these four questions, the first is of most importance to Origen. The topic of God's foreknowledge and human free will comes up repeatedly in his writings. It was a major piece of his answer to what he considered to be the heterodox doctrine of "natures", that is, that all living beings have been given a particular predetermined nature which they cannot change. The answer he gives here is developed from an argument of cause and effect. Because God knows all effects that follow causes, when he sees the latter he knows what will follow. Origen's illustration of this is someone seeing a reckless person choosing to take a slippery path. Knowing that the person will slip and fall does not make the knower responsible for the person's fall. Nor does it cause the person to choose to take the slippery path. "It does not occur because it is known," he says, "but it is known because it will occur" (*Phil* 23.8). This argument is nuanced later in the *On First Principles,* when Origen wrestles with the perennial issue of the hardening of Pharaoh's heart and in the Caesarean homilies on Jeremiah when he deals with the prophet's assertion in Jeremiah 20:7 that God had deceived him so that he had taken a particularly painful course of action. A part, at least, of its Alexandrian context lay in the debate about the role of the stars in human life.

The exposition he gives of the "image of God" in Genesis 1:26 put Origen at odds with those he refers to in some contexts as the simple. One of his characterizations of the simple was that they were people who held views of God which were unworthy. A second, correlative characterization was that they insisted that the text of Scripture must be understood only in a literal sense (*Princ* 4.2.1–2). He asks whether the image of God referred to in Genesis 1:26 exists in the body or in the soul. The simple, he argues, though he does not use this designation here, locate it in the body, which means that God has a body like that of a human being. He singles out the second-century bishop of Sardis, Melito, as an example of a person who held this view. Melito, he says, wrote a treatise with the title, *On God being Corporeal.*[49] Those who locate the image in the human body, Origen argues, read the Bible literally. They use Scriptural references to God's eyes, ears, mouth, sense of smell, arms, hands, feet, and fingers to argue that these describe God's form. They also argue from the Old Testament theophanies to Abraham, Moses, and the saints that God must have a form if he can be seen, and that that form must be human. Origen then shows that such arguments are invalid. Zechariah 4:10, for example, refers to "the seven eyes of the Lord". But we have only two, Origen says, therefore, we are not made according to that image. Or, Psalm 90:4, in the Septuagint, refers to God's "wings". But we have no wings, he comments. "And how can the spherical heaven which is... always in motion be God's throne as they suppose?" Or, how can the earth, in Isaiah's words, be God's footstool (Is. 66:1)? Then, alluding to the scientific view of the earth-centered universe put forward by the Alexandrian astronomer, Ptolemy, Origen proposes the ridicules question, "Since the mid-heaven and the earth contain his body from his knees to his feet but the earth is in the middle of the whole cosmos and is contained by it, as they prove with geometrical proofs, are the feet of God with us or with those in the southern hemisphere?" And how could a physical God whose throne is the vastness of heaven and whose footstool is the whole earth walk in a garden or speak to Moses on the peak of Sinai? "And how", he asks in conclusion, "will someone who holds these opinions about God not be said to be a fool?"[50] Origen himself locates the image of Genesis 1:26 in the " rational soul", and argues that Paul, in 1 Corinthians 15:49, shows clearly that "moral actions characterize the image and not the form of the body".[51]

Origen's arguments must be directed in the first instance at Melito's treatise, and then at those who share Melito's views. Origen has boldly pitted himself against a view held by a venerable luminary in the Christian tradition. Polycrates had listed Melito among the notable bishops of Asia and praised him as a man who had lived in the Holy Spirit (Eusebius, *H.E.* 5.24.5). The unknown author of the "Little Labyrinth" praised the soundness of Melito's Christology against the Monarchian views (Eusebius, *H.E.* 5.28.5). Origen's attack on Melito could not have pleased his bishop Demetrius who, in addition, may have shared Melito's understanding of the image and seen himself within the parameters of Origen's characterizations of the simple.

Origen's exposition of Genesis 3:21 also relates to his understanding of the story of the creation of humanity in Genesis. There is a short catena

[49] *Catenae Graecae in Genesim et in Exodum II* (1986), 73, frag. 73. Eusebius, *H.E.* 4.26.2 and Jerome, *Lives of Illustrius Men* 24, both list this as one of Melito's works also.

[50] *Catenae Graecae in Genesim et in Exodum II* (1986), 73–4, frag. 73.

[51] Ibid, 74, frag. 73.

fragment from the commentary on this verse.[52] This section of the *Commentary on Genesis* would have been composed at Caesarea, but it is a continuation of the agenda that Origen set for the commentary in Alexandria and continues to reflect the theological situation he experienced there. The first works of Origen's writing and publication program in Caesarea were the product of his earlier Alexandrian environment more than that of his new Caesarean environment. This was especially true as he worked on completing projects he had begun in Alexandria.

The fragment begins by posing the question, "What must one think about the 'garments of skin'?" Origen first ridicules the literal interpretation that God, like a tanner, provided leather clothing for Adam and Eve, as "silly" and "unworthy of God". This would have been the interpretation of the simple. He then turns to the Valentinian understanding that the phrase "garments of skin" refers to the physical body.[53] He thinks this view is "plausible" and seems to have held it himself, though he recognizes a problem posed by Adam's statement in Genesis 2:23, "This is now bone from my bones and flesh from my flesh." This statement is made before the garments of skin had been prepared in Genesis 3:21, so how could the latter verse refer to God's preparation of physical bodies for Adam and Eve who already have bones and flesh? Philo had interpreted the "garments of skin" as physical bodies (*Leg* 3.69; *QG* 1.53). Clement of Alexandria did not hold this view for he says it was the view of Julius Cassianus and, he adds, both Cassianus and others who believe as he does are wrong (*Str* 3.14.95.2).

Origen then notes a second interpretation held by others which understands the phrase "garments of skin" to refer to the mortality which Adam and Eve put on as a result of their sin. Those holding this view, however, Origen says, cannot explain why it is God who is the cause of mortality, and not sin, nor can they explain how material flesh and bones were incorruptible prior to the sin which produced mortality. In his sixth homily on Leviticus, however, Origen embraces this interpretation of the "garments of skin".[54] It is possible that he proposed both interpretations in his commentary without rejecting either of them, a practice that he often followed, and that he made use of each interpretation.

---

[52] *Catenae Graecae in Genesim et in Exodum II* (1986), 124–5 (fr. 121). On the question of the genuineness of this text see Vogt (1987), 86–7. On the interpretation of the text see Simonetti (1962), 373–8; Pisi (1987), 322–335; Crouzel (1989), 90–4, 218.

[53] See Irenaeus, *Haer* 1.5.5; *Exc. Ex Theod* 55.1; Tertullian, *Adv Val* 24.

[54] PG 12.469B. See Van den Hoek (2000), 90, n. 15.

The fragment ends with an argument against there being physical bodies in Paradise. If Paradise is a divine region, and not an earthly garden with literal trees, as the simple believed, how could physical bodies have functioned in such an environment? Origen believed that souls are always clothed in bodies appropriate to their environment, a point which, as we will see later, played as important a role in his understanding of the resurrection as it did in his understanding of the creation of humanity.[55] This view of the soul and its body is introduced here to argue against using Genesis 2:23 to prove that the garments of skin could not be physical bodies because they appear too late in the story. There could have been no physical bodies in Paradise. Then Origen adds that "one must not cling to the letter" because the letter of Scripture "tells a falsehood". What he means is that one must not take the physical terminology used in the story of the creation of Adam and Eve literally. There were neither physical bones nor flesh in the Paradise of Genesis 2 and 3.

I began this discussion of the *Commentary on Genesis* by looking at a set of questions posed by Origen regarding the opening verses of Genesis in relation to a similar set that Gnostic groups had posed, and I have called attention to other questions Origen asked of later passages. Origen's answers to these questions sometimes oppose Valentinian viewpoints and sometimes flirt with them. His approach to the opening stories of Genesis, no less than that of the Valentinians, constitutes a rereading of Genesis which proved troubling to both his contemporaries in the faith and later defenders of it.[56] This rereading shows the influence of the Platonizing interpretation seen in Philo and Clement of Alexandria, and, sometimes, even in the followers of Valentinus. It is easy to imagine an ever-widening rift developing between Origen and his bishop Demetrius as Origen moved forward in his publishing program with Ambrose.

THE *COMMENTARY ON THE FIRST TWENTY-FIVE PSALMS* AND THE TREATISE *ON THE RESURRECTION*

I include the treatise *On the Resurrection* with the *Commentary on the Psalms* because of the close relationship between this treatise and the fragment from the commentary on Psalm 1:5. There are only a few fragments of

---

[55] Epiphanius, *Pan* 64.14.7–8; *Cels* 7.32–3.   [56] See n. 30 above.

these two works. For the *Commentary on the Psalms* there is a small set of fragments from a commentary on the first Psalm which are, with a relative amount of certainty, attributed to the Alexandrian commentary.[57] Four of these seem to be from the prologue (*Phil* 2.1, 2.2, Epiphanius 64.7, *Phil* 2.3), two, because the excerptors connect them with the word "blessed", may come from the discussion of Psalm 1:1 (*Phil* 2.4, 2.5), another two, which the excerptors identify with the commentary on the first Psalm, give no hint of where they may have been located in the commentary (*Phil* 3, Eusebius, *H.E.* 6.25.1–2), and finally there is a fragment from the discussion of Psalm 1:5 (Epiphanius 64.9–10.4).[58]

The *Commentary on the Psalms* was undertaken at Ambrose's request. He is addressed in the prologue and Origen's work is said to be the result of his friendly cajoling. In this important text Origen says,

I have said these things in the prologue, holy Ambrose, because I am being compelled by your great desire to learn and shamed by your kindness and humility to undertake a tremendous task which I admit is beyond me and my ability, and because I hesitated for a long time, knowing the danger not only of speaking about holy subjects, but much more of writing about them and leaving the writings to those who come after us. You have brought me to this by enchanting me in all sorts of ways as a friend, and by the incitement of godliness. You shall be my witness to God throughout your lifetime that I have made a careful examination of the things dictated, and a witness to the reason this undertaking has come about. Sometimes I am successful [in my arguments] but at others I am too forceful or appear too daring. But I have tracked down the meaning of what is written without despising the well-put maxim, 'When you speak about God you are judged by God', and the other, 'There is no small danger in speaking even the truth about God.' (Epiphanius, 64.7.1–3).

This text is used by some to argue that the *Commentary on the Psalms* was Origen's first published work because it refers to his reticence to write on "holy subjects".[59] It seems strange to me, however, that Ambrose, a recently converted Valentinian, would make a study of the Psalms his first choice of Biblical books on which he desired a commentary from Origen. We know of no particular use the Valentinians made of the psalms. The Gospel of John and Genesis, both favorite books of the Valentinians,

---

[57] See Nautin (1977), 262–75.

[58] Nautin (1977), 274, argues that because Pamphilus does not cite the comments of Origen on any psalm after the twenty-fifth psalm that he had used only the Alexandrian commentary on the Psalms in his defense of Origen. If this is the case, that adds five additional brief fragments that are extant from this commentary (Nautin's fragments F[3]–J).

[59] Ibid. 263; Trigg (1983), 88.

would have been much more likely choices. The only pointers to the date of the *Commentary on the Psalms* and the two books *On the Resurrection* are in *On First Principles*, where Origen says that he has already written the commentary on Psalm 2:5 (*Princ* 2.4.4) and that he has written "books" on the resurrection (*Princ* 2.10.1). We have previously noted his references to working on the *Commentary on Genesis* in *On First Principles* (1.2.6; 2.3.6). This suggests that work on the prologue to John's Gospel, the opening chapters of Genesis, the early Psalms, the treatise on the resurrection, and the *On First Principles*, was being carried out in the same time frame.

In the fragments from the prologue that precede his statement of hesitation Origen has addressed the issue of the obscurity of all Scripture. The reason for the obscurity of a writing was, as noted earlier, one of the topics commonly addressed in the prologues to commentaries. In this prologue Origen has cited two of his favorite passages on this issue, Revelation 3:7 joined with 5:1–5, and Isaiah 29:11–12, about the sealed book and the key of David, and asserted that these passages apply not just to the Revelation of John and the prophecy of Isaiah but to the entire Bible, which is filled with "enigmas, parables, obscure sayings, and various other forms of obscurity which are difficult for human nature to grasp" (*Phil* 2.2). Then he states his hesitation about undertaking the project in the fragment from Epiphanius. This is followed, in my opinion, by the story which he had learned from the teacher he calls "the Hebrew". "This teacher had compared Scripture to a house whose rooms are locked. One must find the key that will unlock each door. It is a tremendous task, the Hebrew had said, to discover the keys because they are not before their appropriate doors but lie scattered about. Correspondingly, he had continued, the only way to open the mysteries of a passage of Scripture is to search through other Scriptures where the explanations lay scattered about (*Phil* 2.3). Origen's expression of hesitation is addressed, I think, to Ambrose's proposal that he now undertake a commentary on the Psalter. Origen recalls the publishing projects he is already engaged in, how many books he has already produced, how little progress he has made in attaining the goal set for each project, and perhaps also, the conflicts that these written works have already stirred up against him, as he anticipates setting out on a commentary on such a large book as the Psalter. His words are "a disclaimer", as Chadwick called them, in response to "Ambrose's flattering request that he should write an exposition of the Psalms". It is a task beyond his powers, Origen asserts. He then cites the two maxims from the second-century AD Alexandrian treatise, *The Sentences of Sextus*, about the dangers involved in speaking even the truth about God.[60] There is a high degree of likelihood that Origen had already begun to experience some of those dangers.

The fragment from Origen's commentary on Psalm 1:5 discusses the resurrection of the dead in connection with the phrase, "the ungodly will not arise in the judgment".[61] The issue of how to understand the resurrection was pressed on Origen from several sides in third-century Alexandria. Ambrose would have been concerned with the Valentinian understanding, while the simple held a radically different view focused on the resurrection of the flesh. The burial practices of non-Christian Egyptians in Alexandria suggest that it was a fundamental belief of theirs as well, though Origen, so far as we know, did not address the issue from their perspective.[62] The question of the resurrection has been identified as "the storm centre" of second-century Christian debate. Athenagoras, Tertullian, and Justin all produced treatises on it[63] as did the second-century Valentinian, who wrote the *Epistle to Rheginos*.[64] In his treatise, *On the Resurrection of the Dead*, written in the early third century, Tertullian claims this doctrine to be the identifying mark of Christians (*Res* 1.1).

The Valentinians spoke the language of resurrection used by the Church, but gave it new meaning. Tertullian says they understood death to mean ignorance of God and those in this state to be buried in error. The term resurrection was used to describe the process in which a person came to know the truth and was given new life by God. Consequently, those who were baptized were considered to have attained the resurrection (*Res* 19).[65] In the Valentinian *Gospel of Philip* the resurrection is discussed in such a sacramental context as Tertullian describes. "Those who say they will die first and then rise are in error. If they do not first receive the resurrection while they live, when they die they will receive nothing. So also when speaking about baptism they say, 'Baptism is a great thing', because if people receive it they will live."[66] Such reflections seem to have their starting point in Paul's words in Romans 6. Origen sometimes flirts with these Valentinian concepts which grow out of Pauline statements. In the tenth book of the *Commentary on John*, which would have been written after he had left Alexandria

---

[60] Chadwick (1959), 115.

[61] As did his commentary on several other of the psalms in this early commentary, if we accept the argument of Nautin (n. 57 above) that Pamphilus drew only on the Alexandrian commentary in his apology for Origen.

[62] On the latter see Chapter 1, in "Culture", p. 9, where the catacombs of Kom el-Shuqafa are discussed.

[63] Van Unnik (1964), 154–5.

[64] See Peel (1969), 12–17.

[65] See Van Unnik (1964), 162–3.

[66] *Gospel of Phillip* 73.1–7, trans. *The Nag Hammadi Library* (1977), 144.

for Caesarea, but not long after, he takes up Paul's assertion that in baptism we are "buried with Christ" and "as if he has attained some pledge of the resurrection", he says, "'we were raised with him' (Rom. 6:4–5), since he walks in a certain newness of life, inasmuch as he has not yet arisen so far as concerns that anticipated blessed and perfect resurrection". Consequently, Origen says, "there both has been a resurrection and will be a resurrection, if indeed we were buried with Christ and arose with him".[67] Origen's comment, in a non-Eucharistic context, that Jesus "is called 'the resurrection' because he removes all that is dead and implants the life which is properly called life, because those who have genuinely received him are risen from the dead" brings him near to the Valentinian way of talking about resurrection (*ComJn* 1.181).[68]

The author of the *Gospel of Philip* also connected resurrection and the eucharist in reflections on Jesus' words in John 6 in a polemic against those thinking the resurrection would take place in the flesh. He cites Paul's saying about flesh and blood not inheriting the kingdom of God (1 Cor 15:50) and asserts that it is the ingested flesh and blood of Jesus (John 6:53), identified as the *Logos* and the Holy Spirit, which will inherit it. He does speak of a resurrection of flesh, but it is "true flesh", not the flesh we know which is "only an image of the true".[69] Here we certainly have the language of the Church used with a different meaning.

The simple, on the other hand, read the Bible literally and understood it to teach that the present body of flesh will be raised from the dead. In the second-century *Acts of Paul*, which Van Unnik thinks to be "typical of the faith of the average Christian at the end of the second century", Paul is said to have taught that resurrection depends on keeping one's body sexually pure.[70] Besides the ascetic and moral emphasis of this statement, it also suggests that the body of flesh is what is raised. Origen knew the *Acts of Paul*, for he refers to it twice and without criticism both times.[71] In the *Epistle of the Apostles*, which Klijn takes to be a second-century document originating in Egypt, Jesus says, "[A]s the Father awakened *me* from the dead, in the same manner *you* also will arise in the flesh." And a few lines later he adds, "[W]ithout being begotten I was born . . . of man, and without having

[67] *ComJn* 10.231–2, 243, trans. *Origen: Commentary on the Gospel according to John Books 1–10* (1989), 306, 309.

[68] *ComJn* 1.181, trans. *Origen: Commentary on the Gospel according to John Books 1–10* (1989), 70, modified.

[69] *Gospel of Phillip* 56.26–57.8; 68.31–7, trans. *The Nag Hammadi Library* (1977), 141.

[70] *Acts of Paul* 12; Van Unnik (1964), 154.

[71] *Princ* 1.2.3; *ComJn* 20.91. See *New Testament Apocrypha* 2 (1963/1965), 324.

flesh I put on flesh and grew up, that (I might regenerate) you who were begotten in the flesh, and in regeneration you obtain the resurrection in your flesh, a garment that will not pass away."[72] Origen knew Christians in Alexandria who thought that the resurrected body would still be subject to fleshly passions (*Princ* 2.10.3). They anticipated eating, drinking, marrying, and having children after the resurrection (*Princ* 2.11.2).

It is these simple believers that Origen addresses in the fragment on Psalm 1:5. All that Epiphanius has preserved is Origen's attack on their views. The simple claim, Origen asserts, that our present bodies will be raised, unaware of how mutable the human body is in its present form. Will it be the totality of the fleshly materials that have made up our bodies throughout our lives, or the body we have when we die that is raised? Such questions distress and offend them, he says. Some of them respond that such matters must be left to God, while others say that it is the body that dies that rises. Epiphanius stops the citation there, but his remarks make it clear that Origen said considerably more. He refers to Origen's many inadequate arguments supporting a false opinion of the resurrection based on the things human nature experiences (Epiphanius, *Pan* 64.10.9–11.3).

The two major sources for Origen's treatise *On the Resurrection* are found in Epiphanius, who quotes a section from Methodius in which he summarizes Origen's arguments from this treatise (*Pan* 64.12.1–17.1), and in *On First Principles*.[73] When Origen comes to discuss the resurrection in the latter he notes that he has already written books on this subject and says that he will repeat some of his arguments from these former volumes.[74] We may assume, therefore, that much of what appears in *On First Principles* 2.10 is repetitive of the material in his two books *On the Resurrection*.

Origen argues that our physical bodies are in a constant state of flux. Each day food is taken in and eliminated. This material substratum of the body, he says, like a river, is ever changing, but the person remains the same. He refers to that which provides this persistent identity of a body with the philosophical term *eidos*, which is usually translated "form" (Epiphanius *Pan*; (*Princ* 2.10.164.14.4–6). He does not seem to have used the term in precisely the ways that Plato did, but Plato's usages do seem to have influenced what he means. On the one hand, Plato can use *eidos* as a synonym for *idea*,

---

[72] *Epistula Apostolorum* 21; cf. 24, trans. Hennecke and Schneemelcher 1 *New Testament Apocrypha* (1963/1965), 205.

[73] See Dechow (1988), 341, and the other fragments collected in *Origenis Opera Omnia* (1844), 55–64.

[74] *Princ* 2.10.1. Origen refers again to this early work on the resurrection when he discusses the subject in his late Caesarean writing, *Against Celsus* (5.20).

which is also rendered "form" or "idea". Plato defines *idea* as that which something "really is". This can be thought but not seen (*Rep* 507B). On the other hand, Plato can also use *eidos* as nearly a synonym for *sōma*, "body", in the phrase "the human form", which is used to describe the residence of the soul in this life.[75] Form, as Origen uses it in his discussion of the identity between the present body and the resurrected body, has nothing to do with the outward appearance of a person. It imprints the body and is constant from infancy through old age even though the visible body may alter radically. It is this form that is resurrected, changed greatly for the better but, nevertheless, the same (Epiphanius *Pan* 64.14.2–6).

Souls must always be clothed with bodies, Origen thinks, but these bodies, as we noted above in the discussion of bodies in paradise in Genesis 3:21, must be suitable for their environment (Epiphanius *Pan* 64.14.7; *Princ* 2.10.1). He draws much of his argumentation from Paul's discussion of the resurrection in I Corinthians 15:35–50. On Paul's analogy of the identity within the change that takes place when a grain of wheat is sown and produces a new plant, Origen argues that the resurrected body will not be flesh, but will continue to be characterized by whatever characterized the body of flesh (Epiphanius *Pan* 64.14.9–15.4). Like the grain that was sown and grew into a new plant, the resurrected body differs greatly from the body of flesh in size, shape, and intricacy (Epiphanius *Pan* 64.16.7). In a passage which Nautin argued comes from Origen's Alexandrian *Stromata*,[76] Origen explains Paul's analogy of the seed with the Stoic phrase *spermatikos logos*, that is, the principle capable of producing life. He may have had in mind Genesis 1:11–12, which he was reflecting on in this same time frame as he wrote his *Commentary on Genesis*. The Genesis text does not use the Stoic phrase, but speaks of the vegetation God caused to spring forth on the earth as producing fruit containing seed for future propagation. Origen compares the seed of a grape with what it produces.

It is a mere granule, so small that you can scarcely hold it between your two fingers. Where are the roots? Where the tortuous interlacing of roots, of trunk and offshoots? Where the shade of the leaves, and the lovely clusters teeming with coming wine? What you have in your fingers is parched and scarcely discernible; nevertheless, in that dry granule, by the power of God and the secret law of propagation, the foaming new wine must have its origin. You will allow all this in the case of a tree; will you not admit such things to be possible in the case of a person?[77]

---

[75] See *Phaedo* 73a1, 76c12, 87a2, 92a5 (cf. 73d7), and the commentary on these passages in Burnet (1963).

[76] Nautin (1977), 296–300.

[77] Jerome, *To Pammachius against John of Jerusalem*, 26; trans. NPNF, ser 2.6, 437, modified.

Writing somewhat later in *On First Principles*, Origen argues that the substance of flesh survives death and is transformed, so that what had belonged to the earth and had returned to the earth via death is raised and "advances to the glory of a 'spiritual body'" in keeping with the merits of the particular soul.[78] In *On First Principles* 2.11.6–7 Origen outlines what he considers a possible progression to perfection which the saint may take upon departing this life. Always a teacher, he pictures this process on the model of a school. The goal is to attain full knowledge. He thinks that the saints first go to Paradise located somewhere on this earth when they die. Here they are instructed about what they saw on earth and, perhaps, given some inklings about what is to come. The pure in heart, and those who die well instructed, pass through this school more quickly than the others and ascend to the region of the air. This region, based on Ephesians 2:2, which suggests that the air between heaven and earth is populated with rational beings, and 1 Thessalonians 4:17, which speaks of meeting Christ in the air, is a school for the saints for a considerable time. There are a series of dwelling places there (John 14:2), called spheres by the Greeks and heavens by Scripture, through which saints pass, as they learn the lessons taught in each stage until they reach the kingdom of heaven and come to the contemplation of God, their final goal.

Origen's exposition of the resurrection would not have satisfied those Alexandrian Christians who anticipated eating, drinking, and marrying in the life after death. It was clearly not satisfying to later bishops like Epiphanius, who made it the central point of his attack on Origen. We may suspect that Origen's bishop Demetrius was disturbed by it as well. Origen's view has some affinities with the modified Valentinianism found in the *Letter to Rheginos*. There the author speaks of a spiritual resurrection (45.24–46.2) and asserts that the body which experiences aging is not raised (47.17–26). He says, nevertheless, that the person who is saved will receive "flesh" in the afterlife (47.4–13), but it is obviously not the flesh of this life.[79] Pauline texts, primarily from 1 Corinthians 15, stood at the center of Origen's efforts to explain the doctrine of the resurrection of the flesh in a manner both worthy of God and understandable to intelligent people (*Cels* 5.18). His later detractors, as Crouzel aptly put it, failed to understand his teaching, "caricatured it and then criticized their caricature".[80]

---

[78] *Princ* 3.6.5, trans. *Origen: On First Principles* (1973), 251.
[79] See Peel (1969), 42, 48–50, 163.   [80] Crouzel (1989), 249.

THE COMMENTARY ON LAMENTATIONS

Eusebius says that Origen produced a commentary on Lamentations in five books in Alexandria. There are no clear indicators for dating the commentary more precisely. We possess 119 fragments attributed to this commentary.[81] The fragments indicate that Origen interpreted the captivity of Jerusalem to represent the state of the fallen soul. The commentary may have been started when Origen was working on the *Commentary on Genesis* as he reflected on the story of Adam and Eve, and especially on the stories of paradise and the subsequent fall which resulted in their being cast out of paradise. The books of the Genesis commentary on the story of the fall were written after Origen had moved to Caesarea[82] but he was certainly already pondering the meaning of this story in Alexandria.[83]

The first six fragments of the commentary come from the prologue and show that Origen discussed at least three of the topics common to commentary prologues in this work.[84] Origen suggests that the subject of Lamentations is the contemplative soul "becoming subservient to the devil". This, he says, is the captivity being discussed and the one who takes captive. There is, however, an antidote for the situation.

But, if we flee to Christ who, according to the prophet Isaiah, proclaimed 'release to the captives' (Is. 61:1), we will be set free from the captivity, even if the captor has previously bound us. For Jesus came 'to lead those who have been bound out of their bonds and those who sit in darkness out of the prison house' (Is. 42:7; *FragLam* 2).

In his comments on Lamentations 1:1 Origen says explicitly, "Jerusalem . . . is the divine soul" (*FragLam* 8). The commentary which follows (*FragLam* 10, 21, 27) alludes to this definition several times. Babylon, on the other hand, represents the helpless and confused state in which the fallen soul now exists. In commenting on Lamentations 2:9, which speaks of the destruction of the gates of Jerusalem, he says,

Now the senses are the gates of the soul, and when it sins they are overwhelmed by passions and become earthly. And the powers which protect these gates of the soul are relaxed when the mind, which rules as king, and the sovereign powers of reason have been destroyed by the passions, when both the law and order of the soul have perished and the soul becomes Babylon, which means Full of Confusion, since it now has neither divine provision nor help (*FragLam* 52).

---

[81] *Origenes Werke* (1983), 235–79.   [82] See Heine (2005), 137–8.
[83] See *ComJn* 1.121; *Princ* 3.2.1; 4.3.1.   [84] See Heine (2001), 427.

Not only is Babylon given symbolic meaning, but also Babylon's king. Commenting on the tribute that Jerusalem must pay to "wicked despots", Origen says, "And perhaps each time the soul stumbles here, it pays some tribute to Nebuchadnezzar, whose name means 'Dwelling-in, and knowledge of, confinement', and not only to Nebuchadnezzar, but also to his satraps" (*FragLam* 9).

The text of Lamentations, however, is not applied exclusively to the soul. There are a few applications to the Church, which is once referred to as "the daughter of the old synagogue" (*FragLam* 118, cf. 104), and to Christ. Jeremiah is said to have been a type of Christ in the things he suffered from the Jews (*FragLam* 69). The most extensive application to Christ is found in Origen's interpretation of Lamentations 4:20, "The Lord Christ, the spirit of our face, was carried off in the destructions of the people, of whom we said, We shall live in his shadow among the nations."[85] Origen begins by dismissing the applications the Jews made of the passage to Josiah. The identification of "the Lord Christ" with "the spirit of our face" leads him to speak of the prophets. "It is clear", he says, "that Christ was the Spirit at work in the prophets. It is also he who says, when he has become human, 'I myself who speak am present' (Is. 52:6). He is the one who is Spirit, and Lord, and Christ", that is, in Lamentations 4:20. The prophets have forsaken the Jews who, in Paul's words, have a veil on their face when Moses is read so that they do not understand his true meaning, and now live among us "under the shadow of Christ, ... speaking of him and preaching". And, he adds, "The prophetic gift ... to which the termination of all prophecy looks is Christ, that is, is from Christ. For Christ is the end of the law and the prophets" (cf. Rom 10:4; *FragLam* 116).

Origen does not specify precisely what he means in these statements about the prophets now living among us. In *On First Principles*, however, he says that before the advent of Christ the Spirit was bestowed on very few people, and these were primarily prophets. It was these few recipients of the Spirit who understood the truth in the law and the prophets. But since the coming of Christ the Spirit has been poured out on multitudes of believers who are, thereby, capable of understanding the true meaning of the law and the prophets. He attributes the fact that nearly all Christians

---

[85] I have translated the text as Origen read it as shown from the phrases of the text scattered throughout his exposition in *FragLam* 116. This is the most frequently appearing text of Lamentations in Origen's other writings. It is most often the reference to living in Christ's shadow that is used (see *ComCant* 3.5.11–12, 14, 18; 4.2.25; *HomCant* 1.6; *Dial* 27; *ComJn* 2.50; *HomJosh* 8.4; *ComMt* 15.12; *HomNum* 27.12; *Princ* 2.6.7; 4.3.13; *ComRom* 6.3).

understand that circumcision, Sabbath rest, and animal sacrifice are not to be understood literally to the work of the Holy Spirit (*Princ* 2.7.2). It is probably this interpretive insight given by the Spirit to which Origen alludes when he says that the prophets have forsaken the Jews and now live among us.

Origen was, among other things, exploring some of the rich symbolic possibilities in Biblical proper names for his theology in this commentary. I have not been able to find any earlier use by him of either Babylon or Jerusalem in the symbolic manner in which he uses them here. Nor is there any such usage in the earlier works of Philo, which Origen had read.[86] When, however, we turn to the *On First Principles*, which was one of Origen's latest Alexandrian writings, there is a fully developed system of Biblical proper names as symbols of the spiritual life.

In *On First Principles* 4.3.5 Origen lays out what he considers to be the proper method to read the sacred writings. The method he sets forth relates some of the key events, places, and persons found in the literal story in the Old Testament set in tension with the readings that Paul gives of them. The Old Testament is about Israel, a people chosen by God and given a land called Judah with a major city called Jerusalem. Paul, however, indicates that there is a physical and a spiritual Israel, some born of flesh and others of promise, an inward and an outward Israelite. Paul also speaks of a heavenly Jerusalem. When the Biblical prophecies, therefore, speak of Israel or Jerusalem it is these spiritual entities that the careful reader of the Bible will understand. Then Origen moves beyond Paul's examples and applies his principle to other key peoples and places mentioned in the Bible.[87] If Israel and Jerusalem can refer to good spiritual realities, then other places and persons mentioned in the Bible can refer to evil realities, places such as Babylon, Egypt, Tyre, and Sidon, or their rulers, Nebuchadnezzar, Pharaoh, and the prince of Tyre (*Princ* 4.3.6–9).

Origen was beginning to find his way around in this symbolism in the *Commentary on Lamentations*. Already in the first book of the *Commentary on John* he had used the concept of captivity to show our need for the redemptive work of Christ (*ComJn* 1.250), but he does not speak of Babylon there.

---

[86] Philo never uses Babylon in a symbolic manner, and has only one symbolic usage of Jerusalem. The latter is connected with peace and is said to exist only in a soul whose goal is peace and contemplation (*De Somniis* 2.250).

[87] See the later Caesarean *HomEx* 5.1, where Origen states that Paul's interpretations of the Old Testament were intended to be examples for Christians and should be applied to other passages not mentioned by Paul.

He does speak of the captives of evil being in Babylon in the sixth book of the *Commentary on John,* which was probably the next thing that Origen wrote after the *On First Principles* (*ComJn* 6.246), and in the tenth book of the same commentary both Jerusalem and the captivity are used symbolically (*ComJn* 10.174, 291–6). He also, following Paul (Eph. 5:31–2), identified Adam and Eve as Christ and the Church in the ninth book of his *Commentary on Genesis,* which would have been the first book of that commentary written after his departure from Alexandria.[88] This symbolism of proper names in the Bible is in full flower in the homilies Origen later preached in Caesarea. There is a clear stability in the usage that Origen makes of this symbolism. The various names remain in their semantic fields. Babylon, for example, is never used of a good spiritual reality in Origen's system, neither are any of the other names identified with evil entities in the *On First Principles.*

[88] See Heine (2005), 137; Heine (2002), 239–41.

6

The Alexandrian Polemical
and Theological Literature

Origen produced a few works of a polemical-theological nature in Alexandria. Eusebius mentions only those books *On the Resurrection*,[1] the *Stromata,* and the *On First Principles*. The treatise *On Natures* is not mentioned in any ancient list of Origen's works. The only reference to the work is in the writings of Victor, the sixth-century bishop of Capua who cites a brief passage from the third book.[2] The *Dialogue with Candidus*, which Jerome mentions (*Ep* 33.4) and briefly summarizes (*ContraRuf* 2.19), may have been the record of a debate that took place in Athens during the transition period when Origen was leaving Alexandria.[3] While these works are not commentaries, they all appear to have revolved around the exegesis of passages of Scripture. Origen's theology always works from Scripture.

ON NATURES AND THE DIALOGUE WITH CANDIDUS

The *On Natures* appears to have been a treatise against Valentinian determinism. Irenaeus relates that the Valentinian Ptolemy taught that humanity consists of three predetermined natures: a material one that is doomed to perish, a spiritual one associated with the spiritual powers, and an animate or psychic one that is intermediate between the other two and with the help of the spiritual can be saved (*AdvHaer* 1.6.1). The Valentinian *Excerpts of Theodotus* reflects the same understanding of humanity when it says there are many who belong to the material, not many who are psychic, and few that are spiritual. The text then explains the significance of these three categories: "the spiritual is saved by nature, but the psychic has

---

[1] The fragments of this work were discussed in Chapter 5 in conjunction with the "*Commentary on the Psalms*", p. 115.

[2] The text, which is on Gn 4:7 and argues against the view that Cain was lost by nature, is quoted in Nautin (1977), 252.

[3] See Crouzel (1989), 21–2.

free-will, and has the capacity for both faith and incorruptibility, as well as for unbelief and corruption according to its own choice; but the material perishes by nature" (*Excerpt* 56.2–3).[4] It was the final point especially that Origen vigorously opposed. He addresses the doctrine of natures several times in *On First Principles* and in Book 2 of the *Commentary on John,* which suggests that there were still those about in Christian circles in Alexandria who accepted this doctrine.[5] In Books 13 and 20 of the latter commentary written in Caesarea, it is clear that Heracleon had discussed this doctrine in his comments on the Gospel of John. Heracleon had claimed that some people cannot hear the claims of Christ because they are of the essence of the devil. What he means, Origen says, is that these people have a different essence than those "they call psychics or pneumatics".[6] Heracleon's remarks about the essence of the devil also suggest, Origen says, that the devil is what he is because God made him with a particular essence (*ComJn* 20.198). This means, he adds, the devil is not responsible for the way he is; it is the fault of the creator. This, Origen, exclaims, is the utmost absurdity (*ComJn* 20.202).

This latter point of Heracleon about the devil was also one of the issues debated by Origen and the Valentinian Candidus. Candidus proposed that the devil is totally evil by nature and can only perish. Origen replied against this deterministic view that the devil's condition is the result of his own choice and, therefore, he is not unconditionally doomed by his created nature. Candidus then accused Origen of claiming that the diabolical nature can be saved.[7] This debate seems to have provided the basis for the later general charge that Origen believed in the salvation of the devil. Not even Jerome, however, who at the time he related his account of this debate was strongly opposed to much of Origen's theology, understood Origen's reply to Candidus to have been out of order. Origen believed that the devil began as a heavenly being who fell from this state by his own choice.[8] His concern, as always, was to defend the goodness of God. The view that God is responsible for the devil's evil fell into that category of views that Origen labeled unworthy of God.

---

[4]   *The Excerpta Ex Theodoto* (1934), 77, 79.

[5]   See *ComJn* 2.124, 134, 135; *Princ* 1.7.2; 1.8.2–3; 3.1.23; 3.1.8; 3.1.18.

[6]   *ComJn* 20.168–70, *Origen: Commentary on the Gospel according to John Books 13–32* (1993), 241.

[7]   Jerome, *Apology against Rufinus,* 2.19.

[8]   *ComJn* 1.78, 95–7. See *Origen: Commentary on the Gospel according to John Books 13–32* (1993), 59–65.

THE *STROMATA*

The ten books of *Stromata* that Eusebius claims Origen composed at Alexandria have all perished.[9] Jerome says he wrote these books in imitation of Clement's *Stromata* and that in them he confirmed all the Christian doctrines by comparing them with the teachings of Plato, Aristotle, Numenius, and Cornutus (*Ep* 70.4). If Nautin is correct concerning the fragment on the resurrection quoted by Jerome coming from this work, then resurrection was one of the doctrines treated in the *Stromata*.[10] In the *Commentary on John* Origen refers to discussing the ruling principle of the soul in the third book of the *Stromata* (*ComJn* 13.298). Some of the *Stromata* consisted of Biblical commentary. In chapter 13 of his *Commentary on Daniel*, Jerome quotes Origen's comments from Book 10 of his *Stromata* on the stories of Susanna and Bel and the Dragon.[11] In the prologue to the first book of his *Commentary on Galatians* Jerome refers to a supplemental exegetical treatment of Galatians in the *Stromata*. He says that Origen wrote "five volumes in the proper sense" on Galatians and that "the tenth book of his *Stromata* filled out his verse by verse treatment" of the book.[12] Later Jerome uses Origen's comments from Book 10 of the *Stromata* to explain Galatians 5:13.[13] Jerome also has a reference to the sixth book of Origen's *Stromata*, in which he claims that Origen tried to adapt the Christian doctrine of speaking the truth set forth in Ephesians 4:25 to the teachings of Plato. He says that Origen argued, following Socrates, that the raw truth must sometimes be mollified for the good of the hearer. God, he says, never lies, but sometimes speaks in ambiguous language for our good. It may occasionally be necessary for a person, however, in the service of some great good, to lie, as Judith, Esther, and Jacob did in the Bible. Such departures from the truth, however, must, as Socrates said, be treated as medicine and used with great caution.[14] This smattering of textual remnants may give us an accurate impression of the random nature of the *Stromata*.

---

[9] The fragments of what remains are collected in *Origenis Opera Omnia* (1844), 69–78.

[10] See the *"Commentary on the Psalms"* above, p. 115 and n. 57.

[11] See *Jerome's Commentary on Daniel* (1977/1958), 152–6; *Origenis Opera Omnia* (1844), 70–5.

[12] PL 26 (1845/1990), 333.

[13] Ibid, 434–6.

[14] Jerome, *Apology against Rufinus* 1.18. The passage Jerome quotes from Plato is *Republic* 389B. Origen's allusion to using a lie as medicine comes from this passage.

ON FIRST PRINCIPLES

The *On First Principles* is Origen's effort to pull together his understanding of the major doctrines of the Christian faith. There is no reference to Ambrose requesting the work in the prologue material of *On First Principles,* nor is he mentioned elsewhere in the work, which suggests that it was Origen himself who felt the need to write this treatise. It was, I believe, the final treatise he produced at Alexandria, not by his intention, but because of the furor that the work stirred up there. Other writings that were in progress, such as the commentaries on John, Genesis, and the Psalms, were stopped temporarily in order to bring this work to its completion. Origen was disturbed by the disagreements he had uncovered among so many who claimed to be followers of Christ. These were not trivial points of disagreement. They were disagreements on the major doctrines of God, Christ, the Holy Spirit, and the creation.

By listening carefully to Origen's words in *On First Principles,* some of these discordant voices can be heard.[15] Some argue from Scripture that God is a body (1.1.1) while others split the divine nature into parts (1.2.6). Some assert that the God of the Old Testament cannot be the Father of Christ (2.4.1–4), and that the first is just and the latter is good (2.5.1). A number of heretics interpret certain Old Testament texts about God literally and use their interpretation to argue that the creator God is imperfect, but simple Christians make similar errors and believe improper things of God (4.2.1). There are those who teach a doctrine of Christ contrary to that found in Scripture (3.3.4). The Jews don't believe in Jesus because they hold to the literal meaning of the prophecies (4.2.1), while the Ebionites think the purpose of Christ's coming was primarily for the Israelites (4.3.8). Some believe the generation of the Son involved a separation from the Father, others that a part of God's substance became the Son, while still others hold that he was not generated from any substance at all but once did not exist (4.4.1). There are some who argue that the statement in Philippians 2:6–7 refers to the soul of Christ assuming a body from Mary (4.4.5). A few have caused dissension in the Church by focusing on the Holy Spirit as Paraclete without relating the name to the activity to which it refers (2.7.3). A number of Christians think the sun, moon, stars, and the holy angels are predeter-

---

[15] Occasionally, the objectors sound imaginary, raising objections that Origen considers possible objections to what he has presented, but the majority of them appear to represent real issues that he has heard raised.

mined to be what they are, and some heretics apply this also to souls (1.7.2). Some think different kinds of spiritual natures originate from different creators (1.8.2). Some non-Christians think the Christian doctrine of the resurrection ridicules (2.10.1). Some Christians anticipate a resurrected body of flesh like the present one with luxury and pleasure beyond the grave (2.10.3; 2.11.2), others think the perfection of rational natures demands that they not be united with a body at all, while the uneducated believe that the flesh perishes completely after death (3.6.5). Many argue from Scripture that we do not have free will (3.1.15) or that there are diverse natures (3.1.23). Some attribute our sins to the work of hostile powers on our minds (3.2.1), others say that we have two souls, one inclined to evil and one to good, and yet others that our evil inclination comes from the body and not from the soul (3.4.1). There are some who take the words of Genesis 1:2 to mean that God created all things from formless matter (4.4.6).

Because of this cacophony, Origen decided to postpone inquiry into other subjects until he had set forth a "definite boundary line (*lineam*) and clear rule (*regulam*)" on these topics. The basic doctrines, he believed, had been handed down from the apostles in the preaching of the Church. Nothing should be believed which differs from this "ecclesiastical and apostolic tradition" (*ab ecclesiastica et apostolica traditione*) (*Princ* 1. Pref. 2). No earlier Christian had attempted anything like the *On First Principles*. It was a new genre for Christian literature, so far as we can tell.

All Christians, Origen says, look to the teachings of Christ as the only source for knowledge of how to live the blessed life. Christ's teachings are not to be found solely in his words while on earth, however; Christ spoke also in Moses and the prophets, and continued to speak in the apostles after his ascension. It is in the whole of Scripture, therefore, that Christ's directions for living the blessed life are to be searched out (*Princ* 1. Pref. 1). This opening paragraph makes hermeneutics the central question of Origen's work. How should one read this Scripture that in such diverse forms provides the instructions from Christ that every Christian wants and needs?

How to read Scripture is one of the major topics Origen discusses in *On First Principles*, but he doesn't take the subject up systematically until the last book in the treatise. Late in the preface he notes that one of the basic doctrines of the Church is that the Scriptures were inspired by God's Spirit and have a hidden, as well as an obvious, meaning. "What has been written are the forms and images of things secret and divine. The whole Church", he adds in somewhat of an overstatement, "believes that the law in its entirety is spiritual, but that what the law intends is not known to all, but only to those few to whom the grace of the Holy

Spirit is given in a word of wisdom and understanding" (*Princ* 1. Pref. 8). Origen considered himself to be among those few who could penetrate to the meaning hidden within the Scriptural text. It was a gift, however, which had to be repeatedly renewed. Jesus' words about asking, seeking, and knocking are a kind of leitmotif in Origen's exegetical work. Some things, he says, can only be understood when we go to the divine Word himself as suppliants and ask that he graciously enlighten the dark secrets of Scripture (*Princ* 2.9.4). Because almost all of the arguments in *On First Principles* are drawn from Scripture and depend on Origen's understanding of the way Scripture should be read, I begin this discussion with Book 4 of *On First Principles*.

The Apostolic Doctrine of Scripture and Its Interpretation

Origen begins by stating his belief in the divine nature of the Scriptures which consist, he says, of the Old Testament and the New (*Princ* 4.1.1). This is an important statement for it shows that before 230 there was a defined body of Scripture in Alexandria which contained a group of writings referred to as the New Testament and which was treated in the same way as the Old. In a later passage Origen refers to the Gospels, the revelations made to John, and to the apostolic epistles (*Princ* 4.2.3). Only the Acts of the Apostles is missing from this list of what were the later recognized categories of New Testament writings, and Acts is mentioned explicitly earlier (*Princ* 1.3.2).

The divine nature of Scripture is proven by appeal to the traditional early Christian proof from prophecy argument. The prophetic passages common to the tradition are cited and their fulfillment in Jesus argued (*Princ* 4.1.2–6).[16] This fulfillment of the prophetic texts proves both the divine nature of Jesus and the divine inspiration of the prophetic words. Neither the inspiration of the prophetic words nor the spiritual nature of the law could be known before the advent of Jesus (*Princ* 4.1.6).

The statement about the understanding of the inspiration of the prophetic words and the spiritual nature of the law depending on the coming of Jesus is a central premise of Origen's hermeneutic. The meaning of the Old Testament is obscure, he holds, locked to the understanding of the readers; Jesus holds the key of David which unlocks this obscurity. This hermeneutic is attributed to both Jesus and Paul in the New Testament" (Luke 24:44–7; 2 Cor. 3:14–16). We have encountered a statement of it already in the prologue

---

[16] See Heine (2007), 97–141. Origen makes use of the proof from prophecy texts again in *Cels* 1.49–56.

to the *Commentary on the Psalms*.[17] There Origen connects it with a story he had learned from an Alexandrian Jewish-Christian teacher he refers to as "the Hebrew". The Hebrew's story comparing Scripture to a house full of locked rooms was an application of the common Greek hermeneutical assumption of the obscurity of the writings of the highly regarded ancients to the Christian Scriptures.[18] Origen would have encountered the concept also in his work as a *grammatikos*, for they considered their work, as well as that of the exegete, to be the clarification of what was obscure in an ancient text.[19]

The mid-second-century physician Galen said that the obscurity of a text could result either from the material itself being unclear or from the improper preparation or incompetence of the interpreter.[20] Origen believes that Scripture is intentionally obscure, veiled, as Paul had said (2 Cor. 3:14–16). He applies this "veiled" concept specifically to the deeper doctrines he considers hidden in the creation account in Genesis (*Princ* 3.5.1) as well as to Scripture in general (*Princ* 4.2.6). The obscurity of Scripture does not lie in the interpreter's ignorance. It lies in the intention of the Holy Spirit in the composition of Scripture.

Alexandrian Christianity had appropriated this hermeneutic prior to Origen and the teacher he calls the Hebrew. The second-century Alexandrian *Epistle of Barnabas* had called the "land flowing with milk and honey" described in Exodus 31 a "parable" about Jesus, and applied various statements found in Numbers 19 to Jesus. In order to understand the true meaning of these obscure texts, it asserts, one must listen to what the Lord Jesus says (*Barn* 6.10; 8.7). *The Preaching of Peter*, another second-century Alexandrian Christian text, refers to the books of the prophets naming Jesus the Christ "sometimes in parables, at other times in enigmas, and at other times precisely, even using the exact words".[21] Clement of Alexandria also held this view, probably learned from Jewish-Christian teachers in Alexandria as well. "The Scriptures hide their meaning", he says, and adds, "Scripture's style is parabolic" (*Str* 6.126.1, 3). This hiding of ultimate meaning, Clement says, is common to Greeks and barbarians who speak on divine subjects. "They conceal the first principles of things and deliver the truth in enigmas, symbols, allegories, metaphors, and in similar manners" (*Str* 5.4.21.4).

---

[17] See, above in "The *Commentary on the first twenty-five Psalms* and the treatise *On the Resurrection*" in Chapter 5, p. 115. Obscurity is also discussed in the brief fragment from the early *Commentary on the Song of Songs* (see the introduction to Chapter 4, p. 83).

[18] See Mansfeld (1994), 149–61.

[19] See Harl (1982), 369, n. 67.

[20] Cited in Mansfeld (1994), 150.

[21] Cited in Clement, *Strom* 6.128.1. See Harl (1982), 342.

Origen's understanding of the obscurity of Scripture stands in this line of Jewish-Christian tradition in Alexandria. He says that the Spirit had two aims in Scripture. The first was to reveal in mysteries the basic doctrines of the faith for those capable of searching them out. The second was to conceal these mysteries in a narrative that would be helpful to the multitudes incapable of such rigorous study (*Princ* 4.2.7, 8).

The key to unlocking Scripture's mysteries, as already noted, is the advent of Christ (*Princ* 4.1.6) for, as he states in his earlier first book of the *Commentary on John*, the Law and the prophets were not gospel before the coming of Christ because "he who explained the mysteries in them had not yet come".[22] Christ holds the key of David who opens and no one shuts, and who shuts and no one opens (Rev 3:7). The sealed book that John sees in Revelation 3:7, written on the front and on the back, which only the one with the key of David can open, is the whole of Scripture. The description of the book points to the two aims of the Holy Spirit in the composition of Scripture. The writing on the front indicates that its interpretation is easy. This is the narrative of Scripture which the multitudes can understand. The writing on the back indicates that its meaning is "hidden and spiritual". This refers to the mysteries of Scripture for those capable of searching them out.[23] Origen believes that this hermeneutic by which Christ unlocks the obscurities of Scripture derives from Jesus himself and has been handed down by the apostles (*ComJn* 1.34; *Princ* 2.11.3).

A second premise of Origen's hermeneutic appears in his statement that if the "usefulness" of the law and the narrative passages of the Old Testament were obvious we would have no clue that there was a deeper meaning in the text (*Princ* 4.2.9). All Scripture must be useful. The usefulness of a text was another of the topics discussed by a teacher with a student when they began to study a text, and in commentary prologues.[24] Galen, for example, was concerned about the usefulness of Hippocrates' writings in his interpretations, and this often led him to modernize Hippocrates' doctrines in a way that made him "a sort of proto-Galen".[25] For Origen the principle of usefulness was a corollary of his view that every word of Scripture comes from the Holy Spirit. In a homily delivered later in Caesarea he says that nothing in a writing that comes from the Holy Spirit can be

---

[22] *ComJn* 1.33, trans *Origen: Commentary on the Gospel according to John Books 1–10* (1989), 40.

[23] *ComJn* 5.6, cf. also the later Caesarean writings, *ComJn* 13.314–15; *HomEx* 12.4; *HomEz* 14.2; *HomNum* 13.2; *ComMt* 11.11.

[24] See above at "The Biblical Commentaries Produced at Alexandria", in Chapter 4, p. 84 esp. at n. 10.   [25] Mansfeld (1994), 152.

useless (*HomNum* 27.1–2). Again, the concept can be found in Paul that the writings of the Old Testament are useful for the Christian. Paul says that the experiences of the Israelites were symbolic and that they were written down to instruct us (1 Cor. 10:11; cf. 2 Tim. 3:16). Origen cites this passage from Paul when he argues that there is no benefit for the reader to be derived from the literal meaning of John 2:6 which states that there were six water jars with a capacity of 20 or 30 gallons at the wedding in Cana (*Princ* 4.2.6). The principle demands the search for a spiritual meaning hidden in a text which, if read literally, has no usefulness for a Christian reader.

Plato had applied the concept of usefulness to the ancient myths of the Greeks. Because we do not know, he says, the truth about antiquity, in the myths we portray the false as true, so far as possible, and thus make it useful (*Rep* 382D). It is not clear that Paul would have gone as far as Plato in his understanding of the events recorded to have happened symbolically to the Israelites. Origen, however, definitely goes in the direction of Plato when he argues that the authors of the Gospels have sometimes written up spiritual truths as though they were writing about historical events. They altered the historical account, he claims, so that the text would be useful in conveying the spiritual message, thus preserving "the spiritual truth...in the material falsehood".[26]

A third premise of Origen's hermeneutic is that the way one discovers the hidden meaning of a passage of Scripture is by searching for "similar expressions...scattered about in the Scriptures" (*Princ* 4.3.5). Origen expresses the principle in the language of the Hebrew teacher who told him the story about the house full of locked rooms whose keys lay scattered about.[27] The explanations for the obscure mysteries of Scripture likewise lie scattered about in other passages of Scripture and the interpreter must find them (*Phil* 2.3). The approach of interpreting an author by comparing other texts of the same author was a common hermeneutical procedure. One of the literary scholars of the Alexandrian Museum in the third century BC (216–144 BC), Aristarchus of Samothrace, is credited with developing the method in his study of Homer. The principle was generally referred to as interpreting Homer from Homer. In the mid-second century AD Galen stated that his approach to exegesis was to explain each author from the work of that author.[28] Origen regularly used the method. He

---

[26] *ComJn* 10.18–20, trans *Origen: Commentary on the Gospel according to John Books 1–10* (1989), 259.

[27] See above, Chapter 5, under "The *Commentary on the first twenty-five Psalms* and the treatise *On the Resurrection*", p. 115.

[28] See Mansfeld (1994), 148.

could bring texts from any book of the Bible to bear on the interpretation of a particular Biblical text because he considered the Holy Spirit to be the author of all Scripture.

The basic assumption of Origen's hermeneutic is that all Scripture has a spiritual meaning, but it does not all have a literal meaning (*Princ* 4.3.5). There is a grand design in the Biblical narrative expressed in the stories of Israel's captivity and release, her wars in conquering and defending the promised land, and her exile and return. The kings and kingdoms against whom the Israelites fight are symbols of spiritual powers that humans must contend with in their spiritual lives. Origen had begun to work on this spiritual symbolism of the names of kings and kingdoms in the Bible in his earlier *Commentary on Lamentations,* as noted above.[29] Here, in the last book of the *On First Principles,* he spells out the details of this symbolic design of Scripture (*Princ* 4.3.5–13).

The hermeneutic set forth in Book 4 should be read as an answer to the literalistic hermeneutic Origen had encountered among those Christians who anticipated a post-resurrection life in which they would live in luxury with bodies like their present ones. They believed that the earthly city of Jerusalem would be rebuilt from the costly materials described in texts from Revelation, Isaiah, and Ezekiel, that they would reign as kings and princes over earthly cities with foreign servants, and that riches would be brought to them on camels of Midian and Ephah. This, Origen says, is the way people think who believe in Christ but read the Scriptures literally. They derive nothing worthy of the promises of God from this kind of reading (*Princ* 2.11.2).

Even using the hermeneutic he has described, Origen believes that there is a depth of mystery in Scripture that the human mind will never decipher. The person who has progressed the furthest in comprehending the meaning of Scripture will always see the road of understanding stretching out before him to an ever-receding horizon. One can only stand in awe and say with Paul, "O the depth of the wealth and wisdom and knowledge of God! How unsearchable are his judgments and untraceable his ways" (Rom 11:33; *Princ* 4.3.14).

The Apostolic Doctrines of God, Christ, and the Holy Spirit

There is no section on the Trinity in the *On First Principles.* There are only individual references scattered about in the work. It is mentioned first in connection with the baptismal formula (*Princ* 1.3.2). Some of the statements

---

[29] See "The *Commentary on Lamentations*" in Chapter 5, p. 12.

made about the Trinity refer to the separate functions of the three persons and suggest that Origen thought about it on the model of the earlier economic Trinity (*Princ* 1.3.5–8). The Trinity is said to be the source of all things, the source of all holiness, and the seat of essential goodness (*Princ* 1.4.2; 1.6.1). The unity of the Trinity is mentioned (*Princ* 1.3.8; 4.4.5) and, most frequently, its immaterial nature (*Princ* 2.2.2; 2.4.3; 4.3.15; 4.4.2, 5). The totality of these references does not add up to anything like a complete doctrine of the Trinity in the work. Neither is there a complete doctrine of any one of the three persons of the Trinity in the various discussions devoted to them. It is more a problem-solving approach than a systematic one that Origen takes to these doctrines.

In the first chapter, devoted to God, Origen argues a single point: God is immaterial (*Princ* 1.1). We have encountered this subject already in our consideration of his discussion of the image of God (Gn 1:26) in the *Commentary on Genesis*. He returns to it in his treatises *On Prayer* 23, where he refers back to his *Commentary on Genesis*, and *Against Celsus* 6.70–2.[30] The majority of Christians then as now considered God to have a body. Some thought of him analogous to the human body, considering "the cause of all things" to be like themselves, as Philo said (*Deus* 56). In a homily delivered later in Caesarea Origen says that the Jews conceived of God as a person with the members and appearance of a human but, he adds, so do some of our own people (*HomGn* 3.1). This would have been the view of the simple who, as noted previously, made up the majority of the Church. Others thought of God more philosophically, but still materially, as some sort of substance and defended their views with such Scriptures as Deuteronomy 4:24, "Our God is a consuming fire", or John 4:24, "God is spirit".[31] Origen objected to any concept associating God with substance, because this makes God subject to the kinds of things to which substance is subject such as change and corruption. He considered all such concepts unworthy of God.

The one thing that bothered Origen about saying that God is immaterial was that Scripture does not use this term. Does this mean that Scripture does not teach that God is immaterial? Origen solved this difficulty by noting that Scripture speaks of God as invisible which, he argues, is equivalent to immaterial (*Princ* 4.3.15; cf 1. Pref. 8–9). In a fragment discussing the statement "No one has ever seen God", in John 1:18, which may be from the fifth

---

[30] See further references in *Cels* in Heine (2004b), 107–8.
[31] *Princ* 1.1.1. Hällström (1984), 66 suggests that Tertullian (*Against Praxeas* 7.5–9) and his sympathizers represent this view.

book of the Alexandrian portion of the *Commentary on John*,[32] Origen goes
into detail on what Scripture means when it refers to God as invisible.

Perception is twofold, namely sensual and intellectual; the one apprehends material
objects and the other immaterial. For this reason we say that those things that are
assumed by the mind and perceived by it are invisible. We do not mean that they
are not seen but that they are not such by nature as to be seen. For nothing material
is invisible, even if it should be out of sight at some time and not seen. "Invisible"
does not mean "not to be seen", but not to be such by nature that this is possible.
Consequently, "not to be seen" and "invisible" are not convertible expressions. The
fact that the invisible is not seen follows from its being invisible. Many material
objects are not seen although they are visible; they may be hidden or they may not
exist at the time. Since this distinction is correct, we must understand what is said to
concern the invisible. Not even the highest powers see God. This is not because of
weakness on their part, but because of God's immateriality (*FragJn* 13).

Earlier Christian thinkers had discussed the Platonic view that what is truly
real is immaterial and perceptible only by the mind, and had applied this to
God.[33] Alexandrian Jewish philosophers had made this same move in their
thinking about God. Aristobulus (second century BC), whose works Origen
had read (*Cels* 4.51), quotes a fragment of a poem attributed to Orpheus in
which he says that no mortal eye has seen God for he can be seen only by
the intellect.[34] Philo also had referred to God as immaterial and believed
that his nature was not such that it could be perceived by sense perception
(*Mut* 7–9). Both Jewish and Christian thinkers had, therefore, brought the
concept of immateriality into the realm of Biblical revelation and used it of
the God of the Bible prior to Origen.

In a second section on God Origen defends the oneness of the God of
the Bible against a heresy that sounds like teachings of Marcion, although
Marcion is never mentioned (*Princ* 2.4–5). He lists and refutes five arguments the heretics bring against the unity of God: (1) John says that no
one has ever seen God, but Moses saw the God he proclaimed; (2) God is
passionless but the God of the Old Testament has human emotions; (3)
The God of the Old Testament is just, the God of the New Testament is
good; (4) Jesus said a good tree cannot produce evil fruit, nor an evil tree

---

[32] Book six of the commentary begins with a discussion of Heracleon's interpretation of
John 1:16–18 and Origen's rebuttal of this interpretation. There is no in-depth discussion of
the verses presenting Origen's interpretation that one would expect on such important verses.
It appears that this has already occurred in the preceding book and that Origen is concluding
the discussion of the passage by showing how Heracleon misapplied it.

[33] Justin, *Dial* 3.7–4.1; Hippolytus, *Haer* 1.19.1–3; Andresen (1981/1952), 325.

[34] See *Fragments from Hellenistic Jewish Authors* (1995), 166–7.

good fruit, but the fruit of the law is just, not good; (5) Jesus again said, "Only God the Father is good." This, the heretics claimed, must refer to the Father of Christ. The way Origen presents some of these arguments sounds as if he had been in direct conversation with people holding these views. He says, for example, that the heretics quote Jesus' saying about the good tree and then add,

What do you make of this, they say? What sort of a tree the law is, is shown by its fruits, that is, by the words of its precepts. For if the law is found to be good, undoubtedly we shall believe that he who gave it is a good God; if, however, it is just rather than good, we shall think of God as a just lawgiver.[35]

Tertullian relates that Apelles, the disciple of Marcion, had spent a few years in Alexandria after breaking with the teachings of Marcion (*Praescr* 30). Exactly what Apelles' break with the teachings of Marcion involved is not completely clear in the fragmentary references to him that are made. He does seem, however, to have continued to reject the Old Testament and to have considered the God of the Old Testament to have differed from the good God proclaimed by Jesus, both of which figure in the points Origen lists.[36] There must have still been those who held Apelles' views of God in Alexandria in Origen's time. It is not impossible, of course, that there were also followers of Marcion there. Whatever their precise heritage, those holding these views were enough of a factor that Origen thought he must address their arguments in his presentation of the apostolic doctrine of God.

The first chapter on Christ is concerned, like the first chapter on God, with the question of nature (*Princ* 1.2). For Christ, there is a divine nature, and a later assumed human nature. This chapter is about the first. It is not about Jesus of Nazareth, the incarnate Christ. That subject is discussed in a later chapter in Book 2. The Christ discussed in this section is the second person of the Trinity. He is immaterial, just as God is immaterial (*Princ* 4.4.2). In Paul's words, he is "the image of the invisible God" (Col 1:15), which must mean, Origen argues, that the image is invisible as well (*Princ* 1.2.6). Wisdom is the Biblical concept used to identify this nature. There are two primary things said about Wisdom in this respect. First, it has substantial existence, meaning its own existence apart from God, though it is not of a material nature. And second, Wisdom has always existed with God. God has always been Father of the Son, who is born of God but has no beginning. What he seems to mean by this oxymoron is that the Son is

---

[35] *Princ* 2.5.4, trans. *Origen: On First Principles* (1973), 105.

[36] See the fragments from Eusebius, *H.E.* 5.13, Pseudo-Tertullian 6, Filastrius 47, and Epiphanius, *Pan* 44.1 collected in Harnack (1960/1924), 404, 409–10).

dependent on the Father for his being. Much as Philo speaks of the *Logos* as containing the plan of creation like a blueprint in the mind of an architect (*Op* 16–20), Origen says that Wisdom always contained the pre-figuration of all that was to be (*Princ* 1.2.2, 4.4).

How, Origen wonders, is it possible to conceive of this mighty Wisdom of God entering a woman's womb, being born as a human, living among us, and finally dying a shameful death, even though we recognize that he was resurrected (*Princ* 2.6.2)? One must proceed cautiously with the subject of the incarnation, he thinks, so as not to think anything unworthy of the divine or illusory of the human. The ability to explain this, he is sure, exceeds human capacity, including that of the apostles. The key to the incarnation, Origen believes, lies in the soul of Jesus which has eternally clung to God. It mediates between God and human flesh. It was not contrary to the nature of a soul to receive a body, nor was it unnatural for a soul, which is a rational being, to receive God. Throughout Scripture human terms are used of the divine nature, and the human nature is described in terms appropriate to the divine. To illustrate this Origen says the Son of *God* died in virtue of that nature he possessed that was capable of death, while Scripture says that the Son of *Man* will come in the glory of God with the holy angels (*Princ* 1.6.3).

All humanity can attain knowledge of the existence of God, and even of the Son of God, apart from the Scriptures, but no one, Origen asserts, except those familiar with the Scriptures could have an inkling of the existence of the Holy Spirit. He raises the question of the origin of the Holy Spirit and concludes that the Holy Spirit was not created (*Princ* 1.3.3; cf. 4.4.8), contrary to his conclusion in the earlier *Commentary on John*.[37] It is the Holy Spirit, he thinks, who moves over the waters in Genesis 1:2. He also notes that Scripture indicates a great authority and majesty in the Holy Spirit, sometimes even verging on exceeding that of the Son (*Princ* 1.3.2). All our knowledge of God, Origen says, is made known to us by the Son through the Holy Spirit. The Spirit's knowledge of the Father, however, does not come through the Son. Like the Son, the Holy Spirit has always

---

[37] See the discussion above, Chapter 4, in "Monarchians, Heracleon, and the Alexandrian Theological Milieu in Origen's *Commentary on John* 1:1b–3", p. 97. This contradiction may arise from Rufinus' agenda to make Origen acceptable to fourth century orthodoxy. Justinian's *Epistle to Mennam*, cited here by Koetschau (*Origenes Werke: De Principiis* (1913), 52) has Origen saying that the Holy Spirit and the Son were "created beings" (*ktisma*). Justinian's statement, too, however, reflects an agenda, though opposite to that of Rufinus. Nowhere does Origen refer to the Son as created. The Son has no beginning (*ComJn* 1.204). This is the point, Origen thinks, of the use of a form of the verb *einai* in John 1:1 (*ComJn* 2.1–9).

existed with the Father in the Trinity. There is a ranking of order, however, descending from the Father, to the Son, to the Spirit and, while the work of the Father and the Son involves all creation, only the saints can possess the Holy Spirit (*Princ* 1.3.7).

Origen returns to the subject of the Holy Spirit in a supplemental discussion (*Princ* 2.7), just as he returned to additional discussions of the Father and the Son. Here he discusses the work of the Holy Spirit focused primarily on his role in the interpreting of Scripture. Prior to the advent of Christ only prophets received the Holy Spirit, but since his advent the promise of Joel 2:28 has been fulfilled and the Spirit has been poured out on the saints in general. Origen does not understand this outpouring, however, to have resulted in a multiplication of prophets with new revelation. It has resulted rather in a new spiritual interpretation of the law among the multitudes of Christians. He then mentions some who have fastened on the term "Paraclete", which is used of the Holy Spirit in John 14–16, and caused dissensions in the Church. Under the claims they make for the Paraclete they have forbidden marriage and ordained fasting in an outward show of strict religious observance. Origen does not identify the people involved, but the use of the term Paraclete and the things that he says they taught point to the Montanist movement which originated in Phrygia in the late second century and moved from there to Rome and to North Africa, where it found an advocate in Tertullian. It was a prophetic movement which claimed new revelations from the Paraclete demanding a very rigorous ascetic life-style. Origen himself lived a very ascetic life, but he has nothing good to say here of those who imposed their ascetic teachings on others claiming the authority of the Paraclete. When this term is applied to the Holy Spirit in Scripture it should be understood in its meaning as "comforter" because, he says, pointing to the work of the Holy Spirit in aiding the understanding of Scripture, "he provides comfort for the souls to whom he opens and reveals a consciousness of spiritual knowledge".[38]

As I noted at the beginning of this section, there is no complete doctrine of either the Trinity or of the three persons individually in the *On First Principles*. Origen responds to divergences from the rule of faith, as in the case of those separating the God of the Old Testament from the Father of Jesus, or inadequate understandings such as those believing God to have a body, rather than expounding it in its completeness.

---

[38] *Princ* 2.7.4, trans. *Origen: On First Principles* (1973), 119.

The Apostolic Doctrine of Creation

Adapting Philo's appropriation of Plato's theory of forms to the Genesis creation story (*Op* 4.16; 10.36), Origen asserted that Genesis 1:1–2 and 1:6–10 speak of two separate creations (*Princ* 2.3.6; 9.1).[39] The first was the creation of immaterial rational natures or minds which Moses "rather obscurely" refers to as the creation of "heaven and earth" (*Princ* 2.9.1). The second, which refers to the firmament called heaven and the dry land called earth, was the creation of the material heaven and earth. While Origen does not mention it, although Philo does (*Op* 12, 29), the earth created in Genesis 1:1 is said in the next verse in the Septuagint to have been invisible. This was the term, as we have seen above, that Origen understood to be the Biblical equivalent to immaterial.[40] It may have been the presence of this term that suggested the approach he took to Genesis 1:1; and he may have made such a connection in the lost *Commentary on Genesis* to which he alludes (*Princ* 2.3.6).

Because the rational natures had been brought into being from not being, they were necessarily subject to change (*Princ* 2.9.2). Only the uncreated Trinity possesses goodness essentially (*Princ* 1.5.3, 6.2, 8.3). The goodness all created beings possessed was not theirs by nature, but was a gift of the creator who also endowed them with free will so that they might make the goodness given them their own by their own choice. But they could, as well, with their free will, withdraw from the good and sink into evil, for "evil is the absence of good" (*Princ* 2.9.2). They chose the latter, some more, some less, but all turned away from the good.

Because the turning from the good was not uniform, it resulted in three categories of rational natures: holy powers, wicked powers, and those between the two. The names of all of the beings in the first two categories are derived from Scripture. The holy powers include the holy angels called ministering spirits in Hebrews 1:14, the thrones, dominions, principalities, and powers of Colossians 1:16, and others which cannot be named (Eph. 1:21). The wicked powers embrace the devil and his angels (Matt. 25:41), princes of this world (1 Cor. 2:6), and the principalities and powers listed by Paul in Ephesians 6:12. The middle category consists of humans. Here too Scripture notes distinctions between those who are

---

[39] See the discussion of this above, Chapter 5, in "The *Commentary on Genesis*".

[40] See the discussion of God above, in "The Apostolic Doctrine of God, Christ, and the Holy Spirit", and especially *FragJn* 13 quoted there.

the Lord's portion and those who are the portion of angels (Deut. 32:8–9; *Princ* 1.5.1–2). Origen takes pains to make clear that this vast array of differences among created beings is attributable solely to their own choices (*Princ* 1.5.3).

This elaborate explanation of the creation of rational beings was driven by Origen's need to answer the question of natures which was still being forced on the Christian community by followers of Marcion, Valentinus, and Basilides. They argued that the various beings, whether heavenly, earthly, or demonic, were what they were because they had been so created (*Princ* 2.9.5). They applied their argument to the beings in all three categories. They asked why God, if he has the will and the power to produce the good, made some beings of higher rank and others lower. They put the question to the human situation also, asking why some people are born into circumstances that are spiritually favorable, like descendants of Abraham, while others are born into cultures where atrocities are practiced as acceptable activities. The answer to the latter cannot be free will, they argued, because one does not choose where one is born. Either one is put into one's situation because he or she was made with a nature appropriate for that situation, or everything is the result of chance. The issue was not a negligible one. Origen had to wrestle with it even in the commentary he had promised Ambrose on the Gospel of John. Heracleon had used the doctrine of natures to explain why some people reacted negatively to Jesus in the Gospel (*ComJn* 20.168–70, 198). How was Origen to defend the goodness and the providence of God against this attack? His answer, as outlined above, was that because God is good, unchangeable, and the cause of all things, he made all rational beings equal and endowed them with free will. It was the exercise of the latter while the beings were in the immaterial state of the first creation which broke up the uniformity of the creation producing the great diversity in which it now exists (*Princ* 2.9.6). Origen's defense of the goodness and providence of God in creation against the Gnostic doctrine of divinely determined natures turned on the axis of his doctrine of free will.[41]

If my suggestion above is correct, that the *On First Principles* was written out of Origen's desire to clarify and unify the Christian understanding of the teachings of the apostles and to defend these apostolic doctrines against those who were eroding their authority, it is ironic that the publication of this document was the final blow that broke his

---

[41] This is why he devotes the biggest part of book three to free will, looking at texts in Scripture which both support it and which appear to place it in jeopardy.

relationship with the hierarchy of the Alexandrian Church and made him a borderline heretic for centuries. Fortunately he had friends in high places in Palestine who seem to have had a broader and deeper understanding of what he was doing and of what he was capable. His Alexandrian friend Ambrose, whose support made his scholarly theological work possible, also continued to stand by his side. While the end of his Alexandrian experience was a bitter one, his most productive years were yet to come.

7

Settling in Caesarea

Origen moved to Caesarea in AD 232 because of irreconcilable differences with bishop Demetrius of Alexandria.[1] He had friends and supporters in Palestine in Alexander, bishop of Jerusalem, and Theoctistus, bishop of Caesarea. He had visited Caesarea first in 215 when the emperor Caracalla was allowing his troops to massacre the citizens of Alexandria.[2] At that time both bishops had recognized his ability as an interpreter of the Bible and had allowed him to preach in their Churches even though he had not been ordained to the priesthood. This had not sat well with Demetrius in Alexandria who, at this point, appears to have directed his displeasure at the two bishops in Palestine rather than at Origen.[3] It would appear that Origen made another visit to Palestine before he moved there permanently, for Eusebius reports that the bishops of Caesarea and Jerusalem ordained him and, consequently, greatly angered Demetrius.[4]

CAESAREA MARITIMA

Caesarea was a younger and smaller city than Alexandria. It had been built by Herod the Great in the period from 22–10 BC approximately 30 kilometers south of modern Haifa, near the ancient Sidonian settlement known as Strato's Tower. The city was one of Herod's many building projects to honor Augustus Caesar, from whom he had received his right to rule.[5] Caesarea was a seaside city built of white stone (Josephus, *Ant* 15.331).

---

[1] See Bienert (1978), 100–4, who argues that it was Heraclas more than Demetrius who was Origen's primary antagonist.

[2] See Chapter 4.

[3] See Eusebius, *H.E.* 6.19.16–18.

[4] *H.E.* 6.8.4–5. Eusebius notes that his use of this story at this point in his narrative is out of synch chronologically when he says at the end of the account, "These things happened a little later." He inserts the story here, immediately after he relates his story of Origen's self-mutilation, because Demetrius had appealed to the latter to disqualify Origen for ordination in his attack on the action Alexander and Theoctistus had taken in ordaining him.

[5] See Josephus, *Jewish War* 1.401–8; *Antiquities* 15.328–41.

It must have gleamed in the Mediterranean sun as one approached it from land or sea. Much of its economy depended on its harbor. It lacked, however, a natural harbor, so Herod, in one of the more outstanding construction achievements of antiquity, built a large harbor capable of anchoring fleets of ships according to Josephus.[6] He sank huge blocks of stone creating a breakwater 200 feet wide (Josephus, *War* 1.411–12), and used a newly developed form of concrete that would harden under water.[7] It has been surmised that Herod hoped that his new city with its large harbor might challenge, or even surpass Alexandria as the center of trade in the eastern Mediterranean. This did not happen, but it did become a major port city for trade between Rome and the East,[8] and the most economically powerful city in Palestine.

Herod intended Caesarea to be a pagan city. The large central temple to Caesar and Rome signaled this clearly, along with the numerous statues scattered throughout the city. He inaugurated the city with a lavish set of games including "musical and athletic contests, gladiatorial spectacles, wild beasts and horse races".[9] Inscriptions extending into the third century AD attest to the continuation of the games at Caesarea.[10] Coins minted there indicate the presence of numerous pagan cults in the city from the first through the mid-third century: Tyche, which some identify with the Semitic Astarte, Sarapis, the "'imperial trinity'" consisting of "Dionysus, Demeter, and Tyche", Poseidon, Apollo, Zeus, Helios, Ares, Hygeia, Dea Roma, and the imperial cult. A second-century papyrus also attests to the worship of Isis at Caesarea.[11]

Two years after Herod's death Rome annexed his kingdom as a part of the empire and made it a province, with Caesarea the seat of the provincial ruler. The city thus became the most powerful political as well as economic city in Palestine. After the fall of Jerusalem in AD 70 it was "the dominant urban center in the country", and this continued to be the case for centuries.[12] Vespasian elevated Caesarea to the status of a colony because of its loyalty during the Jewish war.[13] After the war the city became predominantly pagan until the late second century. It is the Alexandrian god Sarapis whose image appears most frequently on coins minted at Caesarea in the second century. The century was a time of population growth and economic expansion. The building projects of Vespasian, Hadrian, and Antoninus Pius made their contributions to the needs, adornment, and comforts of the city.[14]

---

[6] *Antiquities* 15.334; Hohlfelder (1992), 799–800.
[7] McKenzie (2007), 46; Hohlfelder (1992), 799–800.   [8] Hohlfelder (1992), 799–800.
[9] Levine (1975), 17.   [10] Foerster (1975), 18.   [11] Ibid., 16.
[12] Levine (1975), 18–19.   [13] Hohlfelder (1992), 800.   [14] Levine (1975), 42.

THE JEWISH COMMUNITY IN CAESAREA

In spite of its original pagan nature, there was a Jewish population in the city in the first century, for in the Jewish war that broke out in AD 66, 20,000 Jewish residents of Caesarea were massacred.[15] In fact, an incident connected with a Synagogue in the city seems to have been the spark that set off the war.[16] Following the war, and through most of the second century, the Jewish presence in Caesarea was small and insignificant. In the last quarter of that century, however, there is evidence again of a significant Jewish population which continues through the fifth century AD. In the late first and early second centuries many rabbis had condemned Caesarea because of its connection with the Romans, who had destroyed Jerusalem and the temple. They pronounced Caesarea impure and equated it with non-Jewish sections of the country. The successive emperors in the Severan line (AD 193–235), however, took several actions which favored the Jews throughout the empire and gave them a more positive attitude towards the Romans. Jews began to move to Caesarea again, and around the end of the second century Rabbi Judah, the compiler of the *Mishnah*, seems to have declared it clean again. This action meant that priests could now be present in Caesarea and not become ritually unclean.[17] It was in this time period that the significant rabbinic schools of Caesarea began to flourish, which elevated the city to the level of Tiberias and Sepphoris as a center of rabbinic study.[18]

Near the end of the second century AD Bar Qappara, who had been a student of Rabbi Judah at Sepphoris, opened a school in Caesarea.[19] On the death of Rabbi Judah, this school became the most prominent of all the rabbinic centers in Palestine.[20] Bar Qappara "advocated the use of the Greek language even in the synagogues and the schools".[21] This view prevailed, for there is abundant evidence that Jews who lived in Caesarea spoke Greek as a second language, and many as their only language. Jewish funerary inscriptions in Greek bear this out.[22] Caesarean rabbis of the fourth century permitted the Shema to be recited in Greek, and the Scriptures to be read in Greek. An inscription found in the Caesarean Synagogue appears to contain a phrase from the Septuagint.[23] One of the first questions that Bardy addressed in his famous study of Jewish traditions in Origen's works

---

[15] Ibid.   [16] Josephus, *Jewish War* 2.284–96; Levey (1975), 43.
[17] Levine (1975), 65–68.   [18] Levey (1975), 44.
[19] Strack (1931/1959), 119; Levey (1975), 55.   [20] Levey (1975), 55.   [21] Ibid., 56.
[22] Bietenhard (1974), 10.   [23] Levine (1975), 70.

was how well Origen knew Hebrew and to what extent he could have entered into discussions with Jewish scholars.[24] This is an irrelevant question concerning Origen's relationship with the rabbis of Caesarea in light of the evidence about the predominance of Greek in the Jewish community there. Origen's discussions with the rabbis in Caesarea would have taken place in Greek.

Approximately two years before Origen's move to Caesarea Rabbi Hoshaya established a school there (AD 230).[25] He died about AD 250,[26] so his and Origen's time in Caesarea was largely coextensive. Hoshaya was considered the preeminent rabbinic authority of his time. His "academy quickly became a center of rabbinic studies. Students flocked there, and R. Hoshaya's twelve outstanding pupils included the most famous names within rabbinic circles in subsequent generations."[27] A rabbinic school could be informal, meeting in the home of the teacher or in other informal settings. "R. Joḥanan...mentions that when studying with R. Hoshaya at Caesarea, students were forced to sit on fish-brine barrels when listening to the sage's lecture."[28]

It is highly probable that Origen had contact and conversations with some of these rabbis, possibly even Hoshaya himself, but no proof exists. More than a century ago Bacher assembled some statements of Rabbi Hoshaya which he suggested may either have had Origen as a direct dialogue partner or have been made in relation to viewpoints held by Origen.[29] But Origen is never mentioned in any of the rabbinic sources Bacher cites. From Origen's side, in the *Contra Celsum*, which was written late in his life in Caesarea, he refers to several earlier conversations with Jews considered to be "wise", but he too never mentions any names.[30] His remark that these conversation partners were considered "wise" by the Jews must mean that they were rabbis who were well-known for their teachings.

The references to conversations with the Jews in the *Contra Celsum* all indicate that they were in polemical settings in arguments related to Jesus. There is a passage in a Greek fragment from Origen's large commentary on the Psalms which he produced in Caesarea; however, that does not seem to have been polemical. In this fragment he names one of his Jewish conversation partners. The discussion concerns how one ascertains the authorship of psalms which are ascribed to no author. Origen relates the conversation as follows:

---

[24] Bardy (1925), 219.   [25] Ibid., 88; Levey (1975), 57; Strack (1931/1959), 120.

[26] Levine (1975), 89.   [27] Levine (1975), 88; see also Bietenhard (1974), 10.

[28] B "Eruvin" 53a, cited in Levine (1975), 103.   [29] Bacher (1891), 357–60.

[30] *Cels* 1.45, 55; 2.31.

I thought that there was one psalm of Moses in the Book of Psalms, which was inscribed, 'Prayer of Moses, man of God'. Later, however, in a discussion concerning certain oracles of God with Ioullus the patriarch and someone the Jews considered wise, I learned that after the first two psalms, throughout the rest of the book, those psalms which lack an inscription among the Hebrews, or have an inscription but lack the name of the author, are considered to have been written by that person whose name is on the preceding psalm.

And as he was talking about these he said first that there are thirteen psalms of Moses. But when I heard what they were, I countered that there are eleven. Then I asked the man who seemed to be wise, and learned that there are eleven, the first of which is the eighty-ninth, beginning, 'Lord you have been our refuge from generation to generation'. He also said the next is a psalm of Moses, which we refer to as the ninetieth.... And he said the ninety-first, which has the inscription, 'Psalm of an ode on the day of the Sabbath', but lacks the name of the one who wrote it, is by Moses.... And he claimed that the ninety-second psalm, which lacks an inscription, is by Moses.... And likewise the ninety-third,... and the ninety-fourth... and the ninety-fifth,... and the ninety-sixth. So too the ninety-seventh, whose inscription has only the word 'Psalm'. The words 'for David', as some copies of the Septuagint have, were neither in the Hebrew text nor in the other versions.... He said that the ninety-eighth psalm... is also by the same person, as well as the ninety-ninth, which has the inscription, 'A psalm for praise', and begins, "Sing joyfully to God, all the earth".[31]

The patriarch Ioullus cannot be identified. Jerome refers to Origen mentioning a patriarch Huillus, whom he says was Origen's contemporary. He says Origen used his interpretation of Isaiah 29:1 in the thirtieth book of his own commentary on Isaiah, which is now lost. In the same passage Jerome also mention's Huillus' view that not only the eighty-ninth Psalm, but also the next 11 psalms were by Moses, which is the view of Ioullus in the Psalm fragment translated here.[32] This makes it relatively certain that the Ioullus of the fragment and the Huillus of Jerome's text are the same person. De Lange thinks that perhaps the text of the Psalm fragment should be emended to read Huillus,[33] but this does not take us any further in identifying the patriarch, for neither name can be identified with any known rabbi of the period. De Lange suggests that Huillus' name is not known because he was head of only a local Jewish community.[34]

---

[31] PG 12.1056B–1057C; also in Rietz (1914), 13.
[32] Jerome, *Against Rufinus* 1.13 (PG 23.408A).
[33] Lange (1976), 23.
[34] Ibid., 24; Bardy suggested that Ioullus is a transcription for Hillel. For his argument see Bardy (1925), 223–4.

Some have suggested that the second man in the dialogue whom Origen refers to as a "wise" man may have been Hoshaya.[35] I think that is likely for the following reasons. There are several times that Origen refers to inquiring of or having discussions with Jews where the term is plural.[36] There are a few instances where he refers to discussions with a single Jew, but the references are indefinite.[37] There are three places, however, where he uses the singular noun with the definite article.[38] One is in the Psalm fragment cited above when he inquires about the number of Psalms of Moses from "the man who seemed to be wise" (*tou parontos dokountos sophou*).[39] The second is a remark on 1 Samuel 2:30 which Origen says comes from "the teacher of the Hebrews" (*ho tōn Hebraiōn didaskalos*), and the third comes from a polemical discussion of Psalm 44:3–8, where Origen says he recalls once causing "the Jew who was thought to be wise" (*ton Ioudaion nomizomenon sophon*) great difficulty when he pressed him with the question of the identity of the God being addressed in these verses. The first and last of these passages involve discussions of psalms, which may suggest that the Jew in question was someone with whom Origen had several discussions during the time he was working on his Caesarean *Commentary on the Psalms*.[40] It is the use of the definite article with the noun in the singular, however,

---

[35] Lange, who mentions this, cites Graetz, Cadiou, and Barthélemy (ibid., 25 and 155, n. 85). He dismisses the suggestion because he thinks the two references are to the same person. The text is relatively clear, however, that Origen is referring to two persons. He says he was having a discussion with Ioullus the patriarch "and with someone (indefinite pronoun *tini*) of those considered wise by the Jews". It would be unusual to name a person and then immediately refer to that person with an indefinite pronoun. Also, it sounds very much like Origen turns to a second person in the conversation when he disagrees with the number of psalms mentioned by Ioullus. He refers to "then inquiring of the man who seemed to be wise" and getting an answer that agreed with his own opinion. It is possible, I think, that the words reported in the fragment from that point on should be attributed to the person Origen refers to as "wise". This does not, of course, mean that the "wise" man was Hoshaya.

[36] I omit here references to Jews who seem to have been Christians, and all references occurring in his Alexandrian works; *Cels* 1.45, 55; 2.31; 6.49; *HomGn* 2.2 (esp. the Greek fragment from Procopius in *Origenes Werke* (1920), 28.16–17). In the Greek fragment the reference is singular but indefinite: *apo tinos tōn par' Hebraiois ellogimōn*, "from one of the famous men among the Hebrews"; *SelEz* 9.2 (PG 13.796B), 9.4 (PG 13.800D–801A), 10.3 (PG 13.743B); *ComJn* 6.83, 212 (Origen may have known these two traditions from Alexandria).

[37] See the Procopius reference in n. 36 above; *HomIs* 9.1; *SelEz* 9.2 (PG 13.800C); *HomEz* 4.8; *ComMt* 11.9.

[38] PG 12.1056B–1057C (on the Mosaic psalms); PG 13.781D–784A on 1 Kgs (1 Sam) 2:30; *Cels* 1.56 on Ps 44:3–8.

[39] This man is first referred to in this discussion with the indefinite pronoun: "someone the Jews considered wise" (*tini tōn chrēmatizontōn para Ioudaiois sophōn*).

[40] Bardy (1925), 234–6 provides several additional passages where Origen either refers to the Hebrews or reflects a view common to them in his discussions of various psalms.

which is most significant. Origen knew and referred to several Jews considered to be wise. *Contra Celsum* 1.56, however, singles out one as especially noted for his wisdom. This must have been someone highly regarded by the Jewish community in Caesarea and, in Origen's time, there was no one considered wiser in rabbinical circles in Caesarea than Hoshaya.[41] The reference to "the teacher of the Hebrews" is also very specific and no one in Caesarea when Origen lived there would fit that description better than Rabbi Hoshaya. I think there is a high degree of probability that Origen had discussions with Rabbi Hoshaya, and that these passages are references to three of those discussions.

THE CHRISTIAN COMMUNITY IN CAESAREA
PRIOR TO ORIGEN

Christianity was most likely first taken to Caesarea by the evangelist Philip in the early thirties. He was one of the seven men chosen to serve the needs of the Hellenistic Jewish segment of the Jerusalem church (Acts 6:1–5). When persecution, set off by Stephen's speech and subsequent martyrdom, scattered the Christians from Jerusalem, Philip went to Samaria as an evangelist and had considerable success among the Samaritans (Acts 8:4–13). He was then sent to preach to the Ethiopian eunuch, on the road between Jerusalem and Gaza. Philip was again successful in his evangelistic work and the Ethiopian was baptized (Acts 8:26–38). Then the account of Philip becomes sketchy. He is said to be at Azotus, the ancient "Philistine city of Ashdod"[42] near the coast, and to have preached the gospel in the towns between there and Caesarea (Acts 8:40). He appears to have settled in Caesarea, for more than twenty years later Paul and Luke stay several days with him in his house there. There was clearly a Christian community in Caesarea at this time, for when the prophet Agabus came from Judea to warn Paul not to go to Jerusalem, Luke says, "We and the people of that place appealed to him not to go up to Jerusalem" (Acts 21:8–12). "The people of that place" who were concerned about Paul's well-being can only be the Christian community there. When Paul set out for Jerusalem in spite of their appeal, Luke says that "some of the disciples from Caesarea" accompanied them as far as their next stopping point (Acts 21:16). Caesarea had a considerable Samaritan population in the

41 See the discussion of Hoshaya above at n. 35 and the references there.
42 Watson (1992), 311.

later empire.[43] Perhaps the city had attracted Samaritans earlier as well and Philip, who had successfully evangelized in Samaria, chose to settle there to work with the Samaritan community.

Peter is the other evangelist reported to have taken the gospel to Caesarea. The famous story of his conversion of the God-fearing Roman centurion named Cornelius is told in Acts 10 and, largely, retold in Acts 11. No mention is made of Philip or of a Christian community in Caesarea in this account. Cornelius is instructed in a vision to send for Peter, who was at Joppa approximately 50 kilometers south on the coast. This story has the symbolic significance for Luke of putting Peter's approval, and consequently that of the Jerusalem Church, on the evangelization of the Gentiles. The accounts concerning Philip and Peter in Acts show clearly that Caesarea was evangelized in the early period of the Christian mission.

Paul's visit to Philip's house in Caesarea on his way to Rome has already been mentioned. He had been in Caesarea earlier, however, when the Jews of Jerusalem made an attempt on his life during his first visit after his conversion. Luke says the brethren took him to Caesarea where they sent him off to Tarsus (Acts 9:28–30). This clandestine removal of Paul from Judea must have involved the Christian community in Caesarea as well as that in Jerusalem, for the Christians taking Paul there would have needed a place to stay with him while arrangements were made for the trip to Tarsus. At the close of his second missionary tour Paul sailed from Ephesus to Caesarea on his way to Jerusalem (Acts 18:21–2). He must have had contact with the Christian community in Caesarea on his arrival, and perhaps with Philip, whose hospitality he would enjoy at the end of his third missionary tour (Acts 21:8–10). Paul was again in Caesarea in the mid-first century, when he was held there as a prisoner for two years. He was allowed some freedoms in this imprisonment, including visits from friends to care for him (Acts 23:23–4; 24:23, 27). Some of these friends had, perhaps, been co-workers of Paul, but many must have been from that group of Caesarean Christians who had appealed to him earlier not to go to Jerusalem, and then had accompanied him on part of his journey when he had set out.

The curtain falls on our knowledge of the first-century Christian community in Caesarea with Paul's removal to Rome and doesn't go up again until late in the second century. What can be observed and surmised about the Christian community of the first century falls under two heads. First, there seem to have been rather close ties between the Christians in Caesarea and those in Jerusalem. Both Philip and Peter came from Jerusalem.

----

[43] Levine (1975), 103.

The Christians in the two cities seem to have communicated with one another and to have helped one another, especially in emergencies such as those connected with Paul. The fact that these were the two leading cities of Judea probably contributed to the relationship as well. The Caesarean Christian community, on the other hand, may have been more open to the evangelization of the non-Jewish population. The Gentile Cornelius is the first named convert of the city, and Philip, who had been a successful evangelist among the Samaritans, resided there. What happened to the Christians of Caesarea in the mid-first century? Were they included in the 20,000 Jews who were massacred there early in the Jewish war, since the Romans, at this time, often did not distinguish Christians from Jews? There is no evidence to answer these questions.

The blackout period on Christian history in Caesarea begins to break up at about the same time that evidence concerning the Jewish community begins to re-emerge there. Eusebius reports on a council held in Palestine about AD 190. It was presided over by Theophilus, bishop of Caesarea, and Narcissus, bishop of Jerusalem. The council sided with Rome, Pontus, Gaul, Osrhoene, and Corinth on the day for celebrating the passion of Jesus. It was to be celebrated on the Friday before the Sunday celebrating the resurrection. The Churches of Asia, whose practice these Churches opposed, celebrated the passion in conjunction with the Jewish Passover, regardless of the day on which it fell (*H.E.* 5.23). In this same context Eusebius reports that the Palestinian bishops, Narcissus in Jerusalem, Theophilus in Caesarea, Cassius in Tyre, and Clarus in Ptolemais, produced a lengthy document concerning the tradition that they had received from the apostles on the subject of the Passover. They ended this document with the claim that the Alexandrian Church celebrated Passover on the same day as they did and they confirmed this by appealing to letters that had passed between the two communities (*H.E.* 5.25).

When Origen visited Palestine in 215 during Caracalla's stay in Alexandria, Theoctistus was bishop of the city (Eusebius, *H.E.* 6.19.17). Little is known about him. The chief thing we know is that he perceived Origen's gift as an interpreter of Scripture, gave him opportunities and responsibilities in the Christian community in Caesarea, and, it seems at least, stood by him when Demetrius and others in the Alexandrian community attacked him. He, along with Alexander of Jerusalem, wrote a letter to Demetrius in defense of their action in allowing Origen to preach, although he had not been ordained when he first visited Palestine (Eusebius, *H.E.* 6.19.17–18). Theoctistus seems to have still been bishop of Caesarea after Origen's death (Eusebius, *H.E.* 7.1, 5). What we know of the Caesarean Christian community in the time of Theoctistus is centered primarily around Origen's activities there as related in Eusebius' *Church History*, the *Panegyric of Gregory Thaumaturgus*, and Origen's own works.

ORIGEN'S EARLY WORK IN CAESAREA AND HIS ALEXANDRIAN PUBLISHING AGENDA

Origen's first activity at Caesarea, after recouping from the battles in Alexandria, was to resume work on the *Commentary on John*. He says he had completed the first five books in Alexandria and had begun the sixth there. This work done on the sixth book, however, had inadvertently been left behind in his troubled departure. He describes his last days in Alexandria as a storm at sea whose winds and waves Jesus had rebuked. It was in this stressful period when he was working on the beginning of the sixth book on John's Gospel that God, he says, delivered him from Egypt as he had done for the Israelites long ago. On first arriving in Caesarea he was too upset by the events in Alexandria to take up the task of a Biblical commentator immediately and, just as hindering, his stenographers were not present. But when he had regained his mental composure and, what he does not mention but should probably be assumed, his stenographers had arrived from Alexandria, he resumed work on the sixth book of the *Commentary on John* from the beginning, assuming that the earlier work done on this book would not be recovered (*ComJn* 6.6–12).

Origen was in Caesarea only three or four years before the outbreak of the persecution of Maximinus (235–8). In this brief interim he seems to have composed Books 6–13, and, perhaps, Books 6–20 of the *Commentary on John*, to have completed the last four books of the *Commentary on Genesis*, which he had taken through the eighth book at Alexandria, written the treatise *On Prayer*, and the treatise *On Martyrdom*.[44] It appears that prior to the persecution he had not assumed any major public role in the Church at Caesarea. It was after the persecution of Maximinus that Origen began what is called the school of Caesarea.[45] It was most likely sometime after this also that he was given the duty of delivering homilies in the liturgical cycle of the Church in Caesarea.

Origen's first work in Caesarea was a continuation of his Alexandrian publishing agenda. He took up his unfinished work on the *Commentary on*

---

[44] See *Origen: Commentary on the Gospel according to John Books 13–32* (1993), Intro., 5–15.
[45] See Eusebius, *H.E.* 6.30.

John which he had begun in Alexandria to provide an alternative to the Valentinian interpretations of John's Gospel.[46] The prologue to Book 6, which he begins in Caesarea, is, again, addressed to Ambrose (*ComJn* 6.6). Once one reads past the prologue to Book 6 in which Origen relates the trouble he experienced at Alexandria and his departure, there is nothing to suggest a break in the interpretation. The first passage he discusses is John 1:19–23, which he calls John the Baptist's second testimony to Christ (*ComJn* 6.13, 43). He begins, however, by prefacing this with a lengthy discussion of John 1:16–18, which he considers, against the view of the Valentinian Heracleon, to constitute John the Baptist's first testimony to Christ (*ComJn* 6.13–42). Heracleon took John 1:16–18 to be the words of the author of the Gospel and not of John the Baptist (*ComJn* 6.13).

Much more was at stake for Origen in Heracleon's argument here than just where to put the quote marks. At stake was the unity of the God of the Law and the Gospel, and the revelation given in the two respective testaments.[47] Pagels has argued that Heracleon had interpreted the statement in John 1:8 that says that John (the Baptist) "was not the light" to refer to the creator God of the Old Testament which the Gnostics labeled the Demiurge.[48] This identification of John the Baptist with the Demiurge is made explicit later in the argument (*ComJn* 6.199). Since Heracleon considered the figure of John the Baptist in the prologue of John's Gospel to represent this very limited divine being, he could not be the true light. And neither could he, as the Demiurge, have made the statement about the invisible God of John 1:18 which, for Heracleon, was a reference to the highest Gnostic deity, their "true God", because the Demiurge of the Gnostic myth was unaware of the existence of this highest God. John 1:18 must, therefore, Heracleon concluded, be a statement made by the disciple who wrote the Gospel, and not a statement of John the Baptist. This argument with Heracleon focused on John the Baptist as a figure of the Demiurge provides the substructure for the sixth book of Origen's commentary. It surfaces next in the discussion of John 1:20–1 (*ComJn* 6.92), then on John 1:23 (*ComJn* 108–18),1:25 (*ComJn* 6.126),1:26 (*ComJn* 6.153, 194–7), 1:27 (*ComJn* 6.198–203), and finally, at the end of the sixth book, on John 1:29 (*ComJn* 6. 306–7).

---

[46] See Chapter 4, in "Ambrose, the Valentinians, and Origen's *Commentary on John* 1:1a", p. 89.

[47] See Heine (2000a), 494–5.

[48] This is based on a very inferential reading of *FragJn* 6 which is on John 1:8. The book of the *ComJn*, where Origen discussed this verse, which she suggests was the third, has been lost (Pagels (1975), 49–51).

After Book 6, of the books I suggested above were composed before the persecution of Maximillan, we have Books 10, 13, 19, and 20. Book 10 covers John 2:12–25. The dialogue with Heracleon continues in much of Book 10, though it is somewhat less pronounced than in Book 6. It does, however, lay out some of Heracleon's key concepts for his reading of the Gospel. The reference to Jesus "going *down* to Capernaum" signifies the Savior's descent to the material realm (*ComJn* 10.48–59). Going "*up* to Jerusalem", on the other hand, refers to his ascent to the psychic realm (*ComJn* 10.210). Here Heracleon's interpretation becomes quite elaborate. The holy of holies within the temple signifies the place of the pneumatics (i.e. the true Gnostics), while the Levites, who serve in the outer court of the temple are those psychics who are saved (*ComJn* 10.211). The merchants and money-changers in the temple are those who, because of their own greed, provide the elements for the worship of the God who occupies the temple of the psychics. Heracleon considered the Jews and "psychic Christians" (the Levites) to worship the creator (*ComJn* 10.212–15).[49] What Origen perceived to be at stake in Heracleon's interpretation of the story of the cleansing of the temple was, as in Book 6, the unity of the God who is the Father of Jesus in the New Testament with the creator God of the Old Testament (*ComJn* 10.216–20). Heracleon took the quotation from Psalm 68:10 in John 2:17 to be the words of the powers Christ cast out of the temple, probably because the words come from the Old Testament, which Heracleon believed was about the Demiurge and his realm (*ComJn* 10.223–4). Origen argues that because another statement from this Psalm is used of Christ at the crucifixion, the statement in John 2:17 must also have been uttered by Christ. In this way he connects Christ, whom Heracleon related to the chief Gnostic deity, with the Old Testament, which Heracleon thought was the book of the Demiurge.

Book 13 is the longest book of the commentary. It covers John 4:13–54. The dialogue with Heracleon dominates this book. Of the thirty pericopae into which Origen divides these verses, only six lack references to Heracleon.[50] The chapter contains the stories of Jesus' conversation with the Samaritan woman and his healing of the centurion's son. Pagels argues that Heracleon understood the story of the Samaritan woman to be a depiction of "pneumatic redemption" and that of the centurion to depict "psychic salvation".[51] We may get an idea of how Origen dialogues with

---

[49] Pagels (1973), 68.
[50] Comments by Heracleon related to the first three pericopae are found in the fourth one. Those lacking comments by Heracleon are John 4:32, 35b, 43–4, 45, and 46.
[51] Pagels (1973), 83–97.

Heracleon's interpretations in this book by looking at how he argues in one of the longer sections he cites from Heracleon (*ComJn* 13.57–74). He begins, it seems, by looking back at what he must have cited from Heracleon in the preceding lost book of the commentary which covered the beginning of John 4. Heracleon seems to have identified the Old Testament Scriptures with Jacob's well and said that they were deficient and passing out of existence. Origen considers him to have denigrated the "ancient words" and to have failed to perceive that they foreshadowed things to come. On the other hand, Origen finds some things in Heracleon's interpretations acceptable. He likes his interpretation of the "leaping water", and he could accept his statement about the Samaritan woman's immediate demonstration of faith, but he is cautious because he thinks that Heracleon might be referring to the woman's actions resulting from her natural state, i.e. as a pneumatic nature, rather than from her free will. On the other hand, Heracleon "distorts the text" when he takes the reference to the woman's husband to mean her consort in the pleroma (*ComJn* 13.62–4, 67–8).

The importance of Heracleon to the *Commentary on John* diminishes significantly in Books 19 and 20. Origen notes once that Heracleon had made no comment on a particular verse (*ComJn* 19.89). References to him appear only at Origen's comments on John 8:21 and 22 in Book 19 and on John 8:38, 43, 44, and 49–50 in Book 20. These two books together, as we have them,[52] cover John 8:19–53. The main issue discussed in these citations of Heracleon is what Origen understood to be the Valentinian doctrine of natures.[53] John 8:44 is the focal point of the disagreement. There Jesus says to the Jews who were arguing with him, "You are of your father the devil." Heracleon understood this to mean, "You have the essence of the devil." He then distinguished between those people the Valentinians classified as *hylic*, i.e. of a material nature and lacking any choice, and those they called *psychic*, i.e. having the nature of soul and capability of some choice. The former have the nature or essence of the devil like a child has the essence of its parent; the latter have the nature of the devil by adoption because they do what he wishes them to do by their own choice (*ComJn* 20.211–18). Origen opposes these views of Heracleon with his understanding of the freedom

---

[52] Book 19 lacks pages at both its beginning and end. The last verse cited at the end of Book 19 is John 8:25 and the first verse cited at the beginning of Book 20 is John 8:37. There must, therefore, be commentary on John 8:25–36 lost from the end of Book 19. There is no way to measure how much is lost from the beginning because all of Books 14–18 are lost.

[53] See Chapter 6, in "*On Natures* and the *Dialogue with Candidus*", p. 127; see also Pagels (1973), 98–113, who thinks Origen did not completely understand Heracleon's teaching on natures.

of the will which all rational beings, including the devil, possess. It is particularly important in Origen's mind that the devil does what he does because of his free will rather than because he is of an essence that does not allow any choices. If the latter were true, he thinks, the devil would be innocent of his actions and should be pitied rather than censured (*ComJn* 20.254). Later, in a homily on Jeremiah preached at Caesarea, Origen cites John 8:44 with no reference at all to Heracleon's doctrine of natures. There he understands the verse as a statement about one's life before God becomes one's father (*HomJer* 9.4).

There is a noticeable drop in interest in Heracleon's views after Book 13 of the commentary. Books 28 and 32, the last two books of the commentary that are extant,[54] do not mention him at all.[55] These two books seem almost certainly to have been written later in Origen's time in Caesarea, and that may be true of Books 19 and 20 as well. The latter two may, at least, have been written after the persecution of Maximinus which began in 235.[56] Why this fading of interest in Heracleon's views in the later books of Origen's commentary? There are at least two reasons that one might think of. First, perhaps Heracleon's commentary was incomplete and he had not commented on those sections of John's Gospel that Origen covers in the later books. If this were the case, however, one would need also to ask why Origen continued his commentary beyond Heracleon's stopping point, for the extent of his commentary on Genesis seems to have been defined by the texts treated by the Gnostics.[57] The other possible reason, which seems more likely to me, is that the importance of the Alexandrian agenda itself had faded somewhat for Origen once he was removed from the Alexandrian setting for a few years and had settled into a new set of issues in a city whose horizons looked somewhat different as a consequence of the vigorous rabbinic community in the city.

It is unfortunate that we have no books preserved of the *Commentary on Genesis*.[58] Origen wrote the first eight books of this commentary in Alexan-

---

[54] Book 32 appears to have been the last book Origen wrote in the commentary, thus ending it at John 13:33 (see Jerome, *Ep* 33.4).

[55] He is also not mentioned in Book 1, but this book begins with a long section treating the kind of topics dealt with by ancient commentators at the beginning of a commentary, and when it does take up the text, it treats in parts, at least, as I argued in Chapter 4, terms and issues that were important to the Gnostics, although Gnostics are not mentioned in the book.

[56] *Origen: Commentary on the Gospel according to John Books 13–32* (1993), intro 5.

[57] See Chapter 5, in "The *Commentary on Genesis*", p. 104.

[58] See Chapter 5, in "The *Commentary on Genesis*", p. 104, where I have discussed fragments from the *ComGn*, including some from books written in Caesarea.

dria and the final four[59] in Caesarea. In the *On Prayer*, which was written in 233 or 234 in Caesarea, he refers to his *Commentary on Genesis* 3:8–9, which seems to have been in Book 10 of the commentary.[60] This means that the *Commentary on Genesis* had either been completed or was near completion a year or so after Origen's move to Caesarea. One cannot make definite statements because of the very fragmentary nature of the remains of this commentary, but it seems very likely that the Alexandrian agenda under which the commentary was begun was carried through in Caesarea.[61]

REFLECTIONS ON ASPECTS OF PIETY AND FAITHFULNESS

Origen's next two works at Caesarea, perhaps written while he was work-ing on the two we have just discussed, have a somewhat different orienta-tion than his previous works. He had been concerned also in his earlier writings about living the faith one holds in Christ, but here he takes up two topics specific to this concern: prayer, and faithfulness in persecution. Origen's life to this point had unfolded in the context of these subjects. Two of Eusebius' stories from Origen's youth bear directly on them. One is about the amazement of Origen's father at his inquisitiveness and eager-ness in studying the Scriptures. Eusebius says Origen's father would, in secret, thank God for considering him worthy to be the father of a son like this (*H.E.* 6.2.9–10). Origen's youth was bathed in the prayers of his father, who must have also taught his son to pray. His later lifework was done in the context of his own prayers and those of his friends. He concludes the prologue to his earliest writing done in Alexandria with a short prayer for God's guidance in discovering the mystical meaning in the words of John's Gospel (*ComJn* 1.89) and at the close of the prologue to the commentary on the first 25 psalms written in Alexandria he asks Ambrose to pray for him in the words of Matthew 7:7, that he might "seek" in a proper manner so that he might have the promise of "finding".[62] A little later in Caesarea, after Origen had again taken up work as a teacher, he exhorts a former stu-dent in a letter to approach the study of Scripture in prayer, using the key given by Jesus in Matthew 7:7 (*EpistGreg* 3.1). In the *Panegyric on Origen*, a

---

[59] *PEuch* 5. Jerome refers to 13 books of the commentary (*Ep* 36.9); Eusebius refers to 12 (*H.E.* 6.24.2).

[60] See Heine (2003), 63–4.

[61] See Heine (2003), 63–73; Heine (2005), 122–42; and Chapter 5, in "The *Commentary on Genesis*", p. 104.

[62] Epiphanius, *Pan* 64.7.4.

student, on departing from Origen's school in Caesarea, speaks of the profound influence Origen had on him and his fellow-students, and concludes by asking Origen to commend them continually to God in prayer (19). He would not have done this had prayer not already been a regular part of the relationship between Origen and his students.

Persecution and martyrdom had also been close to Origen's life from his youth. When he was a teenager his father was arrested and martyred. While his father was in prison Origen wrote him a letter about martyrdom from which Eusebius quotes the statement, "Be careful not to change your mind for our sake" (*H.E.* 6.2.6). Eusebius also relates that Origen would have given himself up for martyrdom at that time had it not been for his mother almost forcefully preventing him (*H.E.* 6.2.3–5). A few years later Origen became widely known in Alexandria for his courageous ministry to martyrs during the local persecutions when Aquila was governor of the city (Eusebiuis, *H.E.* 6.3.3–5). Both prayer and martyrdom were subjects of which Origen had experiential understanding.

In spite of his long experience with prayer, Origen closes the prologue to his *On Prayer* as he does so many of his prologues, by requesting prayer for his understanding of the subject at hand.

[T]he discussion of prayer is so great a task that it requires the Father to reveal it, His Firstborn Word to teach it, and the Spirit to enable us to think and speak rightly of so great a subject. That is why I, who am only a human being and in no way attribute an understanding of prayer to myself, think it right to pray for the Spirit before beginning my treatise on prayer, in order that the fullest spiritual account may be given to me and that the prayers written in the Gospels may be made clear.[63]

Junod called attention to the fact that Origen begins this treatise by talking about impossible things that become possible only by the grace of God.[64] One of these impossible things, Origen says, is to explain the subject of prayer "in a manner that is accurate and worthy of God".[65] Junod thinks, further, that the conclusion of the treatise confirms that Origen "had approached the composition of this treatise with a certain apprehension".[66] Origen certainly expresses some dissatisfaction with the results of his study in this conclusion and anticipates that at a later time and with divine help he might be able to do better. "[I]f you pray for me in my studies", he says,

---

[63] *PEuch* 2.6, trans. *Origen* (1979), 86.

[64] Junod (1980), 81–3.

[65] *PEuch* 2.1. Approximately five lines of text are missing in the manuscript at this point, so we do not know exactly what Origen said about how God makes this possible (*Origenes Werke* (1899), 2:299).

[66] *PEuch* 34; Junod (1980), 85.

"I am not without hope that from God the Giver I can become capable of additional and more divine insights into all these matters and that having received them I shall be able to discuss the same points more nobly, more loftily, and more clearly."[67]

The occasion for the treatise on prayer was a letter from his friend and patron Ambrose and a godly woman named Tatiana (*PEuch* 2.1). They had questions about the validity of prayer which came from the philosophical milieu. They cited two common arguments of the philosophers against praying. "First, if God knows in advance what will happen, and these things must happen, prayer is useless. Second, if all things happen as God wills, and what he wills is inevitable, and nothing he has willed can be altered, prayer is useless."[68] The late second-century Platonist, Maximus of Tyre, had raised an identical objection to the validity of petitionary prayer. His objection, like those cited by Ambrose and Tatiana focused on the relationship between prayer and providence. "[N]othing", he argues, "that falls under the heading of Providence is to be requested or prayed for."[69] Ambrose, Tatiana, and Origen may have known these arguments from Christian sources, too, however. Clement of Alexander attributes teachings against the need for praying to the followers of a Gnostic teacher named Prodicus (*Strom* 7.7.41). He seems to have argued, much as Maximus of Tyre did, that God "will not grant anything to those who pray, if they do not deserve it, nor will he refuse to grant blessings to those who deserve them, even if they do not pray".[70] Petitionary prayer, therefore, is useless. Clement's response is the somewhat lame remark that petitions are still of value even though good things are granted without them.

The treatise on prayer has its roots in the Alexandrian experience of Origen and his friends. The question of the validity of prayer sits in the larger context of the question of divine foreknowledge and human freedom. Origen begins his discussion with philosophical arguments he had used in Alexandria to defend the freedom of the will against the doctrine of determinism. The first is a philosophical argument based on motion.[71] Rational beings, he argues, have the cause of their motion within themselves. To be

---

[67] *PEuch* 34; trans. *Origen* (1979), 170.

[68] *PEuch* 5.6. Junod (1980), 86–7, has noted that Ambrose's question is a "philosophical *topos*". De Faye, (1927), 159 noted a "curious resemblance" between Maximus of Tyre's ideas on prayer and the beginning of Origen's *PEuch*.

[69] *Maximus of Tyre* (1997), 46 (Oration 5.4).

[70] *Maximus of Tyre* (1997), 45 (Oration 5.3); cf. Clement, *Strom* 7.12.73. Trapp calls attention to the similarity with Clement in n. 17 (ibid.).

[71] *PEuch* 6.1; *Princ* 3.1.2; cf. Plato's comments on the self-movement of the soul (*Phaedrus* 245C) and Aristotle's criticism of Plato's view (*De Anima* 1.3).

moved by external forces means that the entity in question is not a living, rational being. To believe, therefore, that humans are moved by a force external to them is to deny that they are living, rational beings (*PEuch* 6.2). The other argument involves praise and blame. Who does not believe that some human actions deserve praise and others blame? This belief assumes that humans freely choose their actions (*PEuch* 6.2; *Princ* 3.1.1, 5). We have already encountered Origen's use of this argument in his discussion of the Valentinian doctrine of natures.[72] This, too, was a philosophical argument used to defend the freedom of the will. Origen's contemporary, the Aristotelian philosopher Alexander of Aphrodisias, used it repeatedly, as did numerous other philosophers.[73]

Origen's next argument concerns praying in the proper manner. The philosophers discussed this also. Maximus of Tyre argued that "God will never stand for you praying for what ought not to be prayed for, nor will he give you what ought not to be given. He oversees the prayers of each and every one of us, . . . and he reviews your words against the standards of what is truly best." He goes on to argue that Socrates, Pythagoras, and Plato all prayed, but they did not petition for things they did not have. Their prayers were conversations with the gods about what they did have, and demonstrated their virtue.[74] Origen's discussion does not parallel this philosophical view exactly, but it too stringently limits petitionary prayer. There are preconditions for praying properly including the disposition of mind one brings to prayer, the way one lives, and the nature of the objects of prayer (*PEuch* 8.1). One of the advantages of prayer is simply that of getting in the frame of mind to approach God in prayer. This, he argues, would be a great gain even if nothing more were accomplished (*PEuch* 8.2).

Origen emphasizes throughout the treatise that one should not pray for little or earthly things (*PEuch* 8.1; 16.2). He bases this on a saying he seems to assume comes from Jesus but which does not appear in any known Gospel, canonical or otherwise.[75] He introduces the saying near the beginning of the treatise and alludes to it in five later passages: "'Ask for things which are great, and those which are small will be added for you', and 'ask for things which are heavenly and those which are earthly will be added for

---

[72] See n. 53 above.

[73] *Alexander of Aphrodisias On Fate* (1983), 65–6, 69, 76–8, 84, 87–8, 90–1, 100 (where prayer is also a part of the discussion), 119, 120–1. Sharples points out that "[t]he incompatibility of praise, blame, punishment and reward with determinism . . . was a standard anti-determinist argument" (ibid., 150).

[74] *Maximus of Tyre* (1997), 48–9 (Oration 5.7, 8). Trapp notes, however, that this is a tendentious argument by Maximus and that Plato's prayers are petitionary.

[75] On his assumption that it is a saying of Jesus, see *PEuch* 27.1.

you' ".[76] It isn't clear whether he considered this one saying or two.[77] It is followed by five additional sayings, all joined by "and", and all sayings of Jesus which can be located in the canonical Gospels. This connection with known sayings of Jesus strongly suggests that Origen considered it a saying of Jesus as well. In his second citation of the saying Origen offers an explanation of what he considers it to mean. The "great" and "heavenly things" are spiritual matters. These things are true. What are "small" and "earthly" are symbols and types of these greater, true spiritual realities. The latter should constitute the subject matter of prayer for anyone who wants to be spiritual. "Small" and "earthly things" are the necessities of the body. These, he says, the Father will supply as they are needed (*PEuch* 14.1). This is accomplished by the angels bringing those who have means together with those who have needs (*PEuch* 11.3–4). One must wonder if he was thinking of the ministrations of the wealthy lady in Alexandria who provided for him after the death of his father, of the services Ambrose continued to provide for him, and of the opportunity to move to Caesarea which Theoctistus provided for him when Demetrius was raging against him in Alexandria.

Origen considered these first issues addressed in his treatise to concern the "problem of prayer". When he thinks he has said all he can on the philosophical problems, he turns to a discussion of the Lord's Prayer that might be classified as a kind of theological commentary on the prayer (*PEuch*18.1). This discussion forms the larger part of the treatise. Here, too, Origen seems to work within an Alexandrian frame of thought. His discussion of the opening phrase of the prayer, for example, "Our Father in heaven" (Matt. 6:9), places the phrase in the context of the Alexandrian philosophical, Christian milieu. He begins by arguing that "in heaven" cannot refer to God being in a place, for the place would then "contain" God and, consequently, be greater than God.[78] Furthermore, those who think of heaven as the location of God also think that he occupies heaven in a bodily manner. This has the consequence of attributing divisibility, materiality, and corruptibility to God because these are all properties of bodies. God cannot, therefore, be a body located in a place (*PEuch* 18.3). Origen then remarks that he has a lengthy discussion of these subjects in his commentaries on Genesis. The *Commentary on Genesis* is not extant, as I have

---

[76] *PEuch* 2.2; 14.1; 16.2; 17.2; 27.1; 33.1.

[77] Clement cites only the first of the two parts (*Strom* 1.24.158.2; 4.6.34.6), as does Eusebius (*Commentary on the Psalms* Ps 16.2), who introduces it as a teaching of "the Savior".

[78] *PEuch* 23.1. For the philosophical and early Christian use of the "containing not contained" argument see Schoedel (1972), 90–9.

already noted.[79] Origen's treatment of Genesis 3:8–9, where this discussion would have been found, would have appeared in one of the later books of the commentary completed after his move to Caesarea.[80] It was, therefore, something he had recently discussed as he finished that commentary which he had started in Alexandria.

Schoedel has noted that the *Teachings of Silvanus* has a similar argument against God being in a place, because this would necessitate that he has a body, which would mean that he is not imperishable.[81] I argued in Chapter 4 that Origen's Christological thinking in the Alexandrian books of the *Commentary on John* shows signs of the influence of the *Teachings of Silvanus*.[82] Furthermore, the first thing he wants to establish as foundational in all thinking about God in the *On First Principles* is that God is immaterial.[83] Zandee has called attention to several passages in Clement of Alexandria where Clement discusses the same points noted above in the *Teachings of Silvanus*.[84] When Origen discusses the phrase, "Our Father in heaven", therefore, he places it in the context of the way he had learned to think about God in Alexandria.[85]

It would be a false impression, however, to think that the entire treatise is devoted to philosophical issues and high theology. Practical issues are often the focus of the discussion. In the section on the clause of the Lord's Prayer, "Forgive us our debts", the discussion moves at the practical and ecclesiastical level. Part of the discussion is about forgiving those who are "in debt" to us (*PEuch* 28.6–7). Another part of the commentary on this clause looks at it in relation to John 20:23, "If you forgive the sins of any, they are forgiven them; if you retain the sins of any, they are retained" (NRSV). Here Origen discusses the forgiveness that comes to people through the agency of the priesthood, and argues, in line with the stricter understanding of the late second-and early third-century Church,[86] that adultery, murder, and other

---

[79] See the section above at n. 58, and Chapter 5, in "The *Commentary on Genesis*", p. 104.

[80] See Heine (2005), 137–40.

[81] Schoedel (1972), 98; *Silvanus* 99.31–100.12.

[82] See Chapter 4, in "Ambrose, the Valentinians, and Origen's *Commentary on John* 1:1a", p. 89.

[83] *Princ* 1.1.1–4; see Heine (2004b), 106–108. See also Chapter 6, in "*On First Principles*", p. 130.

[84] Zandee (1977), 58–62.

[85] I do not mean, of course, that no one outside of Alexandria thought of God this way. See the references cited by Schoedel (1972), 90–4. Schoedel does point out, however, the importance of Philo in transmitting some of the developments in the philosophical discussion of the subject which later became important in the Christian tradition (ibid., 94–8).

[86] See Heine (2004d), 207–8.

more serious sins cannot be forgiven by priests (*PEuch* 28.9). But, he notes, some priests have overstepped their limits and claim the power to forgive even sins in this latter category—idolatry, adultery, and fornication (*PEuch* 28.10). This, he says, is contrary to the Scripture that says, "There is a sin unto death; I do not say that you should pray on behalf of such sin" (1 John 5:16). Origen does not name the priests who claimed power to forgive beyond what Scripture authorized, but he had been to Rome several years earlier when he was living in Alexandria, and this was one of the things that Hippolytus accused Callistus of claiming there.[87]

This issue was a particularly sensitive one for Origen, for in his *Exhortation to Martyrdom* he identifies idolatry as apostasy in persecution. Even those who, in times of persecution, only go through the outward motions of recognizing the pagan gods to avoid death still disobey the command of Exodus 20:4–5 against idolatry, for they "bow down" to the idols even though they do not "worship" them (*ExhMart* 6). Origen calls even this insincere activity in times of persecution fornicating with demons (*ExhMart* 9). Forgiving idolatry by priests in the third-century Church almost always meant forgiving those who had committed apostasy in persecution. Origen's father had suffered death rather than apostatize (*HomEz* 8.4). Origen's firm stand against priests who offered forgiveness to apostates had deep roots in his own personal life.

Echoes of the *On First Principles* can be heard in Origen's discussion of the petition, "Bring us not into temptation". How, he asks, can the Savior ask us to make this request when we encounter temptation at every corner in life? Being tempted is coextensive with life on this earth (*PEuch* 29.1). There is an extensive discussion of the Christian's struggle with the opposing powers in *On First Principles* (3.2). There, Origen distinguishes between the temptations involving "flesh and blood" referred to in 1 Corinthians 10:13 and those involving "principalities and powers" referred to in Ephesians 6:12. The former, which were a Corinthian kind of temptation, involved temptations of the flesh. The latter are temptations of the mind or spirit.[88] This same distinction is present in the discussion of temptation in the *On Prayer*, and the same two Scriptures are used, but the distinction is not explicitly defined as it is in the earlier Alexandrian work.[89] Origen's answer to the dilemma posed by this petition is that being "delivered"[90]

[87] Hippolytus, *Haer* 9.11.20–9.12.26; see *Alexandrian Christianity* (1954), 181.

[88] *Princ* 3.2.4–6; see Heine (2002), 66–8.

[89] *PEuch* 29.2. Origen makes this same distinction later in a homily at Caesarea (*HomJosh* 11.4).

[90] Origen uses the verb "to deliver" from the second clause of the petition, "Deliver us from the evil one", rather than the verb in the first clause of Matt. 6:13, "Bring us not into temptation".

from temptation does not mean not to be tempted, but not to submit when we are (*PEuch* 29.9).

When Origen finishes his treatment of the Lord's Prayer he closes the treatise with a brief discussion of what might be called the mechanics of praying—the proper disposition, posture, and place in which to pray, along with the direction to face in prayer, the time one ought to pray, and the general subject categories that should constitute a prayer (*PEuch* 30–3). These are all more or less physical aspects of praying, but they play a part in shaping and preparing the mind of the praying person to approach God. For example, the general posture of prayer should be standing with hands and face lifted to heaven symbolizing the directing of the mind to God but, if it is a prayer seeking forgiveness of sins, then kneeling is the proper posture, for this represents the mental attitudes of abjection and submission (*PEuch* 30.2–3). Every prayer should begin and end by glorifying God (*PEuch* 33.1).

It is difficult to categorize the treatise on prayer. Works on prayer are often devotional and praise prayer, practical, and describe how it should be done, or apologetic and argue against attacks on the validity of praying. There is little of what one might call devotional in the treatise; there is some treatment of practical aspects, and more argument in defense of prayer. But there is also a large section of commentary on the Lord's Prayer as found in Matthew and Luke. There is no clear structure in the treatise, nor any overarching aim that holds its parts together.[91] The three blocks of material discussed above are not presented in any unified way. Junod's remark is well taken when he says that the work "bears the marks of a work composed with difficulty".[92]

While it is not possible to say in what circumstances Origen wrote the *On Prayer*, the *Exhortation to Martyrdom* was written in a very specific set of circumstances. The Severan family had ruled the empire since AD 193. The wives and mothers of the Severan dynasty were extremely powerful women and, it seems, religious. Michael Grant asserted that "[n]o Roman woman had ever received so much power, privilege and honour as Julia Domna, the wife of the north African Septimius Severus (AD 193–211)".[93] She was the mother of Caracalla (AD 211–17), and her sister, Julia Maesa, was the mother of Elagabalus (AD 218–22). The daughter of Julia Domna, Julia Mamaea, was the mother of Alexander Severus (AD 222–35), the last of the Severan emperors.[94] Julia Domna's father had been a hereditary

---

[91] See Junod (1980), 86, and *Alexandrian Christianity* (1954), 183–4.
[92] Junod (1980), 86.   [93] Grant (1992), 36.   [94] Ibid.; Frend (1984), 272.

priest of the Semitic god Baal. I noted earlier that it was probably under the influence of Julia Domna that Septimius Severus had built a temple to Kybele in Alexandria.[95] Julia Domna gathered a court of sophists, intellectuals, and pseudo-intellectuals about her, including the sophist Philostratus who wrote the life of the religious figure, Apollonius of Tyana.[96] I noted above that the Severan dynasty had taken several actions favoring the Jews.[97] They seem, in general, to have been favorable towards Christians as well. The *Historia Augusta* claims that Alexander Severus had a private chapel that included statues of previous emperors and famous men, "including Apollonius of Tyana, Orpheus, Abraham, and Christ".[98] It was Alexander's mother, Julia Mamaea, who had brought Origen to Antioch to discuss the religion of the Christians.[99]

This peaceful relationship of the Church with the ruling authorities came to an abrupt end in March 235 when Alexander Severus died in a revolution. His position was seized by Julius Maximinus. Herodian says that immediately after seizing power Maximinus set about to eliminate all friends of Alexander from positions of influence.[100] Among those targeted were people of wealth, and leaders in the Church.[101] Görres argued that this persecution of Christians was the result of Maximinus' hostility to the Severan family and its friendly treatment of Christians, especially that of Julia Mamaea.[102] This would have made Origen a potential target because of his earlier connection with Mamaea. He was not arrested, however, but his friend and patron Ambrose and a presbyter in the Church of Caesarea named Protoctetus were.[103]

This persecution of Maximinus and the arrest of Ambrose and Protoctetus were the occasion and circumstances of Origen's *Exhortation to Martyrdom*. Ambrose was clearly a man of great wealth (*ExhMart* 14, 15). He may also have held some kind of high political office. Origen refers to him as "honoured and respected by a vast number of cities".[104] This implies more

---

[95] See Chapter 1, in "Culture", p. 9, and Haas (1997), 143.

[96] *Philostratus and Eunapius* (1989/1921), x–xi.

[97] See above, in "The Jewish Community in Caesarea", p. 147.

[98] *Alexandrian Christianity* (1954), 388.

[99] Eusebius, *H.E.* 6.21.3.

[100] *Herodian* (1970), vol 2, 7.1.1, 3.

[101] Ibid., 7.3.1–4; Eusebius, *H.E.* 6.28.

[102] Görres (1876), 533.

[103] It is not known for certain whether Origen remained in Caesarea during the persecution or if, sometime during it, Theoctistus sent him away to Cappadocia where he was hidden by a Christian woman named Juliana (see *Origen: Commentary on the Gospel according to John Books 13–32* (1993), 7–11).

[104] *ExhMart* 36, trans. *Alexandrian Christianity* (1954), 418.

than just owning extensive property in Egypt. People described in this way were normally political figures. He may have been an office-holder under Alexander Severus, and this, as well as his being a Christian, would have made him a target of Maximinus' persecution.[105] The *Exhortation to Martyrdom* can be dated to the early months of 235. Origen refers to the possibility of being executed in Germany (*ExhMart* 41). Maximinus was in Germany in 235, but he had moved on to Pannonia by the winter of that year.[106] It was his policy to bring political prisoners to his military camp where he himself could try and sentence them.[107]

Origen's overriding concern in this treatise is that his friends remain faithful to their confession. The worst thing one can do, he says, is to recognize another god and not confess the true one (*ExhMart* 10). I noted above in discussing the *On Prayer* that Origen identified idolatry with apostasy. There is more involved, however, than just turning away from the faith. Drawing on the Pauline association of idolatry with the worship of demons (1 Cor. 10:20–1) he argues that the demons depend on the smoke of the sacrifices to survive in Earth's atmosphere. Those, he says, possibly alluding to Gnostic groups, who consider offering the demanded sacrifices as indifferent actions are actually supporting the forces of evil on Earth (*ExhMart* 40, 45.). Others tried to avoid persecution by complying with the demand to worship another god, arguing that the name given to God is indifferent, so one may still worship the supreme God but call him Zeus or Zen, Apollo, Artemis, or Demeter. This is not possible, Origen argues, because names are connected by nature with the objects they describe. What things are called is not the result of mere human convention.[108] The only names that the Christian should use of God are those used by Moses, the prophets, and Jesus (*ExhMart* 46). Origen points out that the words of Matthew 16:24–5 constitute a part of the agreement the Christian enters into with God on receipt of the covenants of salvation. One must deny oneself, take up the cross, and follow Jesus. Our souls can only be saved if we are willing to lose them for the sake of Christ (*ExhMart* 12).

Examples from the persecution literature in the Old Testament, including what are sometimes called the Apocryphal books, Esther, the Daniel stories, and the books of the Maccabees are called into play for encouragement. But it is the teachings and example of Jesus that are cited most

---

[105] If this were true, then it could have been through him that Origen became known to Julia Mamaea, and not by the great fame of Origen as Eusebius relates it (*H.E.* 6.21.3).

[106] Neumann (1890), 228.

[107] *Herodian* (1970), Vol. 2, 7.3.4.

[108] In *Cels* 1.24 Origen identifies these two views with the Stoics and Aristotle, respectively.

frequently in the treatise. One thing is especially noteworthy: there is very little that can be called allegorical interpretation in the *Exhortation to Martyrdom*. The stories and sayings are read and applied literally. This is crisis literature. The sacrifices made by the heroes of the Bible are related for the impact the stories carry on their surfaces. No further, hidden meaning is sought.

The persecution ended with the death of Maximinus in AD 238. Peace returned to the Church. Origen entered into the most productive period of his life, preaching in Caesarea, receiving students, publishing Biblical commentaries, and traveling as an ambassador of orthodoxy to defend the truth in various synods called to correct erring bishops (Eusebius, *H.E.* 6.29. 4–37.1). We have no further information about Protoctetus, who was one of the addressees of the *Exhortation to Martyrdom*, but Ambrose remained faithful and survived the persecution, for Origen is still addressing him as a faithful Christian and the prompter of his published work in the *Against Celsus*, his last written work produced years later in Caesarea.[109]

I consider the four documents or parts of documents discussed in this section to be transitional pieces in Origen's move from Alexandria to Caesarea. In the books of the commentaries on John and Genesis written in this period Origen is still living in Alexandria intellectually and continuing the arguments with the Valentinians he had begun there. It is difficult to identify Origen's intellectual framework in terms of Alexandria or Caesarea in the *On Prayer*. There are certainly Alexandrian elements in it; there is nothing, in my view at least, that one would have to label Caesarean. The *Exhortation to Martyrdom* was written for a specific situation that developed after Origen's arrival in Caesarea. He had been no stranger to persecution and martyrdoms during his time in Alexandria, however, and had certainly thought much about it there. His earliest known writing, as Eusebius has related it, was the letter of encouragement he wrote to his father when the latter was in prison awaiting martyrdom (*H.E.* 6.2.6). There are other hints in the treatise that connect Origen's thought with Alexandria. When he discusses Matthew 19:29 about the multiplication of relationships that those will experience who have left family members, homes, and lands he notes that it does not include a wife, because Matthew 22:30 says that there will be no marrying after the resurrection. He had known Christians in Alexandria who expected to marry after the resurrection.[110] He also indicates that

---

[109] *Cels* Prol. 1, 3.1, 4.1, 5.1, 6.1, 7.1, 8.76.

[110] *ExhMart* 16; *Princ* 2.11.2. Had Origen read Lk 18:29–30, however, he would have seen that the Lukan account does include wives in the list of those left behind.

the renunciation of other gods in Joshua 24:14–15 had been a part of the catechetical instruction that Ambrose had received in Alexandria and that he would have responded to it in the words of Joshua 24:16, "May we never forsake the Lord to serve other gods" (*ExhMart* 17). So the *Exhortation* too, perhaps, should best be considered a Caesarean writing with significant roots in Alexandria.

8

Origen as Preacher in Caesarea

Preaching plunged Origen into the life of the Christian community in Caesarea. Sometime after the persecution by Maximinus had ended, probably
between 239 and 244, Theoctistus gave Origen the responsibility of delivering the homilies in the three-year liturgical cycle of the Church. This
included a daily morning non-eucharistic assembly, Monday through Saturday, in which an Old Testament text was read and a homily was delivered
on the text. Both believers and catechumens were in attendance at these
assemblies. On Sundays, and Wednesday and Friday evenings, there were
eucharistic services in which the Gospels were read and a homily was delivered on the Gospel text. The eucharistic services on Wednesday and Friday
evenings celebrated the end of the fast on those two days each week (*Hom-
Lev* 10.2). The eucharistic services were for believers. Catechumens were
allowed to attend services involving the reading of the Gospels only in the
final weeks before their baptism. The readings of the Old Testament and
the Gospels proceeded systematically through the Scriptures so that their
entirety was covered in the three-year cycle.[1]

On the basis of some cross-references in the homilies, Nautin argued
that Origen's homilies on the Old Testament began with the Psalms and
the Wisdom literature, proceeded to the prophetic books, and ended with
the historical books of Genesis through Judges. The list is not complete
and we do not know if Origen did not complete the cycle, or if the other
homilies have simply not been preserved.[2] Only 20 homilies on Jeremiah
and one on 1 Samuel have been preserved in the Greek language in which
Origen delivered them. There are translations into Latin by Rufinus of 16
homilies on Genesis, 13 on Exodus, 16 on Leviticus, 28 on Numbers, 26
on Joshua, nine on Judges, one on 1 Samuel, and nine on Psalms. There
are also translations into Latin by Jerome of two homilies on the Song of
Songs, nine on Isaiah, 14 on Jeremiah, 14 on Ezekiel, and 39 on Luke. There

---

[1] This reconstruction follows Nautin (1977), 389–409. For my more complete summary of
Nautin's arguments see *Origen: Homilies on Genesis and Exodus* (1981), 19–24.

[2] Nautin (1977), 403–5; *Origen: Homilies on Genesis and Exodus* (1981), 22. For a list of Origen's homilies see Jerome, *Ep* 33.4.6–9.

may also be some additional homilies on the psalms, for Peri has argued that Jerome's 59 homilies on the psalms are little more than translations of some of Origen's homilies.[3]

In Origen's first homily on the thirty-sixth psalm he refers to a ruler whose rule flourished 30 years ago and then withered "like the flower of the grass", to be followed "by another, then another, and another", all of whom had their glory that also withered and was scattered like dust, so that no vestige remains of it (*HomPs 36* 1.2). Nautin has suggested that the man to whom Origen refers who ruled 30 years ago was Septimius Severus.[4] Origen refers to four rulers in this paragraph, all of whom had their moments of glory, he says, and then faded. I think he is referring to the four Severan rulers: Septimius, Caracalla, Elagabalus, and Alexander, skipping over the usurper Macrinus who ruled only one year after he had murdered Caracalla. Septimius Severus died in February 211. The latest date for Origen's sermon, then, if he was using Septimius' death as his point of reference, would be 241. If Origen's preaching at Caesarea began with the Psalms, as Nautin thinks, and if Jerome's list of Origen's homilies on the psalms is complete, his first homily on the thirty-sixth Psalm was his seventeenth homily. Jerome's list begins with the third psalm and skips several, so it may not be complete.[5] On the other hand, Origen surely did not deliver a homily on each of the 150 psalms. The homilies on the other Old Testament books that are preserved have gaps, and sometimes lengthy ones, between the texts of the homilies. It seems to me that we can be relatively confident that the homilies on the thirty-sixth psalm were fairly close to the beginning of Origen's preaching in Caesarea.[6]

ORIGEN'S HOMILIES IN THE SETTING OF CAESAREA'S JEWISH COMMUNITY

One of the things that Origen was thrown into when he took on the responsibility of preaching in Caesarea was a confrontation with the vigorous rabbinic community there. He refers, in one of his early homilies, to the hostility of the Synagogue to the Church. In explaining Psalm 36:1, he quotes and comments on Deuteronomy 32:21, "They have made me

---

[3] Peri (1980), 7–28; Rondeau (1982), 158–61; Heine (forthcoming a).
[4] Nautin (1977), 404.
[5] See n. 2 above.
[6] See Torjesen (1986), 87.

jealous with what is not God and irritated me with their idols; I will make them jealous of a race which is not a race." Origen identifies the "race which is not a race" as the Christians.

Why is it, [he asks], that even now the Jews are not stirred up against the pagans, nor do they hate or grow angry at those who worship idols and blaspheme God, but they have an insatiable hatred of Christians, who have at least forsaken idols and turned to God? In this respect, at least, even if they would not grant in another, the Jews have become like the pagans. Therefore, when you see Jews acting hatefully and in a hostile manner against Christians, know that that prophecy is being fulfilled which says, 'And I will stir them up against those who are not a race.' For we are not a race. Some of us have become believers from one city and others from another, but never, from the beginning of the Christian faith, has a whole race adopted it. We are not a single, whole race, like the Jews or the Egyptians; we have been gathered from individual races here and there. Therefore it says, 'I will make them jealous of a people who are not a race and will provoke them by a foolish race.' And, therefore, they are provoked by us and hate us as if we were a foolish race. They claim to be wise themselves, because the oracles of God were entrusted first to them, and they think about the law of God from childhood to old age and have not, like Christians, just come upon the law of God. But for this very reason 'God chose the foolish things of this world that he might confound the wise' and in this way the statement is fulfilled, 'I will provoke them by a foolish race'.[7]

This homily must have some connection with Christian experience in Caesarea, including Origen's own. Homilies have to connect with the lives of the people to whom they are addressed. If the people in Origen's audience had never experienced any hostility from the Jewish community, they would have left shaking their heads and wondering about the new priest from Alexandria. Origen's reference in this text to the Jewish claim to be wise because of their long-standing relationship with the oracles of God may be reflected also in his comments noted in the preceding chapter about Jewish teachers in Caesarea who were called wise men or sages.[8]

Origen refers again to Jewish persecution of Christians in a homily on Judges, where he says that heretics, who once were a part of the Church, join with pagans and Jews in persecuting Christians (*HomJdg* 8.1). In commenting on Psalm 119:98, "You made me wiser than my enemies concerning your commandment", Origen says,

He calls those enemies who lay claim to the commandments and hate us. They are the Jews of the circumcision, people towards whom we have no enmity. For the

---

[7] *HomPs* 36 1.1; cf. *HomJer* 19.12, and *ComRom* 8.6.
[8] See Chapter 7, in "The Jewish Community in Caesarea", p. 147.

Christian was "made wiser" than these "concerning the commandment" of God because the Christian understands and keeps the law spiritually. On this basis I perceive a deeper meaning in the Lord's words, "Love your enemies", for those who have "a zeal for God but not in accordance with knowledge" are our enemies.[9]

In other homilies Origen alludes to Jewish dismissal of the Gospels and apostolic writings of the Christians (*HomGen* 13.2), and includes Jews with Greeks, philosophers, and common people who speak against the Christians and condemn Jesus (*HomJer* 14.8). In a fragment from what was probably a homily on 1 Corinthians[10] delivered in Caesarea in which he discussed the Pauline statement that no one who speaks in the Spirit of God says "Jesus is accursed", Origen relates this to the Jews.

If you should ever see a Jew interpreting the divine Scriptures and not treating the prophetic words pejoratively as most do, the question may arise if the Spirit of God is in him. So that you may not be in doubt whether the Holy Spirit is in such a person or not, Paul teaches that since every Jew says "Jesus is accursed", and no one speaking in the Spirit of God says, "Jesus is accursed", the person who claims to understand the law and the prophets but curses Jesus does not have the Spirit of God.[11]

Paul, of course, does not say in 1 Corinthians 12:3 that "*every Jew* says 'Jesus is accursed'". There is nothing in the Pauline context to suggest that Paul was thinking of the Jews at all. The application comes from Origen and must have arisen from his experience with the Synagogue in Caesarea.

In Caesarea Origen was forced to think theologically about the relationship between Jews and Christians in ways that he had not had to do in Alexandria. There, in my opinion at least, most of Origen's contacts with Jews were with those who were Christians, such as those who used the *Gospel according to the Hebrews*, and the important teacher in his early life whom he calls simply "the Hebrew". In Caesarea, however, Origen was in contact with a large, vibrant Jewish community. This may be why it is in Caesarea rather than Alexandria that he gives more serious attention to the Pauline epistles, where issues of Jews and Christians are treated in Scripture.[12] It was in Caesarea, at least, that he wrote all his commentaries on Pauline

---

[9] *La chaîne palestinienne sur le psaume* 118 (1972), Vol. 1, 346.

[10] There is no mention of any works by Origen on 1 Corinthians in the ancient literature. Jerome refers to commentaries on several Pauline epistles but mentions none on Corinthians. Among the homilies he refers to 11 on 2 Corinthians but does not mention any on 1 Corinthians (Jerome, *Ep* 33.4).

[11] *Frag1Cor* 47. Text in *Exegetica in Paulum Excerpta et Fragmenta* (2009), 172.

[12] On Origen's attitude towards and use of the Pauline epistles in Alexandria see Chapter 2, in "Christian literature of the second century associated with Alexandria", p. 34.

epistles, including his important commentary on Romans which we will consider in the next chapter.

Not only Origen, but also the people to whom he preached were in regular contact with Jews in Caesarea and some, at least, had some knowledge of Jewish practices and had not figured out completely how to distinguish the two groups religiously. He refers to Christian women who do not bathe on the Sabbath in keeping with Jewish laws, and who eat unleavened bread at Passover (*HomJer* 12.13). Some of Origen's congregation clearly knew the practices of the Synagogue. The law of the Sabbath in Exodus 20 forbids work. The *Mishnah*, however, which had been compiled at the end of the second century, gives specific directions for things forbidden and permitted on the Sabbath. One forbidden thing was entering a bath-house.[13] The Christian women in Caesarea who would not bathe on the Sabbath learned this law from the local Synagogue and not from reading or hearing the Old Testament read. Origen also suggests in a comment on Exodus 12:46 that some Christians in Caesarea may have been in the habit of attending Synagogue services in addition to the services of the Church.[14] In a homily on Leviticus 16 he refers to people in his audience who think they should keep the Jewish fast on the Day of Atonement. "It is necessary now", he says, "to make a few remarks also to those who think that they too must observe the Jewish fast because of the command in the Law" (*HomLev* 10.2; cf. *HomJer* 12.13). Leviticus 16, which describes the activities on the Day of Atonement, is not explicit about fasting. Leviticus 16:29 had been understood by the Jews to refer to fasting on that day.[15] The *Mishnah*,

---

[13] *The Mishnah* (1933/1958), 100 (Shabbath 1.1).

[14] *PG* 12.285D; see Lange (1976), 86, 93; Bietenhard (1974), 50–1. Lange (1976), 86 also cites *HomLev* 5.8 as a text showing that Origen knew Christians who went "to Synagogue on Saturday and to Church on Sunday". He quotes the text as follows: "'The literal interpretation of the Bible is stale; the Christian interpretation is fresh 'If you produce in church today what you learnt from the Jews yesterday, that is to 'eat the meat of yesterday's sacrifice'." I do not think this indicates that Origen is thinking of someone who had been in the Synagogue the day before. For one thing, it comes from a homily on Leviticus which was not one of the texts used for the Sunday homilies (see beginning of this chapter) so that the reference to yesterday would not be to the Sabbath. For another, Origen appears to address these words to priests. He says, "Hear these words all you who are priests of the Lord and give attention to what is said." He then equates the flesh of the sacrifices which the priests received with the word of God which they offer to the Church. They are not to bring "yesterday's" word to the Church. "Yesterday" refers to the literal understanding of Scripture, which Origen equates with the Jewish way of reading Scripture. What they learned "yesterday from the Jews" is a reference to the literal understanding of Scripture, which, Origen says, is not to be offered as food to the Church.

[15] See the note to Lev 16:29 in *The HarperCollins Study Bible, Revised Edition* (2006), 175, where the understanding of *Targum Pseudo-Jonathan* is cited. This understanding is at least as old as Acts 27:9, where "the fast" must refer to the Day of Atonement.

however, forbids eating and drinking on the Day of Atonement.[16] Origen and his audience in the Caesarean Church were in close enough contact with the local Synagogue that they were aware of their religious laws and observances. They were getting their understanding of some of the Jewish law from the practices of the contemporary Synagogue.

When Origen's situation in Caesarea is understood, then the importance of his approach to the Law becomes more understandable. It may be that he had to defend the use of the Law in the Church as well as show how Christians read it differently from the Jews. He begins his tenth homily on Leviticus by asserting that it is proper for the Church to use the writings of Moses because it believes that Moses was a prophet and consequently wrote about future mysteries which were revealed to him in "symbols, figures, and allegories". The Law, he argues following Hebrews 9:10, was valid until "the time of the new order comes". It was like the clay figures which craftsmen make prior to casting the intended images in metal. It is a preliminary necessity, but once the intended work is completed, the clay image loses its value. Origen did not think, however, that the Jewish Scriptures became completely useless with the coming of Christ. They became useless read in their literal sense concerning laws and practices, but they continued to function in the role of prophecy and type.[17] Origen addresses the issue of the Christian way to read the Law, again, in the prologue to a homily on Exodus (*HomEx* 5.1). Here he appeals to the way Paul reads the law in 1 Corinthians 10:1–4. The literal reading and interpretation of the Law makes people Jews, not Christians, he argues. Paul was aware of this and gave a few examples of how Christians should read the Law. Christians should learn from these Pauline examples and apply the principles Paul used in them to the texts of the Law in general.

In some of his homilies Origen reflects, similar to Paul in Romans 9–11, on why non-Jews can now claim to be heirs to the promises made to the Jews and think that God has disinherited the original heirs. "How does it fall to me," he asks, "born it matters not where, a stranger to the so-called holy land, now to preach about the promises of God, and believe in the God of the patriarchs Abraham, Isaac, and Jacob, and, by the grace of God, to accept Jesus Christ who was proclaimed previously by the prophets" (*HomJer* 4.2)? In this particular homily he distinguishes between Israel, whom God divorced, and Judah, who is identified with the Christians

---

[16] *The Mishnah* (1933/1958), 171–2 (Yoma 8.1).
[17] *HomLev* 10.1. Origen may be dependent on Melito of Sardis for this comparison; see Heine (2007), 55.

because Christ descended from Judah.[18] To his credit, Origen continues to follow the storyline in Jeremiah 3 and notes that Judah did not learn from the fate of Israel but continued sinning. This leads him to introduce the Pauline warning from Romans 11:21, "If he did not spare the natural branches, how less likely is it that he will spare us" (*HomJer* 4.4)? Origen concludes this homily by expressing the hope that he and his hearers will live according to the Biblical teachings so that when the "fullness of the Gentiles has been saved, then Israel, too, can enter. For," he adds, quoting Paul again with a statement from John, "'Once the fullness of the Gentiles has entered, then all Israel will be saved,' 'and they will be one flock, one shepherd' teaching us to glorify Christ Jesus himself, to whom be glory and might for ever and ever."[19] In another homily he reflects on this same statement of Paul about the salvation of Israel after the "fullness of the Gentiles has entered", and there he refers to the delayed perfection of Israel (*HomJosh* 26.2). Origen was convinced that the present attitude of the Jews towards the church was a part of God's plan. He was also convinced that this was a temporary attitude and that there would come a time when, as Paul says in Romans 11:26, "All Israel will be saved." This issue is discussed in a fragment of a homily on Luke's Gospel, where the story of the healing of the hemorrhaging woman and the raising of Jairus' daughter are interpreted as symbols of the Christian-Jewish question.

How is it, [Origen asks], that Jesus went off to the daughter of the ruler of the synagogue first, and not to the hemorrhaging woman who met him on the way? And how is it that, although he went off to the former first, the latter was the first healed? For the Son of God came first to the daughter of the ruler of the synagogue, that is, to the synagogue of the Jews, and he found her sick and dying, for the transgressions of Israel were causing her to die. But the hemorrhaging woman who met him on the way, who was full of impurity and who bled "not in her menstrual cycle" (Lev 15:25) but continually, and was sick with a scarlet sin, was the church from the Gentiles. The latter believed in the Son of God before the former. And where he goes, she follows, wishing to touch even "the hem of his garment". Luke adds something that Matthew does not mention, that the daughter of the ruler of the synagogue was twelve years old and that the hemorrhaging woman had been hemorrhaging twelve years. She began hemorrhaging, therefore, at the time the former was born. For she lived in disobedience as long as the synagogue was alive. And her salvation begins at the same time that the former reaches her end. For she is dead for twelve years and the hemorrhaging woman who has believed is healed from her suffering for twelve years. No physician had been able to heal her, for

---

[18] See also *HomJer* 18.4–5.
[19] *HomJer* 4.6; cf. 5.4; 18.5; *HomJosh* 11.3.

many physicians had attempted to heal the Gentiles. The philosophers, for instance, who promised truth, were physicians trying to heal her. But though she spent all her money, none of the physicians were able to heal her. But when she touched the hem of Jesus, who is the only physician of souls and bodies, she was healed immediately by her fiery, hot faith. If we consider our faith in Christ Jesus and think of how great the Son of God is and what we have touched of him, we will see that in comparison to all his hems, we have touched a (single) hem, but nevertheless, that hem heals us and allows us to hear Jesus say, "Daughter, your faith has saved you." And if we are healed, the daughter of the ruler of the synagogue will also be raised, for it says, "When the fullness of the Gentiles shall enter, then all Israel will be saved" (Rom 11:25).[20]

He also uses the Pauline image of the grafting of the wild olive branch onto the root of the good olive tree to express the relationship between Church and Synagogue. We, he says, who formerly worshipped gods of stone have been grafted, down to the present day, onto the root of the faith of the patriarchs (*HomJosh* 7.5).

Bietenhard asked if Origen, in his discussions of Romans 9–11, understood that Paul is treating the problem of the Church and Israel, or if he saw these chapters only as treating the problem of predestination and free will. He answered that, "In the approach and execution of his exegesis, Origen grasped . . . the Pauline intention." Origen saw, he said, that in these three chapters Paul is discussing the Church and Israel, and more precisely he is asking if God had cast off the Jews or not, and if they still had a future and hope.[21]

While Origen speaks of hostilities and hatred of Jews against Christians, and warns his congregation against observing Jewish customs, attending Synagogue services, and reading the Scriptures in a literal way as the Jews do, he also knows that Christians and Jews belong to the same family. They have the same ancestors in the faith. They look to the same Scriptures for instruction, and address the same God in prayer. Before a person can come to baptism in the church he must first have been purified by the Law. Moses is always with Jesus; the Law is always with the Gospels (*HomLev* 6.2). Some Christians had suggested taking God's promise to Abraham that his descendants would be as numerous as the "stars of heaven" to mean the Christians, and the reference to their multitude as the "sand of the seashore" to mean the Jews, giving Christians a higher standing than the Jews. Origen rejects this, insisting that each metaphor can be applied to

---

[20] *Origenes Werke: Die Homilien zu Lukas* (1959), 278–9; *FragLk* 125. See the discussion of this passage in Vogt (1974), 198–9.

[21] Bietenhard (1974), 61.

each people because there had been many righteous men and prophets among the former Jews and there were numerous corrupt people among Christians (*HomGn* 9.2). In a homily on the Song of Songs, he asserts that Synagogue and Church are sisters, and that our Savior is the son of our sister, the Synagogue (*HomCant* 2.3). Origen can argue with the Jews, but he cannot ultimately reject either them or their Scriptures. As Bietenhard remarks, "Origen himself is no enemy of the Jews; he cannot be, because he understood Romans 9–11."[22]

THE AUDIENCE ORIGEN ADDRESSED IN HIS HOMILIES

I noted above that there was a daily morning service, Monday through Saturday, during which the Old Testament was read and a homily was delivered on at least a portion of the text read. The books of the Old Testament were read consecutively in their entirety, probably two or three chapters a day.[23] This reading would have covered the entire Old Testament in approximately three years. *The Apostolic Tradition* of Hippolytus, which may reflect the tradition at Rome in the third century, states that catechumens were to be instructed for three years. This may have reference to attendance at these daily morning services where both catechumens and believers were present, for in the immediately following section in the *Tradition* catechumens are instructed to pray apart from the faithful at the end of the teacher's lesson and, at the end of the prayer, they are not to share in the kiss of peace with the baptized.[24] This implies that both believers and catechumens were in attendance during the instruction.

Origen's Old Testament homilies were clearly not for catechumens alone. Junod noted that the level of the homilies is amazingly high and that Origen placed "great intellectual, moral, and spiritual demands on the Church" in his homilies. He concluded that they were for "the whole Church", including bishops and clerics as well as catechumens.[25] Catechumens were, nevertheless, among those addressed, as some of the passages in Origen's homilies make clear. In his fourth homily on Joshua, which is about Israel crossing the Jordan, he refers to some who are pre-catechumens. He addresses them

---

[22] Ibid., 72.
[23] In his homily on 1 Kings 28 Origen indicates that 1 Kings 25–8 had been read prior to his homily (*Hom1Kg (1Sam)*1).
[24] *The Apostolic Tradition of St Hippolytus of Rome* (1937), 28–9 (sections 17–18). See also *Origen: Homilies on Luke* (1996), xix–xx.
[25] Junod (1994), 78.

as people who are in the process of leaving Egypt. They are obviously non-Jews, for he says they have forsaken idolatry and desire to hear the divine law. Becoming a catechumen involved an initial step of repentance which, for the Gentiles in Caesarea, meant turning away from idolatry, and which Origen characteristically referred to as leaving Egypt (see *HomIs* 1.1). "When you have been added to the number of the catechumens", he says, "and you undertake to submit to the rules of the Church, you have parted the Red Sea and, placed in the encampments of the desert, you apply yourself daily to hearing the law of God and looking on the face of Moses which has been unveiled for the sake of the glory of the Lord" (*HomJosh* 4.1). It is implicit here that the catechumens were expected to be present for the daily readings and homilies on the Law. In these the "veil" that Paul said lies on the face of Moses when the Law is read in the Synagogue (2 Cor. 3:13–16) is removed by the Christian interpretation, and the glory that shone from Moses' face when he descended from being with God can be seen. "But", Origen adds, "when you have come to the mystical font of baptism...then, when the Jordan has been parted by the ministries of the priests, you will enter the land of promise in which Jesus receives you after Moses, and he himself becomes the leader of a new way for you." Here Origen ties two points in the Joshua story to the experience of the catechumens. First, baptism in the Church is administered by the priests, just as it was the ministry of the priests at the Jordan that parted the waters and allowed Israel to cross on dry land. Second, in the Greek translation of the Hebrew Old Testament, Joshua's name is Jesus. It is Joshua/Jesus who leads the people after they cross the Jordan. Moses had died and Joshua had been in charge of Israel prior to the crossing of the Jordan, but Origen, probably because of his use of the crossing the Jordan to symbolize baptism, takes this as the symbolic shift in which the people now look to Joshua rather than Moses. Here Origen's symbolism may have more than one level of meaning. One thing he certainly means is that once a person has been baptized Jesus is the one to whom the person looks from that time on—not to Moses or to any other. He may, at a secondary level, also be suggesting to the catechumens that once they have been baptized they will be a part of the Gospel services of the Church, not just the non-eucharistic services which presented the Old Testament Scriptures.[26] Origen continues to address catechumens, though not exclusively, in the next homily on Joshua. He takes up the battles that

---

[26] For other places where Origen refers directly to catechumens see *HomJosh* 9.9; *HomJer* 27.3, 6; *HomCant* 2.7; *HomLk* 7.8; 21.4; 22.6; 32.6; *HomEz* 5.4; 6.5, 7; 7.4. For some places where he seems to address catechumens, but the term itself does not appear see *HomGn* 10.5; 13.4; *HomJdg* 6.2; *HomIs* 1.1.

await one after baptism. Using the words of Paul in Ephesians 6:12 about battles against principalities and powers, he fashions a kind of template to place over the stories in Joshua that relate the Israelites' battles against the inhabitants of Canaan. The Canaanites are interiorized as the demonic powers which wage war against the new Christian.[27] Origen was, in a sense, warning new converts of what Robert Frost called the frightening possibilities of one's own "desert places".[28]

Beyond catechumens, Origen's congregation at Caesarea was a mixed group.[29] First, it should be noted that there were people to whom he preached who either owned or had access to copies of Scripture where they could reread at their leisure the text Origen had discussed in his homily. He apologizes, in concluding a homily, that he does not have time to discuss all the mysteries in the text considered for the day but, he adds, the hearers may reread the text and dispel some of its mystery by their own inquiries (*HomGen* 10.5). In another homily he encourages his hearers to show some initiative when they read Scripture and apply their own understanding to bring out Scripture's meaning (*HomGen* 12.5). Those in the priesthood who may have been present would certainly have had access to a copy of the Septuagint in the Church. But there must have been others also who had invested in such a large body of codices. This speaks to the level of wealth of some in the Christian community in Caesarea as well as to the level of their education. There were those in his audience who had been educated in the sciences (*HomGen* 13.3). Perhaps it was some of these owners of Scriptural texts who, Origen says, loved the letter of the Law and brought "malicious charges" against his allegorical interpretations, arguing that the truth depends on the literal meaning of the text.[30]

Some who heard Origen preach in Caesarea were priests.[31] He rebukes priests who are lenient towards Christians who sin because they fear what might be said about them.

You who preside over the Church are the eye of Christ's body, [he says], ... You are a pastor; you see the lambs of the Lord unaware of danger to be carried to precipices and suspended over steep places. Do you not run? Do you not call them back? Do you not at least restrain them with your voice and deter them with a shout of reproof?[32]

---

[27] *HomJosh* 5.1–2; 1.7; 13.1; 14.1, 2; 15.1.
[28] "Desert Places", in *The Poetry of Robert Frost* (1969), 296.
[29] See Junod (1994), 57.
[30] *HomGn* 13.3; trans. in *Origen: Homilies on Genesis and Exodus* (1981), 189.
[31] See *HomJer* 12.3, for example.
[32] *HomJosh* 7.6; trans in *Origen: Homilies on Joshua* (2002), 81.

The direct address in these statements demands that there were people in his audience who had the responsibility of looking after the spiritual well-being of others in the Christian community. He addresses priests again when he warns them on the basis of Leviticus 7:5 against bringing the meat of "yesterday's" offering to the Church. This means they should not offer the old, that is, the literal, meaning of the text to the Church, but the new, spiritual meaning (*HomLev* 5.8). Those priests whose lives are moral, who know sound doctrine, and who can communicate the truth of the faith, not only have the name "priest", but deserve the name (*HomLev* 6.6). Jeremiah teaches, he says, that priests must live worthily of their position (*HomJer* 11.3). Frequently, however, they treat their office as a source of pride rather than performing their functions with humility (*HomEz* 9.2). God will demand more of the priests than of the laity because of the responsibility of their office.[33] Some priests seem to have been addicted to wine, for Origen insists that the commands of Leviticus against drunkenness in the priesthood are to be maintained in their literal sense (*HomLev* 7.1).

Hippolytus claimed that Callistus, bishop of Rome from 218–22, regarded the Church to be a kind of Noah's ark which contained both clean and unclean animals.[34] Origen must have found the Christian community in Caesarea, to his chagrin, to have resembled Noah's ark. He knew of Christians who still consulted astrologers and augurs in their attempts to know the future, and who maintained other superstitions (*HomJosh* 5.6; 7.4). Some of the people to whom he preached attended pagan spectacles for entertainment (*HomLev* 11.1), and preferred the circus, horse races, and athletic competitions to hearing the Word of God (*HomLev* 9.7, 9)—Caesarea had a theater, an amphitheater, and quinquennial games from its inception (Josephus, *Wars* 1.415). He reproaches his hearers for concentrating on their flesh instead of their spirit. They cannot plead that they were overcome by fleshly stimuli; they themselves provide the stimuli. They have a fixation on luxury and food, and drink wine in excess. He compares some of the Christians in Caesarea to the Gibeonites in Joshua 9 who deceived the Israelites. They believe in God and show deference to the ministers of the Church but make no attempt to alter the habits of their previous lives.[35] Others rarely put in an appearance at the services of the Church, and when they do, they spend their time gossiping rather than listening to the Word of God (*HomJosh* 1.7).

---

[33] *HomJer* 11.3; *HomEz* 5.4; *FragJer* 50.
[34] *Haer* 9.12.23.
[35] *HomJosh* 10.1; see Völker (1966/1930), 22–3.

Women are rebuked for chattering, interrupting, and having their minds on domestic duties (*HomEx* 13.3). Some people listened to the reading of the Biblical texts but left before the homily explaining the texts was delivered (*HomEx* 12.2).

The tenth homily on Genesis seems to mark a breaking point in Origen's patience with his audience. He spends an extended amount of time speaking directly to their laxity in relation to worship and spiritual matters. Some, he complains, show up at the Church only on feast days and then it is only to enjoy the festival and relax. They have time, he complains, for doing business in the marketplace, for prosecuting lawsuits, and even for visiting the countryside, but few of them, he says, have time for God. Even when they are present, he adds, they gossip, with their backs turned when the Scripture is read. The words of Scripture which have been read to them are mystical, but he is hesitant to explain their secrets for fear that he would be throwing pearls on deaf ears. They may think he is being harsh with them but, he concludes, he "cannot 'whitewash' a falling 'wall'".[36] Origen's irritation at his congregation's laxity towards hearing the word of God comes out again later in the homily. Here he recognizes that what he is saying does not apply to everyone in his congregation. Some, he says "are always present" for the preaching of the word. But others, like the Jews, only observe infrequent festive days.[37]

I think we cannot conclude that Origen was completely happy with his experience of preaching in Caesarea. The lifestyle of much of his congregation was frustrating to the ideals he had for them. Origen saw the life of the Christian as a journey, moving, like that of the Israelites, from Egypt to the promised land. He recognized, again like the Israelites, that this journey was one of constant struggle against powerful adversaries. But he also thought that one should engage in it with all the energies at one's disposal.

> For what good is it for us to have gone forth from Egypt and yet carry around with us the reproaches of Egypt? What good is it to travel through the wilderness, that is, what does it help us to have renounced this age in baptism but to retain the former filth of our behavior and the impurities of our carnal vices? Thus it is fitting, after the parting of the Red Sea, that is, after the grace of baptism, for the carnal vices of our old habits to be removed from us by means of our Lord Jesus, so that we can be free from the Egyptian reproaches.[38]

---

[36] *HomGn* 10.1; trans. in *Origen: Homilies on Genesis and Exodus* (1981), 158; see also *HomEx* 12.2.

[37] *ComGn* 10.3; trans. in *Origen: Homilies on Genesis and Exodus* (1981), 162.

[38] *HomJosh* 26.2; trans. in *Origen: Homilies on Joshua* (2002), 216.

THE GOAL OF ORIGEN'S HOMILIES

Junod has shown that in his homilies Origen's concern is to edify the Church, not to explain the meaning of texts. In the commentaries he focuses on the details of the Biblical text, but in the homilies he chooses for comment those elements in the Biblical text that will let him address topics he considers important to building up the Church.[39] Torjesen has argued convincingly that the organizing center of Origen's homilies is the concept of the journey of the soul.[40] This journey, at the theoretical level at least, consists of three stages: purification, knowledge, and perfection.[41] In Origen's actual exposition within the homilies, however, where he "accommodates himself to the material content of the text", she notes, "there is a multiplicity and diversity of individual steps which are difficult if not impossible to organize into a strict program".[42]

Building up the Church, for Origen, meant administering lessons that were severe as well as those that were instructive and encouraging. He compares the "doubled scarlet" that was offered for the construction of the tabernacle to Christian teaching. The scarlet color suggests fire to him, and fire, he says has double power—heat and light. Christian teaching, he asserts, burns and enlightens at the same time.[43] This appears in a sermon on Exodus, which means that Origen had held the preaching office in Caesarea for some time and had already preached through the Psalms, the Wisdom literature, the prophets, and Genesis. He had already experienced the painful as well as the rewarding aspects of the preaching office. To build up the Church, sins had to be condemned and sinners confronted. In an earlier homily Origen speaks of prophets and teachers in general, but he must be thinking of his own activity in the Christian community in Caesarea. He compares them to physicians and says they are always with the sick and wounded, never with the healthy. Furthermore, those they try to help hate them and want to avoid them. They think of the pain inflicted by the surgeon rather than the healing that follows the pain.[44] Like Paul, the preacher must occasionally make his audience weep for their sins (*HomJer* 20.6).

---

[39] Junod (1994), 65–81; see also Markschies (1997), 60–2, 67–8. See *HomLev* 1.1; 5.12; 7.1, 4; 14.1; *HomEx* 2.4; 4.5; *HomNum* 14.1, etc.

[40] Torjesen (1986), 70–107.

[41] Ibid., 71–3.

[42] Ibid., 77.

[43] *HomEx* 13.4. Origen makes a similar observation on the twofold power of the sun in *ComCant* 2.2.16–18.

[44] *HomJer* 14.1; see Junod (1994), 72.

One of the concepts that Origen refers to regularly in speaking of the soul is that of the image of God. We were made in God's image and we carry that image within ourselves, although it is often unseen. The Son of God, he states, like a great artist, has painted that image within us. We cannot destroy it, but we can obscure it. We paint the "image of the earthly" over it with a brushstroke of covetousness which darkens it, and another of rage, and another of pride, and impiety, and malice. In this way we ourselves paint an image which God did not paint. We need, therefore, the help of the God who says through Isaiah, "Behold I blot out your iniquities as a cloud", so that once the colors with which we concealed the image have been blotted out it can shine forth as it was first created.[45] The reconstructing of the human self as the image of God is the goal of the soul's journey.

Origen uses the metaphors and figures of the Biblical text that the liturgical cycle has dictated for his sermons to develop this journey. In his sermons on the Octateuch it is the activities of the patriarchs, the deliverance of the Israelites from slavery in Egypt, their experiences in the wilderness, and their struggles in the promised land that provide the imagery. The words of Exodus 20:2 are addressed to every soul that has come to despise Egypt, which is the present age: "I am the Lord your God, who brought you out of the land of Egypt" (NRSV). "Egypt", Origen says, "is 'the house of bondage'. But Judaea and Jerusalem are the house of freedom." The overriding metaphor in these homilies is that of the journey from bondage to freedom and the battles that must be fought in winning and retaining that freedom. The same character of metaphor is continued in the homilies on the prophetic books, except that the names change. In the homilies on Jeremiah and Ezekiel the names Nebuchadnezzar and the Prince of Tyre may designate the ruler of this world, as well as Pharaoh, and Babylon may be substituted for Egypt to refer to the realm controlled by the devil.[46]

In other homilies the metaphors change in keeping with the contents of the Biblical readings. In the prologue to the first homily on the Song of Songs Origen uses the metaphor of singing the songs found in the Old Testament to set forth the soul's progress. There the journey begins with singing the song of Moses after crossing the Red Sea, that is, after experiencing Christian baptism (Ex 15:1–21). But the person who sings this song is "still a long way from the Song of Songs".[47] One must continue the "spiritual journey through the wilderness" to the song sung at the well dug by the

---

[45] *HomGen* 13.4; trans. in *Origen: Homilies on Genesis and Exodus* (1981), 193; cf. *HomJer* 2.1; Torjesen (1986), 51–2, 78, 85.

[46] See, for example, *HomJer* 28.1–2; *HomEz* 13.

[47] *HomCant* 1.1; trans. in *Origen: The Song of Songs Commentary and Homilies* (1957), 266.

kings (Num 21:17–18). From there one goes on to the bank of the Jordan
to sing with Moses the song in Deuteronomy 32. Next, one sings the song
of Debborah after fighting to conquer the holy land (Judges 5). The next
song on the journey is that of David when Saul tried to kill him (2 Kings
22), followed by Isaiah's song of the vineyard (Isaiah 5:1–7). When one has
sung all of these songs and had the experiences connected with them, one
finally comes to sing the Song of Songs (*HomCant* 1.1).

These remarks in the prologue to the first homily point to Origen's understanding of the Song of Songs. It stands at the end of the soul's journey. This
is not teaching for catechumens or the recently baptized. This is teaching
for those who have progressed through the earlier stages of the journey and
have reached the goal. It is about the soul's longing for and anticipation of
marriage to Christ, the bridegroom (*HomCant* 2.13). In this context Origen
offers a rare comment about his own experience as a Christian. He notices
how the bridegroom is elusive in the Song of Songs. The bride catches sight
of him and then he is gone. Only someone who has experienced this can
understand it, he says. Then he offers his own testimony.

God is my witness that I have often perceived the Bridegroom drawing near me
and being most intensely present with me; then suddenly He has withdrawn and
I could not find Him, though I sought to do so. I long, therefore, for Him to come
again, and sometimes He does so. Then, when He has appeared and I lay hold of
Him, He slips away once more; and, when He has so slipped away, my search for
Him begins anew.[48]

It is difficult to say exactly what kind of experience Origen relates here.
Many have taken it to be a description of a mystical experience. I have
suggested elsewhere that it is a description of Origen's experience, perhaps mystical, in reading the Bible where sometimes he is successful in his
search for Christ in the text, and at other times he gets a brief insight, or
glimpse of Christ, but then it is gone and he must resume his search.[49] If
this level of experiencing Christ in the Biblical text was the goal towards
which Origen wished to move his congregation at Caesarea by his preaching, then it is easy to see how he became so frustrated with their lack of
interest in listening to the reading and exposition of the Biblical text in the
regular assemblies of the Church.[50]

---

[48] *HomCant* 1.7; trans. in *Origen: The Song of Songs Commentary and Homilies* (1957), 280.

[49] Heine (1997b), 143–4. It has been noted that in his most famous homilies about the spiritual ascent, the twenty-seventh homily on Numbers and the homilies on the Song of Songs,
that Origen is more concerned with overcoming the tendency to lapse than with the actual
ascent to God (Heine (1975), 245, n. 2).

[50] See the section above, "The audience Origen addressed in his homilies", p. 179.

Origen did not think of the Christian life as the achievement of a static stage of perfection. "[W]e are on a journey," he said, "and we have come into this world that we may pass from virtue to virtue."[51] Paul's statement that he is constantly pressing "on toward the goal", "forgetting what lies behind and straining forward to what lies ahead" (Phil 3:13, 14; NRSV) is a basic concept in Origen's understanding of the Christian's life. It is dynamic, rigorously pressing forward but, nevertheless, always under attack, and always liable to failure. "The just person", he says, "strains forward to what lies ahead and forgets what lies behind." At the same time Origen finds it necessary to warn against remembering "what lies behind". He cites Jesus' warnings against turning back to take a garment, about remembering Lot's wife, and about not looking back once one has put one's hand to the plow.[52] He conceived the dangers to a Christian's progress to lie on two levels, which he sometimes designated the Corinthian kind of temptations and the Ephesian kind; the former involving struggles with the flesh, the latter those of the spirit.[53] In his sermons on the Octateuch and the prophets he uses the names of places and hostile peoples to talk about the interior battles that the Christian must fight after baptism. In his sermons on the Song of Songs he depicts the longings, fulfillments, and frustrations of the Christian who has been victorious in the wars against the Canaanites, who has come out of Babylon, and who now longs for the presence of Christ like a bride longs for the sight of her absent groom.

In keeping with his understanding of the Christian life as a journey, Origen describes Christians as people who live in tents rather than houses. Houses have foundations and remain at one place. Tents are for people who are on the move and have not yet reached the end of their journey. Christians are on a journey into the wisdom of God, and the further they progress, the deeper they find it to be. "Travellers . . . on the road to God's wisdom have no houses", Origen says, "because they have not yet reached their goal. They have tents, which they carry with them on their perpetual journeys, their never-ending travels; and the further they go, the more the road before them opens out, until it stretches to infinity."[54]

---

[51] *HomNum* 27.7; trans. in *Origen: Exhortation to Martyrdom* (1979), 254.

[52] *HomJer* 13.3; cf. 18.8; *Die Fragmente aus der Prophetenkatene* 22 (*Origenes Werke* (1983), 245), ibid. 30 (ibid., 249).

[53] See Chapter 7, in "Reflections on Aspects of Piety and Faithfulness", p. 159.

[54] *HomNum* 17.4; trans. in Daniélou (1955), 303.

9

Scholarship and Teaching in Caesarea

Origen flourished as a scholar and teacher during the reign of Gordian (AD 238–44). He was 54 years old when Gordian began to rule and was at the height of his intellectual powers. The scholar, who had been educated in Alexandria, produced the abundance of his fruit in this period at Caesarea. He brought to the challenges of Caesarea his Alexandrian work on the Hexapla which compared the Septuagint, the Old Testament Bible of the Christians, with the Hebrew text and its other Jewish translations into Greek made in the second century, so that textual differences between the Biblical text used by the Jews and the Septuagint text used by the Christians were at his finger tips.[1] He also brought to his work in Caesarea the Hebrew-Christian understanding of parts of the Old Testament that he had learned from the Christian teacher in Alexandria whom he called "the Hebrew",[2] and he brought his extensive reading of Philo, which was one Jewish way of reading the law.[3]

Eusebius says it was during the reign of Gordian that Origen began receiving students at Caesarea and names Theodore, Gregory, and Athenodore as three foreign students who came to him there.[4] He also locates the composition of the commentaries on Isaiah (30 books), Ezekiel (25 books), and the Song of Songs (ten books) in the reign of Gordian. The commentaries on Isaiah and Ezekiel are lost, but the prologue and the first three books of the *Commentary on the Song of Songs* have been preserved in

---

[1] See Chapter 3, in "Origen's Hexapla", p. 73.

[2] See Chapter 2, in "The school of 'the Hebrew'", p. 56.

[3] See Chapter 2, in "Continuity between early Alexandrian Jewish Christianity and the later Alexandrian Christian community", p. 29. Runia (1993), 158, thinks Origen had taken the works of Philo to Caesarea from Alexandria and that this text is the basis of our present text of Philo. Origen cites Philo by name in his late Caesarean work *ComMt* 15.3 and says he "'enjoys a high reputation among intelligent people for many subjects discussed in his treatises on the Law of Moses'", and again in *Cels* 4.51 and 6.21 (Runia (1993), 160). For a list of anonymous references to Philo in Origen see Runia (1993), 161–3.

[4] H.E. 6.30.1. On Origen's school curriculum in Caesarea and the probable nature of the school see Chapter 2, in "The ecclesiastical school directed by Origen in Alexandria", p. 60 where the Caesarean school is treated as a reflection of Origen's teaching in Alexandria. For special studies of the school of Caesarea see Knauber (1968) and Crouzel (1970).

the Latin translation of Rufinus. Eusebius further says that Origen finished the commentary on Ezekiel in Athens and wrote the first five books of the *Commentary on the Song of Songs* there, finishing it when he returned to Caesarea (*H.E.* 6.32.1–2). We know nothing further about the visit to Athens. Eusebius does not mention the *Commentary on Romans* or the other Pauline commentaries. Origen refers to the *Commentary on Romans* in his *Commentary on Matthew* (17.32) and in the *Against Celsus* (5.47; 8.65), both of which were written in the reign of Gordian's successor Philip (Eusebius, *H.E.* 6.36.2). This shows that the *Commentary on Romans* had been composed earlier and, probably, in the reign of Gordian. The original 15 books of the Greek commentary, which have been lost, have been abbreviated to ten books in a Latin translation by Rufinus. A portion of the commentary in Greek, covering Romans 3:5–5:7, was discovered among the papyri found at Tura in 1941.[5] The other Pauline commentaries are lost except for some fragments preserved in quotations of later writers.[6] The *Commentary on Ephesians* was written before that on Romans[7] and the *Commentary on Philemon* may have been his first Pauline commentary.[8] Jerome refers also to commentaries on Galatians, Philippians, Colossians, 1 and 2 Thessalonians, and Titus (Ep 33.4). The last books of the *Commentary on John* were also written in this period—perhaps Books 19–32.[9] It was also either during the reign of Gordian or his successor Philip that Origen composed his large *Commentary on the Psalms* at Caesarea. This work is lost except for fragments excerpted by later writers.[10] It was in this same period of time that Origen probably preached the majority of his sermons at Caesarea.[11]

How could Origen produce such a vast amount of work in the space of six years? There was, in all probability, considerable overlapping in several aspects of this production. In a review of the extensive set of ancient commentaries on Aristotles' works published under the series title of *Commentaria in Aristotelem Graeca*, Praechter argued that the ancient commentaries on Aristotle are largely "transcripts from oral lectures". They are the notes of students taken during the teacher's lectures in which "the tangible traces of the oral lecture have been effaced" in preparing them for publication. One of the changes Praechter notes that took place in this editing process

---

[5] *Le commentaire d'Origène sur Rom. III.5–V.7* (1957).
[6] See Heine (2002), 1–2.
[7] Heine (2000c), 149–57.
[8] Bammel (1995), 505–6; see also Heine (2001), 433–4, and (2000a), 117–33.
[9] *Origen: Commentary on the Gospel according to John Books 13–32* (1993), 15–18.
[10] See Heine (forthcoming a).
[11] See Chapter 8.

was the elimination of direct "address in the second person plural", but, he adds, there is "the occasional overlooked passage" which betrays the original form of oral address to an audience.[12] It is noteworthy that the regular form of direct address in Origen's commentaries is second person singular. There is a first person plural, however, preserved in his rhetorical question related to John 8:37, "If anyone of *us* is seed of Abraham" (*ComJn* 20.45). This may be something that slipped through the editing process. It suggests that these words were originally addressed to a group, perhaps to Origen's students. I think a large portion, at least, of Origen's written corpus produced at Caesarea was delivered as oral address to students. Instead of students' notes, however, we should think of the notes as coming from the shorthand writers Ambrose provided for Origen.[13] These, I suggest, sat among Origen's students and took down his lectures. Eusebius says Origen permitted such transcriptions of his "public lectures" by shorthand writers after he was 60 years old. This is usually taken to be a statement about the recording of Origen's preaching, but there is nothing in the statement that would limit it to that. It is probable, as Nautin argues,[14] that Eusebius has Origen's age incorrect and that it was near the beginning of Gordian's reign that this happened. Eusebius admits that he is relying on hearsay evidence (*H.E.* 6.36.1). I think that early in the reign of Gordian Origen began to use Ambrose's shorthand writers to take down his lectures both in his school and in the Church and that Origen then edited the transcripts before the calligraphers produced the final copies for publication. The *Panegyric to Origen* delivered by his student Gregory on departing the school in Caesarea shows traces of statements that appear in Books 20 and 32 of the *Commentary on John*. I have argued elsewhere that these remarks of Gregory suggest that he had heard Origen delivering the lectures in Caesarea that became Books 20 and 32 of the *Commentary*.[15] There is also evidence that some points made in his lectures on Scripture to his students also found their way into homilies delivered in the Church.[16]

Origen's publishing agenda, begun in Alexandria with Ambrose's support, begins to shift in the later work he does on the *Commentary on John* in Caesarea. The focus on Heracleon and his understanding of the Gospel of John becomes less of an issue. Origen begins to take up the issue, pressed upon him by the presence of the Jewish community in Caesarea, of the

---

[12] Praechter (1909), 523–4; trans. 38.
[13] Gorday (1983), 47, makes a similar suggestion.
[14] Nautin (1977), 401.
[15] Heine (1993b), 261–6.
[16] Ibid., esp. 263–6.

Gentile inclusion in the people of God and what this meant for the status of the non-believing Hebrew community. I called attention in Chapter 7 to the fact that the prominence of references to Heracleon fades in Books 19 and 20 of the *Commentary on John* and is entirely absent from Books 28 and 32. From Book 19 on in the *Commentary on John* Heracleon is a memory for Origen, but the Jewish community in Caesarea is a present reality. The Gnostic doctrine of natures, however, continues to linger in Origen's mind and is repeatedly refuted in his later works. This doctrine bothered him so much because he considered it to necessitate an unworthy view of God. If the devil is what he is by nature and not by his own choice, then all his evil must be attributed to God, who made him that way. If humans are what they are by nature and not by choice, then their evil too must be attributed to God. This, of course, was the issue of theodocy, and that was a concern to a much broader audience than the Gnostics.[17] The doctrine of natures continues to be referred to in the Caesarean works even though other issues were closer to hand.[18]

It is in Caesarea too that the Pauline literature becomes more important to Origen. He takes up Ephesians with its central focus on the inclusion of the Gentiles in the people of God, although he interprets many of the passages in relation to the Gnostic natures.[19] In the interpretation of Ephesians 3:1–7,[20] however, the central argument is that the ancient Hebrew prophets understood what they were prophesying and did not speak in ecstasy and utter things that they had no understanding of themselves. The importance of this argument in Origen's situation is that the Hebrew prophets of old spoke of the inclusion of the Gentiles in the kingdom of God and knew that this was what they were talking about. It is not the Gentile Christians, in other words, who are first speaking of the inclusion of the Gentiles by taking words of the prophets, somewhat as Celsus said they could be taken, and making them mean whatever they want (*Cels* 7.9). The inclusion of the Gentiles was rooted in the understanding of the patriarchs and prophets of Israel. The magisterial commentary on Romans comes not long after the *Commentary on Ephesians*, and in this commentary Origen looks closely at the question of the salvation of Gentiles and Jews. Portions

---

[17] For a discussion of this issue against Celsus, see *Cels* 6.53–6. The most thorough treatment of Origen's views on this subject is in Koch (1932), 96–162.

[18] See, for example, Heine (2002), 123–4, 138, 183–4; *ComJn* 28.179; 32.246; *ComRom* 1.3; 4.12, etc.

[19] See Heine (2002) references in n. 18 above.

[20] This is found only in Jerome's translation, though I think Jerome is reproducing Origen here. See Heine (2002), 141–8. On Origen's understanding of Ephesians 3:5–6 in a discussion that is preserved in his Greek text, see *ComJn* 6.21–8.

of the *Commentary on the Song of Songs* written in this period also reflect these issues and suggest disagreement with the Jews over the interpretation of that book.[21]

In what follows I will examine the evidence for this shifting of Origen's attention to the issue of the Jews in relation to the Christians in the three major extant pieces of literature that were produced during the reign of Gordian: Books 19, 20, 28, and 32 of the *Commentary on John*, the *Commentary on Romans*, and the *Commentary on the Song of Songs*. There are two issues that occupy Origen's mind in relation to the Jews. One is the hostility of the Synagogue to the Church, and the other is the question of the salvation of the Jews. Origen does not consider the Jews enemies to the faith in the sense that he did the Gnostics.[22] He knows that the Jewish Scriptures are fundamental for the teachings of the Church. He repeatedly defends the Jews and their prophets—including Moses—against the attacks of Celsus in the first book of the *Against Celsus*.[23] He also defends the law and the prophets against the views of the Gnostic Heracleon, who would eliminate them in favor of revelation in Christ (*ComJn* 6.13–28). De Lange considered Origen to perceive "the debate between the Church and the Synagogue" to lie solely in "the one question of the interpretation of scripture".[24] This is too narrow, in my opinion, but the question of the way to read the Old Testament was certainly an important part of the debate. The exegetical method Origen had learned in Alexandria became even more important to him in Caesarea as he labored to preserve the heritage of the Hebrew Bible for the Christian community.

ORIGEN AND THE JEWS IN BOOKS 19–32 OF THE *COMMENTARY ON JOHN*

There are no references to the contemporary Jewish community in Book 32 of the *Commentary on John*.[25] That book is commentary on Jesus' last meal with his disciples in John 13. There are no conflict stories between Jesus and the Jews in that text. Books 19 and 20 of the *Commentary on John* also

---

[21] See Heine (1992), 674.

[22] See Vogt (1974), 193–4.

[23] See Lange (1976), 63–4.

[24] Ibid., 82.

[25] There is only one reference to the Jews in this book (32.389–94). It relates to Jesus' remark about an earlier statement he had made to the Jews (John 13:33). There is also only one reference to the heterodox who held the doctrine of natures (32.246).

have no explicit references to the contemporary Jewish community. There are a few references to Heracleon,[26] and occasional references to views of the heterodox.[27] Books 19 and 20 are commentary on John 8:19–53, which relates a rather bitter controversy in the temple between Jesus and the Jews, some of whom were Pharisees and some tentative believers in Jesus. When Origen interacts with the Jews in his comments, it is, formally at least, the Jews in the text of the Gospel of John. I think it is possible occasionally, however, to see the contemporary Jews in the Synagogue in Caesarea standing behind Origen's remarks in relation to the Jews in the text of John. It is Book 28 of the commentary that provides a basis for reading Origen's remarks about the Jews in Books 19 and 20 in this way.

In Book 28 Origen clearly engages the Church–Synagogue issue in his interpretation of the controversies following the resurrection of Lazarus in John 11. The book begins with commentary on John 11:39. The earlier part of the story would have been discussed in Book 27, which is not extant. In discussing John 11:45–6 Origen asks who it was who went to the Pharisees and what their intention was. He thinks it could have been some of those who saw what happened and believed in Jesus and wanted to convert the Pharisees to belief, or it could have been some who did not believe and wanted to stir up the Pharisees against Jesus by reporting what he had done. He opts for the latter (*ComJn* 28.77–85).

Origen begins his interpretation of John 11:47–8 with the literal meaning. The Pharisees and priests feared that the whole Jewish population might be drawn to faith in Jesus, and that this might provoke the Romans to take military action against the Jewish nation and destroy their place, that is, the temple. Origen interprets John 11:48, where this fear is stated, in light of Jewish history subsequent to the Johannine text. The Pharisees and temple authorities did not permit Jesus to live and consequently, he says, "the Romans came and took away their place. For where", he asks, "is that which they call a sanctuary? And they also took away the nation, casting them out of the place, and scarcely permitting them to be where they wish even in the Diaspora."[28] The latter assumes the post-Hadrian situation when the Jews had been banned from being in Jerusalem.

Origen then turns to the anagogical or higher meaning of this text. He finds the anagogical meaning to lie in the Gentiles having been given the

---

[26] See Chapter 7, in "Origen's Early Work in Caesarea and his Alexandrian Publishing Agenda", p. 154.

[27] See, for example, *ComJn* 19.12–16, 27, 32; 20.106, 127, 135, 287–97.

[28] *ComJn* 28.91–2; trans. in *Origen: Commentary on the Gospel according to John Books 13–32* (1993), 313.

position that the Jews held earlier and quotes Romans 11:11, "By their transgression salvation has come to the Gentiles, to stir them to envy." This verse, along with Romans 11:25 about a part of Israel experiencing a hardening until "the fullness of the Gentiles" has entered, is extremely frequent in Origen's discussions of the question of Gentile and Jewish salvation. They are cited exclusively in literature produced in Caesarea.[29] "The Romans" who take away the nation in John 11:48 represent all the Gentiles and are understood to have replaced the Hebrews as the people of God. The prophecy of Hosea 1:9 has been fulfilled in that "the people have become not a people, and those of Israel are no longer Israel, and the seed did not reach the point that they became children".[30]

The reference to seed not becoming children is an allusion back to his earlier discussion of John 8:37–9 (*ComJn* 20.3). The distinction between being "seed of Abraham" and "children of Abraham" is a central issue that Origen treats in Book 20. "Seed" points to generative principles and is a child in potential. "Child" is the realization of the potential in the seed. Being a child of Abraham is not, however, a racial matter. It is one's works that make one a child of Abraham. One who is seed of Abraham can, by diligence, become a child of Abraham. On the other hand, neglect can cause seed of Abraham to cease to be even seed (*ComJn* 20.5, 32). Some, as reported by Daniel, may be "seed of Canaan", and some, according to Wisdom, may be "accursed seed" (*ComJn* 20.33). Since Origen makes explicit application of the seed and children of Abraham to the Church–Synagogue theme in Book 28, it seems that he must have had this same issue in mind in his discussion in Book 20, although it is never made explicit there.

Origen brings his discussion of John 11:47–8 to a conclusion with an application to the current situation in Caesarea and labels the literal practice of the Jewish religion as "type" and the Christian faith as its intended "truth". He begins with a recapitulation of his understanding of the text. "[T]he chief priests" who represent "all the physical worship among the Jews, and the Pharisees" who represent "all the teaching of the law according to the letter, plot against Jesus, the truth. The type, in order to exist, wishes to hinder the manifestation of the truth." Then he contemporizes the text even more, when he says, "Now we must assume that these things are happening now too, and that it is possible to see them in those who, through the preservation of physical Judaism, wish to destroy the spiritual

---

[29] See *Biblia Patristica* (1991), 375–6.

[30] *ComJn* 28.93–4; trans. in *Origen: Commentary on the Gospel according to John Books 13–32* (1993), 313.

teaching of Christ."[31] He is referring to the contemporary Synagogue, and since his primary contact with the Jews and the Synagogue at this time was with those in Caesarea, he must be alluding to the situation in Caesarea. His statement suggests a certain level of hostility between Synagogue and Church.

John 11:50 provides Origen another opportunity to discuss the issue of Jewish and Gentile salvation. Caiphas had said in the Johannine text that it was better for one man to die for "the people" than for the whole "nation" to perish. Origen takes "people" to mean the Jews and "nation" to mean the rest of humanity and states that Jesus' death was not just for "the people" but for all humanity. He makes the same distinction a little later when John 11:52 refers to Jesus' death as being for the "nation" and "to gather the scattered children of God" (*ComJn* 28.178). He rejects the Gnostic view that the "scattered children of God" are those who are spiritual by nature (*ComJn* 28.179–83) and argues that they are the scattered Hebrews—patriarchs, prophets, elect—whether dead or alive, who were or are "righteous in God". These are the "healthy" who need no physician to whom Jesus refers when he says, "The healthy do not need a physician, but only the sick" (Matt. 9:12). Jesus' death, therefore, was for the "nation", that is, "the sick", so that they would not perish, *and* for "the scattered children of God", that is, "the healthy", so that they might be gathered into one with the "nation", and in him, "there might be one flock, one shepherd" (John 10:16) in fulfillment of Jesus' prayer in John 17:21, "As you and I are one, that they also may be one in us."[32] Origen understands this statement of Jesus in John 17:21 to refer to the unity of Jews and non-Jews who believe in Christ.

The statement in John's Gospel that "Jesus...no longer walked about openly among the Jews, but went from there to a town called Ephraim..., and...remained there with the disciples" (John 11:54, NRSV), is another text that Origen interprets in relation to the Church–Synagogue theme. He understands the literal meaning to be a statement against rushing irrationally into martyrdom in that Jesus withdrew from contact with his opponents for a period of time (*ComJn* 28.198–211). The "anagogical meaning", however, is taken to refer to the salvation of the Gentiles and the fate of the Jews (*ComJn* 28.211–22). *Long ago* Jesus walked among the Jews in the

---

[31] *ComJn* 28.95, 97; trans. in *Origen: Commentary on the Gospel according to John Books 13–32* (1993), 313–14.

[32] See Chapter 8, in "Origen's homilies in the setting of Caesarea's Jewish community", p. 172, where I note the use of John 10:16 in this same way in his homilies.

persons of the prophets. *Now* he has departed to Ephraim. This is developed by means of the etymological exegesis of names. Ephraim, Origen says, means "fruitfulness". He was the brother of Manasses, who was the elder of the people "from forgetfulness". Origen associates Manasses and "forgetfulness" with the Hebrews, for he says that after "the people 'from forgetfulness' have been left behind, the fruitfulness of the Gentiles has come about".[33] God has turned Israel, in the language of Psalm 107, into a barren desert, but he has made the desert of the Gentiles into a water source which makes it possible for the "hungry" to live there and build a city called the Church. God has raised up the Gentiles and has "established his family like a flock of sheep".[34] Then he moves back to the imagery of John 11:54, but still thinking of the anagogical meaning, and concludes by saying,

'Jesus', therefore, 'no longer walks openly among the Jews, but has departed from there into the country' of the whole world, 'near the desert' of the Church, 'into the city which is called Ephraim', that is, 'fruitful', 'and there he has remained with his disciples.' *And to this moment, Jesus is with his disciples near the desert in the city called Ephraim.*[35]

These discussions in Book 28 show that Origen was alert to contemporary issues between the Church and the Synagogue whose reflections could be seen in the stories about Jesus' conflict with the Jews in John's Gospel. I suspect that this same reading of the text is also present in some of Origen's remarks about the Jews in the text of John 8 in Books 19 and 20, where no explicit reference to the current situation is made.

Origen understands the discussion between the Jews and Jesus in John 8 to be focused on the question of Jesus' identity. Jesus' statement that the Jews do not know either him or his Father (John 8:19) prompts Origen to assume they had made a statement about knowing who Jesus was. He then introduces into the discussion the kinds of things the Jews knew about Jesus—where he was born, and who his mother and brothers were (*ComJn* 19.10). This information is all present elsewhere in the Gospels. If Origen's statement reflects his knowledge of the Jewish view of Jesus in the Caesarean Synagogue and in the rabbinic school there, it is a much less radical view than the kind of slanderous statements about Jesus' origins

---

[33] *ComJn* 28.214; trans. in *Origen: Commentary on the Gospel according to John Books 13–32* (1993), 336.

[34] *ComJn* 28.218; trans. in *Origen: Commentary on the Gospel according to John Books 13–32* (1993), 337.

[35] *ComJn* 28.221–22; trans. in *Origen: Commentary on the Gospel according to John Books 13–32* (1993), 337, modified.

that Celsus puts in the mouth of his Jewish antagonist which Origen later reports (*Cels* 1.28).

Still discussing the same verse of John, Origen focuses a little later on the Pharisees. They are similar, he suggests, to the heterodox who did not accept that the creator God of the Old Testament was the Father of Christ in that they too did not believe that the God who had given the law was the Father of Jesus (*ComJn* 19.32–3). This was a pointed statement that struck at the center of the Christian–Jewish debate about the identity of Jesus. It is difficult to imagine Origen making this statement in Caesarea and thinking that it related only to the Jews in the Gospel text and not to those in the local Synagogue. In the *Against Celsus* Origen says the Jews pressed the Christians about use of the title "Son of God", for they argued that no such person is ever mentioned by the prophets (*Cels* 1.49). Origen does not, however, develop this line of thought any further in Book 19 in relation to the Jewish rejection of Jesus. He applies the statement instead to his understanding of the way a person progresses in the spiritual life, by beginning with the humanity of Jesus and progressing through the various concepts applied to him in the Bible until one comes to knowledge of the Father himself. The consequence of this is that one cannot know the Father without knowing Jesus.[36]

Book 28 of the *Commentary on John* shows clearly that Origen now has a particular interest in the Pauline question of the inclusion of the Gentiles and the exclusion of the Jews from the people of God as expressed in such verses as Romans 11:11. It is likely that traces of this interest are present in latent form in Books 19 and 20 as well when Origen discusses the arguments that Jesus has with the Jews in John 8. We turn now, however, to the *Commentary on Romans*, where the discussion of this issue becomes much more explicit as Origen takes up the Pauline texts that address the question directly.

ORIGEN AND THE HOPE OF ISRAEL IN THE *COMMENTARY ON ROMANS* 9–11

The *Commentary on Romans*, as all of Origen's writings, ranges widely over a variety of subjects, and is not limited to the question of Jewish salvation. In the prologue to the commentary he says that Paul raises a number of questions of the sort that the heretics latch onto to support their views.

---

[36] *ComJn* 19.34–9. On the "aspects" of Christ see Heine (2004a), 93–5.

One of these views, he says, is that human activity is determined by the particular nature each person has, and not by the individual's own choices. The heretics focus on a few words in the epistle, he asserts, and use these words to dismiss the doctrine of free will which is taught in all Scripture.[37] Whether there were actual persons menacing the faith of the Christians in Caesarea by teaching this, or whether this was a leftover theme from Origen's memories of Gnostic groups in Alexandria is not known. In the midst of his interpretation of Romans 9–11, however, there is a lengthy detour to engage the interpretations of Valentinus and Basilides on the doctrine of natures.[38]

Later in the prologue Origen provides a list of the subjects he considers Paul to treat in the epistle: the law of Moses, the calling of the Gentiles, Israel according to the flesh and not according to the flesh, circumcision of the flesh and circumcision of the heart, the spiritual law and the literal law, the law of the flesh and the law of the members, the law of the mind and the law of sin, and the inner and outer man.[39] At the beginning of the third book of the commentary he makes a statement about his understanding of Paul's purpose in the epistle. He says that the epistle seems incoherent because Paul switches repeatedly from addressing Gentiles to Jews, and vice versa, sometimes speaking favorably and sometimes unfavorably of each group. The coherence of the epistle lies in its central theme of showing "how salvation came to those who lived by the law prior to the coming of Christ or how, *on the basis of Israel's unbelief, salvation would be bestowed on the Gentiles* through the coming of the Savior. Furthermore," he continues, Paul "wants to show that it is not the totality of the Gentiles who are saved, but only those who have believed; nor is the totality of Israel rejected because a remnant of believers is saved."[40] The words I have italicized are an allusion to Romans 11:11. This allusion in this programmatic statement about Paul's purpose in the epistle highlights the importance of these words for Origen's understanding of the epistle. Romans 11:11 and 11:25–6 are the most frequently cited verses from the epistle in the writings of Origen.[41] They shape his understanding of the tension between the Synagogue and the Church and also his understanding of the hope of

---

[37] *ComRom* Prol. 1; *Der Römerbriefkommentar des Origenes* (16:1990), 37.

[38] *ComRom* 8.11; cf. Pagels (1975), 41–2.

[39] *ComRom* Prol. 1, *Der Römerbriefkommentar des Origenes* (16:1990), 41.

[40] My italics. *ComRom* 3.1, trans. modified from *Origen: Commentary on the Epistle to the Romans* (2001), 179. There is a fragmentary Greek text of this section in *Le commentaire d'Origène sur Rom. III.5–V.7* (1957), 1.

[41] See *Biblia Patristica* (1991), 375–6.

Israel: "[T]hrough their stumbling salvation has come to the Gentiles, so as to make Israel jealous" (Rom 11:11; NRSV) and, "[A] hardening has come upon part of Israel, until the full number of the Gentiles has come in. And so all Israel will be saved" (Rom 11:25–26; NRSV). In the following discussion I will focus on the importance of these verses in Origen's *Commentary on Romans* 9–11,[42] but I will also refer to his use of them in his *Commentary on Matthew* and the *Contra Celsum*. The latter works were written a few years later in Origen's life at Caesarea, in the reign of Philip (AD 244–9).

These two texts in Romans 11 allow Origen to view the Jewish rejection of Jesus in a positive light. First, Romans 11:11 shows that the rejection is not a totally bad thing. It functions to produce something good, like the hardening of Pharaoh's heart, which Paul says in Romans 9:17 God used that his name might be proclaimed throughout the world.[43] The Jewish rejection of Jesus has opened the way for the salvation of the Gentiles. Romans 11:25–6, on the other hand, allows him to see that the hardening of Israel's heart is not a permanent condition. There will be an eschatological time of salvation for the Jews[44] and the two peoples will become one.[45] This simplified overview, however, covers a number of complexities in Origen's exegetical moves as he explains the texts of Romans 9–11 with occasional glances at contemporary debates with the Synagogue. It is to these complexities that we now turn our attention as we look at some specific examples of Origen's exegesis treating these themes.

The hardening of Israel and the salvation of the Gentiles

Origen's discussion of the hardening of Israel is not limited to interpreting ancient texts. He sees evidence of it in his immediate situation. "Even now" he says, citing Paul's words in Romans 11:25, the descendants of those Israelites who died in the wilderness in the time of Moses are wandering aimlessly away from the promised land (*ComRom* 7.13). Origen anchors both the theme of Israel's hardening and the salvation of the Gentiles in Old Testament prophecy. He begins to set up the scenario by picking up on the word "promises" (Rom 9:4), which Paul says belong to the Israelites. He notes two prophecies which he interprets in relation to Christ and the Gentiles. The first is the Septuagint text of Hosea 9:12, which says, "There is

---

[42] The commentary on these chapters appears in *ComRom* 7.13–8.13.

[43] Origen uses the analogy of Pharaoh again in *SerMt* 145.

[44] See *ComRom* 8.1 (where it is referred to twice), 8.9 (where it is mentioned four times), 8.10, and *ComMt* 16.26.

[45] *ComRom* 8.9; *FragMt* 428.

woe to them; my flesh is from them." Origen asks why the prophet should refer to woe, and answers in the words of Simeon about the infant Jesus, "This child is destined for the rising and falling of many in Israel" (Luke 2:34; NRSV). He joins with this the words of David, "People whom I had not known served me" (Ps. 18:43; NRSV). On the conjunction of these two statements, both of which he considers to have been spoken in the person of the Messiah, Origen understands that it had been prophesied that the Messiah's own kin would reject him and the Gentiles, whom he had not known, would receive him (*ComRom* 7.13). "I have been found by those not seeking me", Christ says, speaking in Isaiah 65:1 (see Rom. 10:20). This is still true, Origen argues, for the Gentiles have found him but the Jews, "down to this present moment" search the Scriptures in quest of the Messiah but stumble over his cross and fail to find him.[46]

Origen notes some of the contemporary Jewish objections to the way the Christians read the Biblical prophecies. He observes accurately that in Romans 9:25–6 Paul has cited a medley of texts from Hosea 1:9, 2:23, and 1:10 and applied them to Gentile Christians even though Hosea had addressed them to the Jews. He refers to two Jewish objections to this Pauline application. First, he says, they may raise the question of where it has been said to Gentile Christians that they were not God's people so that they may be called "sons of the living God" (*ComRom* 7.18). This objection is grounded in the Jewish insistence that the prophecies must be understood literally. These words were spoken to the Hebrews so they can only be interpreted in reference to the Hebrews. In a later passage he alludes to this same kind of objection the Jews raised against the Christian interpretation of prophecies in relation to themselves and Jesus. Here he asserts that the Scriptures themselves become a snare for the Jews because they insist on taking them literally. He cites Isaiah 45:13 as a prophecy of Christ, where the person spoken of is said to build God's city and release the captivity of God's people. The Jews argue, Origen says, that Jesus did not fulfill this prophecy because "he did not build the city of God, ... nor ... call back the captivity of the people".[47] The Jews had also learned from the Scriptures, according to John 12:34, that the Messiah remains forever. When they saw Jesus die, Origen says, they concluded that he could not be the Messiah (*ComRom* 8.8). This was a hermeneutical issue between the Jews and Christians. The Jews insisted on the literal meaning of the Scriptures and Origen insisted on the intellectual or spiritual meaning. The other Jewish

---

[46] *ComRom* 8.6; cf. *Cels* 2.78.
[47] *ComRom* 8.8; trans. in *Origen: Commentary on the Epistle to the Romans* (2002), 164.

objection Origen notes to the Pauline application of the prophecies of Hosea in Romans 9:25–6 is an objection to the right of non-Jews to use the Jewish Scriptures. "They assert", he says, "that God spoke these things in Judea—for it is in that place alone that God is known—and that none of these things pertain to us, since 'the law speaks to those who are under the law'." Here, again, the insistence on a literal reading of the text is obvious. But the assertion, which Origen quotes from Romans 3:19, about the law addressing (only) those who are under it points to a major problem the Jews had with Christians. The latter did not obey the law of God but still claimed to be the people of the God who had given the law.[48] Origen does not address this larger issue here, but replies only to the literalism involved in associating God with a place.

Origen's allusions to these two particular cases suggest that there was a broad discussion and disagreement between the Synagogue and Church in Caesarea about how to read the Old Testament prophecies. It seems likely to me that this discussion provided the motivation for Origen's commentaries on Isaiah and Ezekiel at this period in his life, and that on the 12 prophets in the following period. He refers later to discussions with the Jews about the referent to be understood in the prophecy in Isaiah 53 (*Cels* 1.55), about their insistence that the title "Son of God" does not appear in the prophetic writings (*Cels* 1.49), and, very generally, about the witness of the law and prophets to Jesus (*Cels* 1.45–6).

Origen interprets Romans 11:12, "Now if their transgression is wealth for the world and their defeat is wealth for the Gentiles, how much more will their fullness be?", by appealing to Deuteronomy 32:8–9. The latter text refers to Jacob becoming the Lord's portion when the boundaries for the nations were assigned. It is the concept of God's "portion" that is the key to this exegetical argument. Origen finds it again in Jeremiah 12:10, where God says through the prophet, "My desirable portion has become an abomination." Because the Lord's portion was now rejected, a new portion had to be found to enter into the riches that had been Israel's and are listed in Romans 9:4: glory, covenants, law, and the service and worship of God. In place of the single nation of the Hebrews, the whole Gentile world became the new portion of the Lord and entered into the riches that had belonged to Israel. This is the present situation, Origen says, and "all the Gentiles are now coming to salvation". But the salvation of the Gentiles is not the final goal of God. "[S]o long as Israel persists in unbelief the fullness of the Lord's portion will not be said to be complete" (*ComRom*

[48] See Heine (2007), 47–74.

8.9). It will not be until "the end time" after "the fullness of the Gentiles enters and Israel has come to salvation through faith" that the "portion of God" will be complete (*ComRom* 8.9). Here, again, Origen sees Israel to be isolated at the present from God's work, to the benefit of the Gentiles, but necessary, nonetheless, to its ultimate completion.

Origen sees the current situation of the Jews to be that of the people invited to the wedding feast in Jesus' parable (Matt. 22:1–10). They make excuses and refuse to attend. But they are angry, nevertheless, because the Gentiles have been invited in their place. They lack the perception to see the meaning of the words God spoke in Isaiah which Paul quotes " 'I have been found by those who did not seek me. . . . But of Israel he says, 'All day long I have held out my hands to a disobedient and contrary people' " (Rom 10:20–1; NRSV; *ComRom* 8.6).

The fullness of the Gentiles and the salvation of Israel

When Origen addresses the hardness of Israel towards the Christian faith and the Gentiles' receptivity of the faith he has his own experience in Caesarea that he can correlate with the Pauline texts. When he takes up the themes of a time when the Gentile inclusion in the people of God will have reached its goal and Israel will become receptive, however, he has only the Biblical texts to use. The completion of the mission to the Gentiles and the ultimate salvation of Israel are eschatological subjects for which Origen had no evidence in his own experience.

There is a wide use of Romans 11:25–6, which speaks of the eschatological salvation of "all Israel" in Origen's later Caesarean writings. In his interpretation of Jesus' parable of the drag net, he identifies the catch of "every kind" of fish with the inclusion of the Gentiles and understands the "fullness" of the net to refer to the "fullness of the Gentiles" (*ComMt* 10.12). In a similar manner, the fruitless fig tree of Matthew 21 is identified with the Synagogue until "the fullness of the Gentiles enters" at the end of the age (*ComMt* 16.26). The calamities the Jews experienced following the condemnation of Jesus are said to continue "until the fullness of the Gentiles shall enter" (*ComMt* 16.3). On the other hand, Romans 11:25 is used to express the eschatological union of believing Gentiles and Jews. "A corner", Origen says, "is the hammering together of two walls. By hammering the 'remnant' from Israel and 'the fullness of the Gentiles' into one, Christ, the stone and the truth, produces this corner, as it has been written, 'This is the Lord's doing' " (*FragMt* 428). And, he claims that Celsus, in his denigrations of the Jews, reveals a total unawareness of God's care for them, of the relationship between their present condition and the blessings befalling the Gentiles, and of their final salvation when the "fullness of the Gentiles" has entered (*Cels* 6.80). These references show that the question of the salvation of the Jews was an important issue occupying Origen's thought in his later years in Caesarea.

By drawing on various motifs found in the Pauline texts in Romans 9–11, Origen constructs a framework for understanding the salvation of "all Israel" in Romans 11:26. He notes the Pauline distinction between "stumbling" and "falling" in Romans 11:11. The Jews have stumbled, he says, but they have not fallen. To fall is a hopeless situation; to stumble is not. He thinks it amazing that Paul can say that the Jews have not fallen after everything that he says about them in the epistle. This distinction, however, is fundamental to the hope of Israel. It allows for their salvation in the eschaton when the fullness of the Gentiles has entered (*ComRom* 8.9).

One of the basic motifs Origen highlights is that of Jewish "jealousy" which Paul says is an intended result of the salvation of the Gentiles (Rom 11:11). He understands this theme to be connected directly with God's words spoken through Moses, "I will make you jealous of those who are not a race" (Deut. 32:21). This anchors, of course, the salvation of the Gentiles and the present situation between Jews and Christians in Moses, the most highly regarded authority of the Jews. Origen identifies those called "not a race" with Christians. True races are constituted by territorial borders, and such things as a common language and customs. Christians, on the other hand, come from all races and are referred to by Moses as "not a race". Moses, therefore, had predicted what is now happening between the Jews and Gentiles (*ComRom* 8.6).

Origen seems to consider the Jewish "zeal for God" discussed in Romans 10:1–3 to be closely connected with the jealousy mentioned in Romans 11:11. He says that the "jealousy" stirred up by seeing the Gentiles being saved, entering into the covenant with God which had previously been theirs, and embracing the law and the prophets in a manner more worthily than they had done—these belong to the list of what Paul considers the advantages of being Jewish in Romans 9:4—will produce a "zeal" in the Jews, in the eschaton, at least (*ComRom* 8.9). Applying Jesus' statement that the one who has will be the recipient of more (Matt 13:12) to Paul's statement about the Jewish zeal for God, he argues that it is better to have a zeal for God, even if it is misdirected, than to have nothing at all, for in the latter case nothing will be received (*ComRom* 8.1).

What constitutes a true descendant of Abraham is another Pauline motif that Origen connects with the salvation of all Israel. Origen is concerned to answer Paul's question implicit in Romans 9:6: "Did God's word fail because the Israelites failed to attain the promise of God?" He first makes the assertion that we have noted him making above in the twentieth book of the *Commentary on John*: not all Abraham's seed are his children. It is not fleshly descent but faith in the promises that constitute the children of Abraham. "Those alone", Origen says, "are considered seed of Abraham who are sons of the promise connected with Isaac, that is, sons of the faith by which Abraham deserved to receive the promise of the future inheritance" (*ComRom* 7.14). Isaac's birth differed from that of all of Abraham's other sons. He was not born naturally. Because of his barren, aged parents, his birth came from the power of God, not from Abraham's flesh. "Isaac, therefore, is rightly said to be a son of God, not a child of the flesh." This same reasoning can be applied to Jacob because God chose him over Esau while the twins were still in their mother's womb. Neither had done anything in the flesh to connect the choosing of Jacob with the flesh (*ComRom* 7.15). What this line of reasoning allows Origen to conclude is that all the descendants of Abraham/Isaac/Jacob have been produced or chosen by God and "adopted" as his children. There is no connection with Abraham in the flesh. The heirs of the promises given to Abraham are *all* adopted children. When he comments on Ephesians 2:12, Origen asserts that those who understand the law spiritually and live according to it have the right "to identify themselves with 'the commonwealth of Israel' even more than the physical Jews".[49] Israel's name, moreover, means one who sees God (Gen. 32:30). One cannot be a true Israelite, therefore, if one has not seen the Christ who claimed that to see himself was to see the Father (*ComRom* 7.14).

What then does "all Israel" mean in Romans 11:26? Origen notes first that there is a mystery about the expression. Only God, the Son of God, and, perhaps, the friends of God, know the precise answer to this question. However, he makes it quite clear that it does not mean all who claim racial descent from Abraham any more than the "fullness of the Gentiles" includes every single person who is non-Jewish. Only those Israelites who have become true Israelites and, in the Spirit, see God with their minds, will be in this "all Israel" saved in the eschaton. Following Paul, he uses the Old Testament prophetic concept of the "remnant" to designate the members of the group called "all Israel". It is similar in meaning to the "fullness of the Gentiles". Those not in the "remnant" are like those not included in "the fullness of the Gentiles".[50]

---

[49] Heine (2002), 132–3.   [50] *ComRom* 8.12; cf. ibid 8.7; *ComMt* 17.5.

Origen is quite clear that the hope of Israel, like the hope of the Gentiles, lies in faith in Christ. The Jews were disinherited, he argues, because they became unbelievers. Their salvation lies in coming to belief (*ComRom* 8.7). Once the fullness of the Gentiles is complete and Israel is jealous of the Gentiles' salvation, the blindness will be dispersed and Israel will see Christ and seek the salvation previously lost because of the blindness (*ComRom* 8.12). Just as the Gentiles were not completely abandoned when they did not believe in God but were later allowed to come to faith, so the Jews have not been completely abandoned in their unbelief but will have an opportunity to come to faith also (*ComRom* 8.13). Commenting on Jesus' words, "For I say to you, You will by no means see me again until you say, 'Blessed is he who comes in the name of the Lord'", Origen says, "These words refer to a spiritual vision based on faith." Then he applies the words to the question of the salvation of the Jews: "For whenever 'the fullness of the Gentiles enters' and they believe in Christ, then those Jews who have believed after these events will perceive the beauty of Christ's deity, as they behold the Father in the Son and declare him to be the redeemer announced by the prophets" (*FragMt* 464).

This vision of the hope of Israel and the importance of Israel in the work of God which he drew primarily from Romans 9–11 must have governed Origen's relationship with the Synagogue in Caesarea. He was quite aware of the tensions between the Synagogue and the Church and spoke openly of them when his exegetical work called for this. On the other hand, he knew that "salvation is from the Jews" (John 4:22; NRSV) and that the Jews were not excluded from God's plan of salvation. It was, it seems, the proximity with the Jewish community in Caesarea that brought these issues to the forefront of Origen's mature theological thinking.

THE IDENTITY OF THE BRIDE AND THE PRE-EXISTENT CHURCH IN THE *COMMENTARY ON THE SONG OF SONGS*

The *Commentary on the Song of Songs* begins with a lengthy prologue which treats topics that were commonly treated in philosophical commentaries on the works of Plato and Aristotle.[51] Origen considers the work to belong to the genre of drama and to be about the love that the bride, who is sometimes the human soul and sometimes the Church, has for the groom she is

---

[51] See Hadot (1987), 99–122; Neuschäfer (1987), 57–84; Heine (2001), 425–6; Heine (1995a), 3–12.

about to wed. The groom is Christ, the Word of God. The other dramatis personae are the maidens who are companions of the bride, the daughters of Jerusalem who deride the bride, and some friends of the groom.[52] The friends are later identified as either the angels or the patriarchs and prophets (*ComCant* 2.8.1).

The subject matter of this book indicates that it is not for those who are in the initial stages of the Christian journey, but for those who have attained a certain level of maturity. The Hebrews, Origen claims, do not allow the young even to hold the book. He adds that it is the practice of the Hebrews to reserve the creation story in Genesis, Ezekiel's description of the cherubim, along with his account of the temple, and the Song of Songs to the very end of a boy's instruction in the Scriptures (*ComCant* Prol.1.4–7).

It is important for Origen to make clear early in the prologue that the things said in the Song of Songs are not to be read in a literal way. He does this by appealing to his understanding of the creation accounts of humanity in Genesis 1:26 and 2:7. He does not understand these to be repetitious accounts, but to refer to two separate creations, one spiritual and the other material. The first, which speaks of man being created "in the image and likeness of God", refers to the creation of the inner person. The second, which speaks of man made from the earth, refers to the creation of the outward or physical person.[53] Scripture commonly, he says, uses terms drawn from the life of the outward person to speak of the inner person (*ComCant* Prol. 2.4–13). It is in this way that the descriptions of the love and desire between the bride and groom in the Song of Songs are to be understood.

When the soul, or inner person, beholds the beauty of the Word and his work it is overcome with longing and wounded by love. But it is a saving wound which ignites the fire of divine love in the soul (*ComCant* Prol. 2.17). This love for the Word by the human soul causes one to behave like God for one wants to do only those things one knows are like God and please him (*ComCant* Prol. 2.41–3). While Origen does not like to use the word passion (*ComCant* Prol. 2.20), his own passion for Christ and the passion he thinks should be present in the Church for Christ is evident throughout the commentary. One of the clearest representations of this is in his discussions of the presence and absence of the bridegroom with the soul. The bridegroom is like a husband who is not always at home with his bride. When

---

[52] *ComCant* Prol.1.1–3. I use the reference system in *Origène commentaire sur le Cantique des Cantiques* (1991 / 1992).

[53] On Origen's understanding of creation see Chapter 5, in "The *Commentary on Genesis*", p. 104 and Chapter 6, in "The Apostolic Doctrine of Creation", p. 142.

he is away the bride yearns for him and searches for him (*ComCant* 3.14.6). Origen sees this absence as an explanation for the soul's inability sometimes to understand obscurities in Scripture. Then, when the meaning is suddenly illuminated, the bridegroom is present, providing understanding. But then he withdraws again. His presence or absence with the soul can be ascertained by the soul's ability or lack of ability to understand Scripture (*ComCant* 3.11.18–19). This discussion is strikingly similar to Origen's description of his own experience with the bridegroom in his homilies on the Song of Songs.[54] He has often experienced, he says, the intense presence of the bridegroom, but then he withdraws and his longing search for him starts again. The love for the bridegroom mediated through Scripture that Origen speaks of in this commentary is something he felt deeply himself.

A cameo of Origen's spiritual hermeneutic

The *Commentary on the Song of Songs* 3.13 is a cameo of Origen's spiritual hermeneutic and may serve as an example of the method he uses throughout the commentary. It contains both a theoretical presentation of his understanding of the way to read Scripture and examples of the practical principles that he uses to dig into Scripture's depths. In the simple words of Song of Songs 2:9, Origen finds concealed teachings about the nature of God, Christology, the Trinity, and salvation.

Everything in the material world, Origen argues, is an image of something in the immaterial world. This is grounded in Paul's statement in Romans 1:20, that God's "eternal power and divine nature, invisible though they are, have been understood and seen through the things he has made" (NRSV). By contemplating material things, one can, therefore, ascend to spiritual things (*ComCant* 3.13.9–14). He then quotes and exegetes Wisdom of Solomon 7:17–21, where the author refers to receiving divine understanding of the material things that make up this world and life in it, including more abstract things such as times, seasons, and human reasoning, and concludes by claiming, in this process, to have received understanding of things hidden and manifest. Origen takes the last statement to be the key to the text, asserting that it shows that each manifest thing is related to something hidden or invisible. This is, he thinks, the only way that someone in the physical world can come to know spiritual realities. God must have included teaching about invisible, spiritual realities in all the physical things he created on this earth so that humans can ascend mentally to spiritual

---

[54] *HomCant* 1.7; see Chapter 8, in "The goal of Origen's homilies", p. 184.

realities and come to understand them by giving careful attention to the things of the visible, physical world (*ComCant* 3.13.16–17).

This divinely created correspondence between things visible in the material world and invisible things should also be understood to apply to Scripture. The same wisdom that produced the world also produced Scripture. Every visible thing described in Scripture is there to convey a spiritual meaning of things that would otherwise be hidden, from the exodus of the Israelites from Egypt to the activities of the Lord in the Gospels (*ComCant* 3.13.28–9).

One way Origen enters this hidden world of Scripture is by using the principle that he had learned from "the Hebrew" in his early days at Alexandria and which he labeled with the Pauline phrase of "comparing spiritual things with spiritual".[55] He searches in Scripture for all the other occurrences of a key word in his text and uses these other contexts to suggest nuances of meaning for the target text. Here his first key word is "young stag" in Song of Songs 2:9 (*ComCant* 3.13.1–7, 30–43). From the other texts using the word "stag" Origen explores the application of this image to Christians and discusses such topics as their being brought to perfection through the Scriptures, the destruction of the serpent of Genesis 3, the overcoming of the effects of the fall, spiritual gifts from the Holy Spirit, the birth of Christ, and the doctrine of the Trinity.

Another way into the mystery of Scripture is by the use of etymology. The Greek noun for "antelope", the other key word in Song of Songs 2:9, is *dorkas*. Origen says the animal has this name because of its extraordinary visual capacity. The noun is derived from the verb *derkomai*, which means to see clearly.[56] This etymology leads him to discuss the fact that only Christ can "see" the Father. This is immediately nuanced, however, by his doctrine of the immateriality of God.[57] First he refers to Jesus' statement that the "pure in heart will see God" (Matt. 5:8) and says that this is possible only as Christ reveals him. This is a reflection of the doctrine he had learned at Alexandria concerning the two seraphim of Isaiah 6 whom "the Hebrew" identified with Christ and the Holy Spirit and said that they concealed God's face and feet with their wings. Origen concluded from this that all knowledge of God comes from Christ through

---

[55] 1 Cor. 2:13; *ComCant* 3.13.8. See Chapter 2, in "The school of 'the Hebrew'", p. 56, and Chapter 6, in "The Apostolic Doctrine of Scripture and its interpretation", p. 132.

[56] Liddell, Scott, and Jones (1961), 445, say the animal has this name because of "its large bright eyes". The Alexandrian poet Callimachus, who in the reign of Ptolemy II worked at cataloguing the Alexandrian library, makes a similar play on the noun *dorkas* (*Hymn 5*).

[57] See Chapter 6, in "The Apostolic Doctrines of God, Christ, and the Holy Spirit", p. 136.

the Holy Spirit (*Princ* 1.3.4). Restricting the vision of God even more, Origen argues that because God is not visible, not even Christ can see him in any physical sense. Seeing God is a mental process, not a visual, physical one, as Jesus himself notes when he uses the verb "to know" rather than "to see" in expressing the Son's perception of the Father (Matt. 11:27; *ComCant* 3.13.44–8).

A final way into the mystery of the text that Origen uses here lies in the order of the key terms in the sentence.[58] He notes that the antelope is mentioned first and then the stag, though the latter is a larger animal than the former. This order, he thinks, has spiritual meaning. Salvation is based on two factors: a person's knowledge of the faith, and the perfection of their works. The antelope, with its clear vision, represents the faith factor. This is the first step in the process of salvation. The stag represents the works by which the deceits of the devil, understood as poisonous snakes, are destroyed.[59] He closes this discussion by returning to the etymology of names in the Bible and noting that "Bethel", the final word in the text means "house of God", and suggests that the reference to "the mountains of Bethel" refers to the books of the law, the prophets, the Gospels, and the writings of the apostles. These are the bases for the vision of faith in God and for learning about the perfection of works.

In this brief section Origen lays out his basic understanding of Scripture as the visible presentation of invisible realities and demonstrates three of the exegetical techniques he uses to ascend from the visible presentation of Scripture to its intended spiritual teachings. In what we would probably consider the rather unpromising statement in Song of Songs 2:9, "My beloved is like an antelope or a young stag on the mountains of Bethel", Origen finds teachings about the lofty subjects of the immaterial nature of God, the revelation of God through Christ, salvation, the essential role Scripture plays in salvation, the Holy Spirit, and the Trinity. This section in the commentary is focused on the bride as the individual soul. We turn our attention now to the bride understood as the Church. It is in this area of application that Origen must reflect on the fact that the Synagogue had identified the bride as a reference to the Jewish people.

---

[58] This is related to the importance given to the sequence of events in a text. See *ComCant* 3.14.9, and on the importance of the sequence in a text in later patristic exegesis see Heine (1995b), 29, esp. n. 74.

[59] *ComCant* 3.13.50. For the ancient belief that deer destroyed poisonous snakes, see Heine (1995b), 97, n. 49.

Church and Synagogue on the identity of the bride

The Song of Songs had been interpreted spiritually by both the Synagogue and the Church prior to the time of Origen.[60] The Jews understood the Song to speak of the relationship between the Shekinah or presence of God, the groom, and Israel, the bride. Christians took Christ to be the groom and the Church the bride. The origins of these interpretations among both groups are obscure. On the Christian side, the fragmentary remains of the commentary on the Song by Hippolytus, the late second-century theologian in Rome, is the earliest clear witness to the spiritual interpretation by the Church. Hippolytus does not take the bride to represent both the individual soul and the Church, as Origen did, but only the Church.[61] On the Jewish side some remarks of the early second-century R. Akiba may be the earliest explicit references among the Jews to Israel being identified with the bride and God with the bridegroom.[62]

There may also be a hint of Jewish–Christian controversy over the identity of the bride as early as the time of R. Akiba, for he says,

As soon as the nations of the world hear some of His praise, they say to the Israelites: "We will join you", as it is said: "Whither is thy beloved gone, O thou fairest among women? Whither hath thy beloved turned him, that we may seek him with thee" (...[Cant.] 6.1). The Israelites, however, say to the nations of the world: "You can have no share in Him", but "My beloved is mine and I am his" (Cant. 2.16), "I am my beloved's and my beloved is mine," etc. (ibid. 6.3).[63]

These comments must have reference to the Church, because there was no hostility among the Jews towards Gentiles becoming Jewish proselytes. The separation between Synagogue and Church, however, was a recognized reality in Palestine long before the time of R. Akiba. His remarks suggest that the Synagogue was viewing the Church as a Gentile phenomenon. The implicit question in the debate was: "Who are the people of God?" There are hints of conflicting interpretations between Jews and Christians concerning the identity of the bride in Origen's *Commentary on the Song of Songs* and in the scattered comments on the Song by the third-century R. Johanan.[64] There have been a few studies attempting to show mutual

---

[60] See Ledegang (2001), 140.

[61] Murphy (1990), 12–15. Origen had traveled from Alexandria to Rome and there had met Hippolytus. See Chapter 4, in "Monarchians, Heracleon, and the Alexandrian Theological Milieu in Origen's *Commentary on John* 1:1b–3", p. 97.

[62] *Mekilta de-Rabbi Ishmael* (1933/1976), 26–7; see also Murphy (1990), 13–14, esp. n. 55.

[63] Ibid.   [64] Also spelled Yoḥanan.

awareness of the conflicting interpretations between these two third-century scholars, if not actual face-to-face discussions.[65]

R. Johanan was "born at Sepphoris in the last quarter of the second century" and died at Tiberias in AD 279.[66] One of his teachers at Sepphoris had been R. Hoshaya before the latter had moved to Caesarea.[67] R. Johanan moved to Tiberias because of a disagreement with one of his other teachers in Sepphoris. There he opened a school and became a famous teacher whose authority was widely recognized. He often visited his esteemed teacher R. Hoshaya in Caesarea during the last 13 years of the latter's life.[68] This would have put R. Johanan in Caesarea at various times between AD 237 and 250, the probable year of Hoshaya's death. It was in the early-to-mid 240s that Origen was completing his *Commentary on the Song of Songs* in Caesarea. These visits would have given Johanan ample opportunities to have learned of Origen's views either from conversations with Origen himself or, indirectly, from R. Hoshaya, who could have known of many of Origen's interpretations of Scripture.

Origen's views of the Synagogue and Church in the *Commentary on the Song of Songs* continue to show the pervasive influence the Pauline statements in Romans 11:11 and 11:25–6 had on his thinking. He cites the verses occasionally in the commentary. It is their teaching concerning the hardening of Israel that will ultimately be dissolved with the consequence that "all Israel" will be saved which causes him, even where the verses are not cited, to see the attitude of the Synagogue towards the Church within the framework of the plan of God.

Origen begins the actual commentary on the Song by identifying the speaker in Song of Songs 1:2 as the Church (*ecclesia*) longing to be united with Christ. This opening identification, however, alerts us to Origen's broader understanding of the term "Church".[69] This is not the Church of the Gentiles which he often intends when he uses this word. It is, he says,

---

[65] Baer (1961), 98–106; Urbach (1971), 247–75; Kimelman (1980), 567–95. The latter study is most helpful because it focuses on R. Johanan, who definitely had opportunity for contact with Origen's views. The first two studies tend to want to demonstrate Origen's dependence on Jewish sources. Kimelman makes the more likely suggestion that, in my opinion, R. Johanan is responding to Origen's views. He states this explicitly in relation to one of R. Johanan's interpretations (581), but it seems to me to be his general view throughout the article. It is not my purpose in this section either to summarize the arguments in these articles or to engage in debate with them. I will, however, occasionally cite points that contribute to my argument.

[66] "Johanan B. Nappaha (Ha-Nappah)" (1904), 211.

[67] See Chapter 7, in "The Jewish community in Caesarea", p. 147.

[68] "Johanan B. Nappaha (Ha-Nappah)" (1904), 212.

[69] This will be discussed more fully below in the final sub-section of this chapter, "The pre-existent Church in the *Commentary on the Song of Songs*", p. 216.

"the combination of all the saints". Prior to the coming of the bridegroom this assembly of saints had been ministered to by angels and prophets. She had received the law from angels, as Paul said (Gal. 3:19), and had learned many details about the coming Christ from the prophets. "Let him kiss me with the kisses of his mouth" (Song 1:2; NRSV) expresses the desire of this Church for the actual presence of the anticipated groom so that she is no longer dependent on angels and prophets but will have his own words from his own mouth (*ComCant* 1.1.5–8). Origen is here speaking of the Israel of the Old Testament as the Church longing for the coming groom.[70]

The concept of Church begins to undergo a narrowing in the commentary on the second half of Song of Songs 1:2, "Your breasts are better than wine." The wine, Origen says, is the teachings the bride had received from the law and the prophets before the appearance of the bridegroom. This wine was good, but the teaching of the bridegroom surpasses that of the ancients (*ComCant* 1.2.8–9, 12, 20). Origen does not make it explicit, but the bride, as Church, now must mean only those of Israel who accepted the new teachings of the groom. When the bride, he says, beholds the treasures of wisdom concealed in the groom she will recognize that they are "much more excellent than was that wine of the Law and the teaching of the Prophets, which she had before".[71]

This same narrower concept of the referents in the word bride / Church appears in the subsequent commentary on Song of Songs 1:3. The "spices" in the Septuagint text are taken to refer to the law and the prophets, which had instructed the young bride about the worship of God. They were the pedagogue mentioned by Paul (Gal. 3:24–5), who prepared her for the coming of the groom in the fullness of time (Gal. 4:4; *ComCant* 1.3.1–2). It seems to me that this narrower understanding of bride in Origen's commentary, after the initial definition of Church, refers to those of Israel who acknowledged Jesus to be the anticipated one in the writings of the prophets and became his followers in the earliest period of the Church.

Conflict enters the commentary at the beginning of Book 2. The "daughters of Jerusalem" vilify the bride as ugly because she is black (*ComCant* 2.1.1). The "daughters of Jerusalem" are differentiated from the maidens who accompany the bride. They are not the bride's friends. The bride now takes on a very specific identification, which differs from the way she was identified in the first book. "This bride" (*haec sponsa*), Origen says, is the Church of the Gentiles. The "daughters of Jerusalem" are the Jews, whom

---

[70] He probably uses this word (*ecclesia*) because it is commonly used in the Septuagint for the assembly of the people of Israel.

[71] *ComCant* 1.2.22; trans. in *Origen: The Song of Songs Commentary and Homilies* (1957), 69.

Paul identified as "most dear because of the election of the fathers, but enemies because of the gospel" (Rom 11:28). Origen's choice of this Pauline statement to identify the "daughters of Jerusalem" suggests the tension he felt in his dealings with the Synagogue. He was vividly aware—primarily because of the Pauline arguments in Romans 9–11—of the importance of the ancestry of the Jews in the divine plan of salvation. But on the other hand, he was also intensely aware of the current hostility of the Synagogue to the Church.

The "daughters of Jerusalem", he says, disdain the bride because she is not descended from Abraham, Isaac, and Jacob, nor had she been a recipient of the teachings of the Mosaic law (*ComCant* 2.1.3–4). The verbs Origen chooses to express this attitude of the Synagogue to the Church are much stronger than anything that appears in Song of Songs 1:5–6. In the Biblical text, the bride says to the daughters of Jerusalem, "*Do not look* at me because I am blackened" (my italics). Origen, however, says the daughters of Jerusalem "despise" the "church from the Gentiles" and "vilify" it "because of its lowly origins". The use of these verbs to interpret the words of Song of Songs 1:5–6 is not the result of a contemplative's perception of the spiritual journey. Origen understands the "mystical" meaning (*ComCan* 2.1.2) of these verses to speak about the relationship between the Synagogue and the Church in the third century.[72]

Origen identifies the Church of the Gentiles with the black bride of Song of Songs 1:5 and then, using the method we noted above he had learned from a Hebrew teacher in Alexandria,[73] turns to other Old Testament passages where Ethiopians are mentioned. In two of these Old Testament passages a black woman is central to the discussion. The first is the Ethiopian woman that Moses married (Num. 12:1). She is a type, Origen claims, of the Gentile Church. The bride, speaking as the Church, says to the daughters of Jerusalem, "I am that Ethiopian. I am black indeed by reason of my lowly origin; but I am beautiful through penitence and faith. For I have taken to myself the Son of God."[74] Miriam and Aaron had opposed Moses' marriage to the Ethiopian. In a homily on Numbers 12 probably delivered about the same time that he was working on the *Commentary on the Song of Songs* Origen identified Miriam with the Synagogue and Aaron with the Jewish priesthood in their opposition to Moses, who is understood as the spiritual law married

---

[72] See "Origen and the Jews in Books 19–32 of the *Commentary on John*" p. 192, above, where a similar understanding is given to the higher meaning of the text in *ComJn* 28.

[73] See above in "A cameo of Origen's spiritual hermeneutic" p. 207.

[74] *ComCant* 2.1.6; trans. in *Origen: The Song of Songs Commentary and Homilies* (1957), 93.

to the Ethiopian (*HomNum* 6.4). Here in the *Commentary on the Song of Songs* Origen notes the incongruence of Miriam and Aaron's objection to Moses taking an Ethiopian wife. They say, "Has the Lord spoken only to Moses? Has he not spoken to us as well?" What they were really objecting to, Origen asserts, was the mystical meaning in which the spiritual law was being united with the Church from the Gentiles. It was the voice of the Synagogue and the Jewish priesthood objecting to the spiritual reading of the law by the Gentile Church (*ComCant* 2.1.22–3). In the homily on Numbers Origen takes the analogy further. Because of the opposition to Moses, Miriam became leprous and was not allowed in the camp for seven days. Origen relates this to Romans 11:25–6 and sees Miriam's time outside the camp to be the present situation of the Jews. But at the "end of the world, when the fullness of the Gentiles has entered, then all Israel will be saved". Mariam's flesh will be restored when she accepts the beauty of Christ and "there will be one flock and one shepherd" (*HomNum* 6.4). That was Origen's eschatological hope for the Jews, but it was not his present situation in Caesarea.

The other black woman of the Old Testament whom Origen relates to this text is the Queen of Sheba, who visited Solomon. She too is a type of the Church of the Gentiles (*ComCant* 2.1.14). In the figure of this type she came to Jerusalem to hear the "true Solomon" and learned the truth about God, creation, the immortality of the soul and future judgment, things which she had not learned from the philosophers (*ComCant* 2.1.27).

Psalm 67:32 (LXX) provides another text that Origen can relate to the Church–Synagogue situation. It refers to Ethiopia stretching out her hands to God. On the basis of Romans 11:11, which states that the salvation of the Gentiles was the result of Israel's offence, Origen thinks that Psalm 67:32 suggests that the Gentiles precede the Jews in their approach to God. Furthermore, he says, returning to his interpretation of Song of Songs 1:4, the daughters of Jerusalem resent this and "envy and disparage" the black Ethiopian (*ComCant* 2.1.42).[75]

Origen argues that Song of Songs 1:6 provides an explanation for the darkness of the bride. It is not a natural condition deriving from creation, nor is it permanent, for in Song of Songs 8:5 in the Septuagint the bride is seen approaching "having been made white". She became dark because, as the people of the Gentiles, she did not stand upright and was, therefore, bypassed by the "Sun of righteousness" (*ComCant* 2.2.4–6). Origen then fleshes out this explanation by reflecting on Romans 11. In an imaginary

---

[75] The other passages Origen cites which contain references to Ethiopians are Zeph. 3:10, Jer. 38:10, and 39:16–18. The themes Origen treats in this section of the commentary are repeated in abbreviated form in his *HomCant* 1.6.

conversation Israel says to the Church of the Gentiles: "Because of my former unbelief you were chosen and the Sun of righteousness looked on you and disregarded me. But now I hope to receive mercy when you become unbelieving." Origen then quotes Paul directly.

For just as you—meaning, no doubt, the Gentiles—once did not believe in God, but have now obtained mercy because of their unbelief; so too they now have not believed in your mercy, so that they also may obtain mercy [Rom. 11:30–31]. And again he says in other words, Partial blindness has befallen Israel until the fullness of the Gentiles should enter (Rom. 11:25; *ComCant* 2.28).

The Caesarean R. Isaac,[76] a disciple of R. Johanan and "a major transmitter" of the latter's sayings, relates a parable in interpreting Song of Songs 1:6 that Kimelman considers to have been in response to Origen's interpretation of the verse. He thinks Origen understood the verse to mean that "the Church has displaced sinful Israel as God's beloved". R. Isaac said,

It happened once that a provincial lady had a black maidservant who went down with a companion to draw water from the spring, and she said to the companion: Tomorrow my master is going to divorce his wife and marry me. Why? Asked the other. She replied: Because he saw her hands stained. Retorted the other: Foolish woman, listen to what you are saying. Here is his wife whom he loves exceedingly, and you say he is going to divorce her because once he saw her hands stained. How then will he tolerate you who are stained all over and black from the day of your birth? . . . . [Israel says to the nations:] If the sun of idolatry has tanned us, you are darkened from birth. While you were still in your mother's womb you served idols.[77]

This story certainly sounds like a reply to an interpretation such as that which Origen had given to Song of Songs 1:6. R. Isaac's story suggests a bitterness on the side of the Synagogue in the debate with the Church about who constituted the people of God. It cannot be missed that the servant girl in the story is considered to hold not just a false, but a stupid opinion about herself and her relationship with her master. Origen's remarks in a homily on Exodus delivered in this same time frame in Caesarea show a similar rancorous attitude on the part of the Church to the Synagogue

---

[76] Strack (1931/1959), 122.

[77] Kimelman (1980), 593, quoting *Song Rab.* 1.6.3. Baer (1961), 100, thinks Origen is responding to the Jewish apology and accusation represented by this story. Urbach (1971), 263–5, thinks Origen's interpretation is drawing on "the midrashic expositions", and suggests that it may reflect an actual "live dialogue with R. Isaac or some other scholar who expounded like him the verse 'I am black but comely'." I think Kimelman's view more likely, that the story is in response to Origen, as the story told by R. Isaac sounds to me more like a response to a contrary interpretation than the kind of story that one would use to interpret this verse if there were no conflicting position.

as he identifies the Gentile Church as the true Israel instead of that Israel "according to the flesh". He says to his Gentile congregation as he interprets Exodus 20:3, a key Biblical passage in Israel's self-understanding, "These words are addressed much more to you who were made Israel spiritually by living for God... For although we are Gentiles in the flesh, in spirit we are Israel."[78] If, however, the Gentile Christians fail to live worthily of this privileged relationship with God, they will suffer the same thing that Israel "according to the flesh" has suffered. Because of "their own sins", they "*deserved* to 'be dispersed through all the nations'. And those who formerly were brought out 'of the house of bondage', now again... are slaves no longer to the Egyptians alone, but to all nations."[79]

This passage from Origen's homily gives support to Kimelman's remark that Origen considered the Church to have "displaced sinful Israel as God's beloved". Other passages that we have considered in Origen, however, suggest that a nuanced version of this is more accurate. Origen thought it was only a temporary displacement. He refers, in fact, in interpreting a later verse, to the calling of the Church coming "between the two callings of Israel". "Israel was called first," Origen says. "Later, when Israel had stumbled and fallen, the church of the Gentiles was called. But when 'the fullness of the Gentiles shall have entered', then 'all Israel', called once more, 'will be saved'" (*ComCant* 4.2.22). Origen gives a definite Christian interpretation to this second calling of Israel, however, when he adds that it will not be "in keeping the law, but in the wealth of faith" (*ComCant* 4.2.23).

Origen's understanding of the relationship between Synagogue and Church, as I noted at the beginning of this subsection, was very strongly influenced by the Pauline arguments in Romans 11:11 and 11:25–26. There was another concept influencing his understanding, however, drawn also, partially at least, from some Pauline statements, that was at work in his understanding of Church and Synagogue. It is to this other concept that I now turn.

The pre-existent Church and Origen's understanding of Church and Synagogue in the Commentary on the Song of Songs

In Alexandria Origen had developed a concept of the Church as existing from the first creation of God.[80] As I noted at the beginning of this section on the *Commentary on the Song of Songs*, he understood Genesis 1 and 2 to speak of

---

[78] *HomEx* 8.1; trans. in *Origen: Homilies on Genesis and Exodus* (1981), 320.

[79] Ibid.; my italics.

[80] See my discussion of 2 Clement and related literature in Chapter 2, "Christian literature of the second century associated with Alexandria", p. 34.

two distinct creations, the first immaterial and the second material.[81] The creation of immaterial rational beings was a creation of beings who were all equal and enjoyed the presence of God equally. There were no Jews or Gentiles in this creation. This was an abstract concept, borrowed partly at least from Plato, which Origen seems to have developed in defense of the Church's doctrine of free-will against the Gnostic doctrine of determinism.[82] It is this community that Origen seems to intend when he speaks of the pre-existent Church, that is, the community of all the immaterial souls that have ever existed enjoying the presence of God. But these souls, each individually it seems, chose to turn from this state of enjoying the presence of God. The degree to which they chose to turn away from God resulted in three subsequent categories of beings: holy powers consisting of such beings as archangels and angels, wicked powers consisting of the devil and demons, and a group between these two extremes consisting of humans. It was this turning away and the situation it created that brought about the creation of the material world for humans, whose souls were clothed with material bodies. The goal of this second creation was to enable the now embodied souls eventually to return to their original condition in the presence of God. "The end", Origen thought, "is always like the beginning."[83]

Origen saw this pre-existent Church alluded to in Paul's remark that God "chose us in Christ before the foundation of the world" (Eph. 1:4, cited in *ComCant* 2.8.4). He also thought that Paul's statement in Ephesians 5:31–32 referred to the pre-existent Church (*ComCant* 2.8.5), as did the statement in Psalm 73:2, in which the Lord is asked to remember the congregation which he had gathered "from the beginning" (*ComCant* 2.8.4).[84] Chênevert is probably correct in his view that this pre-existent perspective on the Church is always present in Origen's thought.[85] It lurks in the background, however, more often than it is in the forefront, and at times, at least, it seems far in the background.

It seems to me that Origen speaks of the Church in four stages in the *Commentary on the Song of Songs*. The first is the pre-existent Church just described, which he must mean when he refers to the Church "before the foundation of the world" (*ComCant* 2.8.4). The second is the Church

---

[81] See above in "The identity of the bride and the pre-existent Church in the *Commentary on the Song of Songs*", p. 205.

[82] See Chapter 6, sub-section "The apostolic doctrine of creation", p. 42.

[83] *Princ* 1.6.2; trans. in *Origen: On First Principles* (1973), 53; see also *Princ* 2.1.3, and the discussion in *Princ* 3.5.4.

[84] For a fuller discussion of these passages and Origen's view of the pre-existent Church, see Heine (2002), 48–56; Chênevert (1969); 25–43, and Vogt (1974), 205–10.

[85] Chênevert (1969), 42–3.

which he identifies with the Israel of the Old Testament, which I noted above (*ComCant* 1.1.5–8).[86] This Church is probably what he intends when he extends its origin back to Adam, and "the beginning of the human race" (*ComCant* 2.8.4), though those preceding Jacob could not technically be called Israelites. This Church experiences a hiatus when the majority of the Hebrews reject Jesus. It is this hiatus that Origen understands Paul to address in Romans 11:11 and 11:25–26. The Hebrew rejection of Jesus triggered the initiation of the third stage of the Church, the Church from the Gentiles. It is the Church in this third stage to which Origen most often refers when he speaks of the Church. But none of the stages are ever dropped completely. Christ came to gather the Gentiles *and* the remnant of Jacob (*ComCant* 2.10.8). It must be remembered also, however, that Origen definitely considered the present state in the Gentile Church to be an advance over the previous state in the Hebrew Church. The elements and laws with which the Hebrews worshipped and obeyed God were only likenesses of the true worship and obedience (*ComCant* 2.8.17–29). Finally, Origen's thought presupposes, even if it does not often express it, a fourth stage of the Church, the Church of the eschaton, when the fullness of the Gentiles has entered and "all Israel" has been saved. In this final stage of the Church there will no longer be Jews and Gentiles, but there will be "one flock and one shepherd" (*HomNum* 6.4 citing John 10:16).

One must notice the similarity of this last assumed stage with the principle that the "end is always like the beginning". And one must wonder how this principle along with his early understanding of the pre-existent Church fueled the confidence he had in Paul's statement that the hardening experienced by Israel would endure "until the full number of the Gentiles has come in", at which time "all Israel will be saved" (Rom 11:25–26; NRSV). On the other hand, I will show in the next chapter that there are signs in Origen's latest works that suggest that he was rethinking some aspects at least of his earlier view that all souls would return to the blissful condition they had enjoyed in the beginning. In other words, some cracks appear to have been developing in the system he had created in Alexandria.

---

[86] See above in "Church and Synagogue on the identity of the bride", p. 210.

10

The Works and Themes of the Senior Scholar

Eusebius says the emperor Philip, who succeeded Gordian, was a Christian and that Origen had corresponded with him and his wife (*H.E.* 6.34, 36). Whether either of these assertions was true or not, the reign of Philip (244–9) was a period of peace between the Church and the empire. Origen was 60 years old when Philip came to power in 244. He produced his final works during Philip's reign. Philip was succeeded by Decius, who initiated a persecution against the Church aimed especially at its leaders. Eusebius, assuming that Philip had been a Christian, says the persecution was the result of Decius' enmity against Philip (*H.E.* 6.39). A Sibylline Oracle, written probably by a Christian, offers some confirmation to Eusebius' view when it asserts that the "murders of faithful men" in Decius' persecution was "because of the former king".[1] Fabian, bishop of Rome was martyred, Alexander, Origen's friend and bishop of Jerusalem, died in prison, as did Babylos, bishop of Antioch (Eusebius, *H.E.* 6.39.1–4). Origen was imprisoned in Caesarea and tortured (Eusebius, *H.E.* 6.39.5). He seems to have survived the persecution, which ended when Decius was murdered, but he died not too long afterwards (Eusebius, *H.E.* 7.1).

The *Commentary on Matthew* and the *Against Celsus* have been preserved from these last years of Origen's life. The latter is complete, with eight books in the Greek text. The *Commentary on Matthew*, according to Jerome's list of Origen's works, consisted of 25 books (*Ep.* 33.4). We have eight books in a Greek text (Books 10–17), which cover Matthew 13:36–22:33. There is, in addition, a later Latin translation by an unknown translator which begins at Book 12.9 (on Matt. 16:13) and continues to Matthew 27:66. This Latin translation thus overlaps a part of the preserved Greek text of the commentary and goes beyond it, providing the additional part of Origen's commentary from Matthew 22:34–27:66.[2] We have, therefore, Origen's commentary, in either Greek or Latin, on Matthew 13:36–27:66. The *Commentary on Matthew* seems to have been written before the *Against*

---

[1] Sibylline Oracles 13.85–8, trans. in *The Old Testament Pseudepigrapha*, 1 (1983), 456.
[2] For details of the Latin translation see Crouzel (1989) 42–3; Vogt (1999), 85–104.

Celsus, but Vogt thinks Origen had not yet finished it when he was working on the *Against Celsus*.[3]

Origen also wrote a commentary on the 12 minor prophets in this period (Eusebius, *H.E.* 6.39.2). He refers, in the *Against Celsus*, to his studies on "some of the twelve prophets", and says he hopes to add other commentaries to these if he is granted the time.[4] He notes some subjects that he is passing over in the *Against Celsus* but will take up, he says, in his "commentaries on the prophets" (*Cels* 7.31). This seems to be an allusion to more anticipated work on the 12 prophets. His work on the 12 prophets is lost.

There are hints in the *Against Celsus* that Origen did not think of it as his final written work. He suggests that he intends yet to treat the events connected with Jesus' burial in a future work devoted to such matters (*Cels* 2.69). He also hints that he may write a work on the subject of whether evil will return after its disappearance (*Cels* 4.69). Even at the end of the treatise he is thinking of the possibility of writing another work against Celsus if it should be discovered that Celsus had actually carried through on his promise to write a sequel to *The True Doctrine* (*Cels* 8.76).

The literature Origen produced during the reign of Philip was that of a senior scholar and theologian. Why did he choose to write on these particular subjects at this time? He provides some reasons for writing the *Against Celsus*. The first, and most obvious, is that his long-time friend and patron, Ambrose, had requested a work from him replying to the treatise of Celsus (*Cels* Pref. 1, 3). Origen was reluctant to undertake the project, suggesting that the best argument against this obscure work of a man long dead was to let it lie in oblivion, and for Christians to continue to live out the teachings of Jesus (*Cels* Pref. 2, 4). But, feeling the pressure of his friend's request, he undertook the work (*Cels* Pref. 3). He says that he is writing for those totally inexperienced with the Christian faith or for those whom Paul called "weak in faith", but not for "true Christians" (*Cels* Pref. 6). The preface, which Origen says he had composed after he had completed approximately half of the first book, speaks somewhat disparagingly of the enterprise (*Cels* Pref. 6). Later, however, he seems to have come to think of what he was doing in the work as having pastoral importance for the Christian community. He says that although the

---

[3] Vogt (1999), 65–7.
[4] *Cels* 7.11. In *Ep* 33.4 Jerome refers to commentaries by Origen on Hosea, Joel, Amos, Jonah, Micah, Nahum, Habakkuk, Zephaniah, Haggai, Zechariah, and Malachi.

work is addressed to an unbeliever, (presumably he means Celsus), he is writing for Christians who are immature in the faith and susceptible, as Paul had said, of being tossed about " 'by every wind of doctrine' " (*Cels* 5.18). The defense, in other words, is to assist those who are young in the Christian faith to stand firm against the sorts of attacks Celsus, and those like him, make on the doctrines that Christians believe. Its intended audience is Christian. The fact that Celsus had presented part of his attack on the Christian faith as the objections of a Jew to Christianity may have contributed to Origen's decision to assent to Ambrose's request. Origen may have seen this as an opportunity to set forth a Christian answer for the Church in Caesarea to some of the objections the Jews there raised against the Christians. It should be remembered that the title of Celsus' book was *The True Doctrine*. Origen is, by contrast, setting forth what he considers to be the true doctrine of the Christians. In his concluding remarks to Ambrose, he says, "It is for the reader...to judge which of the two breathes more of the spirit of the true God and of the temper of devotion towards Him and of the truth attainable by men, that is, of sound doctrines which lead men to live the best life."[5] Doctrine, as noted previously, was never an abstract system for Origen. It was, as this closing statement makes clear, a set of teachings intended to produce Christian character (cf. *Princ* 1. Pref. 1).

The occasion for the writing of the *Commentary on Matthew*, by contrast, must be surmised because the first books of the commentary, where Origen's remarks about such matters usually appear, are lost. There is no mention of Ambrose in any of the preserved books. It may be that Origen himself made the decision to write this commentary. He might have chosen to write on Matthew's Gospel because of the strong Jewish presence in Caesarea. Matthew's Gospel had been considered by the second-century Church to have special connections with the Jewish community. Papias, the second-century bishop of Hierapolis, had asserted that Matthew had collected the sayings of Jesus in the Hebrew language (Eusebius, *H.E.* 3.39.16). Origen was aware of and accepted a tradition very similar to that. In a fragment preserved from the first book of his *Commentary on Matthew* he says that it was Matthew, the apostle and tax-collector, who wrote the Gospel, and that he wrote it in the Hebrew language for Jewish converts to Christianity (Eusebius, *H.E.* 6.25.4). Writing on Matthew's Gospel would have been a natural choice for Origen to make in the Caesarean context.

---

[5] *Cels* 8.76, trans in *Origen: Contra Celsum* (1965), 511.

EXOTERIC AND ESOTERIC DOCTRINES

The *Commentary on Matthew* and the *Against Celsus* provide Origen's most mature thinking about the Christian faith. He believed that, like the doctrines of the philosophers, some of the doctrines of the Christians were exoteric and others esoteric (*Cels* 1.7). These terms, however, have a slightly narrower meaning for him than they have in their general philosophical usage. By exoteric he does not mean doctrines understood by the general population outside the Church, though that population may, in a limited sense at least, be included. He means primarily the doctrines understood by the majority within the Church whom he more usually refers to as the simple. The esoteric doctrines, likewise, are not those understood by the "insiders" in general, but only by those Christians who are philosophically inclined and apply the hermeneutic of allegory to uncover the deeper doctrines in the Biblical texts.

He says that the exoteric doctrines, which are known to "almost the whole world", comprise "Jesus' birth from a virgin,...his crucifixion, and...resurrection,...and...the proclamation of the judgment which punishes sinners according to their deserts and pronounces the righteous worthy of reward".[6] He also believed that the traditional doctrines of the Christians originated with Jesus (*Cels* 5.61). It is clear in the writings of this last period of Origen's life that he did not consider these to be merely the common doctrines that everyone associated with Christians, but that he himself shared these basic beliefs that the majority of second-and third-century Christians held. He believed, for example, in the historicity of the Biblical accounts (*Cels* 2.58; 3.5; but cf. 5.42), in the virgin birth of Jesus (*Cels* 1.32–7; 2.69; 6.73), the divinity of Jesus (*Cels* 3.33), the miracles performed by Jesus (*Cels* 2.48), the death, burial, and bodily resurrection of Jesus (*Cels* 2.61–2, 65, 69), and in a literal consummation and judgment (*ComMt* 12.30; 14.8–12; 16.22). He asserts that all ideas accepted in the Church must "harmonize with the traditional doctrines received from Jesus".[7] There are two important assumptions in this statement: (1) he recognized a common body of traditional Christian doctrines, and (2) he believed that these doctrines were derived from Jesus himself (cf. *Princ* 1. Pref. 2).

The earlier Christian proof from prophecy argument became more important to Origen in his later years.[8] He had cited certain prophetic texts

---

[6] *Cels* 1.7, trans in *Origen: Contra Celsum* (1965), 10.

[7] *Cels* 5.61, trans in *Origen: Contra Celsum* (1965), 311.

[8] See *Cels* 1.33–5, 49–55; 2.37; 3.2–4, 15; 4.2; 5.53; 6.35, 47; 7.7; *ComMt* 10.21. For a general discussion of the proof from prophecy argument in the second century see Heine (2007), 97–141. For a detailed discussion see Skarsaune (1987) and Ungern-Sternberg (1913).

related to Jesus to prove Jesus' deity in conjunction with his argument for the inspiration of the Scriptures in his Alexandrian work, *On First Principles* (4.1.3–6). There he appealed to Genesis 49:10, Deuteronomy 32:21, Psalm 45:1–3, Isaiah 7:14, Micah 5:2, Daniel 9:24, and Job 3:8. All of these passages, with the exception of the Job passage, were common texts used in the second-century proof from prophecy argument. None of them appear elsewhere in Origen's *On First Principles*. They play no role at all in his discussions of Christ in the other sections of the treatise. In the sections of the *Commentary on John* produced at Alexandria he also takes note of prophetic arguments which are more likely, he says, to produce faith in Christ than the stories of his miracles. In this context he alludes to prophecies which speak of the place of Christ's birth, his homeland, his teachings and miracles, and his suffering and resurrection. He praises the prophetic witness, but he does not cite prophetic texts and argue for specific points about Jesus from them (*ComJn* 2.202–9). He quotes Genesis 49:10 once in the first book of the *Commentary on John*, but does not use it as an argument, saying its discussion would be more appropriate for other places (*ComJn* 1.143), and he also alludes to Job 3:8 in the same book (*ComJn* 1.96). Deuteronomy 32:21 is not cited in the *Commentary on John*, nor is Isaiah 7:14, or Daniel 9:24. Micah 5:2 is once alluded to in the *Commentary on John*, but only in the section written at Caesarea (*ComJn* 19.104). The only passage from the prophetic texts appearing in *On First Principles* 4.1 which Origen actually discusses in his Alexandrian works is Psalm 45:1–3. He discusses these verses, however, because he thinks that most Christians misinterpret them. He does not use them in a positive way in his own argument.[9] These observations suggest that while Origen was aware of the proof from prophecy arguments at Alexandria, they played almost no role in the works he produced there.

There are numerous proofs from prophecy texts and arguments, however, in the *Against Celsus* and the *Commentary on Matthew*. One reason for this, of course, is that Celsus had put part of his attack on Jesus in the mouth of an imaginary Jew. The proof from prophecy arguments had originated in earlier Christian–Jewish debates and was especially suitable for Origen's Jewish context in Caesarea, both in answering the objections of Celsus' imaginary Jew and in discussions with his own Jewish contemporaries in the local Synagogue.

Origen considered the argument from prophecy to be the strongest confirmation of Jesus' authority (*Cels* 1.49). All the major Christian

---

[9] *ComJn* 1.280–87. The only place where a phrase from Ps 45:1–3 is used in a positive way by Origen in the Alexandrian works is in *Princ* 2.6.1.

understandings of Jesus had been foretold, from his birth to his crucifixion and resurrection. He argued that Micah 5:2 had foretold that the Messiah would be born in Bethlehem and that this was where Jesus had been born (*Cels* 1.51). Jesus' birth occurred, moreover, at the time prophesied in Genesis 49:10 when rulers ceased from Judah in conjunction with the appearance of "the expectation of the nations". Jesus is the "the expectation of the nations" in Genesis 49:10 in whom the nations/Gentiles have put their trust (Is 49:8–9; *Cels* 1.53; *ComMt* 10.21). Isaiah 7:14, in the Septuagint translation used by Origen and the Church, shows, in his opinion, that Jesus was born of a virgin. Here Origen engages in an argument against the later Jewish translations of Isaiah that did not translate the text to say a "virgin" would conceive, but a "young woman" would conceive (*Cels* 1.33–5). The philological details of his argument against the later translations are not correct, but the length to which he goes shows the importance of the connection of Isaiah 7:14 with the birth of Jesus for him.[10]

Prophecy also confirmed the events of Jesus' ministry for Origen. Celsus had accused Christians of believing Jesus to be the Son of God because he healed the lame and blind, and raised the dead. Origen says, in effect, that is correct, but we make the connection between these events and Jesus' deity because of the prophecy in Isaiah 35:5–6 (*Cels* 2.48). Isaiah 53 shows that the passion of Jesus was not something unexpected, and also provides a rationale for it, namely that it was to benefit humanity (*Cels* 1.54–5). Psalm 16:25–8, the text cited in Acts 2 to confirm the resurrection of Jesus, still functions in this way for Origen. In it he sees a prophesy of Christ's descent to Hades, his resurrection, and ascension (*ComMt* 16.8; *SerMt* 132, 138; *Cels* 2.62; 3.32).

In the opening of the third book, *Against Celsus*, Origen reiterates the points about Jesus that are rooted in the proof from prophecy argument: his birthplace, his virgin birth, his signs and wonders, the swift spread of his message, his sufferings, and his resurrection (*Cels* 3.2). The prophets, he says near the end of the treatise, "foretold the story of Jesus Christ".[11] Christians prove, he argues, that Jesus was the one prophesied by juxtaposing quotations from the prophets and from the Gospels (*Cels* 3.15; 6.35; cf. 5.53; *ComMt* 12.2).

Origen believed these exoteric doctrines accepted by the majority of Christians, or he would not have argued so strenuously for them. He also believed, however, that there were aspects of the faith that went

---

[10] On the inaccuracy of the argument see Kamesar (1990), 57–60.

[11] *Cels* 7.7, trans. in *Origen: Contra Celsum* (1965), 401.

beyond the understandings of most Christians. These were the "esoteric" doctrines that only the philosophically inclined understood. The esoteric doctrines grew out of the exoteric ones. The exoteric doctrines, therefore, were always important, but the esoteric ones represented the true goal of Christian teaching (*Princ* 4.7–8; *Cels* 2.4). Those with above average minds could understand what is hidden "in the law, the prophets, and the gospels".[12] Those who can understand Christian doctrines philosophically perceive such teachings as those about God with a clarity that supersedes that of the majority of Christians (*Cels* 3.79). The wrath of God, for example, has nothing to do with the emotion that humans experience, but is a way of speaking of God's corrective discipline (*Cels* 4.72). The death and burial of Jesus are laden with meanings that reach far beyond the events themselves (*Cels* 2.69). The resurrection of the flesh is "preached in the churches" but "is understood more clearly by the intelligent".[13] The Gospels are not simple, he asserts, except for those who are simple in their understanding. When Jesus says, "Let the person who has ears hear", he is suggesting that there is a deeper meaning in his words. For those capable of hearing these deeper meanings, the Gospels conceal things worthy of God (*ComMt* 10.1–2).

At Alexandria Origen had constructed a kind of hierarchy of Scripture in the first book of his *Commentary on John*. There he argued that among the Scriptures recognized in the Churches the law and the prophets were foundational documents, followed by the apostolic writings, but the Gospels formed the apex of the hierarchy of Scripture (*ComJn* 1.13–24). Towards the end of his life he still worked with that hierarchical understanding of Scripture. The whole of Scripture speaks of Christ. The Gospels, however, do it most clearly and thoroughly. The writings of the Old Testament, nevertheless, are absolutely necessary if Christ is to be properly understood.[14] Discussing the parable of the pearls in his *Commentary on Matthew*, Origen identifies Christ as the expensive pearl and the law and the prophets as the less valuable ones. The law and the prophets are necessary, nevertheless, for bringing one to the knowledge of Christ. Presumable he means, by analogy, that one could not recognize an exceptionally valuable pearl if one did not first know pearls in general. The majority, however, he asserts, incorrectly think they can find Christ without a clear understanding of the law and the prophets (*ComMt* 10.8–9).

---

[12] *Cels* 3.74, trans. in *Origen: Contra Celsum* (1965), 178.
[13] *Cels* 5.18, trans. in *Origen: Contra Celsum* (1965), 277; cf. *Cels* 4.72.
[14] See Vogt (1974), 195–6.

The esoteric doctrines are those which ascend "from the events recorded to have happened to the truths which they signified".[15] They had been of central importance to Origen from his earliest days as a Christian teacher. The *On First Principles* is filled with such doctrines and interpretations of Scripture. What is different in his late life, it seems, is that the exoteric doctrines had become more important to him than they were in his Alexandrian period.

A NEW EMPHASIS ON THE CHURCH AND SOTERIOLOGY

Doctrines about the Church became more important to Origen in his later life.[16] They appear repeatedly in these two last works that we have from him. I think this resulted from two factors. First, Origen was directly involved in the full life of the Church in Caesarea. Bishop Theoctistus assigned him the task of preaching to the common people in addition to his work as a scholar and educator. In Alexandria Demetrius had limited his labor to the classroom, forbidding him the broader exposure of preaching to the populace. In Caesarea Origen had to think about how doctrine related to the lives of the common people who made up the Church. The second factor forcing Origen to think more theologically about the Church in Caesarea was the presence of the active rabbinic school there. In immediate juxtaposition with a very active Jewish community he had to reflect on its relationship to the Church. He did not think of the Church as a community of faith that arose after the death of Christ. It had existed from the beginning of creation, and all the Hebrew saints of the Old Testament were a part of it. In his interpretation of the workers in the vineyard (Matt. 20:1–16), he identifies the vineyard as the kingdom of God which stretches from Adam to his own time and says that "all . . . who perform the works of the kingdom of God in a manner worthy of salvation, will receive the denarius" (*ComMt* 15.35). Moreover, the part of the Church's Scripture which Christians called the Old Testament, had been written by and about the Jewish community.[17] But in his own experience the two faith communities stood over against one another in a hostile relationship. He had to think about how the current chasm between Church and Synagogue fit into the plan of God and how it would be resolved.

---

[15] *Cels* 2.69, trans. in *Origen: Contra Celsum* (1965), 119.
[16] There have been two major studies of Origen's doctrine of the Church: Vogt (1974) and Ledegang (2001).
[17] See Vogt (1974), 194.

The Church and the Jews

We have already noted Origen's reflections on the Church and the Jews in his homilies and in his earlier commentaries produced at Caesarea.[18] In this section attention will be focused on the *Commentary on Matthew* and, to a lesser extent, the *Against Celsus*. It is in the *Commentary on Matthew* especially that Origen reflects on the relationship between the Church and the Synagogue.

Origen recognizes the tension between the two opposing communities but considers them both essential to the plan of God and to the wholeness of the Church. The antagonism between the two communities can be felt in his reply to the remark Celsus put into the mouth of his imaginary Jew when he said that the prophets had not proclaimed "a plague like" Jesus. Origen replies, "He spoke like a Jew, in keeping with their bitterness, when he reviled Jesus without using any persuasive argument at all" (*Cels* 2.29). He can speak quite bitterly of the Jewish attack on Jesus, as when he says,

[E]ven now Jesus is delivered in Jerusalem (and by Jerusalem I mean those people whose hopes are centered on this earthly place) to the Jews who claim to be serving God. And those who are high priests, as it were, and the scribes, who boast that they interpret the divine scriptures, condemn Jesus to death by their evil speech against him. They are always handing Jesus over to the Gentiles, mocking him and his teaching among themselves, and tongue-lashing the worship of God through Jesus Christ. They themselves crucify him by their anathemas and their desire to destroy his teaching (*ComMt* 16.3).

In another context Origen accuses the Jews of imprisoning the prophetic word because they do not receive the one who was the subject of prophecy (*ComMt* 10.22). This latter passage rumbles with undertones of the debate between the Church and the Synagogue while pursuing the exposition of a Biblical text. The same rumblings are heard in the exposition of Matthew 13:57, which speaks of the Jews in the text being scandalized at Jesus, to which Jesus replied that a prophet is dishonored only in his own country. Origen then comments, "And if anyone should perceive Jesus Christ, 'a stumbling-block to the Jews' who persecute him down to the present moment, being proclaimed and believed in by the Gentiles,...he will see that Jesus had no honor in his own country but that he is honored by the Gentiles who are strangers to 'the covenants'" (*ComMt* 10.16; cf. 16.23; 17.14). He concludes these remarks with the significant observation that

[18] See Chapter 8, in "Origen's homilies in the setting of Caesarea's Jewish community", p. 172 and Chapter 9.

in spite of the dishonor, Jesus "'was teaching in their synagogue' *neither separating from it nor rejecting it*" (*ComMt* 10.16, my italics). This, I think, was the problem Origen perceived in his own situation—how to maintain a relationship with the Synagogue in spite of its rejection and dishonor of the Christian faith in Jesus.

Origen finds links between the two communities in the symbolism of various stories in Matthew's Gospel. The donkey and the colt that Jesus sends his disciples to release and bring to him in Matthew 21:1–5 are the Synagogue and the Church of the Gentiles. Jesus wants to release both from their bondage to sin by the teachings of his disciples (*ComMt* 16.15). There are several passages where Origen refers to a commonality between the Church and Synagogue because they share a common scripture. He considers Matthew 21:42, which speaks of the rejected stone becoming the cornerstone, to shame the Jews. They considered themselves to be builders of the people but they rejected Jesus, whom God set to be the stone which "holds together the two corners of the Old and New Testament and the two buildings of the peoples" (*ComMt* 17.12). The parable of the vineyard taken from the first recipients because they were untrustworthy and given to others, which concludes with the statement that "the kingdom of God will be taken from you and given to a nation which produces its fruits", is applied to the Scriptures (Matt. 21:33–43). "'The Lord of the vineyard'", Origen says, "'delivered' this vineyard, which is...the law and the prophets and all divine Scripture, 'to farmers'. The first were that people (for they first 'were entrusted with the logia of God'), but the second was 'the nation producing its fruits,' the church from the Gentiles" (*ComMt* 17.7; cf. *Cels* 2.78). This exposition puts more emphasis, perhaps, on the separation between the two communities, but it recognizes that the Scripture of the Gentile Church was first the Scripture of the Synagogue, and that both are in some way tied together on the basis of this common Scripture.

The relationship between the two communities on the basis of their common Scripture is even more important in an interpretation Origen gives to the passage about levirate marriage in Deuteronomy 25. He suggests that the woman is the human soul, married first to the letter of the law, but bearing no children in this marriage. The brother to whom she is subsequently married is the spiritual law. In this marriage she produces children. Then Origen makes a significant statement about the Church and Synagogue relationship: "The <two> indeed are brothers, and the two laws ***[19] who

---

[19] Klostermann thinks there are some words missing here on the basis of the parallel Latin translation (*Origenes Werke: Origenes Matthäuserklärung* I (1935), 675).

always dwell together have been born from one mother of understanding. For their house has not been divided, but they are 'brothers' and both interpretations dwell in one house, namely the Scripture which contains them." The child, furthermore, is named after the first brother. "For the name of the one born of the spiritual law is the name of the one who died, since he too was called law of God, and the name of the man who died need not be obliterated by the Israel that is discernable and is truly Israel, even though he himself was obliterated" (*ComMt* 17.31). This latter means, I think, that Christians still refer to the law interpreted spiritually as law, even though they consider the law in its literal sense to be dead.

The parable of the two sons asked to work in the vineyard which concludes with Jesus' pronouncement that "the tax-collectors and the prostitutes will precede you into the kingdom" is also understood to speak to the contrast and the unity of the Synagogue and Church (Matt. 21:28–32). This does not mean, Origen argues, that Israel will never enter the kingdom. Otherwise Jesus would not have spoken about "preceding" because this would have been an inappropriate idea if the others were not to follow. This reveals, he thinks, the truth of the Pauline statement in Romans 11:25 that once " 'the fullness of the Gentiles' has entered, then 'all Israel will be saved' " (*ComMt* 17.5).

Origen has an extended discussion of the relationship between the Church and Synagogue and the ultimate resolution of their separation in his exposition of Jesus' teachings about divorce in Matthew 19. The Synagogue, he asserts, was Christ's first wife, but she revolted against her husband and committed fornication with the devil, so he divorced her (*ComMt* 14.17). Origen then nuances this interpretation by turning specifically to the divorce legislation in Deuteronomy 24:1 and seeking the spiritual meaning of this law. He starts with Isaiah's question about the whereabouts of the bill of divorce with which God had dismissed Israel (Isa. 50:1). He takes this to suggest that Israel departed from God without having an actual bill of divorce. Then he turns to the wording of Deuteronomy 24 and says that "later, when an unseemly thing was found in her . . . he wrote her a bill of divorce". The "unseemly thing" was the choice of Barabbas over Jesus and the insistence that Jesus be crucified. "The new covenant, which summoned the Gentiles into the house of him who had cast off his former wife was, in effect, that bill of divorce." He then cites what he considers to be the signs that show that Israel has been divorced and cast out: the destruction of Jerusalem and the temple along with all the acts of worship associated with the temple, the Synagogue's loss of much of its civil authority, and the absence of prophets among the Jews (*ComMt* 14.19).

Origen then takes the metaphor of the divine divorce of the Synagogue further, following the text of Deuteronomy 24:2–3, which presents the scenario that the divorced woman marries another and, in time, the second husband also divorces her. The new husband of the Synagogue, he suggests, is either the devil or an evil power. The goodness of God, however, will bring it about that "at the end of things" the second husband, like the husband assumed in Deuteronomy 24:3, will divorce her. It is at this point that Romans 11:25–6 presents a conundrum for Origen's interpretation, for it speaks of all Israel being saved after the fullness of the Gentiles enters. Deuteronomy 24:4, however, forbids the wife who was divorced and married another to return to her former husband because she is said to be polluted. He is convinced, on the basis of Romans 11:25–6, that there will be an eschatological turning of Israel to Christ, but his elaborate interpretation of the marriage and divorce and remarriage of the Synagogue does not seem to permit it. His thinking is not very clear at this point, but he appears to make some separate suggestions, unrelated to one another, it seems to me at least, for ways to solve the problem and maintain the anagogical analogy of the divorce legislation in Deuteronomy 24 with the situation of the Synagogue. First, he suggests that the first husband may return and take the woman back in an act of saving her. This would involve her being saved after she was defiled. Second, he notes the prohibition in Leviticus 21:14 of a priest marrying a prostitute. This applies, he says, only to priests. He suggests that if one considers the calling of the Gentiles to be the prostitute in question, then one can appeal to the divine command to Hosea to take a prostitute for his wife (Hos 1:2).[20] This is like, he says, Jesus' statement that the priests are free of guilt when they break the law of the Sabbath in performing their duties in the temple (Matt. 12:5). On the basis of Hebrews 9:10, which refers to the temporary nature of the old laws until "the time of the new order comes", he argues that as the Son of man is Lord of the Sabbath, so he is Lord of all the laws and can change them at the proper time (*ComMt* 14.19–20). This last argument seems to be Origen's answer to the dilemma, but he never actually chooses among the suggestions he has made.

This elaborate and detailed reading of the situation of the Synagogue into the divorce legislation of Deuteronomy 24 highlights several aspects of Origen's attitude towards the Synagogue. He is quite explicit in

---

[20] Cf., on this idea, *ComMt* 12.4, where God is said to leave the adulterous synagogue and take a wife of fornication (Hos. 1:2), meaning the Gentiles. The latter are compared to Rahab, the prostitute who received Joshua's spies and was consequently saved.

expressing the Jews' rejection of Jesus, and their role in his condemnation, even though he does it in terms of the Gospel texts. He considers them to be alien to the Church in his time, for the latter is the new bride of the husband Israel had forsaken. He accepts Paul's arguments in Romans 11 about Israel being cut off as a description of the situation he knows. On the other hand, he also accepts Paul's statements about a future salvation for the Jews. Church and Synagogue have had the same husband and at some future time they will be one family.

The rock, the keys, and the gates of Hades

Frend points out that in the third century Rome was being increasingly recognized as the "senior bishopric" and that the western segment of the Church was interpreting Matthew 16:18 to refer to the establishment of Peter's authority.[21] When Origen discusses Matthew 16:16–19, he argues against those who claim that the passage refers exclusively to Peter.[22]

But if you think, [he says,] that the whole Church is built by God on that one Peter alone, what do you say of John, the son "of thunder", or each of the other apostles? Would we then be so bold as to say truthfully that the gates of Hades will not prevail against Peter in particular, but that they will prevail against the rest of the apostles and those who are perfect?...And does not the saying, "Upon this rock I will build my church," apply to all of them? And did Christ give "the keys of the kingdom of heaven" to Peter alone, and no one else of all the blessed ones will receive them? But if the saying, "I will give you the keys of the kingdom of heaven" applies to others, should this not be true of everything previously said as well...? Here, indeed, the words "Everything that you bind on earth will be bound in heaven," etc. appear to be said to Peter, but in John's Gospel, the Savior gives the disciples the Holy Spirit by breathing on them and says, "Receive the Holy Spirit"; [if you dismiss the sins of anyone, they are dismissed, but whose sins you retain shall be retained].[23]

Origen argues that the recognition that Jesus is the Christ the Son of the living God is the result of illumination from the Father in heaven in the case of everyone who makes the confession with understanding. This means that every person who makes this confession is a Peter, and consequently also a rock on which the Church is built (*ComMt* 12.10; cf. *Cels* 6.77; *ComMt* 15.22). This is not, however, a carte blanche endorsement of every single

---

[21] Frend (1984), 400. Cyprian, however, who was a western bishop, acknowledged the importance of the see of Rome but did not acknowledge its superiority (ibid., 352).

[22] See Ledegang (2001), 280.

[23] *ComMt* 12.11. The bracketed words from John 20:22–3 are found in the parallel Latin translation of Origen's text (*Origenes Werke: Origenes Matthäuserklärung* I (1935), 87).

person associated with the Church as a Peter and a rock. Only the virtuous qualify for these titles. There are many people who claim to be a part of the Church but who live in a way contrary to their claim. Here the phrase "gates of Hades", another of the key terms in Origen's exposition, comes into play. Every sin, he says, is "a gate of Hades". Therefore, no one living in sin can be said to be a rock, for the "gates of Hates" are prevailing against that person. False doctrines are also "gates of Hades", and consequently, Marcion, Basilides, and Valentinus can each be said to have built a gate of Hades (*ComMt* 12.12).

The demand for virtuous living appears also in Origen's interpretation of the phrase about the gift of the "keys of the kingdom" with their powers of binding and loosing (*ComMt* 12.14). This phrase too applies "to every Peter". The statement, "I will give you the keys of the kingdom of heaven", Origen argues, must be understood in conjunction with the statement, "The gates of Hades will not prevail against it." Only one against whom the gates of Hades do not prevail receives the gift of the "keys", and these keys are as many as the gates of the virtues, which they open. Origen understands this gift to convey a great clarity of moral perception, which results in a great moral and spiritual authority.

The rock [he asserts], on which Christ builds the church, namely everyone who says, "You are the Christ, the son of the living God", has great authority. His judgments remain firm, as if God were passing judgment in him.... The gates of Hades, however, prevail against the person who judges unjustly and does not "bind on earth" in accordance with the word of God, nor "loose on earth" in accordance with his will. But the gates of Hades do not prevail where one judges justly. It is for this reason that such a person has "the keys of the kingdom of heaven", to open for those who have been loosed on earth, that in heaven they may be loosed and free, and to bind for those bound by his just judgment on earth, that they may be bound and judged in heaven (*ComMt* 12.14).

Origen was aware, of course, that the bishops of the Church used this statement of Jesus to authenticate their authority to forgive or to refuse to forgive sins. He does not argue that this is an improper application of the statement. But he does apply the same basis for the authority to do so to the bishops that he has applied to every Peter. Only the person against whom the gates of Hades do not prevail, that is, the person whose life is not ensnared in sin, can possess the gift of the keys. The authority does not reside in an ecclesiastical office, he argues. It is a moral authority that resides in Christian character. Anyone who does not qualify morally as a true Peter yet thinks he can bind or loose on earth and that his judgments will be honored in heaven is arrogant and does not understand the meaning of the Scriptures (*ComMt* 12.14).

When Origen was living in Alexandria he had visited Rome. Zephyrinus was bishop at the time, and Callistus and Hippolytus were rivals hoping to succeed him. One of the charges Hippolytus later brought against Callistus, when the latter had been made bishop of Rome, was that he assumed the authority to forgive certain sins which should not be forgiven.[24] We do not know if Origen's remarks here reflect this argument about the bishop's authority to forgive sins he may have heard at that time in Rome, or whether he is thinking about the issue in general as it was being practiced in the Church at large. He seems not, however, to be projecting a purely hypothetical situation which he had never witnessed in the actual Church.

When Origen comes to discuss Matthew 18:15–18, he recognizes a priority to the authority given to Peter over the authority granted to bind and loose in these verses.[25] He notes a possible problem between the statement in Matthew 16 and that in Matthew 18 concerning the authority given to those who three times admonish a sinner in Matthew 18:18. It seems to be the same authority given to Peter alone earlier. It isn't completely clear whether he intends Peter exclusively, or all who deserve to be called Peter, in the contrast. He finds an answer to his problem in a textual difference between the two statements. In Matthew 16:19 the word "heaven" is plural, as it regularly is in Matthew when he speaks of the kingdom of heaven. In Matthew 18:18, however, it is singular in some manuscripts as it must have been in the text that Origen used. He thinks there is intentional meaning in this difference. Peter received the keys, not of one heaven alone, but of all the heavens, and consequently, he received a far greater power than is indicated

---

[24] Hippolytus, *Haer* 9.12.20–6.

[25] He also refers to the Church being built on Peter, by whom he seems to mean the one individual, in *ComJn* 5.3, a fragment from the section written at Alexandria, preserved in Eusebius, *H.E.* 6.25.8, as he does also in a Caesarean homily (*HomEx* 5.4) for which, however, we have only the later Latin translation of Rufinus. *FragComJn* 22, on John 1:42, which would have been in one of the early books of the commentary written at Caesarera, between Books 6, which ends with John 1:29, and 10, which begins with John 2:12, also refers to Jesus saying to Peter that he will build the Church on the rock in conjunction with a statement about Peter's name coming from *petra*, which means rock. The fragment is brief, however, and could have been further nuanced by Origen in ways that the excerpter neglected. There is a somewhat similar fragment on Matthew 16:13–18 (*FragMt* 345 II) in which it says that Christ "calls him Peter because of the firmness and stability of his faith, on which [i.e. faith] Christ said he will build the church, since he first established the doctrines of the church among both Jews and Greeks. And the church was built on him." Klostermann suggests that this fragment is related to *ComMt* 12.10–11, but indicates some indefiniteness about the fragment coming from Origen. I can find nothing in the fragment that parallels the Greek text that we have of the commentary on these verses in *ComMt* 12.10–12.

in the statement made to those who three times admonish a sinner in Matthew 18:18, which gives authority only in a single heaven (*ComMt* 13.31).

The death of Jesus and its significance

When Origen discusses the death of Jesus for humanity the first question he asks is who or what died? He looks at this from the perspective of the titles given to Jesus in the Bible.[26] In a book written at Caesarea, probably during the reign of Gordian,[27] he asserts that the *Logos*, who was in the beginning with God, is incapable of death, as is Wisdom, Truth, and all the other titles associated with the deity of Jesus. It was the man Jesus, "born of the seed of David according to the flesh", who died, Origen thinks. It is this man, capable of death, who is indicated by the title "son of man" in the Bible (*ComJn* 32.322; 28.157–60). The prophets, Origen argues against Celsus, did not predict that "God would be crucified"; they make it clear, on the contrary, that it was a man who suffered.[28] When he comments on the statement in Matthew 20:28 that "the son of man...gave his life a ransom for many", he complains that some, "in the fantasy of praising Christ, confuse issues concerning the firstborn of all creation with issues concerning the soul and body of Jesus,...thinking what was seen and present in this life was one and not at all compounded".[29] He then asks if they think that "the deity of the image 'of the invisible God' and the pre-eminence of the firstborn 'of all creation', or...He in whom 'all things have been created'...was given as a ransom for many" (*ComMt* 16.8).

Origen has no concept of the divine dying. Jesus was a being compounded of the divine and the human. Only the human died on the cross. What the Jews destroyed "was not God, but a man....[T]he Word in the beginning with God, who was also God the Word, did not die." "[T]he image of the invisible God, the Firstborn of all creation does not admit of death. But this man, the purest of all living creatures, died for the people."[30] Crouzel is correct when he observes that, for Origen, redemption was the work of Christ's *humanity*.[31] This is not the Gnostic idea, however,

---

[26] See Heine (2004a), 93–5.   [27] See Chapter 9 at n. 9.

[28] *Cels* 7.16; trans. in *Origen: Contra Celsum* (1965), 407.

[29] Hagemann (1864), 309–11, argues that this was the teaching of Callistus. Cf. above, Chapter 4, in "Monarchians, Heracleon, and the Alexandrian Theological Milieu in Origen's *Commentary on John* 1:1b–3", p. 97.

[30] *ComJn* 20.85; *ComJn* 28.159–60; trans in *Origen: Commentary on the Gospel according to John Books 13–32* (1993), 224, 325.

[31] Crouzel (1989), 194–7.

of a phantom body which the true Jesus abandoned on the cross, laughing at those who thought he was suffering there,[32] though both ideas draw on some of the same Greek concepts of deity. Origen's thought differs from Gnostic thought. He does not despise the human Jesus. The humanity of Jesus was a necessary part of the divine plan. He even suggests that Jesus, in his humanity, was exalted to the level of the *Logos* because he glorified God in his death (*ComJn* 32.325–6). In another context he argues that the crucified Jesus Christ is one in soul and body with the "first-born of all creation" "even more than 'he who clings to the Lord is one spirit'" (*ComMt* 16.8).

Assuming a human nature meant dying a human death (*Cels* 1.61; cf. *ComJn* 6.177). The death of Jesus, therefore, was inherent in the incarnation from the beginning. If he had not wanted to die for humanity, he would not have come (*Cels* 2.23). Origen sometimes talks of the death of Jesus for humanity in generic terms. He speaks of it as "benefiting" the human race (*Cels* 1.61; 2.23). This benefit, however, seems to be directly related to what has been called the classic, or "Christus victor" doctrine of the atonement,[33] for Origen speaks of people everywhere being able to escape the hold of demons because of Jesus' death (*Cels* 7.17; 1.31). This imagery, as well as other imagery he uses of the atonement, is drawn from the Bible. Origen cites Colossians 2:15, where Jesus is said to triumph over the principalities and powers on the cross (*ComMt* 12.18). He joins this imagery with Jesus' statement in John 12:31–2 about casting out "the ruler of this world" and drawing "all people to himself" by the power of his forthcoming crucifixion, and understands the two together to refer to Jesus' stripping Satan of his powers so that people may freely come to salvation. Once Jesus "'put off the rulers and authorities and made a show of them by boldly triumphing in the cross', if anyone is ashamed of the cross of Christ he is ashamed of the economy [of salvation] for which those powers were overcome" (*ComMt* 12.18). Christ's triumph over the powers has its practical application when Origen urges people to break the bonds of the passions and vices with which the powers have bound them by crucifying their own "flesh with its passions and desires".[34]

On the basis of Matthew 20:28, Origen speaks of the atonement as a ransom.[35] The obvious question that arises is to whom was the ransom paid? Certainly not to God, he says. Could it have been paid to the devil?

---

[32] See Pagels (1979), 72–3.

[33] Aulén (1961). For his location of Origen within this view, see 38, 49.

[34] Gal. 5:24 (NRSV); *HomGn* 9.3.

[35] I am treating this separately from the Christus Victor doctrine, although Aulén (1961), 47–57, subsumes the ransom under the Christus Victor theme.

He concludes that this was the case, though he recognizes that this view is not without problems. The devil, he says,

> had power over us until the soul of Jesus was given to him as a ransom for us. He was deceived <of course and imagined> that he could have power over it. He did not see that he could not apply torture to constrain it. For this reason "death", having thought it had power over "him, no longer had power" over the <only> one who was free "among the dead" and stronger than the power of death. He was so much stronger that those held by death who wished to follow him were able to be free. Death no longer had any power against them at all, for death cannot assail anyone who is with Jesus (*ComMt* 16.8).

This version of the ransom doctrine of the atonement contains hints of the theory of the deception of the devil which is later associated especially with Gregory of Nyssa.[36] In Origen's discussion it is not the ransom price that frees souls from the devil's grip, but the impotence of death in the presence of the indestructible power of the soul of Jesus, something the devil had not anticipated.[37]

De Faye thought Origen considered the death of Jesus important only for the simple.[38] There is nothing in the *Commentary on Matthew*, which was one of Origen's mature and last works, to suggest this.[39] The death of Jesus was an important element in his understanding of the economy of salvation. He did think that there were also esoteric meanings latent in the exoteric story of the death of Jesus, but he did not consider these to diminish the importance of the death of Jesus for all people (*Cels* 2.69). One might say that he thought of the death of Jesus as he did the second coming. He draws esoteric doctrines from it, but says he does not reject the "simpler understanding" of the event when he does so (*ComMt* 12.30). Origen's discussions of the atonement set it in the context of dealing with the devil, either in the imagery of winning a victory over him, deceiving him, or paying a ransom to him. This understanding of the atoning effect of Jesus' death falls within the parameters that Aulén called the classic doctrine of the atonement and considered to be the primary view held by the writers of the New Testament and the Church Fathers.

---

[36] Aulén (1961), 51–3.

[37] For a slightly different presentation of the ransom through Christ, see *ComMt* 12.28–9.

[38] De Faye (1923), 121. See a criticism of De Faye's view in Aulén (1961), 38.

[39] It should also be noted that all of the texts about the atonement cited above are from the Greek sections of the *Commentary on Matthew*. De Faye (1928), 1–3, thought only the Greek texts of Origen could be trusted and that the Latin texts had been corrupted by their translators.

The power of the virtuous life

Origen never thought of salvation apart from a life that could be said to be worthy of salvation. Jesus is the "great high priest" of Hebrews 4:14 who promised those who truly learned the ways of God and "lived lives worthy of them that he would lead them on to the things beyond this world".[40] One must, as noted above, perform the "works of the kingdom" in a worthy manner to "receive the denarius" of salvation.[41] When he discusses the man without a wedding garment in Jesus' parable (Matt. 22:11–12), Origen identifies this man with those who come to the Christian faith but do not put aside their previous evil practices. They are blamed for having the audacity to enter such a great celebration without putting on "the robe of virtue", the shining garment of which Solomon spoke in Ecclesiastes when he said "Let your garments always be white". Their fate is to be bound and, then, not simply cast out, but cast into outer darkness devoid of all light (*ComMt* 17.24). Celsus had argued that the absence of altars and images among Christians showed that their religion was secretive and suspicious. Origen replied that the virtues formed within Christians by the *Logos* are their images. In being prudent, righteous, courageous, wise, and pious, Christians have set up living images in which God is honored (*Cels* 8.17–18).

Origen did not think that the virtuous life that led to salvation was achieved by one's own power alone. It could not be achieved, however, without one's own efforts. When Jesus tells the disciples to get in the boat and go "to the other side" while he remains behind (Matt. 14:22), he is sending them forth alone into temptations and difficulties. It was up to the disciples to get to the other side, or at least so it seemed. Their experience in the midst of the sea, however, was to teach them that they could not get through the difficulties to the other side without Jesus. They must first do all within their power, struggling on behalf of the virtues, to reach the other side, and when they have done this they become worthy of divine help. The one who reaches the other side does so because Jesus "sails with him", but he must first do all within his power to get there.[42]

Origen was under no illusion, of course, that everyone who claimed Christian faith was a virtuous person. Being a virtuous person demanded continual effort after one came to the faith; and many did not make that

---

[40] *Cels* 6.20; trans. in *Origen: Contra Celsum* (1965), 333.
[41] *ComMt* 15.35, cited above in "A new emphasis on the Church and soteriology", p. 226.
[42] *ComMt* 11.5–6; see also *ComRom* 7.17.

effort. He refers to the Church as a "temple built of living stones", but he knows that "some in it...do not live as in the church, but serve the flesh, and make the house of prayer <built> of living stones a den of thieves because of their wickedness" (*ComMt* 16.21). These deviants from Christian virtue were to be found among the clergy as well as in the laity. He refers to bishops, presbyters, and deacons "who are greedy, tyrannical, ignorant, and impious" and to whom Jeremiah's word could be applied: " 'Those who lead my people...are wise in knowing how to do evil, but they do not know how to do good'" (*ComMt* 16.22; cf. 12.14, *ComRom* 2.2).

Origen held a rigorous view of sin and forgiveness for both those wanting to be initiated into the Christian community and for those who were already a part of it. In the *Against Celsus* he outlines what must have been the catechetical and penitential practices of the Church in Caesarea as well as that in a large part of the rest of the world. He says they first examine those interested in the faith individually to see if they have demonstrated sufficient "desire to live a good life" before they are allowed to receive the "elementary instruction" that leads to baptism. Some people have the specific responsibility of ascertaining if any coming to the "common gathering" practice "secret sins". Those who are accepted into the community are put on a path of daily improvement. Those who sin, and especially those who commit sexual sin, are dismissed from the community. They may be readmitted later if they demonstrate a genuine change in their life, but they have to endure a longer probation time than those initially coming to the faith, and they can never hold any office in the Church.[43]

Koch was of the opinion, and I think he was correct, that this rigorous view of the Christian life was something that Origen inherited from second-century Christianity. He argued that one of the points emphasized in the second century was that Christianity is a new life and traces of this new life should be visible in the Church. The greatest demands were made, therefore, for purity of life.[44]

A NEW LOOK AT ESCHATOLOGY

Vogt thinks that there is a new interest in eschatology discernable in certain passages of the *Against Celsus*. He argues, that in his remarks against Celsus' statements about God needing a rest after creating the world, Origen draws

---

[43] *Cels* 3.51; quoted phrases from *Origen: Contra Celsum* (1965), 165–6.
[44] Koch (1932), 312–13.

on Hebrews 4:9, 5:11, and especially 12:23 to present an understanding of the creation story in relation to the seventh day that is no longer an explanation of the present order of the world, as he had interpreted it in his earlier *Commentary on Genesis* to which he refers in his discussion. Origen now, Vogt believes, on the basis of these passages in Hebrews, thinks of the creation story as pointing to the story of salvation, and especially to the eschatological goal of that story.[45] Vogt further thinks that there is an eschatological reorientation going on in Origen's reply to Celsus' accusation that the Christians' refusal to worship the various gods or demons worshipped by the population at large was a sign of their rebelliousness. Worshipping minor deities who served the greater God, Celsus argued, was not incompatible with worshipping the greater God himself. Origen, Vogt thinks, by using Philippians 3:20, and especially Hebrews 12:23 again, gives an eschatological turn to his defense of the Christian refusal to recognize any other deity.[46] He sees a similar modification of Origen's understanding of Genesis 1:26 going on in *Against Celsus* 5.15–16, 6.63, and 7.66.[47] He also argues that Origen has given an eschatological orientation to the Pauline non-eschatological statement in Galatians 5:17 about the desire of the flesh against the spirit and the spirit against the flesh in *Against Celsus* 8.23.[48] Vogt suggests that these passages amount to a retraction of viewpoints Origen had espoused in his early writings, and compares Origen to Augustine who, in his later life, changed his mind from his earlier strongly Platonic view about a world of sense and a world of spirit. The old Augustine, he says, spoke of a present world and a future world.[49]

Vogt's discussions pick up some minute points in Origen's arguments against Celsus and are very fine-tuned observations. His case seems to me to be valid. Origen appears to have an increased interest in eschatology in the last writings that he produced. What I will argue in this section is that he was also rethinking some of his earlier eschatological assertions about the consummation and the life to come. I will focus particularly on his earlier doctrine of the "restoration" or "*apokatastasis*" of all souls, and teachings directly related to that. I will argue that he continues to use the concept of restoration—the term appears a number of times in the Bible, especially in the Septuagint—but that he is beginning to think of it more in relation to the repentant, who make the kind of effort to live the worthy

---

[45] Vogt (1999), 144–9. The passages he bases this argument on are *Cels* 5.59; 6.51, 61.

[46] Vogt (1999), 150–2; *Cels* 8.5.

[47] Vogt (1999), 154–5.

[48] Vogt (1999), 155–9.

[49] Vogt (1999), 149.

life discussed in the preceding section, and that he begins to consider a limit to the restorative efforts of God when his therapeutic punishments are continually rejected.

In his early Alexandrian work, *On First Principles*, Origen had a neat formula for eschatology: "The end will be like the beginning." Because he had argued that all souls began their existence as rational substances in the presence of God, he concluded that they would ultimately end in that same state; "restored" to what they were in the beginning.[50] This was a comprehensive plan in Origen's mind, involving the "complete restoration of the whole creation" (*Princ* 3.5.7). He supported this view with the Pauline statement in 1 Corinthians 15:28 that in the end all things will be subjected to the Son who, in turn, will be subjected to God, so that, in the final analysis, God will be "all in all". The additional Pauline statement in 1 Corinthians 15:25 that Christ will reign until, in the words of Psalm 110:1, all his enemies have been "put under his feet", is further corroboration of this view, for the putting of his enemies under his feet is not understood to refer to their destruction, but to their salvation and restoration (*Princ* 3.5.7). In a work written when he was still in the process of mental transition from the Alexandrian to the Caesarean milieu,[51] Origen takes Ephesians 2:7, which refers to the abundant wealth of God's grace in the coming ages, to mean that the most heinous sinner who lived in sin his entire lifetime will, in some way beyond Origen's comprehension, receive remedial treatment in the age to come.[52]

Systems based on logic can be tidy. Conclusions follow from premises in regular order. But Biblical texts can be messy, with either too much or too little to fill the necessary space. This can result in their pushing against the limits in which they have been placed, or allowing those limits to collapse because the texts are not sufficient to support them. A good

---

[50] See *Princ* 1.6; 2.10; 3.5–6; Vogt (1999), 19–20. Edwards (2002), 111–14, has questioned whether Origen held this view even in the *On First Principles*, at least in the way that it is usually understood.

[51] See Chapter 7.

[52] *PEuch* 27.15. It is unfortunate that we do not possess Origen's *Commentary on Ephesians*, which was written, it seems, not too many years after the work on prayer, and before the Commentary on Romans (see Heine (2000c), 149–57). There is also nothing on this verse preserved in the fragments from the Ephesians commentary. There is, however, a passage in Jerome's *Commentary on Ephesians* which, in my opinion, is based on Origen's comments on Ephesians 2:6–7. This passage suggests that Origen was still, at the writing of this commentary, thinking of a divine rehabilitating action for the evil powers, at least, in the age to come (see Heine (2002), 127–8).

example of this is the uncertainty Origen expresses at Caesarea about the duration of the punishment meted out to the man without a wedding garment in Jesus' parable because there is no statement about this in the text itself.[53]

Origen had always worked with the Bible before him and he certainly used Biblical texts in conjunction with his arguments in the *On First Principles*. But he seems, in his later years in Caesarea, to have been even more deeply immersed in the exposition of the Bible than in his Alexandrian years. His Alexandrian exposition of the Bible seems to have been limited to special concerns. As a result, he treated Biblical books in a piecemeal manner, focusing only on those parts that he considered to address those concerns, such as the first five chapters of Genesis, which the Gnostics had used extensively. In Caesarea, on the other hand, he appears to have treated Biblical books in their entirety. The *Commentary on Matthew* would appear to have been a commentary on the whole of the Gospel. There is no reason to think that he began with Book 10 of the commentary. Even if the book numbers were eliminated from the discussion, there are none of the things at the beginning of Book 10 which one finds at the beginning of Origen's commentaries. The final part of the commentary that we possess is very near the end of the Gospel (Matt. 27:66), suggesting that it probably reached the end. The Caesarean *Commentary on Romans* also seems to have been a commentary on a complete book, and perhaps also the many lost commentaries that he produced at Caesarea on Pauline epistles, the prophetic books, and the Psalms. The literal meaning of the Scriptural texts also seems to have increased in importance for him in these later years. This may have resulted, partly at least, from his close contact with the Caesarean Jewish community, where the literal teachings of the Hebrew Scriptures were constantly studied and debated. Origen never abandoned the esoteric spiritual reading of Scripture, but he gave some deep thought to issues raised by the literal meaning of the text and did not use these difficulties simply as the excuse to introduce a hidden meaning.

Origen had many opportunities to think about eschatology when he wrote his *Commentary on Matthew*, for there are numerous texts in Matthew's Gospel that refer to the subject. On six occasions Matthew refers to someone being "cast into outer darkness" (Matt. 8:12; 13:42, 50, 22:13; 24:51; 25:30). Chapter 24 contains Jesus' eschatological address, and chapter 25 contains three parables with an eschatological focus.

---

[53] *ComJn* 28.63–5. This passage will be discussed below.

Rethinking the restoration (*apokatastasis*) of all souls

In his recent study of universal salvation in Origen and Barth, Greggs notes that there are several passages in Origen where "salvation seems to be limited", and the concept of restoration applicable only to the saints. He thinks, however, that Hanson's explanation of these texts eliminates any tension they might present to a doctrine of universalism.[54] Hanson's interpretations strike me, however, as tenuous. In what follows I will examine closely three of the passages from Origen's Caesarean period that Hanson cites in support of a doctrine of universalism in Origen. Two of the passages are from the *Commentary on Matthew*; the other is from a homily on Exodus delivered perhaps a few years earlier at Caesarea.

A limitation to God's patience

The first passage is about the meaning of God's wrath and is used by Hanson to show that it is not the passion to which humans apply the term. Origen is interpreting the second commandment which refers to God as "jealous". He comments that when one perceives God chastising or acting in what might be called a jealous manner towards one, he should recognize that God is acting out of concern for that person's salvation. But then Origen adds a note of warning.

> But if you do not recover your senses when you have been chastised, if you are not corrected when you have been reproved, if you despise when you are beaten, know that if you go on sinning continually his jealousy will depart from you and the prophet Ezekiel's words to Jerusalem will be spoken to you: "Therefore my jealousy will depart from you and I will no longer be angry with you." ... If you understand these words, it is the voice of God having compassion when he is angry, when he is jealous, when he causes pain and beatings. ... Do you wish to hear, however, the terrible voice of God when he is displeased? Hear what he says through the prophet. When he had enumerated the many abominable acts the people had committed he adds, "And for this reason I will not visit your daughters when they fornicate nor your daughters-in-law when they commit adultery." This is terrible! This is the end when we are no longer reproached for sins, when we offend and are no longer corrected. For then, when we have exceeded the measure of sinning "the jealous God" turns his jealousy away from us.[55]

Hanson cites this passage to show that Origen understands the wrath of God to mean his "educative discipline", and notes that God's true wrath

---

[54] Greggs (2009), 72–3.

[55] *HomEx* 8.5; trans. modified from *Origen: Homilies on Genesis and Exodus* (1981), 327–8.

is precisely the opposite of anger, for it is present when God turns his wrath away from us.[56] This much is true. What he does not point out is that this passage speaks against his larger argument that Origen believed that all people would eventually be saved. This passage points to an end point for the patience of God's corrective "wrath". Continual disregard for God's discipline of punishment will lead to exceeding "the measure of sinning" and result in God's total disregard for one. When Origen refers to "exceeding the measure of sinning" it seems highly likely to me that he is alluding to the statement in Genesis 15:16 about the Amorites being spared in the time of Abraham because their "sins were not yet filled up". He has a brief comment on this verse in a Greek fragment which probably came from scholia on Genesis produced at Caesarea where he asks, "Why does he say, 'The sins of the Amorites are not yet filled up?'" He answers, "So that he might show that they are cast out with good reason because of their sins" (PG 12.113C). He makes an explicit use of this verse in commenting on Paul's statement that God's forbearance should lead one to repentance.

[J]ust as God made everything in measure, weight, and number, so also there is a definite measure of his patience. We must believe that this measure was squandered by those who perished in the flood and by those in Sodom who were devastated by heavenly fire. It is also on this account that it is said of the Amorites, "For the sins of the Amorites are not yet complete until now" [Gn 15:16].... So then, God bears with everyone patiently and awaits each one's repentance; but this should not render us negligent or make us slow to conversion, since *there is a definite measure to his patience and forbearance.*[57]

This idea of the limit to God's patience, as we will see, reverberates in Origen's wrestling with the concept of being bound and cast into outer darkness in the sayings of Jesus in Matthew's Gospel.

I think Hanson also misinterpreted Origen's commentary on the parable of the laborers and the parable containing the story of the man without a wedding garment at the wedding feast. He says that "the teaching of the parable of the Labourers in the Vineyard... is that everyone shall be saved; and in treating of the man cast into 'outer darkness'... he makes it clear that he thinks that the man must eventually return from the outer darkness".[58]

---

[56] Hanson (1959), 335–6.

[57] *ComRom* 2.3; trans. in *Origen: Commentary on the Epistle to the Romans* (2001), 105–6, my italics.

[58] Hanson (1959), 334.

The man without a wedding garment

To begin with the second of these two passages, Origen was by no means certain that the man without the wedding garment who was bound and cast into outer darkness would, at some point, return. In the twenty-eighth book of the *Commentary on John*, written sometime before the *Commentary on Matthew*, but not more than a few years before it, and definitely written at Caesarea, he refers to this man in conjunction with his interpretation of the resurrection of Lazarus, whose burial bonds Jesus commanded to be loosed when he raised him from the dead. He comments that being bound because one is dead and being bound "as a result of the judgment of the Lord" are not to be considered the same thing. Lazarus fell into the first category, and the man without a wedding garment into the second. Then he raises the question whether the one bound by the Lord's judgment will always be bound and remain in outer darkness or if he will sometime be released. He notes that the Biblical text says nothing of his future release. Origen concludes that the safest path is not to give an opinion on this question since "nothing has been written of him" (*ComJn* 28.63–5).

Hanson approaches the issue from the perspective of the Origen of the *On First Principles*. "[U]niversalism in Origen's thought", he says, "is a necessary conclusion from his basic premises." For Origen to allow even one or two souls to slip through the net of universal restoration would, he asserts, "be for God, the single, simple, primal, unalterable One, to compromise himself with change and becoming and corruption. This is inconceivable, and therefore all must be saved."[59] If Origen's view, at this point in his life, had been so strenuously determined by this philosophical position, he would have had a ready answer for the question of the man's release.[60] But he did not have an answer, because the Biblical text does not give an answer. Origen listens to the Biblical text here and does not force it to fit his earlier system.[61] Hanson did not cite this passage in

---

[59] Hanson (1959), 335.

[60] See Bigg (1968/1886), 231–2, who also cites this passage as an instance showing Origen's "hesitation" concerning the final salvation of all beings.

[61] There is another example of Origen listening to Biblical texts on this subject and not forcing his earlier systematic views on the texts. In *ComJn* 19.64–88 he is explaining Jesus' statement, "I go, and you will seek me, and you will die in your sin." At several points in this rather long discussion Origen notes the finality of the fate of those from whom Jesus departs because of their unbelief so that they consequently die in their sin. The majority who come to faith, he says, do not remain in it and become true disciples. Only a few advance to the freedom which truth brings (*ComJn* 19.66–7). Once the Word has manifest himself and not been received, he departs and then all search for him is vain. All that is left is to die in sin (*ComJn* 19.74). The one who completely destroys with evil the seeds of truth sown in his soul will not

the *Commentary on John*. He refers to the discussion of the parable in the *Commentary on Matthew* (17.24). Here Origen says that this man stands for all those who come to faith but do not lay aside the evil they previously practiced. They are blamed for having the audacity to enter such a great celebration without taking up "the robe of virtue". The fate of this man, and of those like him, is to be bound and not simply cast out of the festivities, but cast into outer darkness devoid of all light,[62] so that, Origen says,

when he has thirsted for light after he has been in the outer darkness, he may wail to the God who is able to show him kindness and rescue him from there, and he may gnash his teeth which, because of evil, have eaten sour grapes and, consequently, are set on edge. For the teeth of the one who ate the sour grapes are set on edge. But even there one must understand the sour grapes to mean the evil of the one who does not <forget the things "behind", nor> stretch out "to the things ahead", but remains in evil when he ought to ripen and make the grapes of virtue sweet.

And he adds, to the whole parable, because of the many who are called and do not become worthy, the words, "For many are called". And because those who enter the wedding feast and recline there are so few, he says, "but few are chosen". And if someone should consider the crowded gatherings of the...churches and scrutinize how many there are who live appropriately and are being transformed "by the renewal of the mind", and how many live frivolously and are being conformed "to this age", he would see that the saying of the Savior is useful when he says, "For many are called, but few are chosen." Elsewhere you can find it said, "Many will attempt to enter and will not be able", and, "Strive to enter through the narrow gate, because few find it" (*ComMt* 17.24).

I think it is less clear here than Hanson thought, that Origen believed that the man would be able to return from the outer darkness. That God has the power to bring him back would have been a given for Origen. But he

---

be able to find him, but will die in his sin (*ComJn* 19.78). Still discussing the same words, he introduces the metaphor of Jesus as a physician despairing of healing those deadly ill with the words, "I go,...and you will die in your sin" (*ComJn* 19.81). Within the same metaphor Origen warns against allowing one's sickness to advance to the incurable stage (*ComJn* 19.82). He brings this discussion to an end by quoting Jesus' words about there being no forgiveness in this age or the one to come for the person who blasphemes the Holy Spirit. Origen concludes, "If...there is no forgiveness in the coming age, neither is there any in the ages which come after it as well" (*ComJn* 19.88; trans. in *Origen: Commentary on the Gospel according to John Books 13–32* (1993), 188).

[62] For other discussions of this phrase in Origen see *SerMt* 69; *FragMt* 157, 158, and the Alexandrian *Princ* 2.10.8.

never says that he will do so.[63] The emphasis on the final saying connected with the parable seems to me to point away from Origen thinking the man would return. If "all" are finally going to be chosen, why call attention to the "many" who fail and the "few" who succeed here, and, especially, then cite two further verses which both emphasize the small number of those who successfully enter. What is the point, in other words, of calling attention to this last statement of Jesus if he thinks that all will ultimately find the "narrow gate" and enter through it?

There is a reference to the outer darkness in a passage in Origen's large commentary on the Psalms composed at Caesarea which also seems to point away from the darkness coming to an end for those who enter it. The passage occurs in the commentary on Psalm 118:91 (LXX), "At your command, the day continues." Origen comments,

> Some ask, Why, since he said elsewhere, "Yours is the day and yours the night" [Ps. 73:16] he does not here too mention the night with the day. If the teaching were about this day, he would not say, "continues", for it does not continue, but comes to an end and is followed by night. But if you understand the new age, the day which is to come, when "the Lord is the eternal light and God is the glory" [Isa. 60:19] of the righteous, then "the day" remains. For the midday "sun will not set on you" [Isa. 60:20]. But in this material world, since all are not righteous, it is not always "the day" and, since all are not sinners, it is not always night. But when the separation of the good from the bad occurs, then there will be that night of the sinners who will depart "into outer darkness" [Matt. 8:12], and "the day" of the righteous, when it "continues" and night no longer follows it. It is of this day, I think, it says, "At your command the day continues, because all things are your servants".[64]

Since the eschatological day of the righteous continues, it seems implicit that the night of sinners will do the same.

The laborers in the vineyard

Hanson's statement that "the teaching of the parable of the Labourers in the Vineyard...is that everyone shall be saved" is oversimplified and overconfident.[65] Origen's understanding of this parable shows him struggling, in my

---

[63] This would be clearer if the *hina* clause were to be understood as a result rather than a purpose clause. Then the words which follow would simply state the result of the man's being cast out, one of which was to cry out to God much like the rich man cries out to Abraham to no avail in Luke's parable of the rich man and Lazarus. Smyth (1963/1920), 562, notes that Plato sometimes introduces local clauses with *hina* "where". This meaning would fit well here, though I am not aware that Origen uses *hina* in this way.

[64] *La chaîne palestinienne sur le psaume 118* (1972), 1, 334.

[65] Hanson (1959), 334.

opinion, with this issue. It is a complicated discussion. First, when he introduces the words to be included as the text under discussion, the Greek manuscript, which consistently does not give the entire text of the passages Origen treats but the opening and closing words of the text to be covered, begins with the opening words of the parable of the laborers in Matthew 20:1 and then says, "and the words which follow, up to the statement, 'For many are called but few chosen'". This last statement does not appear in the parable of the laborers, but is the closing statement in the parable of the wedding guests appearing in Matthew 22:14. It does not seem that Origen intended to treat that entire block of text as one. At the end of his discussion of the parable of the laborers, the next section is again introduced in the normal manner with an indication of the section to be treated. The Latin manuscript containing the parallel to the Greek commentary at this point quotes the entire parable of the laborers but ends it with Matthew 22:14, as follows: "So the last will be first and the first last; for many are called, but few are chosen" (*ComMt* 15.28). It appears that Origen wanted to pull Matthew 22:14 into his discussion of Matthew 20:1–16. The importance of this will appear later.

Origen believes that this parable is packed with mysteries (*ComMt* 15.31). He thinks the first that needs to be explored is latent in the expression "day". Can this mean the "whole present age"? He then considers the implications of this understanding if one joins with it Deuteronomy 32:7, "'Remember the days of old'".[66] This leads him to reflect also on the pondering of the Psalmist who says, "'I remembered and pondered the years of old.... And I said, The Lord will not cast aside forever will he?'" Origen then comments, "And perhaps (to speak rather boldly), the Lord will not 'cast aside forever' (for it is a momentous thing for the Lord to cast aside for one age), but perhaps he will cast aside even into a second age, when so great sin is not forgiven 'neither in the present age nor in the one to come'" (Matt. 12:32). Origen spins this idea out through the ages of the hours mentioned in the parable when the different groups of workers were hired, bringing it to a climax with the words of Ephesians 2:7 referring to the richness of God's grace in the ages to come. He then gives this interpretation of the parable a very specific eschatological setting.

And these things were said because of the day in the parable before us. You can also establish these things from the Epistle of John who declares, "Children it is the last hour..." (1 John 2:18). For the last hour follows the eleventh hour of the parable before us, since the householder in the parable went out about the eleventh hour

---

[66] In Origen's Greek text the same word is used where it is translated "age" in his question, "of old" in Deut. 32:7, and "of old" and "forever" in the following Psalm passage.

and "found others standing, and said to them, Why have you stood here idle the whole day?" (*ComMt* 15.31).

This sounds like Origen is still thinking as he did in Alexandria about a series of future ages or worlds through which those who did not obey God in this life would pass, in a process that would eventually result in their restoration to the presence of God. If this were the end of Origen's interpretation of the parable it would seem rather clear-cut that he still held to the doctrine of the salvation of all created beings. But it is a long exposition that Origen gives to the parable, and this is only the beginning.

The second mystery Origen investigates is the significance of the five ranks of workers who were hired. He suggests that the first, when the householder went out early, should be understood to be Adam and Eve, who were hired at the time of creation to cultivate the vineyard of piety. The second hiring was the rank of Noah and the covenant made with him. This was followed by Abraham and the patriarchs prior to Moses. The fourth hiring was that connected with Moses, and the final was that which took place with the coming of Christ (*ComMt* 15.32). The first application Origen makes of these five ranks is the rather banal one of identifying each of them with one of the five senses (*ComMt* 15.33). Some of them do reappear, however, in more meaningful ways in connection with later discussions. He suggests that there was a connection between the workers hired and the work that needed to be done at the particular time of hiring. When the householder hired the first workers he selected those who were suited for the works starting at early dawn. And so it went with each group hired. "But," he says, "a certain final work remained in the vineyard which needed a fresh, new calling, which vigorously and rapidly completed the remaining work of the vineyard, and this was the work of the new covenant." The denarius which each worker receives is the "coin of salvation" (*ComMt* 15.34).

He also thinks there is a secret doctrine about the soul latent in the question the householder asks those he hires at the eleventh hour: "Why have you stood here the whole day idle?" Since they had wanted to work and had waited the whole day, Origen says, "[T]hey boldly defend themselves and say, 'No one hired us'" (*ComMt* 15.34). He explains the nature of his observation by saying,

[I]f the soul is sown along with the body, how did they stand idle the whole day?... But I am asking also about the things outside the vineyard where the workers are found by the one who goes out to hire them, and I am considering whether the place outside the vineyard is the region of souls before they are joined to bodies, and (whether) the vineyard refers not only to things here, but also to things outside the body where, I think, the workers are hired.... No one (so far as the parable is concerned) who fails to do the works of the vineyard is sent into it. For the householder blamed no one for having worked unsatisfactorily, even though he blamed the one who expected a higher wage (*ComMt* 15.35).

I think Origen's statement is significant that, "No one who fails to do the works of the vineyard is sent into it." He identifies the vineyard as the kingdom of God on the basis of Jesus' statement in Matthew 21:43, "The kingdom of God will be taken from you and given to a nation which produces its fruits." "All", he concludes, "who do the works of the vineyard and complete the works of the kingdom of God in a manner worthy of salvation, will receive the denarius" (*ComMt* 15.35). One must not fail to notice the emphasis on doing the works here, in order to receive the denarius.[67]

Origen brings his interpretation of the parable of the laborers to a close by offering one additional way to read the parable which has occurred to him. He thinks this reading may prove useful to people who are offended by the "deeper and more esoteric narrative", meaning the interpretation which relates it to souls which he has just given. In this final reading of the parable the "day" does not represent the present age, as in the first reading, but the duration of individual lives on earth. The different times at which workers were hired would stand for the different physical ages at which people come to faith: childhood, adolescence, young manhood, the elderly, and those at the point of death. One other point must be noted. This interpretation does not embrace the entire creation, but only those who come into the Church albeit at different times in their lives. It puts an emphasis on the choice the workers make to work, and must, therefore, assume that there are others who chose not to work in the vineyard. In this interpretation it is the *choice* to work and not the *duration* of the work that the householder rewards with the denarius of salvation. Those converted in their youth, when they had to struggle with the passions, are those who are angered because those who were converted on their deathbed, so to speak, receive equal payment with themselves (*ComMt* 15.36).

In this way of reading the parable, Origen says, the Church is the vineyard and the market from which people are called are the places outside the Church from which people are called and sent into the Church. This reading, however, introduces a new question, which is not explicitly mentioned in the parable. What about those called who do not maintain their calling, but are overpowered by passions and depart from the Church? They can no longer be numbered among the workers in the vineyard. What if they

---

[67] See also *ComMt* 12.30 and 14.8.

wish to repent and return to work in the vineyard after they have had their fill of the passions? They cannot defend their absence from the work in the vineyard by saying, "No one hired us." Nor can it be said that they "have stood idle all day". This was a question, of course, which occupied the mind of the second-and third-century Church. These people, Origen borrowing Paul's language says, began "with the spirit" and ended with the "flesh". But now they "want to return again to live anew in the spirit". Origen wants to hold out hope to such people, but he does not think they can be restored to equality with those who have never swerved from the path on which they were set when the householder sent them into the vineyard.

> We are not saying these things to dissuade those who have fallen from getting up or <to hinder> those who have strayed from returning, or those licentious sons who have squandered the substance of the gospel teaching from running back to the father's house. For because they have repented and are constrained by a life that has been turned around, let them have things that are better than those constrained in sins.... For one must surely not assume that they are like those who sinned in youth because they had not learned even the beginning elements of the faith (*ComMt* 15.37).

Origen seems to shift the meaning of "the last" who received payment first from those converted on their deathbeds to those who have returned to the Church after abandoning it earlier. "Therefore," he says, "the house-holder wishes to give even to the last as also to the first the denarius, that is salvation, since he has the right to do what he wishes with his own things, and he reproves the man who has the evil eye because the householder is good" (*ComMt* 15.37). While Origen may not have chosen this reading of the parable as his first choice, he, nevertheless, does not dismiss it, but seems to consider it an important way of reading the parable. This is the old Origen who has accepted the responsibility of pastoring the Church, wrestling with an issue that continued to trouble the Church. With the strong emphasis on living a life worthy of salvation, what should be done about those who failed, who began the process of salvation and then fell away. Could they repent and return? Could they be "restored" to their previous state in the Church?

Origen had given a Church-related interpretation to the concept of restoration somewhat earlier in a homily he preached on Jeremiah at Caesarea. He is commenting on the words of the Lord to Israel in Jeremiah 15:19: "If you return, I will restore you." He first generalizes the promise and says it is made to each person whom God encourages to return. This does not understand the statement as a universal statement made to the whole creation, but as a limited statement made to some. But he then remarks that the words, "I will restore you", seem to contain "a mystery".

"No one", he says, "is restored to a place where he has never been. Restoration is to one's own affairs." "Therefore," Origen continues, "he says to us who have turned away that, if we return, he will restore us. This, in fact, is the meaning of the promise recorded in the Acts of the Apostles, 'Until the times of the restoration of all, of which God spoke of old through the mouth of his holy prophets' in Christ Jesus" (*HomJer* 14.18; Acts 3:21).[68] Is Origen thinking of a general restoration of the whole creation as in the *On First Principles*? Or is he thinking of the restoration of those who repent, whether initially to enter the Church, or a second time to return to the Church? It must be noted that there is an emphasis on individual volition in this text. Origen's application retains the contingency of the statement in Jeremiah, "*If* you return, I will restore."

Origen concludes his interpretation of the parable of the laborers by combining Matthew 22:14 with 20:16: "Many, therefore, of the last will be first and some of those called first will be last. For the called are many, but the chosen are few" (*ComMt* 15.37). Does he intend Matthew 22:14 to be the conclusion only to the last way he has suggested reading the parable, or to the previous esoteric reading as well? Either way, it seems to me that he has used this verse as a filter at the end of the interpretation to separate the "few" who are chosen from the "many" who are called. This way of concluding his interpretation of the parable of the laborers should, it seems to me, put a brake on rushing to the conclusion that Origen saw this parable to teach "that everyone shall be saved".[69]

---

[68] In the *Commentary on Matthew*, Origen uses Acts 3:21 to interpret 1 John 1:5, which, he says, speaks of seeing God just as he is, and asks if it can be taken in the following manner: "For now, even if we should be worthy to see God with the mind and heart, we do not see 'him just as he is', but just as he comes to be with us because of our economy. But at the end of things and of the 'restoration of all of which he spoke through the mouth of his holy prophets from of old' (Acts 3:21), we will see him, not as we do now, as he is not, but as is fitting then, as he really is" (*ComMt* 17.19). There is no necessity in this use of Acts 3:21 to conclude that Origen anticipated the restoration of all creation. All that this usage necessitates is that the saints be restored to that state in which they can contemplate God as he is. In the *On First Principles* he may understand this verse to refer to a general restoration at the end, though all that is used from the verse are the words, "restoration of all" (*Princ* 2.3.5). I can find no reference to Acts 3:21 or any discussion of the end times in the other reference to *On First Principles* given in *Biblia Patristica* (1991), 348. Likewise, there is no quotation of the verse in the reference given to *ComJn* 1.91, only the mention of the "so-called restoration". The phrase, "the restoration of all" appears in *SerMt* 55, but the parallel Greek fragment does not contain the words (*Origenes Werke: Origenes Matthäuserklärung II Die lateinische Übersetzung der Commentariorum Series* (1976), 128). The references to *ComMt* 17.15 and 17.16 are both to the "restoration" of the Church to Christ. There is no necessity to connect these references with Acts 3:21. The references to *HomJer* 14.18 and *ComMt* 17.19, both of which I have already discussed, are the only explicit references to the passage among the eight listings in *Biblia Patristica* (1991), 348.

[69] Hanson (1959), 334.

Did Origen understand this parable to mean that all would eventually be saved, even if they made no choice to live a life worthy of salvation in the present age? One reading he gives to the parable might be taken in that way. The last reading he suggests as a possibility, however, points in a different direction.

But on the other hand

There are, however, passages, especially in the *Against Celsus*, which suggest that the late Origen still held essentially the same eschatological views as the early Origen, and there are others which indicate some ambivalence. For example, he continues to think of God's wrath and punitive measures as disciplinary and corrective in their purpose. Biblical passages which speak of God's anger and wrath are ways God speaks to people who are on the level of children (*Cels* 6.71; cf. 5.16). God's wrath is not emotional, as in humans, but is his way of applying severe methods to correct severe sins. He cites Romans 2:4–5, about those who store up wrath against themselves for the time of judgment by ignoring God's patient calling to repentance, to prove that God's wrath is not an emotional reaction (*Cels* 6.72). God uses evil as a discipline to refine away the impurities in the wicked. It appears that he thought of this occurring in a future age. He refers to God putting such people in a school of virtue "somewhere in the universe" (*pou tou pantos*). When they have purged their nature they progress to the divine realm (*Cels* 6.44). On the other hand, Celsus had accused the Christians of holding the same belief about eternal punishments as the mystery religions. Origen makes a somewhat detailed response to this criticism, but he never denies it outright. He argues instead that there is going to be an age to come in which the righteous will be rewarded and sinners will be punished (*Cels* 8.48). He comments on some other remarks of Celsus and then returns to the subject of eternal punishments and chastises Celsus for not making a better argument that those completely evil will suffer eternal punishments. Again, Origen passes by the opportunity to point out that a true understanding of Christian doctrine does not embrace eternal punishments, if this is what he believed. Instead, he argues that while Christians want to make all people aware of all their doctrines, there are some persons who are so prejudiced against Christians that the only doctrine that resonates with them at all is the doctrine of eternal punishments for the wicked. Nevertheless, he adds, Christians want to convince them that good lives are rewarded with happiness. His concluding statement in this section is that all who live good lives will receive good ends and all who are evil will be subjected to pain and torments (*Cels* 8.51, 52). Nothing is said about those who are evil being improved by the pain and torments.

Celsus had asserted that Christians anticipate going to a "better earth than this one", much like the places spoken of by the inspired men of the Greeks. Origen replies that Moses had preceded all the Greeks with his teaching that God had promised a land of milk and honey. He interprets this promised land, however, much as the author of Hebrews 4:1–11 interpreted the promised rest, insisting that the promise does not refer to the land of Judea which the Hebrews inhabited. The land of Judea, Origen argues, like the rest of the world lies under the curse put on the earth at the fall of Adam and Eve. The land of promise is identified, instead, as the land described in Hebrews 12:22: "[M]ount Zion...the heavenly Jerusalem, the city of the living God". To verify this understanding of the good land promised in the books of Moses, Origen invites his critics to consider the teaching of the prophets, where it is asserted that those who have wandered and fallen away will return to Jerusalem and "be restored to the...city of God" (*Cels* 7.28, 29). This statement echoes Origen's earlier Alexandrian view of the restoration of all who fell away.[70]

There is a similar discussion, also supported by a prophetic text in the last book of the *Against Celsus*. Celsus had expressed the desirability of all peoples being united under one law, but dismissed it as an impossible, foolish wish. Origen argues, to the contrary, that this very thing will happen but not in the physical body. He argues that the time is coming when the *Logos* will overpower every rational nature and perfect each soul so that it will choose from its own freedom what the *Logos* wills. He seems not to have seen that this concept is self-contradictory. In order to get every soul to freely choose what the *Logos* wills, the individual soul's freedom must first be overridden by the *Logos*. He then suggests an analogy in which he expresses both an unrealistic belief in the power of medicine and a slight doubt that this will work for every soul.

And we hold, [he says], that *just as it is unlikely* that some of the consequences of physical diseases and wounds would be too hard for any medical art, *so also it is unlikely* in the case of souls that any of the consequences of evil would be incapable of being cured by the rational and supreme God. For since the Logos and the healing power within him are more powerful than any evils in the soul, he applies this power to each individual according to God's will, and the end of the treatment is the abolition of evil.[71]

---

[70] The following passages are the more important ones in *Princ* on the restoration of all and doctrines closely connected with it: 2.3.5; 3.5.4–7; 3.5.8; 3.6.5–8.

[71] *Cels* 8.72; trans. in *Origen: Contra Celsum* (1965), 507, my italics.

He then raises the question of whether evil, once destroyed, will rise again, but he does not answer it. For Biblical support of the view that evil will be totally destroyed and every soul corrected, he quotes Zephaniah 3:7–13. It is a lengthy quotation and Origen makes brief comments only on verses 9 and 11. The first is that the Lord says after the consummation of the earth, "I will return[72] a language to the peoples for its generation" (Zeph 3:9). He thinks that the condition the prophet says will follow the consummation is analogous to that which existed before the confusion of tongues at Babel. The remainder of the verse gives the reason for the return to one language: "That all may call on the name of the Lord to serve him under one yoke." He joins to this latter statement the remark in Zephaniah 3:11 about the "contempt of pride" being removed by this action which leaves, Origen thinks, a state in which "no longer is there 'wickedness' nor empty words, nor a lying tongue". He thinks Celsus' assertion that a unified humanity is impossible is probably true in this life, but the words of Zephaniah show that it is possible in the future life (*Cels* 8.72).

Origen had used parts of this passage from Zephaniah in other writings he had produced since moving to Caesarea.[73] They are used in eschatological contexts but somewhat differently than here. Zephaniah 3:10, which completes the statement about all peoples "serving the Lord under one yoke" refers to offerings being brought to God from beyond the rivers of Ethiopia. In his other uses of this verse, Origen identifies this statement about Ethiopia with the Church of the Gentiles. It is used in the *Commentary on the Song of Songs* in connection with the statement of the bride, "I am black and beautiful."[74] A similar identification is made in the homilies on Jeremiah, but with a more specific eschatological interpretation. He introduces the words from Zephaniah in the general context of a discussion of the statement in Romans 11:11, about the stumbling of Israel providing a time of salvation for the Gentiles, and the statement in Romans 11:25–6 that when the full number of the Gentiles have entered, then all Israel will be saved. He notes that although Paul had referred to a remnant of Israel chosen by grace (Rom. 11:5), Israel as a whole had been abandoned. Then he suggests applying the same categories of the remnant and those to be saved later to the Gentiles. He notes that Romans 11:25–6 do not say "whenever *all* the Gentiles are saved", but "whenever the *fullness* of

---

[72] For this meaning of the verb *metastrephō*; see Judg. A 5:28 (LXX).

[73] Citations from this chapter of Zephaniah appear only in works Origen produced in Caesarea; see *Biblia Patristica* (1991) 3, 148.

[74] Song 1:5. Zeph 3:8–11 is quoted in *ComCant* 2.1.17; see the discussion in Chapter 9, in "Church and Synagogue on the identity of the bride", p. 210.

the Gentiles has entered" (my italics). "Some (of) Israel",[75] he adds, "will be saved, not after all the Gentiles, but after the fullness of the Gentiles." Then he introduces the words from Zephaniah 3 that we discussed above in the *Against Celsus*, and suggests that the hearer, if he is able, should consider when it will be that "all will serve God under one yoke and bring him sacrifices from the ends of Ethiopia" (*HomJer* 5.4). He does not take the discussion any further.

He also uses the Zephaniah passage in a homily on Joshua. In this context he contrasts how Jesus took possession of the earth on his first visit by sowing the word that caused Churches to spring up, and how he will take possession of it the second time. Paul, he thinks, describes the manner in 1 Corinthians 15:25 when he refers to Christ making "all his enemies his footstool". He recognizes that many have not yet been placed under Jesus' feet. But this must occur, "[f]or the end of things cannot take place unless all things have first been subjected to him". He then quotes three supporting prophetic texts: Psalm 72:11, which refers to "all nations" serving him, Psalm 72:8–9, which refers to the Ethiopians falling down in his presence, and Zephaniah 3:10, which says the Ethiopians will bring him offerings. All will be subjected to Jesus but, Origen argues, it is far better to have been taken by Jesus at his first coming, for these people, he says in the imagery of Joshua's conquest of the land, will "receive the inheritance of the land of promise". The discussion closes with a warning to those still in opposition to Jesus when he comes again: "But when anyone has become subject out of compulsion, then, when even 'the last enemy, death, must be destroyed', *there will no longer be grace for those who are subjected.*"[76] Should this last statement be taken at its face value, that there will be those who will be destroyed without grace, or should it be pressed into the mold of Origen's Alexandrian thought that those who do not repent in this life will pass through additional painful existences until they do so? There is one text in the *Against Celsus* which suggests that Satan, at least, will be destroyed forever. He asserts that Satan had fallen from the blessed condition. "According to Ezekiel he walked blameless in all his ways until iniquity was found in him, and being 'a seal of likeness and a crown of beauty'

---

[75] Origen uses the indefinite pronoun *tis* with Israel here. The noun Israel, of course, is not declined, so it is not possible to say precisely what case is understood here. I have put the "of" in brackets, to suggest that it might be either nominative, "Some Israel", or genitive, "Some of Israel". Husson and Nautin take it as nominative and translate, "Il y a un Israël qui" (*Origène Homélies sur Jérémie* (1976, 1977), 1, 291–3). Smith also takes it as nominative and translates, "For a certain Israel will be saved" (*Origen: Homilies on Jeremiah; Homily on 1 Kings 28* (1998), 46).

[76] *HomJosh* 16.3; trans. in *Origen: Homilies on Joshua* (2002), 154, my italics.

(Ez 28:15, 12–13) in the paradise of God he became, as it were sated with good things and came to destruction, as the Word tells us which mysteriously says to him: 'Thou didst become destruction and shalt not exist for ever' " (Ez 28:19).[77] In the earlier letter that Origen wrote to his friends in Alexandria he vehemently denied that he had ever taught that the devil would be saved. Only a madman, he asserted, could teach such a thing.[78]

There is a basis for thinking that in his later life Origen did think there were limitations on the redemptive work of God. It seems to me a defendable, but not an unquestionable, conclusion that in Caesarea Origen was in the process of rethinking his view of the ultimate salvation or restoration of all beings. If this is true, then we should precede with caution when we encounter discussions of this subject in his late works and not immediately conclude that what he says in these works can be fleshed out with positions he held in Alexandria when he wrote the *On First Principles* and the early books of the *Commentary on John*.

[77] *Cels* 6.44; trans. in *Origen: Contra Celsum* (1965), 361–2.
[78] The letter is preserved by Rufinus in PG 17.624–6. There is an English translation in NPNF 2nd series, 3, 423.

Bibliography: Primary Sources

Alexander of Aphrodisias On Fate (1983), Text, translation, and Commentary by R. W. Sharples (London: Duckworth).

Alexandrian Christianity (1954), Selected Translations of Clement and Origen with Introductions and Notes by J. E. L. Oulton and H. Chadwick, Vol. 2, The Library of Christian Classics (Philadelphia: The Westminster Press).

The Apocrypha and Pseudepigrapha of the Old Testament in English (1,1965/1913; 2, 1968/1913), ed. R. H. Charles (Oxford: Clarendon Press).

The Apostolic Tradition of St Hippolytus of Rome (1937), Vol. 1, ed. by G. Dix (London: Society for Promoting Christian Knowledge; New York: The Macmillan Company).

Biblia Sacra iuxta Vulgatam versionem (1969), 2 vols, ed. by B. Fischer, J. Gribomont, H. F. D. Sparks, W. Thiele, and R. Weber (Stuttgart: Würltembergiache Bibelanstalt).

Catenae Graecae in Genesim et in Exodum II. Collectio Coisliniana in Genesim (1986), ed. F. Petit, CCSG, 15 (Turnhout: Brepols, Leuven: University Press).

La chaîne palestinienne sur le psaume 118 (1972), Vols 1 & 2, SC 189, 190, Intro, Text, and Trans. by M. Harl with the collaboration of G. Dorival (Paris: Les Éditions du Cerf).

Clément d'Alexandrie Extraits de Théodote (1970), ed. and trans. by F. Sagnard, SC 23 (Paris: Les Éditions du Cerf).

Le commentaire d'Origène sur Rom. III.5–V.7 (1957), ed. by J. Scherer, Bibliothèque d'Étude, 27 (Cairo: Institut Français d'Archéologie Orientale).

Exegetica in Paulum Excerpta et Fragmenta (2009), ed. by Francesco Pieri, Opere di Origene 14/4 (Rome: Città Nuova).

Dio's Roman History (1955/1927), Vol. 9, trans. by E. Cary, LCL 177 (Cambridge, Mass.: Harvard University Press; London: William Heinemann Ltd).

Early Christian Fathers (1953), trans. and ed. by C. C. Richardson, LCC 1 (Philadelphia: The Westminster Press).

Eusebius The Ecclesiastical History and the Martyrs of Palestine, Vol. 1 (1927), Vol. 2 (1928), ed. by H. J. Lawlor and J. E. L. Oulton (London: Society for Promoting Christian Knowledge; New York and Toronto: The Macmillan Co.).

Eusebius Werke Achter Band Die Praeparatio Evangelica (1954, 1956), GCS 43,1–2 (Berlin: Akademie-Verlag).

Fragments from Hellenistic Jewish Authors, Vol. 3, Aristobulus (1995), by C. R. Holladay, SBL Texts and Translations 39, Pseudepigrapha Series 13 (Atlanta: Scholars Press).

Gregor der Wundertäter (1996), *Dankrede an Origenes*, trans. by P. Guyot, intro. by R. Klein, FC 24 (Freiburg, Basil, Vienna, Barcelona, Rome, New York: Herder).

Gronewald, Michael (1968), Psalmen Kommentar [Didymus] Teil II Born: Rudolf Habelt Vel

The HarperCollins Study Bible, Revised Edition (2006), Gen. ed. H. W. Attridge (HarperSanFrancisco).

Herodian (1970), 2 vols, trans. by C. R. Whittaker, LCL 454, 455 (Cambridge, Mass.: Harvard University Press; London: William Heinemann Ltd).

Hippolyte commentaire sur Daniel (1947), ed. and trans. by Maurice Lefèvre, SC 14 (Paris: Éditions du Cerf).

Hippolytus Werke 3, Refutatio Omnium Haeresium (1916), ed. by P. Wendland, GCS 26 (Leipzig: J. C. Hinrichs'sche Buchhandlung).

S. Hilarii Episcopi Pictaviensis Tractatus super Psalmos (1891), CSEL 22 (Pragae / Vindobonae: F. Tempsky; Lipsiae: G. Freytag).

Jerome's Commentary on Daniel (1977 / 1958), trans. by G. L. Archer, Jr (Grand Rapids: Baker Book House).

Johannes Philoponos De Opificio Mundi / Über die Erschaffung der Welt (1997), FC 23 / 1, trans. by C. Scholten (Freiburg, Basel, Vienna, Barcelona, Rome, New York: Herder).

La lettre à Africanus sur l'histoire de Suzanne (1983), N. De Lange, in *Origène Philocalie, 1–20 sur les écritures*, M. Harl (Paris: Editions du Cerf).

Lightfoot, J. B. (1926), *The Apostolic Fathers* (London: Macmillan and Co.).

Maximus of Tyre: The Philosophical Orations (1997), translated, with an introduction and notes by M. B. Trapp (Oxford: Clarendon Press).

Mekilta de-Rabbi Ishmael (1933 / 1976), Vol. 2, trans. by J. Z. Lauterbach (Philadelphia: The Jewish Publication Society of America).

The Mishnah (1933 / 1958), trans. by H. Danby (Oxford: Oxford University Press).

New Testament Apocrypha, (1963 / 1959; 1965 / 1964), 2 vols, Hennecke, E. and Schneemelcher, W., eds, trans. by R. McL. Wilson (Philadelphia: The Westminster Press).

Origen: Commentary on the Epistle to the Romans (2001 / 2002), trans by T. P. Scheck, FOTC 103, 104 (Washington, D.C.: The Catholic University of America Press).

Origen: Commentary on the Gospel according to John Books 1–10 (1989), trans. by R. E. Heine, FOTC 80 (Washington, D.C.: The Catholic University of America Press).

Origen: Commentary on the Gospel according to John Books 13–32 (1993), trans. by R. E. Heine, FOTC 89 (Washington, D.C.: The Catholic University of America Press).

Origen: Contra Celsum (1965), trans. by H. Chadwick (Cambridge: Cambridge University Press).

Origen: An exhortation to Martyrdom, Prayer, First Principles: Book IV, Prologue to the Commentary on the Song of Songs, Homily XXVII on Numbers (1979), trans. and introduction by R. A. Greer (New York / Ramsey / Toronto: Paulist Press).

Origen: Homilies on Genesis and Exodus (1981), trans. by R. E. Heine, FOTC 71 (Washington, D.C.: The Catholic University of America Press).

Origen: Homilies on Jeremiah; Homily on 1 Kings 28 (1998), trans. by J. C. Smith, FOTC 97 (Washington, D.C.: The Catholic University of America Press).

Origen: Homilies on Joshua (2002), trans. by B. J. Bruce, ed. by C. White, FOTC 105 (Washington, D.C.: The Catholic University of America Press).

Origen: Homilies on Leviticus (1990), trans. by G. W. Barkley, FOTC 83 (Washington, D.C.: The Catholic University of America Press).

Origen: Homilies on Luke, Fragments on Luke (1996), trans. by J. T. Lienhard, FOTC 94 (Washington, D. C.: The Catholic University of America Press).

Origen: On First Principles (1973), trans. by G. W. Butterworth (Gloucester, Mass.: Peter Smith).

Origen: On Prayer (1954), trans. by J. E. L. Oulton, in *Alexandrian Christianity*, The Library of Christian Classics 2 (Philadelphia: The Westminster Press).

Origen: The Song of Songs Commentary and Homilies (1957), trans. and annotated by R. P. Lawson (New York, N.Y. and Ramsey, N. J.: Newman Press).

Origen: Treatise on the Passover and Dialogue of Origen with Heraclides and his Fellow Bishops on the Father, the Son, and the Soul (1992), trans. by R. J. Daly, ACW 54 (New York and Mahwah, N. J.: Paulist Press).

Origène commentaire sur le Cantique des Cantiques (1991 / 1992), I and II, ed. by L Brésard and H. Crouzel with the collaboration of M. Borret, SC 375, 376 (Paris: Éditions du Cerf).

Origène homélies sur Jérémie (1976), I, ed. by P. Nautin, trans. by P. Husson and P. Nautin, SC 232 (Paris: Éditions du Cerf).

Origène Homélies sur les juges, Text, Introduction, Translation, Notes and Index by P. Messié, L. Neyrand, and M. Borret, SC 389 (Paris: Éditions du Cerf).

Origène Homélies sur les psaumes 36 à 38 (1995), Text by E. Prinzivalli, Introduction, Translation, and Notes by H. Crouzel and L. Brésard, SC 411 (Paris: Éditions du Cerf).

Origenes Werke: De Principiis (1913), GCS 22, ed. by P. Koetschau (Leipzig: J. C. Hinrichs'sche Buchhandlung).

Origenes Werke: Die Homilien zu Lukas (1959), GCS 49, ed. by M. Rauer (Berlin: Akademie Verlag).

Origenes Werke: Homilien zum Hexateuch (1920), GCS 29, ed. by W. A. Baehrens (Leipzig: J. C. Hinrichs'sche Buchandlung).

Origenes Werke: Der Johanneskommentar (1903), GCS 10, ed. by E. Preuschen (Leipzig: J. C. Hinrichs'sche Buchhandlung).

Origenes Werke: Jeremiahomilien, Klageliederkommentar, Erklärung der Samuel- und Königsbücher (1983), GCS 6, ed. by E. Klostermann, revised by P. Nautin (Berlin: Akademie Verlag).

Origenes Werke: Matthäuserklärung I Die griechisch erhaltenen Tomoi (1935), GCS 40, ed by E. Klostormann and E. Benz (leipzig J.C. Hinrichs'sche Buchhandlung).

Origenes Werke: Origenes Matthäuserklärung II Die lateinische Übersetzung der Commentariorum Series (1976), GCS 41 / 1, ed. by E. Klostermann, with E. Benz and U. Treu (Berlin: Akademie Verlag).

Origenes Werke: Die Schrift vom Martyrium, Gegen Celsus, Die Schrift vom Gebet (1899), 2 vols, GCS 2, 3, ed. by P. Koetschau (Leipzig: J. C. Hinrichs'sche buchhandlung).

Origenis Opera Omnia (1844), Vol. 16, ed. C. H. E. Lommatzsch (Berlin: Sumtibus Haude et Spener).

The Oxyrhynchus Papyri (1903), Part III, ed. by B. P. Grenfell and A. S. Hunt (London: The Egyptian Exploration Fund).

Papyrological Primer (1965), van Groningen, M. D. and B. A., 4th edition (Leyden: E. J. Brill).

Patrologiae Graecae 103 (1900), *Photii, Constanntinopolitani Patriarchae Opera Omnia* (Paris: Apud Garnier Fratres Editores, et J.-P. Migne, Successores).

Patrologiae Latinae 26 (1845 / 1990), *Sancti Eusebii Hieronymi Opera Omnia* (Turnholt: Brepols). *Origenis Opera Omnia* (1844).

Das Petrusevangelium und die Petrusapokalypse (2004), ed. T. J. Kraus and T. Nicklas, GCS, n.s. 11, Neutestamentliche Apokryphen I (Berlin / New York: Walter de Gruyter).

Philo 9 (1995 / 1941), LCL 363, trans. by F. H. Colson (Cambridge, Mass. / London: Harvard University Press).

Philostratus and Eunapius The Lives of the Sophists (1989 / 1921), trans. by W. C. Wright, LCL 134 (Cambridge, Mass. / London: Harvard University Press).

Plotinus 1 (1989), trans. by A. H. Armstrong, LCL (Cambridge, MA: Harvard University Press).

Rietz, Gualterus (1914), *De Origenis Prologis in Psalterium* (Ienae: Typis H. Pohle).

Der Römerbriefkommentar des Origenes (16:1990, 33:1997, 34:1998), ed. by Caroline P. Hammond Bammel, Vetus Latina 16, 33, 34 (Freiburg: Herder).

Select Papyri (1934), ed. by E. S. Edgar and A. S. Hunt, Vol. II, LCL (Cambridge, MA: Harvard University Press; London: William Heinemann).

The Acts of the Pagan Martyrs, Acta Alexandrinorum (1954), ed. with commentary by H. Musurillo (Oxford: Clarendon Press).

The Apostolic Fathers, 3rd edition (2007), ed. and trans. by M. W. Holmes (Grand Rapids, Mich: Baker Academic).

The Excerpta Ex Theodoto of Clement of Alexandria (1934), ed. and trans. by R. P. Casey, Studies and Documents 1 (London: Christophers).

The Gnostic Scriptures (1987), trans. by Bentley Layton (London: SCM Press Ltd).

The Nag Hammadi Library in English (1977), trans. by Members of the Coptic Gnostic Library Project of the Institute for Antiquity and Christianity, J. M. Robinson, Director (New York / Hagerstown / San Francisco / London: Harper & Row).

The Old Testament Pseudepigrapha, 1 (1983), 2 (1985), ed. by J. H. Charlesworth (Garden City, N.Y.).

Tractatus Tripartitus Pars I De supernis (1973), ed. by R. Kasser, M. Malinine, H.-C. Puech, G. Quispel, and J. Zandee (Bern: Francke Verlag).

Völker, Walther (1932), *Quellen zur Geschichte der christlichen Gnosis* (Tübingen: J. C. B. Mohr (Paul Siebeck)).

Bibliography: Secondary Sources

Abd-el-Ghani, Mohammed (2004), "Alexandria and Middle Egypt: Some Aspects of Social and Economic Contacts under Roman Rule", in *Ancient Alexandria between Egypt and Greece*, ed. by W. V. Harris and Giovanni Ruffini, Columbia Studies in the Classical Tradition 26 (Leiden/Boston: Brill), 161–78.

Andresen, Carl (1979), "'Siegreiche Kirche' im Aufstieg des Christentums. Untersuchungen zu Eusebius von Caesarea und Dionysios von Alexandrien", *Principat* 23.1, ed. by Wolfgang Haase, in *Aufstieg und Niederegang der römischen Welt* II, ed. by Hildegarad Temporini and Wolfgang Haase (Berlin/New York: Walter de Gruyter).

——(1981/1952), "Justin und der mittlere Platonismus", in *Der Mittelplatonismus*, ed. by C. Zintzen (Darmstadt: Wissenschaftliche Buchgesellschaft), 319–68.

Athanassiadi, Polymnia (1999), "The Chaldaean Oracles: Theology and Theurgy", in *Pagan Monotheism in Late Antiquity*, ed. by Polymnia Athanassiadi and Michael Frede (Oxford: Clarendon Press), 149–83.

——and Frede, Michael (1999), "Introduction", *Pagan Monotheism in Late Antiquity*, ed. by Polymnia Athanassiadi and Michael Frede (Oxford: Clarendon Press), 1–20.

Aulén, Gustaf (1961), *Christus Victor* (New York: The Macmillan Company).

Ausfeld (1904), "Neapolis und Brucheion in Alexandria", *Philologus* 63, 481–97.

Bagnall, Roger S. (1993), *Egypt in Late Antiquity* (Princeton: Princeton University Press).

Bacher, W. (1891), "The Church Father, Origen, and Rabbi Hoshaya", *JQR* 3, 357–60.

Baer, Y. (1961), "Israel, the Christian Church, and the Roman Empire", in *Scripta Hierosolymitana* 7, ed. by A. Fuks and I. Halpern (Jerusalem: Magnes Press, The Hebrew University), 79–149.

Bammel, Caroline (1995), "Origen's Pauline Prefaces and the Chronology of his Pauline Commentaries", in *Origeniana Sexta* (Leuven: Peeters), 495–513.

Bardy, G. (1937), "Aux origines de l'école d'Alexandrie", *Recherches de science religieuse* 27, 65–90.

Bardy, G. (1925), "Les traditions juives dans l'oeuvre d'Origène", in *Revue Biblique*, 217–52.

Barnard, L. W. (1966), *Studies in the Apostolic Fathers and their Background* (New York: Schocken Books).

Barnes, Robert (2000), "Cloistered Bookworms in the Chicken-Coop of the Muses: The Ancient Library of Alexandria", in *The Library of Alexandria: Centre of Learning in the Ancient World*, ed. by Roy MacLeod (London/New York: I. B. Tauris): 61–77.

Bauer, Walter (1934/1971), *Orthodoxy and Heresy in Earliest Christianity*, ed. by R. A. Kraft and G. Krodel (Philadelphia: Fortress Press).

Bell, H. Idris (1937), *Recent Discoveries of Biblical Papyri* (Oxford: Clarendon Press).

——(1948), *Egypt from Alexander the Great to the Arab Conquest* (Oxford: At the Clarendon Press).

Biblia Patristica (1991), 3 *Origène* (Paris: Éditions du Centre National de la Recherche Scientifique).

Bienert, Wolfgang A. (1978), *Dionysius von Alexandrien* (Berlin/New York: Walter De Gruyter).

Bietenhard, Hans (1974), *Caesarea, Origenes und die Juden* (Stuttgart/Berlin/Köln/Mainz: Verlag W. Kohlhammer).

Bigg, Charles (1968/1886), *The Christian Platonists of Alexandria* (Amsterdam: Editions Rodopi; Oxford: Clarendon Press).

Blank, David L. (1982), *Ancient Philosophy and Grammar: The Syntax of Apollonius Dyscolus*, American Classical Studies 10 (Chico, CA: Scholars Press).

Blum, Rudolf (1991), *Kallimachos: The Alexandrian Library and the Origins of Bibliography*, trans. Hans H. Wellisch (Madison: The University of Wisconsin Press).

Borgen, P., Fuglseth, K. and Skarsten, R. (2000), *The Philo Index* (Leiden/Boston/Köln: Brill; Grand Rapids, Mich./Cambridge, U.K.: William B. Eerdmans).

Boulluec, Alain Le (2000a), "Alien wisdom", in *Alexandria, Third Century B.C.*, ed. by Christian Jacob and François de Polignac, trans. by Colin Clement (Alexandria: Harppocrates), 56–69.

——(2000b), "Clement, Origen and the eternal nature of the written word", in *Alexandria, third century BC*, ed. by Christian Jacob and François de Polignac, translated by Colin Clement (Alexandria: Harppocrates), 206–11.

Brown, Peter (1988), *The Body and Society* (London/Boston: Faber and Faber).

Burnet, J. (1963/1911), *Plato's Phaedo* (Oxford: Clarendon Press).

Cadiou, René (1944), *Origen: His Life at Alexandria*, trans. by John A. Couthwell (St Louis/London: Herder).

Campenhausen, Hans von (1969/1953), *Ecclesiastical Authority and Spiritual Power in the Church of the First Three Centuries*, trans. by J. A. Baker (Stanford: Stanford University Press).

Casson, Lionel (2001), *Libraries in the Ancient World* (New Haven/London: Yale University Press).

Chadwick, H. (1959), *The Sentences of Sextus* (Cambridge: Cambridge University Press).

Chênevert, Jacques (1969), *L'église dans le commentaire d'Origène sur le cantique des cantiques*, Studia travaux de recherche 24 (Bruxelles/Paris: Desclée de Brouwer; Montréal: Les Éditions Bellarmin).

Collins, John J. (1993), *Daniel*, Hermeneia (Minneapolis: Fortress Press).

Collins, Nina L. (2000), *The Library in Alexandria and the Bible in Greek*, Supplements to Vetus Testamentum 82 (Leiden/Boston/Köln: Brill).

Crouzel, H. (1970), "L'Ecole d'Origène à Césarée", *BLE* 71, 15–27.

——(1989), *Origen*, trans. by A. S. Worrall (Edinburgh: T. & T. Clark).

Daniélou, Jean (1955), *Origen*, trans. by W. Mitchell (New York: Sheed and Ward).

——(1964), *The Theology of Jewish Christianity*, trans. by John A. Baker (London: Darton, Longman & Todd; Chicago: Henry Regnery).

Dawson, D. (1992), *Allegorical Readers and Cultural Revision in Ancient Alexandria*, (Berkley/Los Angeles/Oxford: University of California Press).

Dechow, Jon F. (1988), "Origen and Early Christian Pluralism: The Context of his Eschatology", in *Origen of Alexandria: His World and His Legacy*, ed. by Charles Kannengiesser and William L. Petersen, (Notre Dame, Ind.: University of Notre Dame Press), 337–56.

De Faye, Eugène (1923, 1927, 1928), *Origène sa vie, son oeuvre, sa pensée*, 3 vol, Bibliothèque de l'école des hautes études 37, 43, 44 (Paris: Éditions Ernest Leroux).

Edwards, Mark (1993), "Ammonius, Teacher of Origen", *JEH*, 169–81.

——(2002), *Origen against Plato*, Ashgate Studies in Philosophy & Theology in Late Antiquity (Aldershot: Ashgate).

El-Abbadi, Mostafa (2004), "The Alexandria Library in history", in *Alexandria, Real and Imagined*, ed. by Anthony Hirst and Michael Silk (Aldershot: Ashgate), 167–83.

Empereur, Jean-Yves (1998), *Alexandria Rediscovered* (New York: George Braziller).

——(2000), "Alexandria rising", in *Alexandria, Third Century B.C.*, ed. by Christian Jacob and François de Polignac, trans. by Colin Clement (Alexandria: Harppocrates), 188–205.

Ferguson, Everett, ed. (1999), *Christianity in Relation to Jews, Greeks, and Romans* (New York/London: Garland Publishing).

Foerster, Gideon (1975), "The Early History of Caesarea", in *The Joint Expedition to Caesarea Maritima*, Vol. I, ed. by C. T. Fritsch (Missoula, Montana: Scholars Press), 9–22.

Fowden, Garth (1993/1986), *The Egyptian Hermes: A Historical Approach to the Late Pagan Mind* (Princeton: Princeton University Press).

Frede, Michael (1999), "Monotheism and Pagan Philosophy in Later Antiquity", in *Pagan Monotheism in Late Antiquity*, ed. by Polymnia Athanassiadi and Michael Frede (Oxford: Clarendon Press), 41–67.

Frend, W. H. C. (1984), *The Rise of Christianity* (Philadelphia: Fortress Press).

Glaue, D. P., ed. (1928), "Ein Bruckstück des Origenes über Genesis 1,28", in *Mitteilungen aus der Papyrussammlung der Giessenere Universitätsbibliothek*, 2 (Giessen).

Goffinet, Émile (1965), *L'utilisation d'Origène dans le commentaire des psaumes de saint Hilaire de Poitiers*, Studia Hellenistica 14 (Publications Universitaires de Louvain).

Gorday, Peter (1983), *Principles of Patristic Exegesis: Romans 9–11 in Origen, John Chrysostom, and Augustine*, Studies in the Bible and Early Christianity 4 (New York/Toronto: The Edwin Mellen Press).

Görres, F. (1876), "Kritische Untersuchungen über die Christenverfolgung des römischen Kaisers Maximinus I. des Thraciers", *ZWT* 19, 526–74.

Grafton A. and Williams, M. (2006), *Christianity and the Transformation of the Book* (Cambridge, Mass/London: The Belknap Press of Harvard University Press).

Grant, M. (1992), *A Social History of Greece and Rome* (New York: Charles Scribner's Sons).

——(1986), *Gods and the One God* (London: SPCK).

——(1986), "Theological Education at Alexandria", in *The Roots of Egyptian Christianity*, ed. by Birger A. Pearson & James E. Goehring, Studies in Antiquity & Christianity (Philadelphia: Fortress Press), 178–89.

——(2003), *Second-Century Christianity*, 2nd edition (Louisville/London: Westminster John Knox Press).

Grant, R.M. (1957), *The Letter and the Spirit* (London: SPCK).

Green, Henry A. (1986), "The Socio-Economic Background of Christianity in Egypt", in *The Roots of Egyptian Christianity*, ed. by Birger A. Pearson and James E. Goehring, Studies in Antiquity & Christianity (Philadelphia: Fortress Press) 100–13.

Greggs, Tom (2009), *Barth, Origen, and Universal Salvation* (Oxford: Oxford University Press).

Griggs, C. Wilfred (1991), *Early Egyptian Christianity from its Origins to 451 C.E.*, Coptic Studies 2 (Leiden/New York/København/Köln: Brill).

Guimier-Sorbets, Anne-Marie and Seif el-Din, Mervat (2004), "Life after death: an original form of bilingual iconography in the necropolis of Kawm al-Shuqafa", in *Alexandria, Real and Imagined*, ed. by Anthony Hirst and Michael Silk (Aldershot: Ashgate), 133–141.

Haas, Christopher (1997), *Alexandria in Late Antiquity: Topography and Social Conflict* (Baltimore and London: The Johns Hopkins University Press).

Hadot, I. (1987), "Les introductions aux commentaries exégétiques chez les auteurs néoplatoniciens et les auteurs chrétiens", in *Les règles de l'interprétation*, ed. by M. Tardieu (Paris: Editions du Cerf), 99–122.

Hagemann H. (1864), *Die Römische Kirche* (Freiburg: Herder).

Haines-Eitzen, Kim (2000), *Guardians of Letters* (Oxford: Oxford University Press).

Hällström, Gunnar af (1984), *Fides Simpliciorum according to Origen of Alexandria*, Commentationes Humanarum Litterarum 76 (Helsinki: Societas Scientiarum Fennica/The Finnish Society of Sciences and Letters).

Hanson, R. P. C. (1954), *Origen's Doctrine of Tradition* (London: SPCK).

——(1959), *Allegory and Event* (Richmond, Virginia: John Knox Press).

Harl, Marguerite (1982), "Origène et les interpretations patristiques grecques de l' 'obscurité' biblique", *Vigiliae Christianae*, 36, 334–71.

Harnack Adolf (1:1904; 2:1905), *The Expansion of Christianity in the First Three Centuries*, trans. by J. Moffatt (New York: G. P. Putnam's Sons/London: Williams and Norgate).

——(1960/1924), *Marcion* (Darmstadt: Wissenschaftliche Buchgesellschaft).

Harrington, Daniel J. S. J., (2002), "The Old Testament Apocrypha in the Early Church and Today", in *The Canon Debate* (Peabody, MASS: Hendrickson).

Heine, Ronald E. (forthcoming a), "Restringing Origen's Broken Harp: Some Suggestions Concerning the Prologue to the Caesarean Commentary on the Psalms", in *Harp of the Spirit*, ed. by B. E. Daley (Notre Dame, Ind.: Notre Dame University Press).

——(1993a), "Stoic Logic as Handmaid to Exegesis and Theology in Origen's Commentary on the Gospel of John", *JTS*, 89–117.

—— (1993b), "Three Allusions to Book 20 of Origen's *Commentary on John* in Gregory Thaumaturgus' *Panegyric to Origen*", in *Studia Patristica* 26, ed. by E. A. Livingstone (Leuven: Peeters Press), 261–6.

—— (1995a), "The Introduction to Origen's *Commentary on John* Compared with the Introductions to the Ancient Philosophical Commentaries on Aristotle", in *Origeniana Sexta*, ed. by Gilles Dorival and Alain Le Boulluec (Leuven: University Press), 3–12.

—— (1995b), *Gregory of Nyssa's Treatise on the Inscriptions of the Psalms* (Oxford: Clarendon Press).

—— (1997a), "Origen on the Christological Significance of Psalm 45 (44)", in *Consensus: A Canadian Lutheran Journal of Theology* 23.1, 21–37.

—— (1997b), "Reading the Bible with Origen", in *The Bible in Greek Christian Antiquity*, ed. and trans. by Paul M. Blowers (Notre Dame, IN: University of Notre Dame Press).

—— (1998), "The Christology of Callistus", *JTS* n.s. 49, 56–91.

—— (2000a), "In Search of Origen's Commentary on Philemon", in *HTR* 93.2, 117–33.

—— (2000b), "Recovering Origen's Commentary on Ephesians from Jerome", in *JTS* n.s. 51.2, 478–514.

—— (2000c), "Evidence for the Date of Origen's Commentary on Ephesians", in *ZAC* 4, 149–157.

—— (2001), "The Prologues of Origen's Pauline Commentaries and the *Schemata Isagogica* of Ancient Commentary Literature", in *Studia Patristica* 36, ed. by M. F. Wiles and E. J. Yarnold (Leuven: Peeters), 421–39.

—— (2002), *The Commentaries of Origen and Jerome on St Paul's Epistle to the Ephesians*, OECS (Oxford: Oxford University Press).

—— (2003), "Origen's Alexandrian Commentary on Genesis", in *Origeniana Octava*, ed. by L. Perrone, Vol. 1 (Leuven: University Press).

—— (2004a), "Epinoiai", in *The Westminster Handbook to Origen*, ed. by J. A. McGuckin (Louisville/London: Westminster John Knox Press), 93–5.

—— (2004b), "God", in *The Westminster Handbook to Origen*, ed. by J. A. McGuckin (Louisville/London: Westminster John Knox Press), 106–13.

—— (2004c), "Heracleon", in *The Westminster Handbook to Origen*, ed. by J. A. McGuckin (Louisville/London: Westminster John Knox Press), 120–1.

—— (2004d), "Articulating Identity", in *The Cambridge History of Early Christian Literature*, ed. by F. Young, L. Ayres, and A. Louth (Cambridge: Cambridge University Press), 200–21.

—— (2005), "The Testimonia and Fragments Related to Origen's Commentary on Genesis", in *ZAC* 9, 122–42.

—— (2007), *Reading the Old Testament with the Ancient Church* (Grand Rapids, MI: Baker Academic).

—— (forthcoming a), "Origen and the Eternal Boundaries", in *Die Septuaginta und das frühe Christentum*, ed. by H. Lichtenberger and S. Caulley (Tübingen: Mohr/Siebeck).

Heine, Ronald (1975), *Perfection in the Virtuous Life*, Patristic Monograph Series 2 (Philadelphia: The Philadelphia Patristic Foundation).

Heisey, Nancy R. (2000), *Origen the Egyptian* (Nairobi, Kenya: Paulines Publications, Africa).

——(1992), Review of *Origène: Commentaire sur le Cantique des Cantiques*, Vol. I, in *JTS* ns 43.2, 673–5.

Hengel, Martin (2002), *The Septuagint as Christian Scripture*, trans. by M. E. Biddle (Grand Rapids, MI: Baker Academic).

Hill, Charles E. (1999), "The *Epistula Apostolorum*: An Asian Tract from the Time of Polycarp", *JECS*, 1–53.

——(2001), *Regnum Caelorum*, 2nd edition (Grand Rapids, Michigan/Cambridge, U.K.: William B. Eerdmans.

Hohlfelder, Robert L. (1992), "Caesarea", in *The Anchor Bible Dictionary*, ed. by D. N. Freedman, Vol. 1 (New York/London/Toronto/Sydney/Auckland: Doubleday), 798–803.

Hornschuh, Manfred (1960), "Das Leben des Origenes und die Entstehung der alexandrinischen Schule", *ZKG* 71, 1–25, 193–214.

Jakab, Attila (2001), *Ecclesia alexandrina* (Bern/Berlin/Bruxelles/Frankfurt am Main/New York/Oxford/Wien: Peter Lang).

Jellicoe, Sidney (1968), *The Septuagint and Modern Study* (Oxford: Clarendon Press).

"Johanan B. Nappaha (Ha-Nappah)" (1904), in *The Jewish Encyclopedia*, ed. I. Singer (New York London: Funk and Wagnalls Company).

Junod Eric (1980), "L'impossible et le possible: Étude de la déclaration préliminaire du *De Oratione*", in *Origeniana Secunda*, ed. by H. Crouzel and A. Quacquarelli (Rome: Edizioni dell'Ateneo).

——(1994), "Wodurch unterscheiden sich die Homilien des Origenes von seinen Kommentaren?", in *Predigt in der alten Kirche*, ed. by E. Mühlenberg and J. van Oort (Kampen—the Netherlands: Kok Pharos), 50–81.

——(1995), "Que savons-nous des 'scholies' $[\Sigma XO\Lambda IA\text{-}\Sigma HMEI\Omega\Sigma EI\Sigma]$?", in *Origeniana Sexta*, ed. by G. Dorival and A. Le Boulluec, BETL, 118 (Leuven: University Press – Peeters).

Kamesar, Adam (1990), "The Virgin of Isaiah 7: 14. The Philological Argument from the Second to the Fifth Century", *JTS*, 51–75.

Kimelman, Reuven (1980), "Rabbi Yohanan and Origen on the Song of Songs: A Third-Century Jewish-Christian Disputation", in *HTR* 73 (1980), 567–95.

Klijn, A. F. J. (1986), "Jewish Christianity in Egypt", in *The Roots of Egyptian Christianity*, ed. by Birger A. Pearson and James E. Goehring, Studies in Antiquity and Christianity (Philadelphia: Fortress Press), 161–75.

——(1988), "Das Hebräer- und das Nazoräerevangelium", in *Aufstieg und Niedergang der Römischen Welt*, ed. by W. Haase and H. Temporini, Part II: Principate, Vol. 25.5 (Berlin/New York: Walter de Gruyter).

Klostermann, Erich (1896), "Die Mailänder Fragmente der Hexapla", *ZAW* 16, 334–7.

Knauber, Adolf (1968), "Das Anliegen der Schule des Origenes zu Cäsaraea", *Münchener Theologische Zeitschrift* 19, 182–203.

Koch, Hal (1932), *Pronoia und Paideusis* (Berlin and Leipzig: Walter de Gruyter & Co.).

Koester, Helmut (1982), *Introduction to the New Testament 2: History and Literature of Early Christianity* (Philadelphia: Fortress Press; Berlin/New York: Walter de Gruyter).

Lake, K. and New, S. (1932), *Six Collations of New Testament Manuscripts*, HTS, 17 (Cambridge/Harvard University Press).

Lane Fox, Robin (1987), *Pagans and Christians* (New York: Alfred A. Knopf, Inc.).

Lange, N. R. M. De (1976), *Origen and the Jews* (Cambridge/London/New York/Melbourne: Cambridge University Press).

Latham, E.C. ed. (1969), *The Poetry of Robert Frost* (New York/Chicago/San Francisco: Holt, Rinehart and Winston).

Layton, Richard A. (2004), *Didymus the Blind and His Circle in Late-Antique Alexandria* (Urbana and Chicago: University of Illinois Press).

Ledegang, F. (2001), *Mysterium Ecclesiae*, BETL 156 (Leuven: Peeters).

Lesky, Albin (1966), *A History of Greek Literature*, 2nd edition, trans. by J. Willis and C. de Heer (New York: Thomas Y. Crowell Company).

Levey, Irving M. (1975), "Caesarea and the Jews", in *The Joint Expedition to Caesarea Maritima*, Vol. I, ed. by C. T. Fritsch (Missoula/Montana: Scholars Press), 43–78.

Levine, Lee I. (1975), *Caesarea under Roman Rule*, Studies in Judaism in Late Antiquity 7 (Leiden: Brill).

Lewis, Naphtali (1963), "The Non-Scholar Members of the Alexandrian Museum", *Mnemosyne*, 257–61.

—— (1983), *Life in Egypt under Roman Rule* (Oxford: Clarendon Press).

Liddell, H. G., Scott, R., Jones, H. S. (1961), *A Greek-English Lexicon* (Oxford: Clarendon Press).

Lietzmann, Hans (1953), *A History of the Early Church* I & II, trans. by B. L. Woolf (Cleveland/New York: Meridian Books, The World Publishing Company, original, 1937, 1938).

Löhr, Winrich A. (1996), *Basilides und seine Schule*, WUNT 83 (Tübingen: J. C. B. Mohr (Paul Siebeck)).

Luttikhuizen, Gerard P. (2003), "The Critical Rewriting of Genesis in the Gnostic *Apocryphon of John*", in *Jerusalem, Alexandria, Rome: Studies in Ancient Cultural Interaction in Honour of A. Hilhorst*, ed. by F. G. Martínez and G. P. Luttikhuizen (Leiden/Boston: Brill), 187–200.

Mackie, E. C. (1904), *Luciani Menippus et Timon* (Cambridge: Cambridge University Press).

MacLeod, Roy (2000), "Introduction: Alexandria in History and Myth", in *The Library of Alexandria: Centre of Learning in the Ancient World*, ed. by Roy MacLeod (London/New York: I. B. Tauris): 1–15.

McKenzie, Judith (2007), *The Architecture of Alexandria and Egypt c. 300 BC to AD 700* (New Haven and London: Yale University Press).

Maehler, Herwig (2004), "Alexandria, the Mouseion, and cultural identity", in *Alexandria, Real and Imagined*, ed. by Anthony Hirst and Michael Silk, (Aldershot: Ashgate), 1–14.

Mansfeld, J. (1994), *Prolegomena: Questions to be Settled before the Study of an Author, or a Text*, Philosophia Antiqua 61 (Leiden/New York/Köln: Brill).

Markschies, Christoph (1992), *Valentinus Gnosticus?*, WUNT 65 (Tübingen: J. C. B. Mohr (Paul Siebeck).

——(1997), "'...für die Gemeinde im Grossen un Ganzen nicht geeignet...'?", *Zeitschrift für theologie und kirche* 94.1, 39–68.

Marlowe, John (1971), *The Golden Age of Alexandria* (London: Victor Gollancz Limited).

Marrou, H. I. (1964/1956), *A History of Education in Antiquity*, trans. by George Lamb (New York: Mentor Books).

Mendels, M. D. (1992), "Susanna, Book of", in *ABD* 6 (New York/London/Toronto/Sydney/Auckland: Doubleday), 246–47.

Moore, Carey A. (1992), "Daniel, Additions to", in *ABD* 2 (New York/London/Toronto/Sydney/Auckland: Doubleday), 18–28.

Murphy, Roland E. (1990), *The Song of Songs*, Hermeneia (Minneapolis: Fortress Press).

Nautin, Pierre (1977), *Origène* (Paris: Beauchesne).

Neumann, K. J. (1890), *Der Römische Staat und die allgemeine Kirche bis auf Diocletian* I (Leipzig).

Neuschäfer, Bernhard (1987), *Origenes als Philologe* (Basel: Friedrich Reinhardt Verlag).

Neymeyr, Ulrich (1989), *Die christlichen Lehrer im zweiten Jahrhundert* (Leiden/New York/København/Köln: Brill).

Norelli, E. (2000), "Origene (vita e opera)", in *Origene Dizionario la cultura, el pensiero, le opera*, ed. by A. M. Castagno (a c. di) (Roma: Città Nuova), 293–302.

Orru, Cécile (2002), "Ein Raub der Flammen? Die königliche Bibliothek von Alexandria", mit einem Nachwort von Wolfram Hoepfner", in *Antike Bibliotheken*, ed. by Wolfram Hoepfner (Mainz am Rhein: Verlag Philipp von Zabern), 31–8.

Pagels, E. H. (1973), *The Johannine Gospel in Gnostic Exegesis: Heracleon's Commentary on John* (Nashville & New York: Abingdon Press).

——(1975), *The Gnostic Paul* (Philadelphia: Fortress Press).

—— (1979), *The Gnostic Gospels* (New York: Random House).

——(1986), "Exegesis and Exposition of the Genesis Creation Accounts in Selected Texts from Nag Hammadi", in *Nag Hammadi, Gnosticism, and Early Christianity*, ed. by C. W. Hedrick and R. Hodgson (Peabody, MA: Hendrickson), 257–85.

Paget, James Carleton (1994), *The Epistle of Barnabas*, WUNT 2.64 (Tübingen: J. C. B. Mohr (Paul Siebeck).

——(2004), "Jews and Christians in ancient Alexandria from the Ptolemies to Caracalla", in *Alexandria, Real and Imagined*, ed. by Anthony Hirst and Michael Silk (Aldershot: Ashgate), 143–66.

Painchaud, L. (1996), "The Use of Scripture in Gnostic Literature", *JECS* 4, 129–47.

Pearson, Birger A. (1986), "Earliest Christianity in Egypt: Some Observations", in *The Roots of Egyptian Christianity*, ed. by Birger A. Pearson and James E. Goehring, Studies in Antiquity & Christianity (Philadelphia: Fortress Press), 132–59.

——(1992), "Christianity in Egypt", in *ABD* 1 (New York/London/Toronto/Sydney/Auckland: Doubleday), 954–66.

——(2004), *Gnosticism and Christianity in Roman and Coptic Egypt*, Studies in Antiquity & Christianity (New York/London: T & T Clark International).

——(2006), "Egypt", in *The Cambridge History of Christianity* 1, ed. by M. M. Mitchell and F. M. Young (Cambridge: Cambridge University Press), 331–50.

Peel, M. L. (1969), *The Epistle to Rheginos* (London: SCM Press Ltd).

Peri, V. (1980), *Omelie Origeniane sui Salmi*, ST 289 (Rome: Biblioteca apostolica vaticana), 7–28.

Perrone, L. (1995), "Perspectives sur Origène et la littérature patristique des 'Quaestiones et Responsiones'", in *Origeniana Sexta*, BETL 118, ed. by G. Dorival and A. Le Boulluec (Leuven: University Press – Peeters).

Pisi, P. (1987), "Peccato di Adamo e Caduta dei Noes nell' Esegesi Origeniana", in *Origeniana Quarta*, ed. by L. Lies, Innsbrucker theologische Studien 19 (Innsbruck,Wien: Tyrolia Verlag), 322–35.

Pollard, T. E. (1970), *Johannine Christology and the Early Church* (Cambridge: Cambridge University Press).

Praechter, K. (1909), "Die griechischen Aristoteleskommentare", *BZ* 18, 516–938; trans. as "Review of the *Commentaria in Aristotelem Graeca*", by V. Caston in *Aristotle Transformed*, ed. by Richard Sorabji (Ithaca: Cornell University Press, 1990), 31–54.

Reynolds, L. D. and Wilson, N. G. (1968), *Scribes & Scholars* (London: Oxford University Press).

Ritter, A. M. (1987), "De Polycarpe à Clément: aux origins d'Alexandrie chrétienne", in *ΑΛΕΞΑΝΔΡΙΝΑ*: Hellénisme, judaïsme et christianisme à Alexandrie. Mélanges offerts au P. Claude Mondésert (Paris: Éditions du Cerf).

Roberts, Colin H. (1954), "Early Christianity in Egypt: Three Notes", in *The Journal of Egyptian Archaeology* 40, 92–6.

——(1979), *Manuscript, Society and Belief in Early Christian Egypt* (London: Published for The British Academy by The Oxford University Press).

Roncaglia, Martiniano Pellegrino (1977), "Pantène et le didascalée d'Alexandrie: du judéo-christianisme au christianisme hellénistique", in *A Tribute to Arthur Vööbus: Studies in Early Christian Literature and its Environment, Primarily in the Syrian East*, ed. by Robert H. Fisher (Chicago: The Lutheran School of Theology), 211–33.

Rondeau, M.-J. (1982), *Les commentaires patristiques du psautier* I, OCA 219 (Rome: Pontificium Institute Studiorum Orienta).

Rowlandson, Jane and Harker, Andrew (2004), "Roman Alexandria from the perspective of the papyri", in *Alexandria, Real and Imagined*, ed. by Anthony Hirst and Michael Silk (Aldershot: Ashgate), 79–111.

Rudolph, Kurt (1983/1977), *Gnosis*, trans. by R. M. Wilson (San Francisco: Harper & Row).

Runia, David, T. (1993), *Philo in Early Christian Literature* (Assen: Van Gorcum; Minneapolis: Fortress Press).

Scheidel, Walter (2004), "Creating a Metropolis: A Comparative Demographic Perspective", in *Ancient Alexandria between Egypt and Greece*, ed. by W. V. Harris and Giovanni Ruffini, Columbia Studies in the Classical Tradition 26 (Leiden/Boston: Brill), 1–31.

Schoedel, William R. (1972), " 'Topological' Theology and Some Monistic Tendencies in Gnosticism", in *Essays on the Nag Hammadi Texts in Honour of Alexander Böhlig*, ed. by Martin Krause (Leiden: Brill), 88–108.

——(1975), "Jewish Wisdom and the Formation of the Christian Ascetic", in *Aspects of Wisdom in Judaism and Early Christianity* (Notre Dame/London: University of Notre Dame Press), 169–99.

Scholten, Clemens (1995), "Die alexandrinische Katechetenschule", *Jahrbuch für Antike und Christentum* 38, 16–37.

Schwyzer, Hans-Rudolf (1983), *Ammonios Sakkas, der Lehrer Plotins*, Rheinisch-Westfälische Akademie der Wissenschaften, Vorträge G 260 (Opladen: Westdeutscher Verlag).

Scott, Alan (1991), *Origen and the Life of the Stars* (Oxford: Clarendon Press).

Siegert, Folker (1998), "The Philonian Fragment *De Deo*", in *The Studia Philonica Annual* 10, ed. by David T. Runia (Atlanta: Scholars Press).

Simonetti, M. (1962), "Alcune Osservazioni sull'Interpretazione Origeniana di Genesi 2,7 e 3,21", *Aevum* 36, 370–81.

Skarsaune, Oscar (1987), *The Proof from Prophecy: A study in Justin Martyr's Proof-Text Tradition: The Text-Type, Provenance, Theological Profile* (Leiden: Brill).

Smith, Morton (1973), *Clement of Alexandria and a Secret Gospel of Mark* (Cambridge, Mass.: Harvard University Press).

Smyth, Herbert Weir (1963/1920), *Greek Grammar*, revised by G. M. Messing (Cambridge: Harvard University Press).

Snyder, H. Gregory (2000), *Teachers and Texts in the Ancient World* (London and New York: Routledge).

Staden, Heinrich von (2004), "Galen's Alexandria", in *Ancient Alexandria between Egypt and Greece*, ed. by W. V. Harris and Giovanni Ruffini, Columbia Studies in the Classical Tradition 26 (Leiden/Boston: Brill), 179–215.

Stählin, Otto and Treu, Ursula (1980), *Clemens Alexandrinus Register*, GCS 39/1 (Berlin: Akademie-Verlag).

Staikos, Konstantinos Sp. (2004), *The History of the Library in Western Civilization, I From Minos to Cleopatra*, trans. by Timothy Cullen (Kotinos: Oak Knoll Press/HES & De Graaf Publishers BV).

Stark, Rodney (1997), *The Rise of Christianity* (HarperSanFrancisco).

——(2006), *Cities of God* (HarperSanFrancisco).

Stead G. C. (1980),"In Search of Valentinus", in *The Rediscovery of Gnosticism*, ed. by Bently Layton (Leidon: Brill), 75–102.

Strack, Hermann L. (1931/1959), *Introduction to the Talmud and Midrash* (New York: Meridian Books, and Philadelphia: The Jewish Publication Society of America).

Swete, Henry Barclay (1902/1968), *An Introduction to the Old Testament in Greek*, revised by R. R. Ottley (New York: KTAV Publishing House, Inc., reprint of Cambridge University Press).

Tarn, W. W. (1967), *Hellenistic Civilisation* 3rd edition, revised by W. W. Tarn and G. T. Griffith (Cleveland and New York: The World Publishing Company).

Tcherikover, Victor A. and Fuks, Alexander, eds. (1957–64), *Corpus Papyrorum Judaicarum*, 3 vols (Cambridge: Harvard University Press).

Torjesen, Karen Jo (1986), *Hermeneutical Procedure and Theological Method in Origen's Exegesis*, Patristische Texte und Studien 38 (Berlin/New York: Walter de Gruyter).

Trapp, M. B. (2004), "Images of Alexandria in the writings of the Second Sophistic", in *Alexandria, Real and Imagined*, ed. by Anthony Hirst and Michael Silk (Aldershot: Ashgate), 113–32.

Trigg, J. W. (1983), *Origen* (Atlanta: John Knox Press).

Turner, E. G. (1968), *Greek Papyri: An Introduction* (Princeton: Princeton University Press).

Turner, J. D. (1986), "Sethian Gnosticism: A Literary History", in *Nag Hammadi, Gnosticism, and Early Christianity*, ed. by C. W. Hedrick and R. Hodgson, Jr (Peabody, MA: Hendrickson Publishers), 55–86.

Ungern-Sternberg, A. F. von (1913), *Der traditionelle alttestamentliche Schriftbeweis 'De Christo' und 'De Evangelio' in der alten Kirche bis zur Zeit Eusebs von Caesarea* (Halle: Verlag von Max Niemeyer).

Urbach, Ephraim E. (1971), "The Homiletical Interpretations of the Sages and the Expositions of Origen on Canticles, and the Jewish-Christian Disputation", in *Scripta Hierosolymitana* 22, ed. by J. Heinemann and D. Noy (Jerusalem: Magnes Press, The Hebrew University), 247–75.

Vallance, John (2000), "Doctors in the Library: The Strange Tale of Apollonius the Bookworm and Other Stories", in *The Library of Alexandria: Centre of Learning in the Ancient World*, ed. by Roy MacLeod (London/New York: I. B. Tauris), 95–113.

——(1996), *Studies in Gnosticism and Alexandrian Christianity*, Nag Hammadi and Manichaean Studies 39 (Leiden/New York/Köln: Brill).

Van den Hoek, A. (1990), "How Alexandrian was Clement of Alexandria? Reflections on Clement and his Alexandrian Background", *HeyJ*, 179–94.

——(1995), "Clement and Origen as Sources on 'Noncanonical' Scriptural Traditions during the Late Second and Earlier Third Centuries", in *Origeniana Sexta*, ed. by G. Dorival and L le Boulluec (Leuven: Peeters), 93–113.

Van den Hoek, A. (1997), "The 'Catechetical' School of Early Christian Alexandria and Its Philonic Heritage", *HTR* 90.1, 59–87.

——(2000), "Philo and Origen: A Descriptive Catalogue of their Relationship", in *The Studia Philonica Annual* 12, 44–121.

Van Unnik, W. C. (1964), "The Newly Discovered Gnostic 'Epistle to Rheginos' on the Resurrection: II", in *JEH* 15, 141–67.

Vogt, H. J. (1999), *Origenes als Exeget* (Paderborn/München/Wien/Zürich: Ferdinand Schöningh).

——(1987), *Warum wurde Origenes zum Häretiker erklärt?* in *Origeniana Quarta* ed. L. Lies, Innsbrucker Theologische Studien, 19 (Innsbruck, Wien: Tyrolia Verlag), 78–99.

——(1974), *Das Kirchenverständnis des Origenes* (Köln/Wien: Böhlau Verlag).

Völker, Walther (1966/1930), *Das Vollkommenheitsideal des Origenes*, Beiträge zur historischen Theologie 7 (Tübingen: J. C. B. Mohr (Paul Siebeck); Nendeln: Kraus Reprint).

Watson, JoAnn Ford (1992), "Philip", in *ABD* 5, ed. by D. N. Freedman (New York/London/Toronto/Sydney/Auckland: Doubleday), 311–12.

West, M. L. (1999), "Towards Monotheism", in *Pagan Monotheism in Late Antiquity*, ed by Polymnia Athanassiadi and Michael Frede (Oxford: Clarendon Press), 21–40.

Williams, M. A. (1996), *Rethinking "Gnosticism"* (Princeton: Princeton University Press).

Zahn, Theodor (1975/1888–92), *Geschichte des Neutestamentlichen Kanons*, Bände 1 und 2 (Hildesheim/New York: Georg Olms Verlag).

Zandee, J. (1977), *The Teachings of Silvanus and Clement of Alexandria* (Leiden: Ex Oriente Lux).

Index